PARTINGS
HOW JUDAISM AND CHRISTIANITY BECAME TWO

Edited by Hershel Shanks

BIBLICAL ARCHAEOLOGY SOCIETY

WASHINGTON, DC

Library of Congress Cataloging-in-Publication Data

Partings : how Judaism and Christianity became two / edited by
Hershel Shanks.

pages   cm

Includes bibliographical references and index.

1. Christianity—Origin. 2. Church history—Primitive and early
church, ca. 30–600. 3. Judaism—History—Talmudic period, 10–425. 4.
Judaism—Relations—Christianity. 5. Christianity and other religions—
Judaism. I. Shanks, Hershel, editor of compilation.
II. Vermes, Geza, 1924–2013. The Jewish Jesus movement.

BR129.P37 2013

270.1—dc23   2013031380

Design by AURAS Design

ISBN 978-1-9353359-8-6 (hardcover)
ISBN 978-1-9353359-7-9 (paperback)

ON THE COVER: Judea Capta coin commemorating the fall of Jerusalem
to the Romans in 70 C.E. Judea is depicted as a mourning woman
and a bound male captive, both shown beneath a palm tree.
Photo by Erich Lessing.

This book could not have been produced
without the enthusiastic, encouraging
and generous support of

George S. Blumenthal

Samuel D. Turner, Esq.

Michael Steinhardt

Contents

Illustrations

Color Plates

Maps

The Authors

James H. Charlesworth is George L. Collord Professor of New Testament Language and Literature at Princeton Theological Seminary and also serves as director of the Princeton Theological Seminary Dead Sea Scrolls Project. He is a specialist in the Apocrypha and Pseudepigrapha of the Old and New Testaments, the Dead Sea Scrolls and the historical Jesus. Among his many books are *The Bible and the Dead Sea Scrolls,* 3 vols. (Baylor University Press, 2006), *Resurrection: The Origin and Future of a Biblical Doctrine* (T & T Clark, 2006) and, most recently, *The Good and Evil Serpent* (Yale University Press, 2010), winner of *The Christian Century's* award for best biblical book.

Bruce Chilton is Bernard Iddings Professor of Religion at Bard College in Annandale, New York. An expert on the New Testament, early Judaism and the Targumim (Aramaic translations of the Hebrew Bible), he has authored, coauthored or edited more than 50 books, including his popular *Rabbi Jesus: An Intimate Biography* (Doubleday, 2000) and a recent critical introduction to *The Targums* (with Paul Flesher; Fortress Press, 2012). He is also the author of many popular and scholarly articles.

Shaye J.D. Cohen is Nathan Littauer Professor of Hebrew Literature and Philosophy in the department of Near Eastern Languages and Civilizations at Harvard University. Before arriving at Harvard in 2001, he was the Ungerleider Professor and Director of Judaic Studies at Brown University. A specialist in the emergence of Rabbinic Judaism, he has written or edited several books and many articles, including *From the Maccabees to the Mishnah: A Profile of Judaism* (Westminster Press, 1987; second edition, 2006) and *The Beginnings of Jewishness* (University of California, 1999).

James D.G. Dunn is Emeritus Lightfoot Professor of Divinity at Durham University in England. A New Testament scholar of international repute, he has written extensively on Jesus and Paul, particularly *The Theology of Paul the Apostle* (Eerdmans, 1998), *A New Perspective on Jesus* (Baker, 2005) and *The New Perspective on Paul* (Eerdmans, revised edition, 2008). He also authored the widely cited *The Partings of the Ways Between*

Christianity and Judaism (SCM, second edition, 2006). His most recent trilogy on *Christianity in the Making* emphasizes the Jewishness of early Christianity and traces its emergence from early Judaism.

Arye Edrei is professor of law at Tel Aviv University where he teaches courses on the history and philosophy of Jewish law. Although his main fields of interest are Talmudic jurisprudence and 20th-century Jewish law, he also writes with scholar Doron Mendels (see below) on the development of Jewish identities in the Diaspora. Edrei serves as coeditor of *Dinei Israel: A Journal of Science and Jewish Law*, published jointly by Tel Aviv University and Yeshiva University in New York.

Steven Fine is professor of Jewish history at Yeshiva University in New York and also heads the university's Center for Israel Studies. He is an expert in Jewish history of the Greco-Roman world and focuses on the relationship between ancient Jewish literature, art and archaeology, as well as how modern scholars understand and interpret early Jewish history. He has authored more than 60 articles and several award-winning books, including *Art and Judaism in the Greco-Roman World: Toward a New Jewish Archaeology* (Cambridge University Press, 2005; revised edition, 2010).

Lawrence T. Geraty is professor of archaeology and Hebrew Bible as well as president emeritus at La Sierra University in Riverside, California. An accomplished field archaeologist who directed the Tell Hisban excavation and is founding director of the Madaba Plains Project in Jordan, he is also an ordained minister in the Seventh-day Adventist Church and taught for 13 years at the denomination's seminary at Andrews University. From 2002 to 2006, he also served as president of the American Schools of Oriental Research. His first published article was on the topic of his contribution to this volume.

Matt A. Jackson-McCabe is chair and associate professor in the department of Religious Studies at Cleveland State University in Ohio and is a specialist in early Christianity. His publications include *Logos and Law in the Letter of James* (Brill, 2001; SBL, 2010) and *Jewish Christianity Reconsidered* (ed.) (Fortress Press, 2007).

Robert A. Kraft is Berg Professor of Religious Studies, Emeritus, at the University of Pennsylvania. A wide-ranging authority on early Judaism and Christianity, his research explores Jewish and Christian literatures of the Greco-Roman period, including the Dead Sea Scrolls, the works of Philo of Alexandria and of Josephus, and the writings of early Christianity's Gnostic and other groups. His recent book, *Exploring the Scripturesque: Jewish Texts and Their Christian Contexts* (Brill, 2009), brings together and updates a selection of his major articles and scholarly contributions. (For more, visit his webpage at http://ccat.sas.upenn.edu/rak/kraft.html.)

AnneMarie Luijendijk is associate professor of religion at Princeton University where she teaches courses on the New Testament and early Christianity. Her research uses literary texts and documentary sources to reveal little-known social histories of the earliest Christians. Her first book, *Greetings in the Lord: Early Christians and the Oxyrhynchus Papyri* (Harvard University Press, 2008), investigates papyrus letters and documents of early Christians in the ancient Egyptian city of Oxyrhynchus. Her second book, *Forbidden Oracles? The Gospel of the Lots of Mary* (Mohr Siebeck, forthcoming 2013), explores the concept of divination in a previously unknown Coptic manuscript.

Doron Mendels is professor emeritus in the department of History at the Hebrew University of Jerusalem. He is the author of many books and articles about Hellenism, Judaism and Christianity, including *The Rise and Fall of Jewish Nationalism: Jewish and Christian Ethnicity in the Ancient Land of Israel* (Doubleday, 1992) and his recently published *Why Did Paul Go West? Jewish Historical Narrative and Thought* (Bloomsbury, 2013). His research deals primarily with the history and development of Jewish ethnic and national identity during antiquity, from the time of Alexander the Great to the reign of Constantine.

Eric M. Meyers is Bernice & Morton Lerner Professor of Religion at Duke University and director of the university's Center for Jewish Studies. He has directed digs in Israel and Italy for more than 37 years and has published (with his wife Carol Meyers) several reports on early synagogues, including *Excavations at Gush Halav* (Eisenbrauns, 1991) and *Excavations at Ancient Nabratein* (Eisenbrauns, 2009). He was editor-in-chief of *The Oxford*

Encyclopedia of Archaeology in the Near East (1997) and most recently wrote (with Mark Chancey) *Alexander to Constantine* (Yale University Press, 2012), part of the *Archaeology of the Land of the Bible* series.

Annette Yoshiko Reed is M. Mark and Esther Watkins Assistant Professor of the Humanities at the University of Pennsylvania and acting director of the university's Center for Ancient Studies. Her broad-ranging research spans Second Temple Judaism, early Christianity and the history of Jewish/Christian relations and identity in late antiquity. She is the author of *Fallen Angels and the History of Judaism and Christianity* (Cambridge University Press, 2005) and also edited (with Adam H. Becker) the widely acclaimed *The Ways That Never Parted: Jews and Christians in Late Antiquity and the Early Middle Ages* (Mohr Siebeck, 2003; Fortress Press, 2007).

Hershel Shanks is founder and editor of *Biblical Archaeology Review*. He has written numerous books on the Bible and biblical archaeology, including *The Mystery and Meaning of the Dead Sea Scrolls* (Random House, 1998), *Jerusalem's Temple Mount* (Continuum, 2007), *Jerusalem: An Archaeological Biography* (Random House, 1995) and *The City of David: A Guide to Biblical Jerusalem* (Tel Aviv: Bazak, 1973; reprinted many times). His autobiography, *Freeing the Dead Sea Scrolls and Other Adventures of an Archaeology Outsider*, was published by Continuum in 2010. He is a graduate of the Harvard Law School and a member of the District of Columbia bar.

Joan Taylor is professor of Christian origins and Second Temple Judaism at King's College London. Her research combines history, archaeology and textual studies to explore a variety of subjects pertaining to early Jewish and Christian life and society, from the Dead Sea Scrolls and the diverse communities of Second Temple Judaism to the historical Jesus and the subsequent development of orthodox and Jewish-Christianity. Her book *Christians and the Holy Places: The Myth of Jewish-Christian Origins* (Clarendon, 1993; revised edition, 2003) earned a 1995 Irene Levi-Sala award for best book on the archaeology of Israel.

Geza Vermes was fellow of the British Academy and director of the Oxford Forum for Qumran Research at the Oxford Centre of Postgraduate Hebrew Studies. He was also professor emeritus of Jewish studies at Oxford

University, where he taught from 1965 to 1991. He was the editor of the *Journal of Jewish Studies* and authored and edited numerous books on both the Dead Sea Scrolls and the Jewish background of the historical Jesus, beginning with *Jesus the Jew* (Fortress Press, 1973) and continuing with his most recent works, *Jesus: Nativity-Passion-Resurrection* (Penguin, 2010) and *The Story of the Scrolls* (Penguin, 2010). His widely acclaimed *Complete Dead Sea Scrolls in English*, available in the Penguin Classics series, celebrated its golden jubilee in 2012. He passed away in May 2013 at age 88.

Lily Vuong is assistant professor of philosophy and religious studies at Valdosta State University in Valdosta, Georgia. Her research focuses on early Christianity, with a particular emphasis on New Testament Apocryphal and Pseudepigraphal writings. She has contributed several important chapters to major edited volumes and is currently working on her book *"Raised in the Temple of the Lord": Mary, Purity, and the Protevangelium of James* to be published with Mohr Siebeck. She is also editing (with Nathaniel DesRosiers and Jordan Rosenblum) the upcoming *Religious Competition in the Third Century: Jews, Christians, and the Greco-Roman World* (Vandenhoeck and Ruprecht Press, 2013).

Pamela Watson is senior lecturer in archaeology at the University of New England in Armidale, New South Wales, Australia. As codirector of the Pella Hinterland Survey (1994–1996), she and colleague Margaret O'Hea conducted an extensive study of the natural and manmade caves surrounding the site of Tabaqat Fahl (Pella) in modern Jordan, a site many believe served as refuge for early Christians fleeing the Roman siege of Jerusalem in 70 C.E. In addition to publishing on the Pella Hinterland Survey, Watson has contributed to several volumes on the ongoing Pella excavations, focusing especially on the site's Byzantine occupation.

Margaret H. Williams is honorary research fellow in the Centre for the Study of Christian Origins at the University of Edinburgh. Her research focuses on Jewish life and religion during the Hellenistic and Roman periods, especially in the large Diaspora communities of Rome and Asia Minor. She is the author of numerous articles and book chapters, as well as *The Jews Among the Greeks and Romans: A Diasporan Sourcebook* (Johns Hopkins University Press, 1998).

Abbreviations

Antiquities	Josephus, *Antiquities of the Jews*	**JPS**	Jewish Publication Society
Apion	Josephus, *Against Apion*	**JRA**	*Journal of Roman Archaeology*
ASOR	American Schools of Oriental Research	**JRS**	*Journal of Roman Studies*
		JSJ	*Journal for the Study of Judaism*
AUSS	*Andrews University Seminary Studies*	**JSOT**	*Journal for the Study of the Old Testament*
BAR	*Biblical Archaeology Review*	**JT**	Jerusalem Talmud, or Yerushalmi (Palestinian Talmud)
BASOR	*Bulletin of the American Schools of Oriental Research*		
		JTS	*Journal of Theological Studies*
BR	*Bible Review*	**Loeb**	*Loeb Classical Library* (Cambridge, MA: Harvard University Press)
BT	Babylonian Talmud, or Bavli		
CBQ	*Catholic Biblical Quarterly*		
EJ	*Encyclopaedia Judaica*, 2nd ed., 22 vols., ed. Fred Skolnik (Detroit: Macmillan, 2007)	**NTS**	*New Testament Studies*
		R.	Rabbi
		SBL	Society of Biblical Literature
GLAJJ	*Greek and Latin Authors on Jews and Judaism*, 3 vols., ed. Menahem Stern (Jerusalem: Israel Academy of Sciences and Humanities, 1974–1984)	**TSAJ**	*Texte und Studien zum Antiken Judentum*
		TynB	*Tyndale Bulletin*
		VC	*Vigiliae Christianae*
HTR	*Harvard Theological Review*	**War**	Josephus, *The Jewish War*
JBL	*Journal of Biblical Literature*	**WUNT**	*Wissenschaftliche Untersuchungen zum Neuen Testament*
JECS	*Journal of Early Christian Studies*		
JIWE	*Jewish Inscriptions of Western Europe*, 2 vols., ed. David Noy (Cambridge: Cambridge University Press, 1993–1995)	**LXX**	Septuagint
JJS	*Journal of Jewish Studies*		

EDITOR'S NOTE: Quotations of biblical verses and passages reflect the individual translation preferences of each author.

THE ROMAN MEDITERRANEAN

Milan

ITALY

Rome

SARDINIA

MACEDONIA

Constantinople

Thessalonica

GREECE

SICILY

Corinth

Athens

Ep

Carthage

Mediterranean Sea

Crete

NORTH AFRICA

Cyrene

Al

Ox

0   500 mi

ROMAN PALESTINE

Mediterranean
Sea

Sidon

Damascus

Tyre

Akko

Capernaum ● Bethsaida
GOLAN

Magdala ● ● Gamla

GALILEE
Sea of Galilee

Sepphoris ● Tiberias ● Hippos-Sussita

Beth
Shearim ● Nazareth

Megiddo ● Gadara ● Abila

DECAPOLIS

Caesarea

Scythopolis ● Pella

Samaria/
Sebaste ● Gerasa

Shechem

Mt. Gerizim ▲

SAMARIA

Jordan River

Joppa

Lydda PEREA

Yavneh Philadelphia

Jerusalem
Bethlehem ● Qumran

Horvat 'Ethri ● JUDEA

Beth Guvrin ● Machaerus

Gaza Hebron ● NABATEA

Ein Gedi Dead
Sea

Masada

IDUMEA

N

0   40 mi

Acknowledgments

IN MANY WAYS, THIS VOLUME FOLLOWS ON THE BIBLICAL ARCHAEOLOGY Society's widely acclaimed books *Ancient Israel* and *Christianity and Rabbinic Judaism*, now in their third and second editions, respectively. As such, the contributors to *Partings* had to meet an enormous challenge: Conveying the most recent scholarship on how and when Judaism and Christianity went their separate ways, with an equal eye toward maintaining the accessible style and tone that have made those previous works so successful. This group of esteemed scholars has not just met but exceeded that challenge.

The editing and final production of this masterful volume owes much to the talents, expertise and labors of the staff of the Biblical Archaeology Society and its associates. BAS publisher and president Susan Laden skillfully oversaw and managed all of the moving parts that make an edited volume like this possible. The overall editing of the volume was expertly led by associate editor Glenn J. Corbett who not only brought all the pieces together, but also did a remarkable job selecting and captioning the book's many illustrations. He was assisted throughout by administrative editor Bonnie Mullin who communicated with authors, ensured deadlines were met, proofed and edited the book's extensive notes, and generally kept everyone on the same page. The book's detailed maps and plans were designed by Dorothy R. Willette. Connie Binder provided the book with its thorough and very useful index. And production manager Heather Metzger patiently guided the work through the final stages of design and publication. A special thanks goes to Dr. Theodore (Ted) Feder, president of Art Resource, for providing several splendid images of the Roman catacombs and the paintings at Dura-Europos. Finally, the design and layout of the book fell to our longtime creative designer Rob Sugar and his excellent team at AURAS Design, especially Melissa Schmidt.

From all these efforts, I hope we have produced an engaging story of how Judaism and Christianity became two.

Hershel Shanks

Introduction

WHAT BECAME CHRISTIANITY STARTED OUT AS A MOVEMENT
within Judaism. It was not long, however, before the two began to diverge.
Yet in some ways they remained joined at the hip, although ultimately
going their separate ways.

This book attempts to describe that process—the "partings"—plural.
It was a complicated, even messy process. The basic premise of this book
is that the parting occurred in different ways in different places and at
different times. Thus, more than one parting. Or did they ever really part?

To those who say our book is not well organized, I reply that that is
because our subject is not well organized. We have not identified a single
storyline around which to describe a process that occurred over approximately half a century and more, from the birth of the Jesus movement in
Jerusalem to the Byzantine period—and even beyond, to modern times.

The subject can be approached in numerous ways—historical,
ideological, archaeological, theological, geographical (e.g., how and
when the parting occurred in Rome or Egypt), or from the viewpoint
of specific events, like the supposed Christian flight to Pella or the change
of the Christian holy day from the Sabbath to Sunday. Why I included
one subject and excluded another can be considered arbitrary or simply
a misjudgment. And those who dig intensively into this volume will
notice some (though mostly minor) differences among the scholars I
have included. That is surely an expectable part of the picture.

But what is presented here should be enough to give the reader (and
student) a broad understanding of the subject, guided by the insights of
world-class scholars. While we cannot claim to be exhaustive, I hope we
can at least claim to be incisive.

We begin with two magisterial chapters that in effect set the stage.
The first, by the late Geza Vermes, describes the complicated world of
Judaism at the time of Jesus and locates the Jesus movement within that
world ("The Jewish Jesus Movement").

This is followed by James (Jimmy, as he is generally known) D.G. Dunn's
chapter that traces the equally complicated beginnings of the break between

the two faiths ("From the Crucifixion to the End of the First Century").

Bruce Chilton's following chapter ("The Godfearers: From the Gospels to Aphrodisias") is driven by a (varying) concept—the Godfearers—rather than a time period. In one incarnation or another, the Godfearers—from the time of the Gospels (late first century C.E.) to fourth-century Anatolia and later—are known sometimes as a kind of half-Jew, sometimes as a kind of Christian, sometimes as neither, sometimes as something in between. Sometimes we learn of their existence only when they are chastised for their Jewish leanings by their clerical critics.

Did the Christian community flee east across the Jordan (and thus preserve itself) to avoid the catastrophe to the Jews of the Roman destruction of Jerusalem in 70 C.E.? Pamela Watson gives an authoritative assessment of the archaeological evidence ("The Christian Flight to Pella? The Archaeological Picture"). I won't prematurely reveal her conclusion.

Joan Taylor ("Parting in Palestine") demonstrates the continuation of both Judaism and what became Jewish-Christianity even after the devastation of the First Jewish Revolt in 70 C.E. The situation was far different, however, after the Second Jewish Revolt (132–135 C.E.), when Jewish-Christians naturally sought to avoid the Hadrianic burdens on Jews and, hence, parted.

Subsequent chapters are often, but not always, geographical, describing the developments in particular areas. As Annette Yoshiko Reed and Lily Vuong note, early conflict between Jesus' Jewish and non-Jewish followers occurred in Antioch, Paul's call to be the "apostle to the gentiles" occurred on the road to Damascus, and it was in Antioch that Ignatius coined the term *Christianismos*—the Greek word from which "Christianity" ultimately derives. Roman Syria was central to the development of early Christianity and its parting from Judaism—a situation that contrasts sharply from developments in the West. All this—and its aftermath—is described in their chapter on "Christianity in Antioch: Partings in Roman Syria."

Returning to Palestine, Eric Meyers adduces the archaeological evidence that the parting occurred much later in Galilee than scholars had once supposed ("Living Side by Side in Galilee"). Although a nascent Christian community surely lived in the Holy Land in the early years, archaeological evidence of a specifically Christian presence before Constantine in the fourth century C.E. is sparse, especially in Galilee. Even after Constantine, the evidence suggests Christianity expanded there slowly and Christian and

Jewish communities shared the area peacefully, if separately.

By contrast, the separation of Christians from Jews started much earlier in Rome. Each reacted to Roman power in its own interest, which sometimes coincided and sometimes conflicted with the other. Roman reaction to Jews and Christians also varied from time to time and from situation to situation. The effect of the Jewish revolts, of Nero's persecution of Christians, and of the varying attitudes of Rome toward its Jewish and Christian populations forms a complicated *pas de deux*—or perhaps *pas de trois* would be more accurate. The *fiscus Judaicus* and its repeal, together with the imperial city's Jewish and Christian catacombs, reflect the complex relationship between Jews and Christians and the relationship of both to Rome. All this is described by Margaret H. Williams in her chapter on "Jews and Christians at Rome: An Early Parting of the Ways."

In Egypt, the Jewish community was largely obliterated by the Romans in the early second century C.E., leaving Christianity to develop without hindrance (or support) from its ancestor religion. Nevertheless, the Christian community, sometimes inexplicably, absorbed much from Judaism. With a candid admission of how little evidence we have, Robert A. Kraft and AnneMarie Luijendijk give a sensitive account of the hazy process by which Christianity emerged in Egypt ("Christianity's Rise After Judaism's Demise in Early Egypt").

Matt Jackson-McCabe ("Ebionites and Nazoraeans: Christians or Jews?") explores two groups who might be thought to reflect odd combinations of Jewish and Christian attributes, which illustrates just how complicated our subject can be. The Ebionites, who some believe grew out of the Nazoraeans (but see Jackson-McCabe's chapter for a critique of this traditional view), were Christians who observed the Torah and yet rejected Paul's apostleship! Christians or Jews?

In a way, Shaye J.D. Cohen's chapter ("In Between: Jewish-Christians and the Curse of the Heretics") could be the beginning of this book—or at least of *a* book. It starts with a helpful definition of terms, especially focusing on the different groups involved in what we usually think of as the "parting." This sets the scene for the group on which he focuses— Jewish-Christians, a group truly in between. Their relations with other groups illuminate the entire picture. In this connection, in an extensive discussion of allegedly anti-Christian cursing, he analyzes the famous "curse of the heretics," or the *Birkat ha-Minim*.

Just when we think we get the picture, along comes Steven Fine to mix things up and remind us that things are not always what they seem. Jews and Christians were not only reacting in different ways that are difficult to interpret, but this often occurred in a larger context that was sympathetic to one or the other and to which the other reacted. They were sometimes intensely antagonistic to one another, especially after the Christianization of the Roman Empire ("The Complexities of Rejection and Attraction, Herein of Love and Hate").

Lawrence (Larry) Geraty analyzes the Christian abandonment of the Sabbath, a fundamental move that definitively separated Christianity from Judaism. It thereby avoided the stigma of being Jewish in a Roman society. But why Sunday? ("From Sabbath to Sunday: Why, How and When?")

In their chapter ("Social Organization and Parting in East and West"), Arye Edrei and Doron Mendels investigate differences in Jewish and Christian social organization that affected their relationship with each other in both regions. These hitherto unidentified social differences also illuminate why Christianity thrived in the West, and Judaism developed largely and differently in the East.

In a concluding chapter, James Charlesworth suggests that the ways never parted. Christianity grew out of Judaism and in so many ways this bond remained over the centuries ("Did They Ever Part?"). So much of the doctrines of Christianity, once thought to set it apart from Judaism, is now revealed to have Jewish roots shared by both.

The authors of this volume are very different from one another. They are young and elderly (I dare not say old). They are men and women. They are American, British, Israeli, Australian and New Zealander; their backgrounds, as reflected in their names, are even more diverse. They are religious and secular and neither and both. But they are all leading scholars committed to an unbiased investigation of the evidence.

As a group, I think they have captured a picture of an enormously complicated development that resonates with unusual interest and relevance to this day. No one will come away from this book without nourishment. Imbibe and enjoy.

Hershel Shanks
May 2013
Washington, D.C.

1

The Jewish Jesus Movement

GEZA VERMES

TO GRASP THE FUNDAMENTALS OF THE PARTING OF THE WAY, THAT is to say of how Judaism and Christianity became two, some essential preliminary questions need to be answered. How is one to define the Judaism into which Jesus was born shortly before the death of Herod the Great in 4 B.C.E.? Did Jesus intend to divorce the movement inspired by him from his inherited Judaism? Did Jesus plan to found a new church, and did nascent Palestinian Christianity consider itself distinct from the main body of Judaism?[1]

Let us consider Judaism first. As a religion, it was practiced by persons born into the Jewish nation and by gentile proselytes who were willing to profess the uniqueness of God and embrace all the religious obligations of the law of Moses. It may be taken for granted that a certain amount of missionary activity was pursued among gentiles in various periods of Jewish history. During the time of Jesus, for example, the Scribes and Pharisees crossed sea and land to make one convert (Matthew 23:15), but how widely proselytizing was practiced in those days and how deeply the eschatological idea of Israel as the light to the nations penetrated Jewish consciousness continue to be matters of scholarly debate.[2]

Formal, organized Judaism was built on a twofold foundation:

(1) the Torah or divinely revealed law, the pedestal of the entire spectrum of religiously inspired life; and (2) on the Jerusalem Temple, the center of ritual worship. Beside and beneath this structured Judaism were also currents of less formal religion, linked to and fed by the prophets, the influential mouthpieces of God, and further sustained down to the age of the rabbis by Jewish holy men.[3] This charismatic religion often came into conflict with that of the ruling hereditary priests who were the officially recognized teachers, judges and performers of ceremonies. Since the middle of the second century B.C.E., sacerdotal monopoly was contested by lay intellectuals, the Pharisees, who claimed authority on account of their learning; they challenged the ruling class of the Temple, the adherents of the Sadducee or Zadokite chief priesthood, even in matters of cultic worship.[4]

From the political and religious points of view, the Jewish society of the age of Jesus was far from unified. Our principal informer, the first-century C.E. Jewish historian Flavius Josephus, speaks of the religious schools or divisions (*haireseis*) of the Pharisees, Sadducees and Essenes, all three traced back to c. 150 B.C.E.,[5] and the religious-nationalistic party of the Zealots/Sicarii, who came into being as a reaction against the Roman census imposed on Judea in 6 C.E. and whose revolutionary activity affected Jewish land up to the fall of Jerusalem in 70 C.E. and of Masada in 73/4 C.E.[6] Together the size of all these groups was modest compared to the total Jewish population of Judea and Galilee, estimated to be about a million people, let alone to that of the whole Diaspora, which was probably several times larger.*[7] There were approximately 4,000 Essenes[8] and 6,000 Pharisees, mostly in the Judean cities.[9] The large majority of the priests and Levites together with their wealthy and influential lay sympathizers formed the party of the Sadducees. Their estimated number, surmised in the Letter of Aristeas and Josephus, hardly exceeded 20,000.[10] Taken together, Pharisees, Essenes and Sadducees would still constitute only a small fraction of the total nonaffiliated Jewish population of Palestine, the common people or people of the land (*'amme ha'aretz*), who were to varying degrees under the influence of the priests or the Pharisees.

The size of the Jewish Diaspora in the age of Jesus is even more problematic than the Jewish population of the Holy Land. Whether living

*Magen Broshi, "Estimating the Population of Ancient Jerusalem," *BAR*, June 1978.

in the Greco-Roman world (in particular Syria, Asia Minor, Italy, Egypt and North Africa) or under Parthian-Persian hegemony in Mesopotamia, the non-Palestinian Jews remained attached to the basic ancestral religious tradition and a fair number of them occasionally visited Jerusalem during the three annual pilgrimage festivals of Passover, the Feast of Weeks (Shavuot) and the Feast of Tabernacles (Sukkot).[11] For Diaspora Jews, as for the Palestinian Jews who lived at some distance from Jerusalem, the physical setting of regular religious activity was the local synagogue; the Temple, on the other hand, constituted the spiritual magnet and focus that united the dispersed Jews into a single "people of God" even if it was expressed through a single journey to the Holy Land in a lifetime.

Despite the bond of the Torah and the Temple, however, the Jewish people in the age of Jesus was not a monolithic body; it included, in addition to the religious parties mentioned above, a large number of splinter groups or sects. Rabbinic tradition mentions 24 varieties, but this is probably an artificial figure, the counterpart of the 24 divisions of the priesthood.[12] In the eyes of the Jerusalem officialdom the first Jesus followers were also a sect (hairesis), that of the Nazarenes (Acts 24:5).

Two of the dissident factions were definitely connected with the Temple and seem to have sprung from schisms in the ranks of the Jerusalem priesthood in the course of the second century B.C.E. The first schism was created by Onias IV, son of the deposed pontiff Onias III, and his followers. Unable to succeed his murdered father, Onias IV fled to Egypt and founded a rival Jewish temple in Leontopolis. Josephus reports that this sanctuary continued to function until the Romans put an end to it in 73 C.E., three years after the destruction of the Jerusalem Temple.*[13]

The second schismatic community was the famous sect of the Essenes, known since antiquity thanks to Philo, Josephus and Pliny the Elder,[14] and identical, in the opinion of the majority of experts, with the inhabitants of the Qumran settlement, who bequeathed to us the Dead Sea Scrolls.†[15] So in more than one sense, the parting of the ways antedated the birth of Jesus. During the age of Jesus even Palestinian Jewry was politically

*Pieter W. van der Horst, "Jewish Funerary Inscriptions—Most Are in Greek," *BAR*, September/October 1992.
†Kenneth Atkinson, Hanan Eshel and Jodi Magness, "Another View: Do Josephus's Writings Support the 'Essene Hypothesis'?" *BAR*, March/April 2009; Steve Mason, "Did the Essenes Write the Dead Sea Scrolls?" *BAR*, November/December 2008; Edna Ullmann-Margalit, "Dissecting the Qumran-Essene Hypothesis," *BAR*, March/April 2008.

QUMRAN. Many scholars believe the site of Khirbet Qumran located along the northwest shore of the Dead Sea was settled by the Essenes, one of several sectarian groups that broke with the Jerusalem Temple and its established priesthood. The Qumran community's extensive library of biblical books, commentaries and sectarian writings is preserved in the famous Dead Sea Scrolls, first discovered in 1947 in caves near the site.

and administratively fractured. After the death of Herod in 4 B.C.E., Judea and Samaria were turned into a Roman province directly ruled by a governor appointed by the emperor; Jesus' Galilee, on the other hand, enjoyed partial autonomy under the Herodian ruler Antipas, who had his own army, tax collectors and administrative machinery. Not surprisingly, Galilee became a hotbed of anti-Roman revolutionary plotting simply because it was not directly governed by the Romans. Jesus launched his movement in the tetrarchy of Herod Antipas (4 B.C.E.–39 C.E.), under the reign of the emperor Tiberius (14–37 C.E.), the governorship of Pontius Pilate (26–36 C.E.) and the high priesthood of Joseph Caiaphas (18–36 C.E.).[16]

The charismatic prophet Jesus the Jew

To reconstruct the religion practiced and preached by Jesus of Nazareth, we need to scrutinize our earliest sources, the Gospels of Mark, Matthew

KEY FIGURES FROM JESUS' LIFE. Several important figures mentioned in the Gospel accounts are also known from artifacts and inscriptions of the early first century C.E. This fragmentary Latin dedicatory inscription found at Caesarea (left) refers to "Pontius Pilate, the Prefect of Judea" who oversaw Jesus' trial and execution. An inscription carved in Aramaic on the side of this ornately decorated limestone ossuary (right), or bone box, refers to Caiaphas, the name of the Jerusalem high priest who turned Jesus over to the Roman authorities.

and Luke (the Synoptics), with an occasional side glance at the more recent and historically generally less dependable account of John, the Fourth Evangelist. The apocryphal Gospel of Thomas, probably compiled in the first half of the second century C.E. and displaying Gnostic tendencies, yields in my view no trustworthy supplements to the canonical Gospels.

We have no dependable information concerning the childhood, youth, education and early adult life of Jesus. The tales about his birth and infancy and the single episode of the 12-year-old boy's Passover pilgrimage to Jerusalem in the midst of his family constitute an inextricable mixture of legend and popular storytelling.[17] His entry into real history is linked to the ministry of John the Baptist, another character surrounded in the Gospels by an air of mystery and miracle, the staple ingredients of charismatic Jewish storytelling.[18]

John the Baptist and Jesus

John, despite the Evangelists' attempt to subordinate him to Jesus, appears in fact as the dominant figure at the beginning of the gospel narrative (Luke 1). His birth is portrayed as miraculous in Luke's infancy story. He is said to have been the son of Zechariah, an elderly priest, and of Elizabeth, a relative of the mother of Jesus, a sterile woman already beyond child-bearing age. The start of the Baptist's public career is put precisely by Luke to the 15th year (28/9 C.E.) of the Roman emperor Tiberius (Luke 1:5–24,39–80, 3:1–2).

John is depicted in the Synoptics as an eremitical prophet, preaching repentance and purification in the wilderness near the Jordan River and encouraging Jews to undergo baptism in view of the approaching kingdom of God. A detached echo of the New Testament story may be heard in Josephus, for whom John was a good man who exhorted his compatriots to be righteous and also to purify their bodies through baptism or immersion in the Jordan River. John's furry clothes and leather girdle recall the biblical prophet Elijah (2 Kings 1:8). His diet was frugal, consisting of locusts and field honey, the latter being possibly the sweet juice of the carob, known also as St. John's bread (Mark 1:6; Matthew 3:4). John's association with Elijah is alluded to by Mark and his identification with the legendary returning Elijah is expressly attributed to Jesus (Mark 1:2; Matthew 11:13–14).

The aim of this new Elijah was to preach penitence in view of the impending arrival of God's reign on earth: "Repent, for the kingdom of heaven is at hand" (Matthew 3:2; Mark 1:15). The Evangelists see in John's message the fulfillment of the prophecy contained in Isaiah 40:3, announcing the approach of the divine king in the desert: "The voice of one crying out in the wilderness: 'Prepare the way of the Lord, make his paths straight'" (Mark 1:3; Matthew 3:3; Luke 3:4).

The same theme appears in the Dead Sea Scrolls. Relying on the same words of Isaiah 40:3, the Qumran community chose withdrawal to the arid shore of the Dead Sea and return to the divine law as the ideal condition for preparing for the establishment on earth of the kingdom of God.[19]

John's short career ended violently when Herod Antipas ordered his decapitation (see Plates 1 and 2).* According to the Gospels, the tetrarch's displeasure was provoked by John's declaring invalid his marriage to Herodias, his sister-in-law (Mark 6:17–29; Matthew 14:3–12). Josephus, on the other hand, suggests that the eloquence of John appeared a potential

*For the historical and archaeological background to this story, see Győző Vörös, "Machaerus: Where Salome Danced and John the Baptist Was Beheaded," *BAR*, September/October 2012.

threat to Antipas's rule and his beheading was a preventive measure.[20]

The episode of a heavenly voice (*bat qol*) accompanying the baptism of Jesus by John attests an intense eschatological and messianic expectation. The celestial declaration about Jesus' filial status is given in two forms. One is addressed to Jesus ("You are my beloved Son"; Mark 1:11; Luke 3:22), and the other is audible to John and to all the bystanders ("He is my beloved Son"; Matthew 3:17).

Jesus entered the public domain by joining the followers of John. Mark reveals nothing about John's preaching apart from the general theme of repentance and the exhortation to baptism (Mark 1:4). Matthew offers a summary proclamation, "Repent, for the kingdom of heaven has come near," together with a reprimand addressed to the Pharisees and Sadducees (Matthew 3:2). Using an Aramaic pun, John threatened them with the loss of their elect status as Jews: "Do not presume to say to yourselves, 'We have Abraham as our father'; for I tell you, God is able from these stones (*abnaya*) to raise up sons (*bnaya*) to Abraham" (Matthew 3:7–10; Luke 3:7–9). John also advised the multitude to be generous to the needy, the tax collectors to be fair, and the soldiers to be content with their wages and abstain from violence (Luke 3:10–14).

The Baptist was an eschatological prophet, who saw himself entrusted with the task of persuading his fellow Palestinian Jews to revert to a life of justice in preparation for God's approach. We are told that he was surrounded by a circle of disciples among whom figured Jesus (Mark 2:18; Matthew 9:14; Luke 5:33; John 3:25). Jesus no doubt inherited from the Baptist his leading ideas, first and foremost the need of repentance for those who seek the kingdom of heaven. We learn from the Fourth Gospel that the original disciples of John complained about a rival group of Jesus' followers, but were silenced by their master (John 3:22–30). In fact, Jesus was not competing with John, and it was only after the imprisonment of the Baptist that Jesus launched in Galilee the penitential campaign initiated by John in the Jordan Valley (Mark 1:14; Matthew 4:12).

Jesus' original activity was characterized by "the power of the spirit" (Luke 4:14), and the essence of his teaching reflected that of John in whose footsteps Jesus set out to inaugurate the reign of God over Israel and the world. "The time is fulfilled, and the kingdom of God has come near; repent, and believe in the good news" (Mark 1:15; Matthew 4:17).

Portrait of Jesus the Jew

1) The charismatic healer and exorcist

While scholars agree that the Gospels are not strictly speaking historical documents, the basic depiction of Jesus as a prophet presents a perfectly credible image of the charismatic "man of God" that we encounter in the Bible and in extrabiblical Second Temple literature including the Dead Sea Scrolls and the writings of the rabbis. To this material must be added the authentic part of Josephus's Testimonium Flavianum, where Jesus is described as a "wise man" and the "performer of paradoxical deeds."*[21] From all this comes the portrait of a Galilean holy man who exclusively addressed "the lost sheep of the house of Israel" (Matthew 10:6). He referred to non-Jews as dogs and explicitly turned down the request of the exorcized gentile demoniac from the Transjordanian city of Gerasa to join the company of his disciples (Matthew 10:5, 15:24, indirectly confirmed by Mark 7:26–27; Luke 8:38–39; and Mark 5:18–19).

From the New Testament accounts, Jesus emerges as an itinerant spiritual healer, exorcist and preacher who was highly popular in Galilee. His charismatic activity consisted in the cure of the sick that often also entailed the expulsion of evil spirits to use the language of the Jews of that age. Demonic possession was linked in the mind of Jesus' contemporaries to nervous and mental diseases. For them sickness, sin and Satan were interconnected realities. Sin, brought about by the devil, caused sickness. In consequence, the healing of a disease was tantamount to forgiveness of sin and both cure and pardon were brought about by exorcism.

Multiple charismatic therapy is summarily alluded to in the Synoptic Gospels: "He healed many who were sick with various diseases" (Mark 1:34; cf. Mark 3:10).

The change in the sick person's physical condition is sometimes ascribed to the person's coming into contact with Jesus' body or with his garments (Mark 3:10, 6:56, etc.). When resuscitating the young man from Nain, Jesus "touched the bier" before issuing the command that he should rise (Luke 7:14). In the case of a woman suffering from a flow of blood, touching the robe of Jesus resulted in a cure, but not without Jesus apparently noticing that some mysterious power had surged from him (Mark 5:25–33).

The charismatics did not feel compelled to protect their ritual purity

---

*John P. Meier, "The Testimonium: Evidence for Jesus Outside the Bible," *BR*, June 1991.

by keeping at a distance the dead or unclean bodies. Again and again, Jesus deliberately reached out toward these patients. Thus, when begged by Jairus to save his daughter, Jesus "took her by the hand" and ordered her to rise from the dead (Mark 5:23,41). The spine of the woman, who was humpbacked for 18 years, was straightened when Jesus placed his hands upon her (Luke 13:12–13).

It is worth pointing out that twice in the Synoptics and once in John's gospel Jesus is credited with practices known from ancient popular medicine. A deaf-mute was cured after Jesus had put his finger into the man's ears and transferred his saliva to the man's tongue while uttering the Aramaic healing word "*Ephphatha,* that is, be opened" (Mark 7:33–34). Likewise Jesus is said to have restored the vision of a blind man from Bethsaida by placing his spittle on his eyes and laying his hands on him (Mark 8:22–23). In one of the few healing narratives of the Fourth Gospel, Jesus cures a man who had been blind from birth by smearing on his eyes mud produced from the mixture of dust and Jesus' saliva (John 9:6). According to talmudic tradition human saliva was endowed with therapeutic effect especially for the treatment of eye troubles.[22]

The least magical-sounding form of charismatic healing was achieved by a direct word of command: The thaumaturgist spoke and the illness vanished. Healing from a distance is referred to in the case of the centurion's servant whose sickness disappeared when Jesus told the officer: "Go; be it done for you as you have believed" (Matthew 8:13).

The climax of charismatic healing attributed to Jesus is attained through the resuscitation of recently deceased persons. Two such cases are the revival of the daughter of Jairus, and that of the son of a widow from Nain, both reawakened by Jesus' direct command (Mark 5:21–24,34–43; Luke 8:40–42,48–55; Matthew 9:18–19,23–26; Luke 7:11–17). The raising of Lazarus in the Fourth Gospel substantially differs from the synoptic revival accounts. The resuscitation takes place not within hours from death but several days later (John 11:28–44), and the stress lies not on the story itself, but on its apologetic value: Raising the putrefying body of a man dead already for four days serves to demonstrate Jesus' supernatural status. This is evidence for the developing faith of early Christianity rather than for the portrayal of the historical Jesus. It is noteworthy that the Fourth Evangelist does not record a single exorcism; in John's view such a primitive activity was below the quasi-heavenly dignity of Jesus.

The success of exorcism and of healing depended on the possessed or sick person's faith in the charismatic power of Jesus. Lack of such belief impaired the ability of the exorcist or healer. Thus no cures were performed in Nazareth because of the unwillingness of the co-citizens of Jesus to recognize his special mastery over sickness and the devil. In fact, even his relatives remained incredulous and thought he was out of his mind (Mark 3:21, 6:5). The words conveying Jesus' reaction evolved into a proverb: "A prophet is without honor only in his hometown, and among his own kin, and in his own house" (Mark 6:4; Matthew 13:57).

The Synoptic accounts repeatedly lay down faith as the prerequisite for the efficacy of the charismatic action and the ultimate cause of the cure (Mark 5:34, 10:52; Matthew 9:28–29; Luke 7:50, 17:19). Jesus frequently proclaims after a healing act: "Your faith has made you well"; "Your faith has saved you"; "According to your faith let it be done to you" (Mark 5:34, 10:52; Matthew 9:29; Luke 7:50, 17:19).

In sum, the portrayal of Jesus as an exorcist and healer and his link with the figures of Moses and Elijah (Mark 9:4; Matthew 17:3; Luke 9:30) firmly place him in the ideological framework of a charismatic Jewish prophet of the biblical and early post-biblical period.[23]

2) The charismatic teacher

Jesus was also admired as a powerful and inspiring teacher. His audiences found his preaching striking and distinctive. On the first recorded occasion, the listeners expressed their amazement because of the peculiar character of his sermon. They called it a new teaching with authority (Mark 1:22,27; Luke 4:32,36) because unlike the synagogue preachers, who supported their assertions with suitable scriptural citations, Jesus confirmed his words by charismatic healing and exorcisms. It is noteworthy that the Synoptic Gospels ascribe to him a surprisingly small amount of Bible interpretation. Paul's letter to the Romans yields twice as many scriptural quotations as Mark, Matthew and Luke taken together.[24]

The kingdom of God

The central essential feature of the religion preached by Jesus concerned the imminent onset of a new age, called the kingdom of heaven or the kingdom of God. The first words placed on his lips in the Gospels relate to this subject and the prologue of the Acts of the Apostles asserts that the last topic he discussed with his inner circle concerned the restoration of the kingdom (Mark 1:15; Matthew 4:17; Acts 1:3). The expression "kingdom of God" figures about a hundred times in the Synoptic Gospels, but apart from a passing reference in the conversation with Nicodemus in John 3 it is totally ignored by the Fourth Evangelist. Not being a philosopher, Jesus abstained from defining the kingdom of God; he preferred to delineate it in colorful parables, comparing it to this-worldly realities, although never to anything connected with politics or warfare (see Mark 4:26,30; Matthew 13:33,44,45,47, etc.). Jesus' attention was focused not on the nature of the kingdom, but on the ways that would secure admittance into it.

His teaching was especially concerned with the imminence of the final age as is clearly stated in well-known sayings such as: "Truly I tell you, there are some standing here who will not taste death until they see that the kingdom of God has come with power" (Mark 9:1; Matthew 16:28; Luke 9:27) and "The kingdom of God is in the midst of among you" (Luke 17:21). The nearness of the end is further asserted in the concluding phrase of Jesus' instruction to his 12 apostles concerning the imminence of the final day, as well as in the so-called eschatological discourse, "Truly I tell you, this generation will not pass away until all these things have taken place" (Mark 13:30; Matthew 24:34; Luke 21:32).

The idea of the kingdom of God grew out of old biblical traditions and arose from the combined concepts of God as the ruler of Israel, the Israelite nation as God's people, and the Jewish king and later the royal Messiah as God's ultimate lieutenant on earth. In the Hebrew Bible, God's kingship was expected to be established either through military conquest of the foreign nations by the Jewish messianic king or directly by God without human agency. The first witnesses of this notion were the prophets known as the Second (Isaiah 40–55) and the Third Isaiah (Isaiah 56–66), who flourished in sixth century B.C.E.

The Book of Daniel (completed in the 160s B.C.E.) and the literature of early post-biblical Judaism (Apocrypha, Pseudepigrapha and the Dead Sea Scrolls written between 250 B.C.E. and 100 C.E.) enveloped the kingdom idea in the eschatological traits of a cosmic battle culminating in the triumphal manifestation of the divine king. The religious enthusiasm generated by these ideas led again and again to revolutionary action, culminating a generation after the ministry of Jesus in the great uprising against Rome (66–70 C.E.). During the early period of the rabbinic era (100–300 C.E.)

the concept of the kingdom of God with political connotations continued to linger notwithstanding the disastrous Bar-Kokhba rebellion (132–135 C.E.) during the reign of the emperor Hadrian.

The kingdom of heaven, incorporating the restored earthly kingdom of Israel, was seen in the early centuries C.E. as the counterpart of the Roman Empire, although the apolitical rabbis did not envision the establishment of God's realm through the sword, but through submission to the law of Moses, "the yoke of the Torah." The well-known Aramaic prayer, the Kaddish, dating to the earliest rabbinic times, implores God to set up his kingdom "in your life and in your days ... speedily in a near time."[25]

Jesus' kingdom of God is situated between the apocalyptic and the rabbinic representations, but being of nonbellicose character, it rather foreshadows the pacific dream of the rabbis than the cataclysmic reality of the apocalyptic visionaries.

Nor did Jesus' preaching of the kingdom of God involve any theological speculation keen to discover the moment when God would reveal himself. This is in contrast to what we find incorporated in the Book of Daniel's 70 weeks of years (i.e., 70 x 7 = 490 years), culminating in the installation of the "abomination of desolation" in the Temple of Jerusalem at the end of the present era. A similar calculus figures in a slightly distorted form in the Qumran Damascus Document,[26] and in an early rabbinic world chronicle,[27] both presenting historically inexact, but theologically correct, time schedules in which the final end would occur 490 years after Nebuchadnezzar's conquest of Judea.

Early Christianity inherited a similar computation in the so-called Synoptic Apocalypse (Mark 13:5–20; Matthew 24:4–22; Luke 21:8–24). This eschatological discourse is a literary composition more likely attributable to the primitive church than to Jesus. Paul, too, devised an amazingly detailed time schedule for the final age, the *eschaton*, crowned with the *Parousia*, the second advent of Christ (2 Thessalonians 2:1–10). Such a calculating mentality is irreconcilable with the stance of Jesus, who opposed mathematical flights of fancy and premonitory giveaways: "The kingdom of God is not coming with signs to be observed" (Luke 17:20; cf. Mark 8:11–13; Matthew 12:38–39, 16:1–4; Luke 11:16,29).

For Jesus, the date of the arrival of the kingdom was a mystery with which only God was acquainted (Mark 13:32; Matthew 24:36). The followers of Jesus had to be prepared day and night. He was convinced that the kingdom of God was imminent and had indeed already begun. His charismatic standpoint tolerated no procrastination. His apostles were not to waste their time on unresponsive Jews (Mark 6:11; Matthew 10:14; Luke 9:5, 10:11), but had to hurry to the hopefully more promising next place. As good and evil were seen as coexisting in Jesus' parables of the kingdom, one must conclude that it was located at the furthest edge of the present era.

According to Jesus, this largely hidden reality of the kingdom was already bursting into the open through charismatic phenomena such as exorcisms performed through the finger of God (Matthew 12:28; Luke 11:20). His followers were exhorted to believe that the kingdom of God was almost in sight, just around the corner.

God the Father

The next step in the reconstruction of the Jewish religion of Jesus takes us directly to the God whose kingdom Jesus was preparing. He did not offer a theological definition of God any more than he determined the idea of the divine kingdom. According to Jesus' existential thought, God is what God does. For him, the Almighty was first and foremost a caring God. Natural catastrophes remained outside his vision.

Christians unfamiliar with Judaism often falsely assume that the contemporaries of Jesus felt that God was distant from them and did not perceive or address him as their Father. They have also an erroneous appreciation of what the term "son of God" signified in those days. A well-known New Testament scholar declared that the invocation of God as Father was "unthinkable" in the prayer language of the Jews of Jesus' age.[28] To clarify these issues, one must first focus on the notion of the fatherhood of God in general. The frequency and variety of the phrases used by the Evangelists, "my Father" or "your Father" (spoken by Jesus or his disciples) and even the all-inclusive "our Father" and the vocative "Father!" suggest that this manner of speaking was in no way surprising.

As a matter of fact, anyone familiar with scripture and post-biblical Jewish writings will know that describing God or appealing to him as "Father" is attested from the earliest times down to the rabbinic era. The personal names in the Bible such as Abi-el ("God is my Father") or Abi-jah ("My Father is Yah [the Lord]") witness a familiarity with the notion of divine paternity, and from the mid-sixth century B.C.E.

onward the idea is positively formulated (Isaiah 63:16, 64:8; Psalm 89:26; 1 Chronicles 29:10). God is not infrequently spoken of or addressed as "Father" in the Apocrypha,[29] the Pseudepigrapha[30] and the Dead Sea Scrolls,[31] too.

In public prayer in the Temple and the synagogue God was usually invoked formally as "Lord," "our God" or "King of the Universe," but one must bear in mind the famous supplication *Avinu, Malkenu* ("our Father, our King"), a formula already traditional in the early second century C.E., and "our Father who are in heaven" (*Avinu she-bashamayim*), a customary phrase on the lips of the rabbis. Early synagogue prayers, too, are regularly directed toward the divine Father.[32] In brief, it can safely be concluded that calling on God as Father was traditional in Jewish circles; it was not, as has been repeatedly claimed by ill-informed or biased New Testament interpreters, an innovation introduced by Jesus.

The renowned German New Testament scholar Joachim Jeremias propounded the thesis that the formula carried a peculiar nuance that linked it exclusively to Jesus.[33] According to his theory, the Aramaic word *abba* (father) was originally an exclamatory formula derived from the babbling of infants (*ab-ba*, like da-da or pa-pa, and *im-ma*, like ma-ma). Although using this kind of language toward God would have struck conventional Jews as disrespectful, Jesus, Jeremias asserted, conscious of his unique closeness to the deity, was brave enough to address the Almighty as "Dad." Although this peculiar thesis has been shown to be a misconception,[34] it nevertheless continues to be repeated despite the fact that it is philologically groundless and from the literary-historical point of view erroneous.

The conclusion one may draw from the foregoing observations is that for Jesus the Lord of creation was first and foremost a loving Father. The nonmention of the suffering innocents is typical of Jesus' optimistic outlook regarding the end time. He believed that at the last moment the all-encompassing love would eliminate the miseries of the world and God would be recognized by all as their benevolent Father.

As a negative confirmation of the association of Jesus' attitude to God and the address "Father," on only one occasion—when his trust appears to have faltered, when on the cross it suddenly dawned on him that God was not going to intervene—the invocation *Abba* is replaced by the less filial "my God," in the bitter cry, "*Eloi, eloi*, why have you forsaken me?" (Mark 15:34; Matthew 27:46).

Son of God

The concept that is reciprocal to "God the Father" is "Son of God." In fact, any male human being speaking of God as Father necessarily imagines himself to be his son. However, the matter is not as simple as that. The title "Son of God" has at least five different meanings in the Hebrew Bible in relation to humans, and a sixth one regarding angels, who are also often designated as "sons of God." In the broadest sense, the title "Son of God" could be applied to every male Jew from the earliest layers of biblical tradition (Exodus 4:22; Deuteronomy 32:18–19; Hosea 11:1, etc.). At a later stage, the sense of the expression became progressively restricted first to pious Jews,[35] and more specially to saintly miracle workers and charismatic Hasidim. Close to the summit of the scale, it applies to the kings of Israel. Finally at the top of the pyramid we find the King Messiah, son of David.[36] In Jewish parlance, "Son of God" is always used in a metaphorical sense.

It is essential, however, to stress that one meaning is never attested because it is incompatible with Jewish monotheism. This is the nonmetaphorical, indeed literal, employment of "Son of God," implying not so much the holder's closeness to God owing to election and piety, but his actual participation in the divine nature. As far as the gospel terminology is concerned, with the exception of a single saying, Jesus is never recorded calling himself "Son of God" in the Synoptics.

In that single passage, Jesus is identified as pre-eminently "*the* Son" (*ho Huios*) (Matthew 11:25–27; Luke 10:21–22). The self-designation occurs in a prayer in which he declares, thinking of himself, that "no one knows the Son except the Father and no one knows the Father except the Son." This unparalleled dictum echoes the theology of the Fourth Gospel and is no doubt a later insertion, for if such a "high Christology" had been genuinely part of Matthew and Luke (or the hypothetical source known as Q*), one would have expected it to figure more than once in the Synoptic Gospels.

The charismatic Judaism preached by Jesus

Seeking to guide his followers toward the kingdom of God, Jesus laid down firm doctrinal directives for his disciples. He did not offer a systematic plan, but handed out special rules and commands. Taken

*See Stephen J. Patterson, "Q," *BR*, October 1993.

together, they amount to the eschatological charismatic religion of Jesus. How did this religion relate to the inherited Judaism of Jesus?

In fact, his religious behavior appears to have coincided in all essentials to that of his Palestinian Jewish contemporaries. We are told that he was circumcised when he was eight days old, and his mother presented him in the Temple of Jerusalem and offered the sacrifice prescribed by the law of Moses (Luke 2:22–24; cf. Leviticus 12:1–8). According to the Synoptic Gospels, he regularly attended the local synagogue on the Sabbath, where he often taught the assembled gatherings, healed the sick and practiced exorcism. He was a popular, much-sought-after religious figure, who attracted large Jewish crowds although his charismatic nonconformity was sometimes criticized by the synagogue and Temple authorities. The Infancy Gospel of Luke ends with the episode of the 12-year-old, legally adult Jesus making his pilgrimage to the Temple with other members of his family in conformity with the prescription of the Torah (Luke 2:41–50).

According to the Synoptics, Jesus' contact with the Temple of Jerusalem during his public career was limited to the single visit at the Passover, which turned out to be fatal. The Gospel of John, on the other hand, brings Jesus to Jerusalem during several Passovers as well as on the occasion of the autumnal Feast of Tabernacles and even once at the festival of dedication (Hanukkah), which did not demand obligatory pilgrimage to Jerusalem. But John's chronology is incompatible with that of the Synoptics which, with the exception of its special timetable relating to the arrest, trial and execution of Jesus,[37] appears to be preferable. On one occasion Jesus is described as paying the annual contribution toward the maintenance of the Temple out of miraculously found money (Matthew 17:24–25). Jesus is also portrayed as observing various external Jewish customs such as having tassels attached to his cloak in conformity with the law of Numbers 15:38 (Matthew 9:20; Luke 8:44; Matthew 14:36; Mark 6:56). In other words, he behaved and looked as an ordinary Jew of his age.

There are three issues on which Jesus' observance of the Torah has been questioned by scholars. It has been argued that Jesus discarded the biblical dietary laws (Matthew 15:10–11; Mark 7:15–20) and thus abandoned a principal tenet of the Jewish religion.[38] But this argument is specious. In his figurative speech, Jesus maintained that the true cause of uncleanness was not external, but internal. It was not caused by the consumption of forbidden food, but by disobeying God's commandment. The source of impurity was the heart, out of which sprang thoughts leading to every breach of the law, and not by comestibles which, whether kosher or not, ended up in the latrine. Jesus' words were misinterpreted by a glossator of the text, who then inserted the phrase, "Thus he declared all foods clean" (Mark 7:19) for the benefit of later generations of non-Jewish-Christians. (This notation is absent from the parallel passage in Matthew 15:17.)

Nothing in the New Testament regarding the early stages of the Christian movement suggests that Jesus intended to annul the distinction between clean and unclean food. If it had been known among his early Jewish followers that Jesus had such an idea in mind, Peter would not have been described as so shocked by the thought of touching nonkosher meat (Acts 10:14). Also Paul's hand would have been strengthened in his rejection of the Jewish ritual and dietary laws by the knowledge that he was faithfully following the teaching of the Lord.

Healing after synagogue service on the Sabbath was another controversial subject. No one actually accused Jesus of breaking the Sabbath law, but one can hear occasional grumbles, implying an oblique criticism of Jesus (Luke 13:14). In fact, the complaint is largely irrelevant. As a rule, Jesus healed by word of mouth and/or by touch, neither of which amounted to "work" prohibited on the Sabbath. Moreover, according to a basic principle of Judaism, the saving of life superseded the Sabbath. Of course a pedantic reader could ask whether some of the illnesses treated by Jesus were actually life-threatening, but even according to the most severe rabbis, in case of doubt legal presumption favored intervention even when the complaint was no more than a throat ache.[39] The rabbinic dictum, "The Sabbath is delivered up to you and not you to the Sabbath"[40] is equivalent to the saying of Jesus, "The Sabbath was made for humankind, and not humankind for the Sabbath" (Mark 2:27).

The third controversial issue concerns the termination of matrimony, authorized by Jewish law, but forbidden by Jesus (Deuteronomy 24:1–4). However, in disapproving of divorce, even at the price of causing upset to his own apostles (Mark 10:1–12; Matthew 19:1–12), Jesus intended to lay emphasis on the ideal of lifelong union between one man and one woman as it was instituted by God at the beginning and restore the original monogamous and indissoluble form of marriage during the brief interim period leading to the inauguration of the kingdom of God.

In addition to these three notorious cases, the so-called "antitheses," a set of sayings contained in the Sermon on the Mount (Matthew 5:21–48), are sometimes cited by New Testament interpreters as revealing Jesus' disregard of the Jewish law. In these antitheses various Old Testament commandments are introduced with the words, "You have heard that it was said to the men of old" or something similar and followed by Jesus' statement, "But I say to you."

The term "antithesis" used by modern gospel specialists to designate the passages in Matthew is a misnomer if it is taken in the strict sense. In none of the passages is the opposite of the scriptural saying advocated. Jesus did not replace "You shall not kill" or "You shall not commit adultery" with "You shall kill" or "You shall commit adultery." What he had in mind was to underscore the inner significance of the biblical teaching by outlawing not only the sinful act, but also the inner motivation inspiring it.

Did then Jesus oppose any of the tenets of the Torah? Some Jews, who dislike Jesus, say so, as do also some Christians, who disapprove of Judaism. However, two gospel sayings survive in Matthew and Luke, which demonstrate that for Jesus Judaism and the Torah were not passing phases in the divine plan, but they were there to last:

> Do not think that I have come to abolish the Law or the Prophets; I have come not to abolish but to fulfill. For truly I tell you, until heaven and earth pass away, not one letter, not one stroke of a letter, will pass from the Law.
>
> (Matthew 5:17–18)

Some have argued that this is the voice not of Jesus, but of Matthew buttressing the beliefs of the primitive Judeo-Christian church as opposed to Pauline Christianity. But the same purpose cannot be ascribed to the non-Jewish Luke, who in many other cases advocated this point of view and nevertheless catered to the interests of gentile Christianity.[41] Indeed, Luke was not less but rather more emphatic than Matthew regarding the lasting character of the Torah: "It is easier for heaven and earth to pass away, than for one stroke of a letter in the Law to be dropped" (Luke 16:17).

Moreover, if it had been known in the early church that Jesus was ready to discard large segments of the Torah, Paul would have not encountered Judeo-Christian opposition when he decided to exempt his gentile converts from the observance of the Jewish ceremonial law and circumcision.

Jesus was definitely not against the Mosaic law. Rather he tried, like other Jewish teachers before and after him, to summarize the Torah. He selected the Ten Commandments as the kernel of Judaism as did his Jewish contemporary, Philo of Alexandria (Mark 10:17–19; Matthew 19:16–19; Luke 18:18–20).[42] Like Philo and the famous rabbi Hillel among others, Jesus also proposed the so-called Golden Rule as his one-article code of morality:[43] "Whatever you wish that men would do to you, do so to them; for this is the Law and the Prophets" (Matthew 7:12).

Finally, to an honest seeker who was "not far from the kingdom of God," Jesus disclosed the great commandment, the combination of two fundamental precepts of the Torah, the love of God and the love of the neighbor (Mark 12:28–34, quoting Deuteronomy 6:4–5 and Leviticus 19:18).

In short, the religion of Jesus was the religion of Moses and the biblical prophets, but a religion adapted for the requirements of the final age in which Jesus and his generation believed themselves. In this religion of Jesus, customary priorities were reversed: Not only did he embrace prophetic preferences, placing the poor, the orphans, the widows and the prisoners before the conventionally devout, but he also offered privileged treatment to the sick and to the pariahs of society. In his view, God preferred the prodigal son, the repentant tax collector and the harlot to the always well-behaved bourgeois conformist (Matthew 11:19; Luke 7:34; Mark 2:17; Matthew 9:13; Luke 5:32; Matthew 10:5, 15:32; Luke 15:4–7).

In the hierarchy of access to the kingdom of God, those animated by the trustful simplicity of a child, inspired by absolute reliance on a caring heavenly Father, are as highly valued by Jesus as the truly repentant sinners (Matthew 18:3; Mark 10:15; Luke 18:17). The hopeful gaze of a little one impresses God more than the self-assurance of a sage (Matthew 11:25; Luke 10:21). As has been remarked in connection with charismatic healing, faith/trust is the dominating virtue in the religion of Jesus. A hungry son never imagines that his father might give him a stone or a snake when he has asked for bread or fish (Matthew 7:9–10; Luke 11:11–12).

This stress laid on a childlike attitude toward God is peculiar to Jesus. The same sentiment of confidence is at the heart of Jesus' attitude to prayer. Without trust, supplications to the heavenly Father are meaningless words; with it everything moves to the sphere of the possible. Jesus assured his followers that faith as small as a mustard seed could move mountains (Mark 11:23–24; Matthew 21:21–22). The best expression of his total reliance on God is found in the memorable formula of the Lord's Prayer: "Your will be done" (Matthew 6:10).

Privacy was another prominent feature of Jesus' instructions on prayer. He himself is repeatedly depicted as choosing solitude for communicating with God (Mark 1:35; Luke 5:16; Mark 6:46; Matthew 14:23; Luke 6:12; Mark 14:35; Matthew 26:39; Luke 22:41). He disapproved of pompous or ostentatious prayer. He advised his followers to perform good deeds and speak to God without being seen by other witnesses and without presenting God with a lengthy shopping list (Matthew 6:6).

For Jesus, citizenship in the kingdom depended on total devotion to the cause. A seeker of the kingdom, like anyone desirous to acquire a precious pearl or a treasure hidden in a field, must be ready to sacrifice everything he had (Matthew 13:44–46). Finally, using hyperbolic imagery, the Jesus of the Synoptics asserts that a man had to castrate himself or get rid of an eye or a limb if that was the price required for entry into the kingdom of God (Mark 9:45–47; Matthew 18:9, 19:12).

Filial trust and readiness to give all one possessed had to be followed by wholehearted action. Attention was to be fixed on today (Matthew 6:11; Luke 11:3). The march toward the kingdom was not to be interrupted or held up even for the short time needed for burying one's father (Luke 9:60; Matthew 8:22). Neither was the new recruit allowed to dream nostalgically about the past. His eyes had to be fixed on the ultimate goal: "No one who puts his hand to the plow and looks back is fit for the Kingdom of God" (Luke 9:62).

The religion taught by Jesus was a reformulation of traditional Judaism in the framework of charismatic eschatology. It did not include a vision of a lasting future. When the end was expected at any instant, sagacious planning for the future appeared to be fatuous. First, personal property was to go overboard; there was no time simultaneously to serve God and Mammon. One must be prepared for rifts in the family in the age leading to the manifestation of the kingdom of God. Hence, in Jesus' mind, if duties toward one's family hampered progress in the advancement toward God, then parents, spouses, siblings and children were to be sacrificed. Finally, expressed as an extreme hyperbole, the disciple had to be ready to abandon his nearest and dearest and even sacrifice his own life: "Whoever comes to me and does not hate father and mother, wife and children, brothers and sisters, yes, and even life itself, cannot be my disciple" (Luke 14:26).

Did Jesus found a church?

In sum, the Judaism preached by Jesus focused on the disciples' striving for God's impending kingdom, and within it for the encounter with the loving and solicitous divine king and Father. There is no indication in the Gospels that he foresaw a lengthy future before the dawning of the great day of the Lord. It is quite remarkable that the word "church" (*ekklesia*) designating an institution intended to continue the mission of Jesus and the idea of baptism as a gateway into the church are completely absent from the Gospels of Mark, Luke and even John, and appear only in three odd passages in Matthew where we read:

> On this rock I will build my church, and the powers of Hades shall not prevail against it.
>
> (Matthew 16:18)

> If [your brother] refuses to listen to [two or three people who try to correct him], tell it to the church; and if he refuses to listen even to the church, let him be to you as a gentile or a tax collector.
>
> (Matthew 18:17)

> Make disciples of all the nations, baptizing them.
>
> (Matthew 28:19)[44]

The idea of a second coming of Christ in a far distant future was alien to early stages of Christian thinking.

The religion proclaimed by Jesus was a wholly theocentric one in which he played the role of the man of God par excellence, the prophet of prophets, the shepherd of the flock, the leader, revealer and teacher without being himself in any sense the object of worship as he later became in the full-fledged Christianity created by Paul and John, and especially by the church from the second century onward. The Judaism practiced and preached by Jesus himself, surrounded by an aura of charisma was meant to be a passport allowing the devout without let or hindrance and without the need for any other go-betweens to enter directly into the kingdom of God. The religion of Jesus was meant to regulate a short-term interim period, which would end with the angelic trumpets marking the inauguration of the kingdom of God. It did not envisage the cross.[45]

TEMPLE WARNING INSCRIPTION. Found in 1935 in Jerusalem's Old City, this fragmentary limestone slab was once part of a balustrade that surrounded the inner courts of the Temple. The stone bears a Greek inscription warning gentiles not to enter. The full text of the inscription reads: "No foreigner may enter within the railing and enclosure that surround the Temple. Anyone apprehended shall have himself to blame for his consequent death."

The shock inflicted on the disciples by the execution of Jesus was overcome relatively quickly through the belief in his resurrection and the charismatic experience of the descent of the Holy Spirit at the first Pentecost 50 days after Passover. This resulted in the replacement of the eschatological D-day from the inauguration on earth of the kingdom of God by Jesus to its launch by Christ at the moment of his *Parousia*, or second coming. However, in the minds of the first followers of Jesus, the period of expectation was not changed in any significant way. Accompanied by his angels, the Lord was to reveal himself during the lifetime of those who had known him before his crucifixion. St. Paul and his Thessalonian disciples looked forward to being eyewitnesses of the universal resurrection, marking the descent from heaven of the glorified Jesus surrounded by an angelic host (1 Thessalonians 4:15–17). The end was still expected to be imminent.

This chronological perspective brings us back to the final question raised in the opening paragraph of this chapter: Did nascent Palestinian Christianity consider itself part of the main body of Judaism?

The answer must be unhesitatingly affirmative. The Judeo-Christians considered themselves Jews and their outward behavior and dietary customs were Jewish. In fact, they faithfully observed all the rules and regulations of the Mosaic law. At worst, they were seen by other Jews as representatives of one of the many sects that flourished in the Holy Land in the first century C.E.

The apostles and the whole Jesus party continued to frequent the religious center of Judaism, the Temple of Jerusalem, for private and public worship every day (Acts 2:46). This attachment to the sanctuary was the most tangible proof of the Jewishness of the Jerusalem church in the sense that all its members were of Judaic ancestry. If Jesus and the leaders who followed him had entertained the idea of gentiles becoming members of the movement, the Temple of Jerusalem, which was of forbidden access to non-Jews under instant pain of death,*[46] would not have been chosen as the principal site of daily devotion. The gospel evidence and the relevant passages in the Acts of the Apostles testify without a shadow of doubt that the movement initiated by Jesus and continued by the early Palestinian church was a purely Jewish entity. There was no sign of any fissure in the united body of Jesus' followers until the acceptance of the principle that non-Jews could become full members of the Jesus movement without first passing through Judaism.

Paul's successful missionary activity among gentiles is the primary source of the parting of the ways.

Excursus: Why was Jesus crucified?

How are we to understand Jesus' tragic end in light of the evidence assembled in the foregoing pages? In this reconstruction, Jesus did not commit any breach of religious law that would carry a death sentence nor was he involved in political or messianic agitation against the Roman state. Why then was he condemned to crucifixion? I have analyzed the reasons for this tragedy in detail in my book, *The Passion*;[47] a few brief comments will suffice here. The disturbance caused by Jesus at the Temple

*Strata, "Inscriptions Show Ancient Jerusalem Was a Global City," *BAR*, July/August 2011.

made the priestly leaders nervous; on their shoulders lay the responsibility for the maintenance of law and order in a Jerusalem then filled to the brim with pilgrims just before Passover; they grasped the opportunity to arrest Jesus after sunset away from the city center. It was done without provoking popular unrest. After a summary interrogation at night, Jesus was hurried in the early hours to the residence of Pilate. He was charged with agitation and summarily and unjustly sentenced and executed as a revolutionary by the prefect of Judea.

The historical probability of such a scenario is reinforced by Flavius Josephus, who presents the case of Jesus as one of the outrages committed by Pilate.[48] But Josephus implies that in the politically stormy years of the first century C.E. in Judea a Jew could easily run the risk of losing his life without breaking any law, Jewish or Roman. It was enough to appear as a potential political threat. According to the *Jewish Antiquities*, John the Baptist was executed by Herod Antipas because his eloquence, his ability to fire the enthusiasm of crowds, could easily lead to revolution in the unsettled social climate of Palestine.[49]

The story of another Jesus, Jesus son of Ananias, confirms that unwisely toying with danger during a pilgrimage feast in first-century C.E. Jerusalem could have a virtually lethal effect. We learn from Josephus[50] that during the days leading to the Feast of Tabernacles, in 62 B.C.E., this "rude peasant" imitated the prophet Jeremiah and day and night loudly proclaimed woe to Jerusalem and the Temple. The authorities, sensing potential trouble, detained him and tried to silence him by administering a severe beating, but this was to no avail. As soon as he was released, he started again. Worried that this Jesus, son of Ananias, might after all be a divinely inspired prophet, yet not wishing to be held accountable for a possible tumult, the Jewish leaders, imitating their predecessors in the days of Pontius Pilate, handed over the troublemaker to the Roman procurator Albinus. As in the case of the Jesus of the Gospels, this other Jesus was given a fresh scourging followed by interrogation before the governor; this later Jesus remained obstinately silent. The down-to-earth Albinus concluded that Jesus son of Ananias was mad and let him go, but if the governor had been in a less tolerant mood, this second Jesus would also have been crucified.

So if the question is put again, "Why was Jesus condemned to death?" the most likely answer in the context of the religious, historical and political circumstances of late Second Temple Judea is this: Jesus' downfall was precipitated by the fracas he caused in the sanctuary at Passover, when Jewish tradition expected the arrival of the Messiah. This made him appear dangerous in the eyes of both the chief priests and of Pilate and that was enough for another Jew to end his life on the Roman cross.

From the Crucifixion to the End of the First Century

JAMES D.G. DUNN

The imagery to be used

TO SPEAK OF "THE PARTING OF THE WAYS" IN WHAT EMERGED from first-century Judaism can be misleading. This phrase assumes that the historical actuality is faithfully (or adequately) represented in the splitting of one way (Judaism) to become two ways (Christianity and Rabbinic Judaism). But the Judaism at the beginning of the first century C.E., better expressed as Second Temple Judaism, was not a single "way." A number of "ways" were pursued by Jews in the Second Temple period. They all confessed the one God of Israel, believed that Israel was God's elect nation, celebrated their Judean/Jewish ethnic identity, were committed to obey the Torah, and acknowledged the centrality of the Jerusalem Temple and cult. But they did so in different ways. Their expression of these shared beliefs was different. Their praxis, as or more important than their beliefs, varied significantly. So much so that many scholars think it more accurate to speak of *Judaisms* during this period.[1] Some of these Judaisms are well known—Sadducees, Pharisees and Essenes, in particular. But there were other strands or paths, represented, for example, by the Enoch cycle of literature, apocalyptists, mystics, Hellenizers, Diaspora Judaism, and not forgetting "the people of the land" and the Samaritans.

Equally problematic is the use of the term "Christianity" for what was happening in the first century. This word does not appear until early in the second century, first coined, so far as we can tell by Ignatius of Antioch.[2] Linguistically speaking, Christianity did not yet exist in the first century! In the Acts of the Apostles the movement of Jesus' followers is referred to as a "sect" (Acts 24:14, 28:22), "the sect of the Nazarenes" (24:5). Significantly, this is the term Acts also uses, as does the Jewish historian Josephus, for the "sects" of the Sadducees, Pharisees and Essenes.[3] In other words, Acts regarded the early movement inspired by Jesus as one of the sects or factions that made up and were part of late Second Temple Judaism.

Equally significant is the fact that the first believers in Messiah Jesus are described as those "who belong to the way."[4] The image clearly reflects the Hebrew idiom of walking (*halak*) along a path, an image, untypical of Greek thought, which Paul nevertheless continued to use.[5] This emphasis on the right way to follow is reflected even more strongly in the Pharisaic/rabbinic understanding of *halakhah* (law), as referring to the rules/rulings (derived from the written Torah) that determine how individuals should act ("walk") in particular situations.[6] And the Qumran sect used the term in much the same way as it appears in Acts;[7] the Qumranites liked to think of themselves as "the perfect of way (*derek*), who walk in perfection of way (*derek*)."[8] In other words, just as the Qumranites represented one of the "ways" of being a Jew, one of the component parts of diverse Second Temple Judaism, so the movement that sprang from Jesus was seen as another "way" of living out the covenant obligations of the people of Israel.

The issues posed by the imagery of "the parting of the ways" are further complicated by the fact that it is not clear, or at least cannot simply be assumed, how the Rabbinic Judaism that became the normative expression of Judaism between the second and fourth centuries (and later) relates to the diverse expressions of Second Temple Judaism. The rabbis can rightly be regarded as the direct heirs of the Pharisees. But are they the heirs of the other forms of Second Temple Judaism, of the other ways of being Jewish?[9] And is Christianity, which became the state religion of the Roman Empire in the fourth century, the direct (and only) heir of "the sect of the Nazarene," the people of "the way" (of Jesus)? Was there a direct, linear connection in each case? Was there one way in each case that led without side-roads and bypasses to the fourth-century outcome? Or did the ways wander hither and thither?[10] Did the ways fragment? How in any case do we relate Jewish-Christianity within the big picture?[11] And did other ways merge into the way(s) emerging from the first century? The issue of Gnostic Christianity at once raises its head.

Of course, by late antiquity and the beginning of the Middle Ages there were two distinct entities—Christianity and Judaism. So some sort of division(s) or split(s) or parting(s) had taken place by then.[12] How to describe these divisions/splits/partings? In fact, no single imagery can adequately describe such a complex historical process or development.[13] Perhaps the simplest imagery to use is the process in which the parts of a garment pull apart over time, the threads that begin to break under the stresses of "wear and tear," or the popping of rivets as heavy seas put unbearable strain on the metal plates of a ship, and so on. Such imagery is still inadequate, but focusing on the strains and tensions between Jews and believers-in-Jesus, including not least Jewish believers-in-Jesus, seems most likely to bring to light what became the irreconcilable features that brought about the emergence of two different (and opposed) identities. And since our knowledge of Pharisaic Judaism (30–70 C.E.) and of the beginnings of Rabbinic Judaism (70–100 C.E.) in relation to followers of Jesus is so thin, when drawing from rabbinic sources, we will have to depend more than is comfortable almost exclusively on Christian sources.[14]

What happened to Jesus

If we have turned our back on the liberal Protestant view that Jesus himself had renounced Judaism and its law,[15] we still have to face up to the claim that Jewish responsibility for, or at least attitude to, Jesus' death already drove a knife into the unsplit fabric.[16] And it is uncomfortably true that the gospel writers and the Acts of the Apostles do emphasize the role of the high priests and the people in bringing about Jesus' death (e.g., Acts 2:23, 3:14–15). But that already takes us into the second half of our time sequence (30–100 C.E.) and can be partly explained by the early Christian apologetic desire to play down Roman responsibility for Jesus' death. We will return to these texts in due course. For the moment, the question is whether the crucifixion of Jesus put a serious strain on the relations of Jesus' disciples to the Jewish authorities and religious leaders.

Here we should note that the only reference Paul makes to Jewish attitudes to Jesus' crucifixion is in 1 Corinthians 1:23: "We proclaim Christ crucified, a stumbling block to Jews." Implied also in Galatians 3:13 is the probability that many Jews regarded someone crucified as accursed by God. How serious an accusation was that? We know from 4QpNah[um] 1.7–8 that the Qumranites regarded the crucifixion by Alexander Jannaeus of his Pharisaic opponents in the same way.[17] In other words, this kind of dismissive insult was another example of the factional vituperation that was all too common among the Second Temple factions.[18] But the fact is that, according to Acts (and in this Acts is confirmed by Paul's letters), Jewish believers-in-Jesus remained in Jerusalem until the First Jewish Revolt against Rome, relatively undisturbed for some 30 years, apart from one or two spells of persecution. The fact that these first followers of Jesus revered their leader as a martyr (cf. Romans 5:6–8), using sacrificial imagery in referring to his death (cf. Romans 3:25, 8:3), rather as the deaths of the Maccabean martyrs were probably already spoken of (cf. 4 Maccabees 17:21–22), probably put them in the category of oddball enthusiasts to be tolerated rather than rooted out.

The same probably applies to the first believers' conviction that Jesus had been raised from the dead, that in the case of Jesus the resurrection of the dead, expected by the Pharisees for the end of this age, had already begun (Romans 1:4; 1 Corinthians 15:20). When nothing more happened (the general resurrection did not come), the believers in Messiah Jesus were probably dismissed as enthusiastic eccentrics—not a belief to be respected, but neither one to be extirpated. That this belief became so fundamental to Christian identity, and probably was from the beginning, did not make it or the believers any less Jewish.

The same is true of the belief that Jesus was Messiah. A crucified Messiah was, as we have seen, probably an oxymoron for most Jews, but it was no less Jewish than Bar-Kokhba being hailed by the famous rabbi Akiba in the Second Jewish Revolt a hundred years later,[19] and evidently could be largely tolerated, since it appears not to have aroused the nationalistic spirit as did Bar-Kokhba. On the contrary, believers in Jesus Messiah were victims rather than proponents of nationalistic politics. The arbitrary execution of James, one of the leaders of the new sect (Acts 12:2), was probably one sign of Herod Agrippa's flexing his own political muscles in the 40s.[20] And in 62 C.E. the other James, the brother of Jesus, was probably the victim of the factionalist fanaticism that was to destroy the chances of success for the first revolt against Rome (Josephus, *Antiquities* 20.200–201).

Somewhat surprisingly, the further conviction among the first believers in Jesus, that he had been exalted to the right hand of God, in fulfillment of Psalm 110:1,[21] likewise did not seem to attract much notice or abuse.[22] Paul alludes at various times to the opposition that his gospel provoked among Jews and traditionalist Jewish believers in Jesus.[23] But apart from 1 Corinthians 1:23 and Galatians 3:13, Paul gives no hint that early Christian beliefs in Jesus' exaltation provoked Jewish hostility. In fact, in the early years the reflection among believers-in-Jesus on what had happened to him was quite consistent with and similar to reflections elsewhere within Second Temple Judaism as to what had happened to such exceptional individuals as Enoch, Elijah, the righteous martyrs, and Ezra and Baruch.[24] These were characteristically Jewish reflections about agents of God. Of course, Christian claims for Jesus became more and more unacceptable to belief in God as one (the *Shema'*),[25] and we will have to return to the subject below. But there is nothing to indicate that the earliest beliefs in Jesus' exaltation were already a seam-tearing stress in the wineskin of Second Temple Judaism.

The Hellenists

The first obvious breaking of threads comes with the Hellenists to whom Luke introduces us in Acts 6:1. As "Greek-speakers" (= "Hellenists"), that is, probably those who could function comfortably only in the international *lingua franca* of the day (Greek), they were almost certainly Jews from the Mediterranean Diaspora who had settled in Jerusalem. That they were also "Hellenizers" in the old sense made so offensive to Judeans in the buildup to the Maccabean revolt (1 Maccabees 1:11–15; 2 Maccabees 4:13) cannot be assumed. Hellenistic culture had already crept quite deeply into Palestine, and a large proportion of Jews (in Jerusalem at any rate) could operate comfortably in Greek.*[26] Even so, if there was

*See Martin Goodman, "Under the Influence," *BAR*, January/February 2010.

in Jerusalem a substantial body of Diaspora Jews influenced by Greek culture, that must have contributed significantly to the uneasy factionalism within Jerusalem in the 30s and 40s.

The new sect of the Nazarene evidently appealed to many of these Hellenists,[27] who presumably became members of the sect by baptism in the name of Jesus. "The way" practiced by these first believers-in-Jesus seems to have been particularly attractive to them.[28] The Acts account has many lacunae in it, but its thrust is clear enough. One of the Hellenist members of "the way" was Stephen, who became a bold spokesman for his new faith in Messiah Jesus (Acts 6:8–10). If we follow the clues provided by Luke, it would appear that Stephen spoke out against the Temple, with its accompanying laws and customs.[29] The accusation against Stephen, in fact, strongly suggests that he took up some teaching or saying of Jesus, understood as a condemnation of the Temple (Acts 6:11–14).[30] And in the speech attributed to Stephen, the accusation against him is taken up in forthright terms: "The Most High does not dwell in houses made with human hands" (Acts 7:48). That language would have been highly insulting in that although the human role in constructing the Temple was hardly to be denied, the phrase "made with human hands" was the phrase used in Jewish Greek to refer to an idol, "the thing made with hands."[31] Did Stephen condemn the Temple as idolatrous? Even if Luke has exaggerated the offensiveness of Stephen's views,[32] an attitude that regarded the Temple, any temple, as unnecessary to and a distraction from the worship of God (as the quotation in Acts 7:47–50 from Isaiah 66:1–2 implies) was bound to be offensive.

How serious was this dismissal of the Temple as the focus of worship for the covenant people? It is likely that Stephen, or the Hellenist believers-in-Jesus more generally, developed the view of Jesus' death as a sin-offering, perhaps even equivalent to the Day of Atonement sacrifice. The implication, which Paul hints at and which Hebrews was to make much of, could already have been present: that Jesus' death as a sin-offering rendered all further sin-offerings unnecessary. That is, the sacrificial cult of the Jerusalem Temple was deemed to be no longer necessary for the believers in Jesus Messiah. We cannot attribute such views to the earliest Jerusalem disciples, since the clear implication of passages like Acts 3:1, 21:20–26[33] and Matthew 5:24 is that the Jerusalem believers-in-Jesus continued to participate in the Temple cult.[34] The

THEODOTUS INSCRIPTION. Theodotus, son of Vettenus, commemorated his rebuilding of a synagogue with this first-century C.E. Greek inscription that was excavated in a Jerusalem cistern. Because the inscription is in Greek and mentions accommodations for "those who have need from abroad," the synagogue may have been used primarily by Greek-speaking Jews ("Hellenists") of the Mediterranean Diaspora. These Hellenists, some of whom became the first believers-in-Jesus, likely contributed significantly to the evolving schisms within Second Temple Judaism.

creedal statement that Paul taught following his conversion, "that Christ died for our sins according to the scriptures" (1 Corinthians 15:3), may therefore have been a Hellenist formulation.[35] So the Hellenists' negative attitude to the Temple may have been still more radical, and the stress on one of the principal seams of Israel's religion would have been all the greater.[36]

However, it should be noted that any pulling apart here was a pulling apart *within* the Jesus sect as well as between the Hellenists and the main body of Jews. For the more traditionalist Jewish believers-in-Jesus seem to have remained largely loyal to Temple (and Torah) when the Hellenist believers-in-Jesus began to pull away from such traditionalist loyalties. Any "parting" then was not between the new sect as such and the rest of the Jews, but between two strands of the new movement. Moreover, we should recall that the status and role of the Temple had already been questioned by the Qumran sect, who regarded their own community as a substitute for the corrupt Temple in Jerusalem.[37] And we should recall that Rabbinic Judaism had to cope with the destruction of the Temple in 70 C.E. and with its absence thereafter, and that they did so by aligning Judaism around Torah and rabbi, instead of around Temple and priesthood. As crucial as was the Jerusalem Temple to Second Temple Judaism, its continued physical presence and cult was not crucial to the Judaism that endured.

The incoming of gentile believers

The consequence of Stephen's stand and execution, according to Luke, was a severe persecution of the Hellenist believers-in-Jesus (Acts 8:1–3). Most think that the principal targets would have been the Greek-speakers (easier to pick out), and the persecuting mission to the Hellenistic city of Damascus (Acts 9:2), which Paul himself confirms (Galatians 1:13–17), also supports the implication that the Hellenists were the main target. The Diaspora Jew Saul (later Paul) took a leading part in persecuting those whom he regarded as recalcitrant (and more dangerous) fellow Diaspora Jews.

The driving out of the Hellenists (who still regarded themselves as Jews) evidently had major consequences for the expansion of the new movement—into Samaria (Acts 8) and crucially up the Mediterranean coast into the principal city of the region, Antioch (Acts 11:19). There, according to Acts, they made the breakthrough of preaching to other Greek-speakers, who were not Jews (11:20).[38] That development set in train a sequence of events that resulted in more and more non-Jews joining the new sect. That Jewish believers-in-Jesus were so open to so many gentile recruits is rather surprising, and one may presume that the more culturally Hellenistic Jewish believers found communication with fellow Greek-speakers more natural than did their more traditionalist counterparts in the new sect. A contributory factor would almost certainly have been that over the years many gentiles had evidently been attracted to Judaism[39]—not least to its understanding of God as invisible (not depictable in a wooden image/idol), to its strong moral standards, to its custom of observing one day in seven as a rest day.[40] These are known, and probably were already known at that time, as "Godfearers"[41]—that is, non-Jews who attached themselves in some degree to the local (Diaspora) synagogues, and who observed at least some of the Jewish customs and festivals.*(See Chapter III, "The Godfearers: From the Gospels to Aphrodisias," by Bruce Chilton.) But the reason given by both Paul and Acts is that the influx of gentile baptisands was a manifestation of "the grace of God" (Galatians 2:9; Acts 11:23), with clear indications that these new believers had been "given the Holy Spirit" just as the first believers had (Galatians 3:2–5; Acts 10:44–48, 11:15–18). The first believers-in-Jesus were evidently convinced that the acceptance of the gentiles was approved by God and demanded by divine initiative.

This broadening out of the new sect's membership to non-Jews must have itself caused a further strain on the fabric of Second Temple Judaism. For ethnicity has always been at the heart of Jewish identity, the (physical) seed of Abraham, the bloodline descending from Abraham, Isaac and Jacob.[42] Non-Jews could be absorbed into that line of descent by becoming Jews, and a widespread hope was that gentile pilgrims would flood to Zion at the end of the age.[43] But as the core of the "Jew (*Ioudaios*)" was the geographical entity "Judea" (*Ioudaia*), so the core of Judaism was the ethnic Jew. Paul knew this well (Galatians 2:15) and tried to shift the definition of "Jew" and also of "Israel" to include those who were not ethnic Jews: "Jew" denoted inner disposition toward God, not something physical (Romans 2:28–29); "Israel" denoted those called by God, which could include gentiles as well as Jews (Romans 9:6–12,24). But did he succeed in such redefinitions? Could he succeed? Understandably, Paul's defense of his mission strategy (1 Corinthians 9:19–23)—to Jews, as a Jew; to those outside the law, as one outside the law—has been as much denigrated as it has been admired. Did the influx of gentiles in itself inevitably change the character of the sect of the Nazarene and accelerate any pulling apart from both mainline Judaism and the diversity of Second Temple Judaism?

If such longer-term consequences were implicit or inevitable in the early days of Paul in his role as "apostle to the gentiles" (Romans 11:13), Paul himself would certainly have resisted them. He might well have described himself more fully as "apostle *of Israel* to the gentiles".[44] In particular, he saw his conversion-commission as of a piece with Jeremiah's commission to be "a prophet to the nations" (Jeremiah 1:5), and as an

*See Louis H. Feldman, "The Omnipresence of the God-Fearers," *BAR*, September/October 1986. For a more recent treatment, see Angelos Chaniotis, "Godfearers in the City of Love," *BAR*, May/June 2010.

acting out of the servant's commission to be "a light to the nations" (Isaiah 49:6).[45] And since the servant is identified as Israel (Isaiah 49:3), one can justifiably conclude that Paul saw himself as both an apostle to the gentiles and as an apostle of Israel, his mission to the gentiles as helping to fulfill Israel's own God-given role. Similarly, when he speaks of the gospel being already preached beforehand to Abraham, Paul was thinking of the promise made to Abraham that "All the gentiles shall be blessed in you" (Galatians 3:8).[46] That is to say, he saw his mission, precisely his mission to the gentiles, as the fulfillment of God's promise to Abraham. These promises to Abraham, particularly the promise of seed and land, were (and still are) so fundamental to Judaism's identity.

But the third strand of the promise (blessing to the nations) has been much more neglected. Paul here speaks with an authentically Jewish voice, calling for his fellow Jews to recognize that the gospel of Jesus Christ was God's way of fulfilling his promise to bless the nations through Abraham. Nor should we forget that Paul's great hope, as articulated in Romans 9–11, was that the success of the gospel for gentiles would provoke Israel to accept the gospel for themselves.

All these were viable hopes during Paul's own mission, but they never cut much ice among Jews as a whole and with the emerging mainstream Judaism in particular. However scripturally valid and theologically sound, history soon judged such hopes to be unrealistic. Under Paul the new Jewish sect was moving too far away from the central identity markers of Judaism.

Circumcision, the law and table fellowship

The problem of Jewish identity markers came to its sharpest expression in the issue of whether the new sect should require circumcision of their gentile converts.[47] The issue had its roots in the very first outreach to gentiles. For it would appear that circumcision was not demanded of gentile converts from the beginning of the mission to the gentiles. Luke makes no mention of the issue in his description of the breakthrough in Antioch (Acts 11:19–24), but the reason for dispensing with circumcision had already been explained (Acts 10:44–11:18), and Luke presumably assumed it would be taken for granted. Certainly it is unlikely that circumcision was initially required of gentile converts and then dropped; such a change of tactic would certainly have left some mark in the disputes that followed. In any case, when the issue did arise, presumably when the number of uncircumcised gentiles was becoming a large proportion of the new sect's membership (Galatians 2:1–10; Acts 15), Paul's practice of accepting gentile converts without circumcision was accepted by the Jerusalem leadership, despite vigorous protests from a more traditionalist Jewish faction. Whether these more traditionalist views gained more strength and were behind the attempts subsequently made to amend Paul's mission by insisting that his gentile converts be circumcised (Galatians; Philippians 3) remains unclear. But Paul certainly brushed off such attempts and insisted on shifting the significance of circumcision from the fleshly rite to its spiritual equivalent (Romans 2:25–29; Philippians 3:3). The argument had some good scriptural precedent,[48] but it presumably cut as little ice with his main Jewish interlocutors as his redefinitions of "Jew" and "Israel."

The point is that circumcision is central to the identity of the Jew and of Judaism, the *sine qua non* for all males who are heirs of the covenant promises given to Abraham and the patriarchs (Genesis 17:9–14). It had been one of the make or break issues when the Maccabeans rebelled against the Syrians (1 Maccabees 1:60–61). It was a, if not the, defining characteristic of Judaism, of being full members of the covenant people, heirs of the promise to Abraham. Paul reflects this when he makes the distinction between Jews and gentiles the distinction between "circumcision" and "uncircumcision" (not "circumcised" and "uncircumcised").[49] So to abandon this requirement, this identity marker of the covenant people, even with good cause, was bound to be a major stress factor in the continuing identification of the new sect with its parent Judaism.

Complaints leveled against Paul from the Jewish side have focused more on Paul's attitude to the Torah. What became a defining feature for Lutheranism in particular—that Paul saw the gospel as the polar opposite of the law, that Paul had abandoned the law as any kind of means of grace—was regarded by most Jews as proof that Paul was a renegade and apostate from Judaism. Both the Lutheran interpretation and Jewish reaction have some basis in Paul's writings. We cannot ignore his attitude to the law as expressed, in particular, in Romans 7:5, 10:4; 2 Corinthians 3; and Galatians 2:19. But, as on other subjects, Paul's attitude to the law is far more nuanced. It is the law's protective role in relation to Israel, which Paul regarded as at an end (Galatians 3:19–29).

He defended the law as holy and just and good, while acknowledging that it had been abused by the power of sin (Romans 7:7–8:4). He saw faith, the Spirit and love as the keys to fulfilling the law (Romans 3:27–31, 8:1–4; Galatians 5:6). Circumcision was now relatively unimportant, but keeping the commandments of God was still of first importance (1 Corinthians 7:19). Here again Paul's teaching was liable to serious misinterpretation (by both the unsympathetic and the over-sympathetic). He no doubt saw himself fully within the priorities and precedents provided by Jesus. But with gentile believers being so exempted from the Torah (and halakhic) practices that were regarded as priorities by most fellow Jews, the report in Jerusalem circles that Paul was regarded as one who taught Diaspora Jews to forsake Moses (Acts 21:21) sounds like a genuine echo of tradition-alist Jewish believers-in-Jesus' suspicions of Paul. However sound Paul's theology, it was probably hard, if not impossible, to dispel the belief that he himself had forsaken Moses, and with him all his gentile converts.

The breaking point, however, was probably not Paul's theology as such, so much as the practices he encouraged in the Diaspora communi-ties that he founded or regarded as part of the gentile mission. For in both Corinth and Rome (1 Corinthians 8, 10; Romans 14:1–15:6), Paul attempted to build single communities embracing both traditionalist Jews and gentiles who had no respect for such Jewish scruples. He defended the right of such traditionalist Jews to maintain their scruples, but made it clear that he thought such scruples were no longer necessary. He urged the less scrupulous to willingly limit their freedom to make room for the more scrupulous. But such communities must have found it hard to get along as partners with any local synagogues. There are strong indications of this in Colossians 2:16–23, where it would appear that the local synagogue regarded the Christian congregation as disqualified from any claim on Israel's heritage.[50] It was all very well to claim that in Christ "there is no longer Jew or Greek" (Galatians 3:28), but for those who saw their identity as "Jew," the consequent strain and undermining of identity would probably have been too much. Was it inevitable that the more gentile Paul's churches became, the less Jewish they became, too?[51]

An alternative way of incorporating gentiles within the covenant people is indicated in the speech attributed to James, the brother of Jesus and leader of the Jerusalem church, in Acts 15:13–31; and with it another way of tackling the issue of Jews and gentiles eating together (15:20,29).

In fact, Acts 15 seems to short circuit the two problems to which Paul refers in Galatians 2:1–14—whether circumcision should be required of gentile converts (Galatians 2:1–10), and on what terms could gentile and Jewish believers share table fellowship (2:11–14). In the citation from Amos 9:11–12, Acts 15:16–17 presents the influx of gentiles as integral to the restoration of Israel. And "the apostolic decree" (the "rules of association" between Jews and gentiles) that follows (Acts 15:20) is primarily drawn from the Torah legislation regarding "the resident alien," that is, the non-Jews who were permanently resident in the land of Israel (Leviticus 17:8–9,10–14, 18:26).[52] Here was a solution to the problems posed by the influx of gentiles to a sect that may well have regarded itself as representative of eschatological Israel. It did not require the gentiles to proselytize, to be circumcised. And its main condition for table fellowship was that the gentile believers should eat kosher meat, from which the blood had been properly drained (Leviticus 17:10–14; Acts 15:20,29). Paul was willing for such a compromise in his letters to Corinth and Rome, where gentiles were almost certainly in the majority; but he had resisted such a policy fiercely when it amounted to a Jewish majority, insisting that gentiles accepted such rules as part of the gospel (Galatians 2:14–16).[53] And he never refers to "the apostolic decree" in his letters.

According to Acts, the "apostolic decree" was addressed to churches in Syria and Cilicia (Acts 15:23), that is, to the churches that had been established during Paul's early mission (Galatians 1:21), when he was in effect a missionary of the Antioch church (cf. Acts 13:1–4, 14:26–28). And we know from the church fathers that through the second century many gentile Christians seem to have observed the terms of "the apostolic decree," shying away from the flesh of pagan sacrifices and abstaining from the blood of animals.[54] So we may have to envisage a twofold practice, or a twofold rationale for the same or a similar practice, enabling Jewish and gentile Christians to share in table fellowship. The "apostolic decree" model would ensure that Christians who observed it were thinking and acting Jewishly. But to what extent it delayed the tearing of the seam attributed to Paul is not so clear.

Other possible tipping points

There are numerous points in the history of Christianity's beginnings that proved to be significant at least with hindsight. We have already noted several—particularly the belief that Jesus had been raised from the dead and exalted to God's right hand; Stephen's or the Hellenists' breach with the Temple; the breakthrough to and influx of gentile believers, with consequent dilution of or departure from Jewish identity markers. The significance of other possible "tipping points" is less clear.

At first sight the designation of the new sect as "Christians" (Acts 11:26) should be significant, especially if it indicated that "Christian" was seen to be distinct and different from "Jew." But the new coinage, *Christianoi* ("Christians") is a Greek form of the Latin, *Christiani*; that is, the name was almost certainly coined by a Latin-speaker or one accustomed to the Latin formation.[55] This implies that it was coined by the Roman authorities in Antioch, on the analogy of Herodians (*Hērōdianoi*) or Caesarians, the party of Caesar, or possibly members of Caesar's household (*Kaisarianoi*).[56] The "Christians" were so called, then, because they were perceived to be partisans of "Christ," followers of "Christ," members of the Christ party.[57] Those so referred to would not be "Christians" as distinct from Jews. Rather, the term would refer to Jewish synagogue communities or subgroups that had embraced gentile believers, that is, Jews as well as gentiles. What distinguished them, from the authorities' perspective, was not their ethnicity but their commitment to Messiah/Christ Jesus.

We may compare the famous Suetonius reference to Emperor Claudius's expulsion of the Jews from Rome in 49 C.E., since they "constantly made disturbances because of the instigator Chrestus (*impulsore Chresto*)" (*Claudius* 25.4). Most take it for granted that Suetonius refers to disturbances regarding Christ, not caused by Christ (or "Chrestus").[58] The point is that the disturbances took place *within* the Jewish community in Rome, presumably between members of one or more of the several synagogues in Rome. And it was as Jews that they were expelled;[59] the Christ faction in Rome, Jews who were also Christians, were still functioning as part of and within the Jewish community. Some think that the expulsion of 49 C.E. had already effected the separation of the believers-in-Jesus from the Roman synagogues.[60] But Paul wrote to Roman believers, a group that included Jews as well as gentiles: As many as half of those named and greeted in Romans 16 were probably of eastern origin and very likely Jewish;[61] and Romans 14:1–15:7 seems to reflect a situation in which more traditionalist Jewish believers, who had been expelled from Rome, had been returning, following Claudius's death, and were receiving a cool or cold reception from the more liberal gentile believers who had been undisturbed by the Claudius decree and now formed the majority of the new movement.[62] As for the puzzling account of Paul's time in Rome (Acts 28), the only reason that makes sense of Luke's failure to explicitly include believers-in-Jesus in his description of Paul's final entry to and imprisonment in Rome is that the believers-in-Jesus were included in the description of Paul's continuing contacts with the Jewish community in Rome (28:17–24). There were still close links between the groups of Jesus-believers and the synagogue in Rome.

Here we should note the strong likelihood that the new faith in Jesus Messiah first reached Rome through Jewish merchants,[63] and that the first believers-in-Jesus were almost entirely Jewish.[64] This would have meant that the Jesus-believers met in the synagogue, or functioned as house groups or tenement groups within the larger Jewish community. Non-Jews becoming part of these groups would not necessarily have changed that basic character of the gatherings of Jesus-believers in Rome. Here, too, we need to ask what would have been the *legal status* of these new groupings of believers-in-Jesus. The Roman authorities were notoriously suspicious of unauthorized groups, or *collegia*, voluntary associations. Jewish synagogues were a recognized exception, their rights of assembly and national practices permitted. Any development of particular interest groups within the synagogue would raise no eyebrows, and even some breach with a particular synagogue community was likely to be regarded by the authorities as an internal dispute, Jews with Jews, as in the famous case in Corinth recorded by Luke (Acts 18:12–17). In the highly sensitive context of the capital city itself, there would be all the greater motivation for the new groups of Jesus-believers, including gentiles, to shelter under the protection of the legal status of the synagogue, to avoid drawing unfavorable attention to themselves.[65] Such a policy would certainly have been consistent with the quietist social policy that Paul himself urged on the recipients of his letter to Rome (Romans 12:14–13:7).

All this has bearing on the next possible indication that a rent had occurred between Christians and Jews. I refer to Tacitus's description of the persecution of Christians in Rome by Emperor Nero in 64 C.E., following the great fire of Rome. According to Tacitus, Nero tried to divert suspicion from himself (as the possible arsonist) by making the Christians the scapegoats: He "substituted as culprits, and punished with the utmost refinements of cruelty a class of men, loathed for their vices, whom the crowd styled Christians" (*Annals* 15.44.2). Evidently the Roman populace had become aware of the Christians in Rome, perhaps as a result of a more vigorous evangelism displayed by the Christians that may be alluded to in Philippians 1:12–18.[66] Most infer from Tacitus's description that the Christians were already widely recognized as a body distinct from the Roman synagogues;[67] but the reference suggests rather that Nero's agents looking out for plausible scapegoats became aware of the Christians from marketplace gossip. There is no hint that they were regarded as "Christians" as distinct from Jews, or that the Jewish synagogues played any part in inciting the persecution.[68] The fact that Sulpicius Severus (beginning of the fifth century) was able to report that a few years later Titus determined to destroy the Jerusalem Temple "in order that the religion [singular] of the Jews and Christians should be more completely exterminated" (*Chronicle* 2.30.7),[69] implies that from an outsider's perspective the religions of Jew and Christian, though different, were not yet disentangled.

Another potential tipping point is, of course, the fall of Jerusalem and the destruction of the Temple, the disastrous climax to the Jewish revolt against Rome in 70 C.E. Here the impact on Judaism was immense, with most of the principal factions of Second Temple Judaism losing all power and sooner or later disappearing effectively from the scene, leaving the rabbis, the heirs of the Pharisees in particular, as the principal heirs of Judaism as such. The impact on the Christian churches is much harder to detect. Apart from the Matthean version of the parable of the wedding banquet (Matthew 22:2–14), with its clear allusion to the destruction of Jerusalem (22:7–8), there are only hints and possible allusions. Notably, there are no Christian heart-rending laments over the disasters that had befallen the Jewish people and the destruction of the Temple, such as we find in 4 Ezra and 2 Baruch. The implication is that the fall of Jerusalem and destruction of the Temple made little impression among the Diaspora groupings of believers-in-Jesus—presumably since they were both geographically remote and, probably as a consequence of continuing Hellenist influence, spiritually remote from the Jerusalem cult, other than as providing a way to make sense of Jesus' death. Since the history of Diaspora Jewish communities following the failure of the First Jewish Revolt is unclear,[70] prior to their coming under the influence of emerging Rabbinic Judaism,[71] it is also unclear whether Christian disinterest in the fall of Jerusalem and the loss of the Temple was a significant factor in determining relations between Jews and Christians in the western Diaspora.

What was the impact of the 70 catastrophe on the Jerusalem community of believers-in-Jesus itself? That is probably the most critical issue in this whole discussion. Apart from anything else, we have no idea whether the Jerusalem disciples were at all involved in the revolt and how their attitude to the revolt affected their relation to fellow Jews. Josephus tells us that when at the instigation of Ananus the high priest, James, the brother of Jesus, was arbitrarily executed in 62 C.E., not long before the outbreak of the revolt in 66, "Those of the inhabitants of the city who were considered the most fair-minded and who were strict in observance of the law were offended at this" (*Antiquities* 20.201). So whether and to what extent members of the sect of the Nazarene were caught up in the increasingly savage internecine factionalism of the period remains obscure.

A more promising line of inquiry is "the flight to Pella" tradition, to the effect that early in the war the main body of Christians in Jerusalem fled from Jerusalem across the Jordan to the Perean city of Pella, one of the cities of the Decapolis.[72] (See Chapter IV, "The Christian Flight to Pella? The Archaeological Picture," by Pamela Watson.) Pella is remembered by Epiphanius as the seat of the Jewish-Christian sects. These were noted for their high regard for James, devotion to the law, and suspicion/ denigration of Paul—a striking echo of Luke's portrayal of the Jerusalem believers in Acts 21:20–21.[73] Equally notable is the fact that the other principal name for such sects is "Nazoraeans," which obviously reflects, retains and maintains the tradition of the first Christians being known as the "Nazarenes" (Acts 24:5). That is to say, there may well be a direct line of continuity between the more conservative traditionalists under James and the subsequent teachings of Ebionites and Nazoraeans.[74] (For further discussion, see Chapter X, "Ebionites and Nazoraeans: Christians or Jews?" by Matt A. Jackson-McCabe.) This observation takes us well beyond our cut-off point of 100 C.E., but it is a reminder that Christianity began as Jewish-Christianity, and that the Jewish-Christian sects of the next few centuries formed a sort of bridge between the diverging trajectories of Christianity and Rabbinic Judaism—a very rickety bridge, since the developing orthodoxies of both Christianity and Rabbinic Judaism despised and disowned such sects as heretical.

Another tipping point should not escape notice: the likely impact of the *fiscus Judaicus*, the tax levied by Emperor Vespasian following the failure of the Jewish revolt, the equivalent of the former Temple tax (two drachmas), still to be paid by all male Jews, but now (the Jerusalem Temple having been destroyed) to be paid to the temple of Jupiter Capitolinus in Rome.*[75] Under Emperor Domitian (mid-80s C.E.), this tax was strictly enforced and exacted with great severity, to include the prosecution of those "who without publicly acknowledging that faith yet lived as Jews, as well as those who concealed their origin and did not pay the tribute levied upon their people" (Suetonius, *Domitian* 12.2).[76] (See Chapter VIII, "Jews and Christians at Rome: An Early Parting of the Ways," by Margaret H. Williams.) Under Domitian many "who drifted into Jewish ways were condemned" on the charge of atheism and suffered severe penalties (Dio Cassius, *Roman History* 67.14.2). This would presumably have come as a shock to any Jewish believers-in-Jesus who were trying to disown their Jewish identities (concealing their origin).[77] But it would almost certainly have provided a strong motivation to many gentile believers-in-Jesus to deny that they had converted to Judaism and to distinguish themselves more clearly as non-Jews to avoid paying the tax. It is true that Domitian's successor, Nerva, repealed Domitian's legislation (97 C.E.) and quashed the practice of permitting slaves and freedmen to accuse others "of adopting the Jewish mode of life" (*Roman History* 68.1.2). But nevertheless the encouragement to pull apart Christian and Jewish identity endured for some ten years and may well help to explain how the early second-century Roman writers, Tacitus (*Annals* 15.44.2) and Suetonius (*Life of Nero* 16.2), not to mention Pliny the Younger (*Epistulae* 10.96), could refer to "Christians" (for the first time in non-Christian writings) as a clearly identifiable and distinct body.[78]

A final possibly pre-100 tipping point, the *Birkat ha-Minim*, is probably best dealt with in discussing John's gospel below.

*On the *fiscus Judaicus* and its reform under Nerva, see Schlomo Moussaieff, "The 'New Cleopatra' and the Jewish Tax," *BAR*, January/February 2010.

The implications of some New Testament writings

The bulk of the New Testament writings span the last few decades of the first century C.E. So they are promising sources in which to seek for indications of further stress points between Christianity's Jewish matrix and its developing identity. Most of these New Testament writings have a strongly Jewish character. The letter of James is addressed to "the twelve tribes who are in the Diaspora" (James 1:1); and 1 Peter is not dissimilarly addressed to the "elect sojourners/exiles of the Diaspora" (1 Peter 1:1). At the other end of the spectrum, in the Book of Revelation, the letters to the churches in Smyrna and Philadelphia refer dismissively to "those who say they are Jews and are not," but are a/the "synagogue of Satan" (Revelation 2:9, 3:9)—indicating a serious rupture between at least these particular churches and the synagogues in the same city. Yet in the last members of the Pauline corpus, the Pastoral Epistles, the issues provoked by Paul's insistence on a Jewish gospel for gentiles seem to have largely faded into the past. But there are plenty of indications that the issues at the heart of the parting-of-the-ways question were more lively in other New Testament writings.

(1) With Luke's Acts the issue is posed whether the final scene (Paul under house arrest in Rome) marks a decisive break between Paul and his fellow Jews, with the gospel now seen as solely for the gentiles (Acts 28:28). So several have argued.[79] But that would cut across the solution to Jewish/gentile fellowship to which Luke had given prominence in Acts 15, and which he presumably presented as the way forward for future Jew/gentile fellowship in Christian assemblies. Moreover, Luke speaks of a turn to the gentiles on two occasions prior to Acts 28 (13:46–47, 18:6), and on both occasions Paul continues his normal practice of preaching first in the Jewish synagogue. There is nothing to indicate that Paul (or Luke!) was altering his tactics in that final scene. Rather he depicts Paul as speaking positively of "the ancestral customs" (28:17) of "my nation" (28:19), and of his imprisonment as "for the sake of the hope of Israel" (28:20). And Luke, we recall, had restricted his account of Paul's time in Rome to his social intercourse and communication with the Jews of Rome (28:17–28). The implication of the closing verses (28:30–31; Paul "welcomed all who came to him, proclaiming the kingdom of God and teaching about the Lord Jesus Christ"), therefore, is that the "all" who came to Paul would have included the only people with whom he had

communicated when he first arrived. Luke's picture, then, is entirely consistent with a mission that continued, and should continue, to reach out to both Jews and gentiles despite repeated Jewish obduracy.[80]

(2) More intriguing is Matthew's gospel. Here there has been a long-running debate as to whether Matthew writes *intra muros* or *extra muros*, that is, from still within the Judaism of the 80s C.E. or as already outside its walls.[81] There are various factors to be considered here. Does the fierce polemic against "Scribes and Pharisees" in Matthew 23 indicate a sharp break between the church(es) for whom Matthew writes and the rabbis attempting to reconstitute Judaism after 70 C.E.? Or should we rather speak of a continuation of the often equally acerbic disputes of the Second Temple period? Again, does Matthew's repeated reference to "their synagogues" (distinctive of Matthew) imply a sharp distancing by Matthew of the synagogue from the church(es) for which he was writing? Or are the references simply to the synagogue(s) of the people in the town or area being visited (Matthew 4:23, 9:35, 12:9, 13:54), or to "their" or "your" synagogues" as distinct from "our synagogues" (Matthew 10:17, 23:34)?[82]

More striking are the passages that seem to indicate that the Jewish people as a whole have been rejected by God (particularly Matthew 8:11–12, 21:43, 22:7–8, 23:37–39). But the first reference is again more reminiscent of the warnings made within the factionalism of the Second Temple period, that other factions were betraying their covenant obligations and in danger of losing their status as belonging to God's favored nation.[83] The second, Matthew makes clear, was directed against the chief priests and scribes (Matthew 21:45), a not untypical prophetic warning that the leaders of the people were failing in their responsibility. And the last two are more readily understandable as allusions to the catastrophe of 70 C.E. than as a rejection of the people as such.[84]

Matthew also has, for example, retained the strong note that Jesus saw his mission as restricted to Israel (Matthew 10:5–6, 15:24); he insists more strongly than any other of the Evangelists that Jesus was a devout Jew whose faithfulness to the law, or to the spirit of the law, exceeded that of the Pharisees (5:17–20); there is a degree to which he presents Jesus as the new Moses;[85] and the extended mission of the final "great commission" is to "all nations" (28:19).

It is fairly clear, then, and generally agreed, that the communities that Matthew represented or for which he wrote were at loggerheads with the emerging rabbinic leadership of post-70 Judaism.[86] What is not clear, however, is whether this was an in-house debate, an extension of Jesus' own disagreements with various Pharisees, one of the sequence of disagreements not untypical of the factional disputes that marred Second Temple Judaism; and whether we can speak of the rabbinic opponents ejecting the believers-in-Jesus from the synagogue, whether they even had the power or authority to do so. In fact, Matthew himself was obviously strongly motivated to present Jesus as wholly within any boundaries that could/should be drawn around Judaism. Implied is his hope still to win his fellow Jews for Jesus. So far as Matthew himself was concerned, the debate was still *intra muros.*

(3) Still more intriguing is the Gospel of John. John seems to go out of his way to present the traditional icons of the religion of Israel as passé. In particular, John interprets the disputed saying of Jesus, "Destroy this temple and in three days I will raise it up," as a reference to "the temple of his (Jesus') body," which his disciples only realized after Jesus' resurrection (John 2:19–22). The implication is obvious, that for his first disciples, Jesus himself had replaced the Temple. In the same spirit is the preceding story, of Jesus transforming the water reserved for the Jewish rites of purification into high quality wine (2:6–10). Similarly, in the encounter with the Samaritan woman, the water from Jacob's well is contrasted unfavorably with the living water that Jesus offers the woman (4:6–15). And, not least, in the great bread of life discourse, Jesus far outshines Moses, since Moses gave bread that provided only temporary nourishment, whereas Jesus himself is the bread from heaven that gives life to the world (6:32–35,48–51,58). All these, however, are claims drawn up within Israel's own terms of reference and hopes for the future. So are they to be interpreted as a disparagement of Israel's icons, a distancing of the Jesus movement from its native Judaism? Or are they rather invitations to the Jews of John's time to see in Jesus the fulfillment of Israel's prophetic visions and hopes?

The issue is sharply posed by John's talk of "the Jews." For "the Jews" are regularly depicted as hostile to Jesus, and in John 8 in particular, "the Jews" are scarified by Jesus as children of the devil, not children of Abraham (8:39–44). It is easy to draw from this that from John's perspective "the Jews" are sharply to be distinguished from Jesus and his disciples; the ways have already parted between the Johannine believers-in-Jesus and the Jews. However, the situation reflected is not quite so clear-cut. For one thing, in many passages "the Jews" seems to be a way of referring to the Jewish authorities.[87] And in many other references "the Jews" seems to denote the Jewish/common people, "the crowd."[88] What is particularly striking about the central section of John's gospel is that this crowd of Jews is divided about Jesus, who he was, and whether he should be believed in, some of them explicitly coming so to believe.[89] In this section a strong impression is given that "the Jews"/the crowd are divided, and have not yet made up their minds with regard to Jesus.[90] All this raises the question whether John saw this still to be the case, that although "the Jews" (authorities) were set against Jesus and his disciples, "the Jews" (the crowd) were still open to persuasion.[91]

The question is posed afresh by the unique Johannine use of the term *aposunagogos*, "expelled from the synagogue." The parents of the blind man "were afraid of the Jews; for the Jews had already agreed that anyone who confessed Jesus to be the Messiah should be put out of the synagogue" (9:22); "many, even of the rulers, believed in him, but because of the Pharisees did not confess it lest they be put out of the synagogue" (12:42); Jesus' disciples should anticipate being put out of the synagogue (16:2). This has invited the hypothesis that what came to be known as the *Birkat ha-Minim*, "the blessing (or malediction) against the heretics" had already been pronounced by the post-70 rabbinic authorities.[92] The reasoning is that no follower of Jesus could take part in the recitation of the *Shemoneh 'Esreh*, the Eighteen Benedictions, since the 12th benediction would be pronouncing a curse on himself and his fellow Christians. Here we have, for the first time from the Jewish side, an indication of action taken to divide Christian from Jew, to make it impossible for Jewish believers-in-Jesus to continue functioning as Jews, acceptable members of the Jewish community.

The issue is fraught, since it is likely that the specific reference to the Christians (the *Notzrim*) was a later addition to the *Birkat ha-Minim*.[93] (For further discussion, see Chapter XI, "In Between: Jewish-Christians and the Curse of the Heretics," by Shaye J.D. Cohen.) Even so, it is likely that Jewish believers-in-Jesus were early on regarded as *minim* by the progenitors of Rabbinic Judaism.[94] This would certainly be consistent with subsequent warnings against *minim* in rabbinic traditions, some of whom certainly seem to be Christian Jews.[95] And it is hardly irrelevant that subsequently Jerome was able to refer to "the Minaeans" (= *minim*) who were active in synagogues cursed by the rabbis (Jerome, *Epistles* 112.13). Without settling the issue of when the *Birkat ha-Minim* began to be said and in what form in rabbinic synagogues, therefore, we can at least acknowledge the likelihood that in the process of defining Judaism more scrupulously/narrowly, the post-70 rabbinic leaders included Christian Jews in those forms of Second Temple Judaism that they regarded as unacceptable (*minim*) and to be sloughed off. Something like this, even if only limited to the Johannine congregations, seems to be inferred in John 9:22 ("[T]he Jews had already agreed that anyone who confessed Jesus to be the Messiah would be put out of the synagogue"). In which case, we have one of the clearest examples of a parting between Christianity and Judaism, or more accurately between a group of Johannine churches and a group of synagogues already controlled by emerging Rabbinic Judaism.

The other aspect of the debate over John's gospel that cannot escape notice is that the Christian claims for Jesus seem to have become, it would appear for the first time, a breaking point for some/many Jews. This is clearest in two passages: John 5:18, where "the Jews" seek to kill Jesus "because he ... was calling God his own Father, thereby making himself equal to God"; John 10:30–31, where "the Jews" take up stones to stone Jesus in response to Jesus asserting that "the Father and I are one." In all the earlier tensions caused by early Christian beliefs in Jesus, there are no indications that any provoked such a fierce reaction from Jewish authorities. But here claims being made for Jesus by his followers seem to have been recognized for the first time as a threat to the unity of God, to the fundamental Jewish creed (*Shema'*) that God is one (Deuteronomy 6:4). This would presumably be the principal factor that predisposed post-70 rabbis to determine that these Jewish believers-in-Jesus were *minim*, and consequently to be expelled from the synagogue. Even then the matter was not final, since it is quite likely that the second-century Christological controversies were in part at least controversies between a Christianity and a Judaism that were attempting to define themselves over against each other.[96]

(4) Finally we should consider the letter to the Hebrews. The main theme of this letter is twofold. It presents the tabernacle and cult that Moses was commanded to set up during Israel's wilderness wanderings as copies and shadows of the way into the divine presence in heaven.

The instruction to Moses to furnish the tabernacle "according to the pattern/archetype shown you in the mountain" (Exodus 25:40) quite naturally suggests a link to Plato's conception of the heavenly world of ideas that form the archetypes of which earthly equivalents are but imperfect copies (Hebrews 8:5, 9:23–24), a foreshadowing of "the good things to come" (Hebrews 10:1). Particularly in mind was the Day of Atonement ceremony, the only day of the year when the high priest could enter the Holy of Holies in the tabernacle, where the presence of God was most real (Leviticus 16). Here the writer's claim is clear, that what happened to Christ, his death and his exaltation to heaven, was the reenactment of what in the earthly Jewish cult and the Day of Atonement ritual was a mere copy and shadow (Hebrews 9:6–14). That is, Jesus was the real high priest; Jesus' death was the real Day of Atonement sacrifice; and his entry into heaven was the entry into the divine presence itself (Hebrews 9:24–26, 10:10–12). His priesthood was unique—an order of priesthood, the order of the mysterious figure Melchizedek (Genesis 14:17–20), a priestly order for which only one who was "without father, without mother, without genealogy, having neither beginning of days nor end of life ... a priest forever" could qualify (Hebrews 7:3). Only Jesus the Son of God (Hebrews 1:2–3) was thus qualified for that priesthood. Which meant that his sacrifice had a similarly eternal character, which meant that what it achieved was once-for-all (*hapax*) and valid for all time (Hebrews 9:26–28). This meant that all other sacrifices had been made redundant and were no longer necessary (Hebrews 9:8–10, 10:1–4). For Christ's entry into the real Holy of Holies, before the heavenly throne of God, meant that the way into the very presence of God had been opened up once for all, for all who came in Christ's train to "draw near to the throne of grace" for themselves, without any further priestly mediation (Hebrews 4:16, 7:25, 10:1,22).

The date of the letter is disputed. But it looks as though it was written for Jewish believers ("to the Hebrews") grieving over the loss of the Jerusalem Temple,[97] though perhaps also gentile Godfearers who had initially been attracted to Judaism by its Temple ritual. This would explain why the letter writer focuses on the tabernacle. He does not make his case on the grounds that the Temple had been destroyed. He goes to the scriptural basis and instructions that governed both the pre-Temple tabernacle and the two temples that followed. By so doing, the tabernacle was the scriptural blueprint for the priestly and sacrificial cult on which he could focus entirely, without any distraction regarding the geographical site and what had happened there. The only Jerusalem he was concerned with was the heavenly Jerusalem (Hebrews 12:22).

The consequences for relations between what Jesus had brought into effect and traditional Judaism were substantial. By limiting the function of the Jerusalem cult to the past, to what was merely copy, indeed, an imperfect copy and shadow of the heavenly reality, the writer dismissed the traditional cult as passé and finished. Christ's sacrifice was the real thing that Israel's traditional cult had only foreshadowed. Christ had once-for-all and forever opened the way into the very presence of God in heaven, for others to follow and "draw near"—in contrast to Israel's high priest who alone could enter into the Holy of Holies and only on one day each year, and then have to withdraw back to where the veil intruded. Consequently there was no need for that frustratingly annual ceremony to be endlessly repeated. The "new covenant" for which Israel had longed (Hebrews 7:22, 8:7–12, 9:15, 12:24) was now in operation and had made the first covenant "obsolete; and what is obsolete and growing old will soon disappear" (Hebrews 8:13). Christ was the high priest who made all priests, all orders of priesthood, redundant (no one else could qualify for the Melchizedek priesthood). Christ's sacrifice made the continuation of a sacrificial cult unnecessary. The Christianity that Hebrews promulgated superseded the Judaism of tabernacle and Temple.

In short, Hebrews sounds the first note of the "supersessionism" that, from the second century onward, became mainstream Christianity's attitude to Judaism.[98] The fact that Hebrews still worked with the imagery of priest and cult, and on the blueprint of the Torah tabernacle (Hebrews 8:5), is a reminder of just how Jewish was the mental and social world that the writer and the recipients of his letter inhabited. And the heroes of faith in Hebrews 11 are a rollcall of Israel's notables. But its attitude to the precursor that was Judaism, the old covenant, was so disdainful that few if any traditionalist Jews would have found it acceptable, and even Jewish believers-in-Jesus may have found it off-putting. That doubts remained over the apostolicity of Hebrews for some centuries in the West[99] may also imply that many Christians may have been uncomfortable with its dismissive attitude to what still counted as Christianity's mother faith.

Conclusion

We certainly cannot speak of the "parting of the ways" between "Christianity" and "(Rabbinic) Judaism" in the first century C.E. There were a variety of strands in Second Temple Judaism that partly overlapped and partly held themselves apart as distinctive. The beginnings of Christianity consisted of two predominant strands that held together in some tension, but that may have begun to pull apart in the last decade or two of the first century, in large part due to the devastation to Jerusalem believers-in-Jesus caused by the suppression of the Jewish revolt. But we cannot be sure of how coherent and united were the assemblies of Jesus-believers scattered through the eastern end of the Mediterranean, and we know too little about beginnings of Christianity in Alexandria and eastern Syria to be able to speak with full confidence about the "Christianity" that was presumably evolving there before the end of the first century. Likewise we know too little about the Rabbinic Judaism that survived the catastrophe of 70 C.E. and in the final years of the first century began to redefine Judaism—though the *Birkat ha-Minim* may tell us something.

What should not be forgotten is that despite the First Jewish Revolt, Judaism was widely recognized and respected as an ancient national religion, with synagogues often in prominent positions in Mediterranean cities. In contrast, the Christian house groups and tenement churches were, throughout this period, minor players in backstreets rather than on main thoroughfares. In the face of Roman suspicion of voluntary associations and new cults, especially from the East, the Christian groups were probably sheltered under the relative protection of the status accorded to the Jews. From the warnings and urgings of later Christian leaders for members of their congregations to desist from attending synagogues on Saturday and observing Jewish feasts,[100] there must have been many Jewish believers-in-Jesus who still regarded themselves as Jews, and many gentile converts who thought they were entering an offshoot of the very venerable religion of the Jews. And if such attitudes persisted into the fourth century, then we can be sure that it was a much more common attitude in the second half of the first century.

We can certainly see a fair amount of evidence of tensions between the forerunners of Christianity and the forerunners of Rabbinic Judaism, seams beginning to pull apart, threads beginning to break—over the Temple and the Jewish way of life in particular. Also evident are the early indications of Christianity's distinctives that would prove unacceptable to most Jews, particularly the growing esteem and veneration accorded to Jesus. On some points and in some places, a falling out took place between synagogue and church. But most, if not all, of these were little different from the sorts of tensions and fallings-out of the factions and sects of Second Temple Judaism. Of a parting of the ways between Judaism and Christianity in the late first century, especially a final parting of the ways, we cannot speak with any historical or social or theological validity.

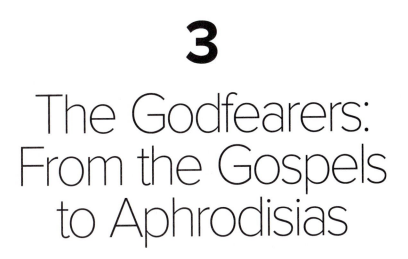

3

The Godfearers: From the Gospels to Aphrodisias

BRUCE CHILTON

THE TERM "GODFEARERS" DESIGNATES NON-JEWS WHO, DESPITE their identity as gentiles, sympathized with the religion of Israel. The difference between cooperative and uncooperative non-Jews is signaled within the Torah itself. For example, when Abraham sojourned in Gerar, he says that he came to the conclusion that "there is no fear of God in this place" (Genesis 20:11). The result of that judgment was dramatic, leading Abraham to tell Abimelech, the local king, that Sarah was his sister, in the belief that Abimelech would kill him if he knew he and Sarah were married.

But how much did a person need to sympathize with Judaism to qualify as a "Godfearer"? In this chapter, we will see that, although the basic factor of acknowledging the God of Israel remained constant, answers to that question varied over time. In addition, even within a given period policies varied from place to place, and teacher to teacher. Although for the most part it was agreed that Godfearers, as gentiles, were not required to keep the covenant of circumcision, even that issue proved to divide leaders in nascent Christianity, when the movement was faced with the question: Could gentile Godfearers be baptized into the name of Jesus? We will see varying policies emerge in response to this question, framed by Pharisees who were part of Jesus' movement, by the teaching of James, the brother of Jesus, and by Paul of Tarsus.

In addition to the dispute over whether gentile followers of Jesus needed to keep the covenant of circumcision along with baptism, Christians during the first and second centuries argued over whether those baptized should eat food purchased in the marketplace and notionally sacrificed to a pagan god. The depth and persistence of that dispute is a measure of how much the status of Godfearer was assimilated by gentile believers.

Even as the status of "Godfearer" permitted Christianity to negotiate the place of gentiles within the movement, while maintaining its loyalty to the scriptures of Israel and the law of Moses, another force was at work that affected usage of the term. In a theology that was at its time of origin unusual, Paul had argued that those who were baptized were themselves like Abraham, who "believed in the Lord" (Genesis 15:6; Galatians 3:6). Believers who imitated Abraham by believing in Christ and being baptized in his name themselves joined the "Israel of God" (Galatians 6:16). Although Paul's position caused contention within the first century, by the second century a predominantly gentile church accepted his theology and went on to teach that the true inheritance of Israel belonged to the church, not to Judaism. From the point of view of this teaching, "Godfearers" had to be observed with caution, to assure that they were not aligning themselves with Judaism, rather than the church's fulfillment of the promises to Israel.

Two countervailing streams of usage, then, took up the term "Godfearers." One stream, continuing Judaic practice, helped to negotiate the place of gentiles within Christianity, as a movement that aimed to bring the light of Israel to the nations. The other, derived from Paul's teaching, took up an at best ambivalent and sometimes negative stance toward "Godfearers," since their orientation could lead them to embrace Judaism rather than an increasingly gentile Christianity. In this chapter we will see these two streams of usage in their relationship and conflict.

In Roman times

Judaism in the period prior to the Gospels was well established in the Greco-Roman world (as well as in the East). Rome's alliance with the Maccabees in 161 B.C.E. at the time of the Roman Republic (see 1 Maccabees 8) established Judaism as a *religio licita*, and this had a profound impact on the Mediterranean Diaspora.[1] The appeal of Judaism extended not only to those who wished to convert to the whole of the religion as proselytes, but also to a group called "Godfearers" (*theophoboumenoi*) or "Godworshipers" (*theosebomenoi*). These Godfearers accepted the God of Israel but without practicing all of the commandments specifically obligating Israelites in the Torah. The Godfearers remained gentiles but embraced the monotheism and the ethical precepts of the scriptures of Israel (especially in their Greek translation, the Septuagint).

The Septuagint also included some works not included in the Bible of Judaism in Hebrew and now described as Apocrypha. The Greek Diaspora also produced a number of supplementary works usually called Pseudepigrapha because the literature is often fictively attributed to writers before the time of the documents. A prominent example, illustrating the place of Godfearers in some Diaspora thinking, are the books attributed to the Sibyl—the premiere prophetess of Greco-Roman culture. She was a pivotal figure of global prophecy, and Diaspora Judaism claimed her as its own.

The Sibylline Oracles were written in Greek near the beginning of the common era but never included in the Bible (either in Greek or in Hebrew). Sibyl is presented as Noah's daughter-in-law. Sometimes made-up history is the most accurate measure of an ancient people's faith, because it shows us what people wanted to believe. That may well describe the situation here.

For Jews in the Diaspora, the most noble non-Jewish people (such as the mantic Sibyl), even if they did not fully embrace Judaism by circumcising their males, were those who acknowledged the God of Israel by following the commandments of Noah (the so-called Noahide laws): refraining from idolatry, from consuming blood and from promiscuous sexuality. These were the Godfearers who, like their Jewish contemporaries, provided a counterpoint to the pagan religions of Greco-Roman cities.

Avoiding idolatry and blood, of course, meant not taking part in many popular sacrifices. In the bustling marketplace, even ordinary meat might appear under the icon of a god or goddess to whom it had been notionally sacrificed at the moment of slaughter. Both Jews and Godfearers avoided that, just as they insisted that animals for consumption be killed by cutting their throats rather than strangling, so the meat was well bled. Even avoiding promiscuity was not an easy matter; marriage with relations outside the immediate family—forbidden by the Torah (Leviticus 18:6–18)—was often encouraged in the Hellenistic world.

Jews and Godfearers stood apart from the ordinary life of Hellenistic cities. Often Jews, Godfearers and ordinary gentiles sat apart in the theaters and stadiums. Inscriptions carved in ancient stone benches of theaters and stadiums in Asia Minor as well as synagogue dedications indicate that "Godfearers" were recognized within their cultures. The evidence comes from Sardis, Philadelphia, Miletus, as well as an extremely important find from Aphrodisias discussed below.[2]

Jews and their sympathizers also kept the Sabbath, which opened them to charges of laziness. Their food laws were also seen to be odd. Why would anyone prohibit eating a meat as good as pork? Hostile gentiles from the time of Antiochus IV Epiphanes (second century B.C.E.) made the pig into a primary symbol of impurity for Jews, rather than just one animal among many proscribed in the Torah. In times of persecution, gentiles would attempt to force pork into the mouths of their hapless victims. Gentile mockery included the taunt, "Do they worship pigs or something?" Otherwise respected authors such as Petronius, Cicero and Plutarch provide notorious examples of this kind of vituperation.[3]

Yet Judaism offered access to a rational deity: a single creator, consistent with philosophy and moral in character. Even the most anthropomorphic images of Israel's God competed favorably with Zeus and company.

Synagogues were "gatherings," as the term *sunagoge* means in Greek, but increasingly they also became buildings, whether in converted private homes or purpose-built. Godfearers attended these meetings in synagogues. Wealthier Godfearers even arranged for donations, and their gifts were a matter of pride for donor and recipient alike.[4]

Each of these synagogues stood in stark contrast to the ornate temples of Greco-Roman cities. The pagan acropolis dominated the urban landscape in city after city, lavishly decorated with statues and altars and the paraphernalia of sacrifice, while modest synagogues nestled in the midst of Jewish neighborhoods, advertised by their plain design and aniconic simplicity.

WWW.HOLYLANDPHOTOS.ORG

VANNI ARCHIVE/ ART RESOURCE, NY

MILETUS THEATER INSCRIPTION. "Place of the Jews and the Godfearers" reads this second-century C.E. Greek inscription from Miletus in Asia Minor (modern Turkey). The inscription, carved into seats in the city's theater reserved for members of these two groups, indicates that Jews and Godfearers—gentile sympathizers and supporters of Judaism—were often classed together in Roman society.

The confidence that Jews and Godfearers together were part of God's providence comes to expression in the fourth book of the Sibylline Oracles (4:24–34):

> Happy will be those of earthly men who will cherish the great God, blessing before eating, drinking and having confidence in piety. They will deny all temples and altars they see: purposeless transports of dumb stones, defiled by animates' blood and sacrifices of four-footed animals. But they will behold the great renown of the one God, neither breaking into reckless murder, nor transacting what is stolen for gain, which are cold happenings. They do not have shameful desire for another's bed, nor hateful and repulsive abuse of a male.

What is especially striking about this prophecy is that it is directed to all people of Asia and Europe (4:1) through the mouth of the Sibyl

(4:22–23), the legendary oracle of mantic counsel. Her utterance here is explicitly backed up by the threat of eschatological judgment for all peoples (4:40–48): The Sibyl is not only cast as a Godfearer, but articulates the apocalyptic prophecy that emerged in Judaism in works such as Daniel in the Hebrew Bible and 2 Esdras in the Apocrypha.

At a much later period (c. the sixth century C.E.), the Talmud identifies Godfearers with the rules in Leviticus regarding non-Israelites who reside in the land: They are to desist from offerings to other gods and from the use of any altar but that in the Temple (Leviticus 17:7–9). They are to abstain from blood (Leviticus 17:10–13) and avoid the sexual relations described in chapter 18. These prohibitions were elaborated into the so-called Noahide commandments (BT *Sanhedrin* 56b), binding upon all humanity, much like the Sibylline Oracles.

The time lag between the Sibylline Oracles and the Talmud shows that the category persisted through the period of concern here (that is, until the sixth century C.E.). But it also shows that what a Godfearer had to do to qualify for that status varied and yet needed to be specified. Time and location made for variations. A blanket refusal of idolatry, for example, would have been difficult if not impossible for a prominent Roman citizen, since swearing an oath to the genius of the emperor and burning incense in front of his image were obligatory as was the sponsorship of large civic sacrificial festivals.

Despite these difficulties, and allowing for variations in practice, it remains striking that, from a Greco-Roman point of view, we can see that God-fearing was perceived as a common phenomenon. The most famous expression comes from Juvenal, the second-century poet:

> Some who had a father who reveres the Sabbath, worship nothing but the clouds, and the divinity of the heavens, and see no difference between eating swine's flesh, from which their father abstained, and that of man; and in time they take to circumcision.
> (Juvenal, *Satire* 14.96–99)[5]

Here, keeping the Sabbath—perhaps even relaxing instead of working on the Sabbath—is portrayed as a bad example that a father may set for his sons. Once he has provided this bad example, all manner of ills might follow, including a renunciation of idolatry (worshiping "nothing but the clouds"), an aversion to pork and ultimately circumcision.

In the Book of Acts

Juvenal lived between 60 and 140 C.E., just when the Acts of the Apostles emerged. This book firmly ensconced the Godfearers in the New Testament.

Acts describes the apostles' outreach to gentiles and to those on the fringes of Judaism. This occurred even prior to Paul's impact. In particular, Peter's conversion of the Roman centurion Cornelius (like Paul's conversion, detailed three times in Acts, in chapters 10, 11 and 15) represents a programmatic outreach to gentiles prompted by visionary experience.

Acts documents a shift in Peter's evangelistic operations from Jerusalem to the coastal cities of Lydda, Joppa and Caesarea (Acts 9:36–10:6), cities dominated by Hellenistic culture that also served as centers of Roman military control. After Peter achieved spectacular success by healing a lame man and restoring to life a faithful and generous Christian widow (Acts 9:32–43), Cornelius, a Roman military officer who was attracted to the God of the Jews ("a devout man who feared God"—Acts 10:2) was told by an angel to contact Peter. A vision came to Peter—and was repeated twice—instructing Peter to overcome his ritual and ethnic prejudices against gentiles. Messengers from Cornelius arrived with an invitation to Peter and his associates to spend the night with him. This of course would violate Mishnaic purity laws (which limit the circle of those from whom hospitality might be accepted[6]), but Peter nevertheless accepts the invitation. Peter's explanation is that these gentiles (Cornelius and his associates) believed; they had been given the gift of the Spirit and had been baptized. Peter then reached a key insight: God treats everyone, Jew and gentile, on the same basis so everyone who trusts in Jesus will receive forgiveness of sins (Acts 10:1–48). These events were reported to the Jerusalem apostles, whose natural prejudices were overcome, and who concluded, "God has also given the gentiles repentance for life" (Acts 11:18).

This precedent is used in Acts to show that Paul's basic policy of gentile inclusion was not solely his invention, but was endorsed by the authoritative Jerusalem-based apostles. In Antioch Paul himself cites Peter's involvement with non-Jews (Galatians 2:11–13). Paul differed from Peter not in his contact with non-Jews, but in his refusal to require them to observe the same regulations of purity that Peter, Barnabas and James, the brother of Jesus, had insisted on. Paul treated non-Jews as belonging to

Israel by virtue of their baptism into Christ, and events proved that he did not insist on usual practices current among Godfearers. Peter, in contrast, was willing to reach out to gentiles, but only if they acknowledged and respected the Torah of Moses, although they would not need to accept the covenant of circumcision that was binding on Jews.

By this point, Godfearers had become a vital category. Cornelius, a Roman centurion stationed in Caesarea, is described as "pious and *fearing God* with all his house" (Acts 10:2). Cornelius's emissaries to Peter underscore this description by saying he is "a just man both *fearing God* and attested by all the nation of the Jews" (Acts 10:22). Peter concludes that God does not discriminate: "In every nation the one who *fears him* and does justice is acceptable to him" (Acts 10:35).

This is the basis on which Paul and Barnabas speak to those who fear God as a class of people (see Galatians 2). In the Antioch synagogue, Paul addresses "Israelites *and* those who fear God" (Acts 13:16). He confirms this usage by calling them "sons of the race of Abraham and those among you *fearing God*" (Acts 13:26). A related usage employs the verb *sebomai* ("worship") rather than *phobeomai* ("fear") (Acts 13:43,50, 16:14, 17:4,17, 18:7).

Thomas Kraabel describes these as "technical terms" that have been used to conclude that there was a large and well-defined gentile penumbra around Jewish practice of the first century.[7] But there is an ambiguity here. In Greek, the term *kai* means "and," but it can also mean "even" or "also." So Acts 13:16, which refers to "Israelites *and* those who fear God," might refer to Israelites *and* God-fearing gentiles (two different groups) or to Israelites who also fear God. On the other hand, Acts 13:26 seems emphatic in the distinction between Jews and non-Jews who fear God. In short, are there two groups or a subgroup of Jews who also fear God? This basic problem, masterfully dealt with by Kraabel, is also treated by Ralph Marcus and Louis Feldman in relation to Josephus's usage of Godfearers.[8]

Complicating things still further, the passage in Acts just discussed may be inconsistent with Acts 13:43, which refers to the *sebomenoi* or God-worshiping people. This group designates proselytes (that is, converts) to Judaism, not merely gentile sympathizers who fear God and worship him.

As portrayed in Acts, the Godfearers hold the place of gentile belief only until their conversion to Christ. This theological feature of Acts is well appreciated in Luther's translation, where he amalgamated several Greek terms into the single description, *Gottesfürchtig*.[9] Given the theological utility of the term, Kraabel seems wise to advise scholarship not to turn the Godfearers into a large, well-defined demographic group. Nevertheless, these sympathizers with the synagogue who could not or would not convert to Judaism undoubtedly constituted a fruitful field of prospects for nascent Christianity.

Acts 15 records a meeting of the apostles in Jerusalem that deals with two disputed issues, circumcision and purity. As to the first item on the agenda, Peter declares that since God gave his holy spirit to gentiles who believed, no attempt should be made to add the requirement of circumcision (Acts 15:6–11). Paul could scarcely have said it better himself.

The second item on the agenda (purity) is settled on the authority of James, Jesus' brother, not on Peter's. (The outcome is *not* in line with Paul's thought.) James first confirms the position of Peter, but then he states his position in a very different way: "Symeon [Peter's real name] has related how God first visited the gentiles, to take a people in his name" (Acts 15:14). James's perspective here is not that all who believe are Israel (the Pauline definition), but that in addition to Israel, God has established a new people, an additional people, in his name.

According to James, the distinction between those from among the gentiles and those from Israel can be explained in two ways. The first is to use scripture; the second is to assess the requirement of purity. The logic of both, however, inevitably involves a rejection of Paul's position.

According to James, what the belief of gentiles achieves is not the redefinition of Israel (as in Paul's thought), but the restoration of the house of David. The argument is possible because of Jesus' Davidic genealogy and, therefore, that of his brother James.

According to Hegesippus, the second-century church historian (as cited by Eusebius in *Ecclesiastical History* 2.23), when James preaches that Jesus is the Son of Man who is to come from heaven to judge the world, the people who agree cry out, "Hosanna to the Son of David!" This reflects the fact that James's view of his brother was based on Davidic descent and that Jesus was a heavenly figure who was coming to judge the world. Taken together Acts and Hegesippus indicate that James's position was that Jesus was restoring the house of David because Jesus was the agent of final judgment.

In James's view, gentiles remain gentiles; they are not to be identified with Israel. His position was not anti-Pauline, at least not at first. His focus was on Jesus' role as the ultimate arbiter within the Davidic line. The line of demarcation between Israel and non-Israel was but a natural result of seeing Jesus as the triumphant branch of the house of David.

In James's understanding, gentile belief in Jesus was a vindication of his Davidic triumph, but it did not involve a fundamental change in the status of gentiles vis-à-vis Israel. But gentiles must nevertheless "abstain from the pollutions of the idols, and from fornication, and from what is strangled, and from blood" (Acts 15:20). These rules naturally separate believing gentile Godfearers from their wider environment.

As a result of James's insistence, the meeting in Jerusalem decides to send envoys and a letter to Antioch to require gentiles accepted by the Jesus movement to honor the prohibitions set out by James (Acts 15:22–35). For James believing gentiles who honor the law in this way do not change their status as gentiles. They are not Jews.

Paul addressed Godfearers, as well to Jews,[10] and held that together they made up "the Israel of God" (Galatians 6:16). But why does Paul not use the term "Godfearer"? Superficially, that might appear strange until Paul's own theology is factored in. For Paul all who believe, both Jews and gentiles, are sons of Abraham and are therefore "Israel" (Galatians 6:16; Romans 11:26). From this it follows that "not all those from Israel are Israel" (Romans 9:6). That assertion calls into question not only the status of Godfearers, but also that of Israel itself. This is perhaps the most radical development in all of Paul's thought: his contention that faith in Christ made all believers into Israel, the people of God, so that the social distinction between Jews and Greeks did not matter from God's point of view. "There is not one Jew or Greek, not one slave or free, not one male or female, since you are all one in Jesus Christ" (Galatians 3:28); from that perspective, Godfearers were not a serious category at all, as they were for James and as they appear in the Book of Acts. Instead, Paul wants to dissolve that designation with his assertion of all believers as Israel.

Justin Martyr, Aphrodisias and John Chrysostom

The second-century Christian theologian Justin Martyr reflects a thorough supersessionist doctrine often referred to as replacement theology. He says bluntly in his *Dialogue with Trypho*:

> For these words have neither been prepared by me, nor ornamented by human art; but David sang them, Isaiah evangelized them, Zechariah proclaimed them, and Moses wrote them. Are you acquainted with them, Trypho [who is a Jew]? They are contained in your Scriptures, or rather not yours, but ours. For we are persuaded by them; but you, though you read them, do not recognize the mind that is in them.
>
> (Justin Martyr, *Dialogue with Trypho* 29.2)

In Justin's *Dialogue*, Trypho is portrayed as becoming lost in the minutiae of the prophetic text, limited to the immediate reference of scripture, enslaved by its specification of laws.

Justin clearly believes that with the defeat of the Bar-Kokhba rebellion (the Second Jewish Revolt against Rome—132–135 C.E.), Judaism is coming to an end. Justin declares two comings of Christ: In the first he would be suffering. After that Justin tells Trypho the Jew, "There would be neither prophet nor king in your race, and—I added—that the Gentiles who believe in the suffering Christ will expect his coming again" (*Dialogue* 52.1). Once these sufferings of Christ had been accomplished,[11] Israel would no longer have a place in God's purpose. As Rodney Werline has explained: "For Justin, then, circumcision is the sign for the recent historical national disaster for the Jews."[12] To this extent, Justin stands not simply for supersession or replacement theology, but for the elimination of Israel as commonly understood on the basis of the prophetic spirit.

While Paul famously still hopes that "all Israel will be saved" (Romans 11:26), Justin is categorical—by means of Isaiah 51:4 and Jeremiah 31:31— that "there is to be an ultimate Law and Covenant superior to all, which now must be kept by all people who claim God's inheritance" (*Dialogue* 11.2–3). This eternal covenant (Isaiah 55:3–4) establishes who is a true, spiritual Israelite *and* Judahite, and who is not (*Dialogue* 11.5), taking the place of all other aspirants to those names. As Philippe Bobichon has said, this is a claim of substitution rather than of fulfillment.[13]

Yet as Christian theology moved in the direction of superseding Judaism, Judaism refused to be superseded. Indeed, in the subsequent centuries there is clear inscriptional evidence for "Godfearers" in Aphrodisias. They have been identified as gentile donors to the synagogue, for example, by Irina A. Levinskaya:

JEWISH AND CHRISTIAN GRAFFITI FROM APHRODISIAS. A close look at the numerous graffiti carved into the walls and columns of ancient Aphrodisias in Asia Minor reveals the city's diverse ethnic and religious makeup. Carved among the city's monuments are distinctive Jewish emblems, including a nine-branched Hanukkah menorah (left) as well as Christian symbols like this Byzantine cross carved in relief (right).

> The inscription from Aphrodisias for the first time established as a fact what previously had been discussed as a possibility, i.e. that the word *theosebes* could designate a gentile sympathizer with Judaism.[14]

Although this finding is supportable, as we will see, recent research shows that we need to qualify it somewhat.

In recent articles, Angelos Chaniotis has shown that in Aphrodisias marks of Jewish presence were by no means limited to the synagogue.*[15] He has documented graffiti on walls and columns that include menorahs and palm branches. In addition, he discusses in detail the 9-foot-tall pillar on which the designation of *theosebeis*, referenced by Levinskaya, actually appears. As Chaniotis observes, a surprising number of donors are designated as Godworshipers or Godfearers, but the column, although it may have served as a doorjam at the synagogue, remains of

---

*See Angelos Chaniotis, "Godfearers in the City of Love," *BAR*, May/June 2010.

ANGELOS CHANIOTIS

APHRODISIAS INSCRIPTION. This 9-foot-tall marble pillar probably stood at the entrance to Aphrodisias's main synagogue. Two of its faces are inscribed in Greek with the names of at least 120 donors who commissioned the memorial. Among the donors are many Jews, but also a surprising number of Godfearers (*theosebeis*) and proselytes. While some scholars date the pillar to c. 200 C.E., recent studies suggest it was erected several hundred years later, probably in the mid- to late fourth century.

uncertain provenience. Further, the column itself was inscribed with its list of 120 donors (Jews, proselytes and Godfearers) in stages, and Chaniotis argues for dating the work in the period after Constantine, rather than in the third century.

This is a case in which observing the limits of archaeological certainty strengthens the value of excavation for social history. The longer the period in which the work of inscribing was pursued, and the further afield from the synagogue it was placed, the more evident, as Chaniotis says, that "the Godfearers in the Aphrodisias inscription reflect the continuation of religious competition and exchange into late antiquity." As he points out, one of the *theosebeis* was called Gregorios, a characteristically Christian name. God-fearing, in other words did not merely lead gentiles to become Christians, as in the paradigm of the Book of Acts; Christians could also be drawn to the synagogue by the fear of God. Research over a long period of time, which includes literary, inscriptional and historical evidence, suggests in the words of A. Andrew Das that "references to God-fearers frequently identify gentile individuals or groups with varying degrees of interest in Judaism—from patrons who are also worshiping other gods, to those interested in certain Jewish customs, to uncircumcised gentile sympathizers devoted to the Jewish God, to actual proselytes."[16]

The evidence from Aphrodisias and other sites enables us to go beyond the question of older scholarship, "Were there gentile Godfearers or not?" There clearly were, at least in Aphrodisias (and the evidence from elsewhere is consistent with what is found in Aphrodisias). Not only is the grammatical form distinct from reference to Jews, but the Godworshipers are listed separately from Jews on the monument. Their names are preponderantly Hellenistic. The most probable reason for the inscription is to honor donors.[17]

The *theosebes* (Godfearer) is also distinguished in the Aphrodisias inscription from the proselyte, who "by purificatory immersion in the ritual bath, and (say the rabbis) by circumcision, has become a Jew, with all the legal and religious rights, privileges, duties and disabilities of a Jew."[18] The formal distinction between proselytes and Godworshipers is clear, as Reynolds and Tannenbaum point out:

> According to Talmudic law the proselyte has cut off his ties with his gentile family, takes a new, Jewish name (our three proselytes have Jewish names), and is supposed to call himself the son of Abraham rather than the son of his gentile father ...[19]

Whether or not Godworshiper/fearer was a technical term in the first century, it had become so by the time of the inscriptions from Aphrodisias.

What emerges at Aphrodisias might indicate a long-established usage, or a new application of a traditional term in a new environment of social construction. Usage of "Godfearers" in relation to gentiles in synagogues might correspond to either understanding. And references in the Hebrew Bible to those who fear God are variously rendered in the Septuagint as *phoboumenoi* ("fearers") and *sebomenoi* ("worshipers"). At any given moment, the terms might be technical or simply an evocation of an attitude of sympathy toward Judaism.

Although only three proselytes are listed in the Aphrodisias inscription, 54 *theosebeis* (Godfearers) and 69 Jews are listed.[20] Projecting this figure, the result would be to imagine Godfearers making up a considerable proportion of the synagogue population in the Diaspora.

By the time of the Aphrodisias inscription, it is clear that Godfearers had been embraced within Judaic usage. Equally, and on the other hand, Christian theology had incorporated the usage of Acts to portray God-fearing among gentiles as a way station toward faith in Christ. As Godfearers are understood in Acts, any movement toward Judaism would be, for the later Christians, a movement in the wrong direction, especially by those who had already accepted baptism and become a member of the Jesus group.

This may help to explain the virulence of the attack of John Chrysostom (347–407 C.E.) against Judaism. In his eight homilies titled *Against the Jews*,[21] the bishop of Antioch reveals that he knows Christians are attracted to Jewish practices. Chrysostom complains in these homilies about Christian participation in Jewish festivals and their acceptance of Jewish customs. Were these Christians attracted to synagogues afresh, or had they been Godfearers previous to their baptism? Were they practicing a form of Christianity that continued to be faithful to Judaic practice? These and other factors have been weighed in assessing the impact of Chrysostom's preaching.[22]

Chrysostom tells of a Christian woman who went to a synagogue to swear an oath (*Against the Jews* 1.3.4), which suggests that Jewish practice was revered for its integrity as well as for its integration within Christian practice and culture in late antiquity. The same attraction is echoed in the *Apostolic Constitutions* from Syria. This source of church law from the third century sets out that clergy who pray in synagogues or take part in Jewish festivals should be deposed from their office (8.47, 65, 71).[23]

To Chrysostom and the *Apostolic Constitutions*, practices like this are to be condemned as Judaizing. At one time the verb *ioudaizein* (which means, "to Judaize") had been a fairly neutral description of behaving in a way that emulated Judaism or supported Judaism.[24] But by the middle of the fourth century, the Council of Laodicea had called for "Judaizers," particularly those who keep the Sabbath and Jewish feasts, to be "anathematized from Christ," in that they should honor only "the day of the Lord."[25] As Steven Fine has suggested in an article that discusses this policy in regard to a recently discovered double inscription (see picture on p. 247), "Is our menorah, with a cross roughly superimposed upon it, a visual expression of a broader pattern whereby Christian cultural boundaries were asserted at Laodicea—in this case, to the distinct disadvantage of the local Jewish community?"[26] (For further discussion, see Chapter XII, "The Complexities of Rejection and Attraction, Herein of Love and Hate," by Steven Fine.)

This background helps to explain why for Chrysostom, Judaizing is "the Galatians' disease" (*Against the Jews* 2.2.3, cf. 1.1.5 and 1.4.4). The phrase invokes the language of Paul writing to the Galatians, where the apostle used "Judaize" in the specific sense of denying Christ. In Paul's view, because all were made one in Christ—whether Jew or Greek, slave or free, male or female (Galatians 3:28)—gentiles should not behave as if they were Jews. They were already "the Israel of God," in Paul's words (Galatians 6:16). A return to any principle but Christ enslaved them and excluded them from that spiritual reality (Galatians 5).

For Chrysostom, Israel is a thing of the past. Chrysostom compares those who Judaize to soldiers who fraternize with the enemy (*Against the Jews* 1.4.8–9). From having been a privileged field of recruitment in Acts, Godfearers now become diseased Christians, on the cusp of heresy.

Conclusion

By now it should not be surprising that "God-fearing" refers to more than one social or religious profile. In Acts, James insists that followers of Jesus are to avoid idols, blood, food sacrificed to idols and fornication (Acts 15:29), much as Godfearers are described in the Sibylline Oracles (4:24–34). Hundreds of years later at Aphrodisias, we know Godfearers as donors to the synagogue—which invites a consideration of benefaction in relation to their religious commitment[27]—and hear John Chrysostom lead the Pauline charge against any "Judaizing" that draws gentiles from the orthodoxy of the church.

The differences involved among Godfearers and attitudes toward them remain striking. Godfearers need to be characterized case by case. Attitudes toward this group within the Christian sources clearly went through a radical change. By the time of Chrysostom, a supersessionist view of Israel meant that sympathy toward Judaism was no longer promoted, not even permitted. Instead of merely parting from the path of benevolence toward Godfearers, Chrysostom represents a reversal of direction as compared to the program of Acts, with a characterization of Judaizers as traitors.

A fundamental conflict emerged within Christian sources of the ancient period. The view of God-fearing as a way for gentiles to access the promises to Israel contradicted the view of God-fearing as a mistaken confusion of those promises for the practices of Judaism. Both these perspectives share the assumption that "Israel" represents a truth that transcends any religion, so that even non-Jews can find a way to it. At the same time, the way to that truth is differently understood: Should gentiles imitate Jews, or embrace an identity that they have been offered apart from Judaism? The great dichotomy between James's policy, which used the Godfearers as a model for gentile Christians, and Paul's approach, which insisted upon their independent identity, remains to this day. Because Christianity defines itself in terms of the heritage of Israel, the issue of how Judaism stands in relation to that heritage is an issue that refuses to go away. The Godfearers occupy the place in history where that issue was most persistently addressed.

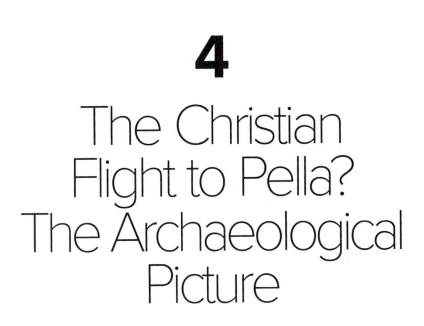

4

The Christian Flight to Pella? The Archaeological Picture

PAMELA WATSON

THERE HAS BEEN MUCH DEBATE OVER THE HISTORICITY OF THE reported migration of the members of the church of Jerusalem to the Transjordanian city of Pella before the destruction of Jerusalem in 70 C.E. Confirmation of this episode, often referred to as the "flight to Pella," has been of particular interest to those investigating the nature and chronology of the divergence of Christianity from Judaism.[1] If it occurred, the migration to Pella could be seen as an early signal of distinction of one entity from the other, whether evidence of a sharp break or part of a process of separation that began in the first century.

The general issue of separation is highly contentious, generating a diversity of arguments.[2] The intention here is not to engage in theological and textual arguments but to consider evidence from the physical domain (rarely referenced in recent literature) that has a bearing on the question.

Archaeological information from recent surveys and excavations at Pella allows a useful re-evaluation of earlier claims for evidence supporting a Jewish-Christian presence here at this time. This in turn can be weighed beside the textual and theological interpretations.

The site of Pella was consistently settled for thousands of years, from Neolithic through Ottoman times, resulting in much construction, destruction and rebuilding within the urban area of the site. The dynamic layering and disruptions entailed in the physical evolution of the settlement presents a fragmented, incomplete pattern of material evidence for interpretation by archaeologists. Although it has been excavated for many decades, such a large and complex site has only been sampled; the independent processes of survival and discovery can be serendipitous on a number of counts. This caveat governs any attempt to integrate the narrative worlds of ancient texts with current archaeological evidence. A further caveat is the difficulty of identifying emerging belief systems and ideology through material remains, particularly when such expressions are embryonic and not easily distinguished from the everyday social context.

Archaeological information on pre-Constantinian Christianity in Transjordan is also limited by the covert nature of the movement as a proscribed religion.[3] Nevertheless, where explicit public physical remains are lacking, archaeology offers instructive insights into local and regional social, economic and cultural systems, allowing a more accurate reconstruction of this first-century world than provided by literary analysis alone.[4] Judith Lieu's focus on the "social realia" in her exploration of the (singular) "parting" model advocates a perspective that sits well with the types of evidence produced by archaeology.[5] As will be seen in the following account, physical remains can suggest lines of interpretation, but the evidence of specific identification is often elusive.

The tradition of the early Christian "flight to Pella"

The historian of the early church, Eusebius, writing around 325 C.E., provides the earliest clear reference to the migration of the Jerusalem Christians to Pella at the time of the First Jewish Revolt against Roman rule (66–70 C.E.):

> [T]he people of the Church in Jerusalem were commanded
> by an oracle given by revelation before the war to those in

the city who were worthy of it to depart and dwell in one of the cities of Perea which they called Pella. To it those who believed in Christ migrated from Jerusalem, that when holy men had altogether deserted the royal capital of the Jews and the whole land of Judea, the judgment of God might at last overtake them for all their crimes against Christ and his Apostles and all that generation of the wicked be utterly blotted out from among men.

(Eusebius, *Ecclesiastical History* 3.5.3)[6]

This claim was reproduced with some variations by Epiphanius a few decades later.[7] Eusebius places Pella in Perea, while Epiphanius vacillates between Perea and the Decapolis. The actual location is within the borders of the Decapolis, but by the fourth century these earlier regional distinctions were vague. The original source or sources used by the fourth-century historians are debatable, although one candidate is the second-century Christian apologist Aristo, from Pella itself.[8]

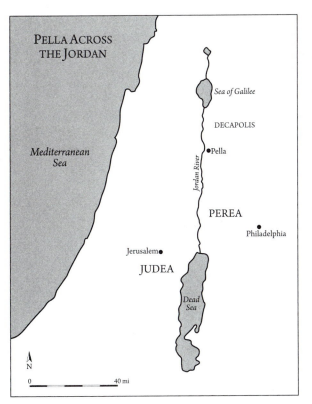

The tradition of the flight to Pella was generally accepted until the second half of the 20th century. At that time and continuing to the present, considerable debate has ensued, without resolution either way.[9] If archaeological evidence were to be found for the presence of Jewish-Christians in the first century C.E. at Pella, the argument might be settled.

Pella in the Hellenistic to early Roman period

Pella is located in the eastern foothills of the north Jordan Valley, overlooking the junction with the Jezreel Valley, on the western margins of biblical Gilead. The settled urban area comprises two hills: a main city mound to the north (Khirbat Fahl) and a naturally higher citadel hill to the south (Tell al-Husn). The intervening valley (Wadi Jirm) runs westward down to the Jordan Valley and contains a perennial spring that has attracted settlement to the site from its earliest origins.[10]

The conquest of the Middle East by Alexander the Great in 333–332 B.C.E. brought the region of Pella under the strong influence of Greek/Hellenistic culture for the first time. The similarity of the ancient city's Semitic name "Pihil"[11] to the birthplace of Alexander, Pella in Macedonia, may have influenced the choice of the Hellenized name bestowed by the Greeks, later Arabized to "Fihl" (the current village is Tabaqat Fahl). Succeeding centuries saw the region torn between the competing claims of Alexander's successors, the Ptolemies and the Seleucids. While there are few remains of the third-century Ptolemaic period, the late Hellenistic Seleucid period is well attested in the archaeological record both within and around the city. Fortresses and defensive walls on surrounding hills indicate a concern for defense, whether against incursions from the east or against the expansionism of the Hasmonean kings. Domestic remains indicate the town was prosperous, well-populated and highly integrated into the Hellenistic world. The capture of the city by the Hasmonean ruler Alexander Jannaeus in 83–82 B.C.E. was recorded by Josephus, who adds that the city was destroyed because the inhabitants refused to change to Jewish customs.[12] Continuing archaeological discoveries of a major destruction layer in different areas of the main mound of the city confirm both the extent and the date of this calamity. Importantly, excavations on the citadel hill of Tell al-Husn since the late 1980s suggest that only the main mound was devastated; no fiery destruction layer appears on the citadel and the elusive early Roman levels that have not been located on the main mound are found on the more defensible hill.[13] This now confirms a continuity of occupation in the city after the destruction wrought by Jannaeus; Pella remained a viable entity to be liberated by Pompey from Hasmonean control in 63 B.C.E. and brought into the province of Roman Syria.[14] It was included in the group of Hellenized cities referred to as the Decapolis.[15]

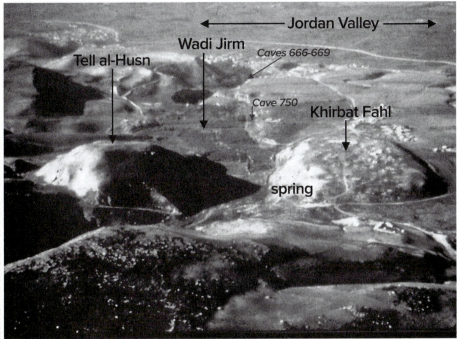

PELLA ACROSS THE JORDAN. This aerial photo shows the main features of the multi-period site of Pella in modern Jordan, including the location of its main areas of settlement and the various cave complexes that could have served as refuge for early Christians fleeing the destruction of Jerusalem in 70 C.E.

The next reference of note is in relation to the pillaging of the villages and cities of Syria, including the Decapolis cities of Pella, Scythopolis, Gerasa, Gadara and Philadelphia, by bands of Jews seeking revenge for the slaughter of the Jews in Caesarea in 66 C.E.[16] Unlike the Jannaeus event, no eloquent destruction of this date can be identified so far in the archaeological record of Pella. As noted earlier, this may be due to an accident of survival or it may be an indication of lesser damage. The earliest Roman public buildings such as the odeon and the bathhouse in the wadi are dated to the late first century C.E.[17] By this time, the public image of a Greco-Roman city is clear.

The search for evidence

For 19th-century European travelers and explorers of the Holy Land, and for 20th-century archaeologists who were steeped in and often

northern apse

PELLA'S WEST CHURCH.
The 1967 excavations of Robert H. Smith focused on a Byzantine church complex west of the main mound, which he called the West Church (left). Below the church's northern apse (at upper left in the photo), Smith discovered a stone-lined grave containing a finely carved Christian sarcophagus (below) that he dated to the late first or early second century C.E. While the interred body dated to the late Byzantine period, Smith believed the sarcophagus had simply been reused and was originally part of a first-century mausoleum that had held the remains of an early Christian refugee.

motivated by biblical history, the "flight" references endowed Pella with a particular status and mystique. They hoped that the existence of one of the earliest Christian communities established outside Jerusalem and the Galilee could one day be verified by physical evidence. Traveling to Pella in the 1880s, the German explorer Gottlieb Schumacher thoroughly investigated the site and its surroundings.[18] He found caves and tunnels southwest of the site in the northern cliffs of the western Wadi Jirm.[19] They exhibited worked features, which convinced him that he had found obscure habitation caves and escape tunnels that he attributed to the Jewish-Christian refugees. He thereby added to the story by equating the concept of refuge and fear in uncertain times with living in caves as anchorites and organizing secret escape routes. The tunnels, he claimed, led for considerable distances (up to 60 feet) into the plateau before their constriction forced him to stop his exploration. Remarkably, fresh air was always present, suggesting they were all leading to an ultimate chamber or outlet. He claimed that the alignments of the tunnels led in a north-easterly direction, converging on an extrapolated point at the sixth-century "West Church" of the city. Another series of caves, which he labeled the "anchorite caves," were in a separate location east of the tunnels and closer to the urban site. One that was better preserved had a cross-vaulted ceiling and two ventilation/light shafts (see p. 81).[20]

In the 1930s, John Richmond explored and described Pella and its surrounds. He reaffirmed the existence and interpretation of these caves and tunnels and thought that their clearance would provide "the best chance of finding archaeological evidence of early Christian life at Pella."[21] In 1958, American archaeologists Robert Funk and Neil Richardson excavated two small soundings on the main tell in order to ascertain the periods represented at the site. They were notably intrigued by the potential to trace the history of the early Christian community at the site and to verify the Eusebian claim.[22]

Concerted archaeological excavation of Pella was initiated in 1967 and work initially concentrated on the obvious public buildings and main tell. The American archaeologist Robert Houston Smith was inspired by the biblical connections and began his work at the West Church. Here he found, lying at an odd angle beneath the Byzantine floor of the northern apse, a decorated Christian sarcophagus whose stylistic features, he argued, could only belong to the late first or early second century C.E. The interred body was found to be of seventh-century date, but there was evidence for reuse, a not uncommon practice in these times. A Christian cross was incised on the edge of the sarcophagus. For these and other contextual reasons he believed it must originally have come from a mausoleum that preceded the church on the site, and may have been the cause of the church's location. He concluded it must have been the repository of a renowned person dating back to the early Christian migration of the first century C.E.[23] Smith's findings at the West Church thereby added credibility to Schumacher's tunnel hypothesis without actually confirming the connection.

With attention focused elsewhere, no investigation of the Schumacher caves and tunnels had been made since Richmond's investigation in the 1930s, and their location, which had only been generally defined, was lost in the subsequent agricultural developments, crop growth and new settlements. In 1996, however, systematic field-walking during the Pella Hinterland Survey (PHS)[24] located all the previously discovered sites and a few more. Their careful examination has allowed us to lay a few myths to rest and inevitably to pose more questions.[25]

Schumacher's "anchorite cave"

Schumacher's "anchorite" cave (designated PHS site 750; Schumacher's drawing is shown opposite) is situated in the lower northern cliffs, about a third of a mile southwest of Pella, adjacent to dense orchards in the wadi floor (marked on photo on p. 77). In Schumacher's time, the door, facing southeast, was overhung with stalactites that are no longer present. He mentions other caves nearby, some of which were either inaccessible or too choked with precipitates and collapse. They are now so overgrown by thick jungle that they cannot be investigated and are no longer visible. In 1996 a sounding was excavated to the bedrock floor of the cave, producing only one identifiable pre-modern artifact, a Roman-period pottery sherd. This was found in collapse debris under the topsoil, but could have fallen in from above. The deposit above bedrock was only 6 inches thick. From Richmond's description and our observations, the cave has long been reused for shelter and storage by the local inhabitants, and there were no original floor deposits. The interior displays obvious pick marks in its shaping, including primitive vaulting, but is less regular and clear cut than Schumacher's drawing shows. Five lamp niches have been cut into the walls. Passages A and B are rock-cut and function more for light and air, although it is possible to squeeze through Passage A. The doorsill was raised and contained another step down to the interior. The bedrock surrounds of the rectangular doorway in the tuffaceous limestone are badly eroded; Richmond believed it had been subsequently enlarged.[26] The cave opens onto a

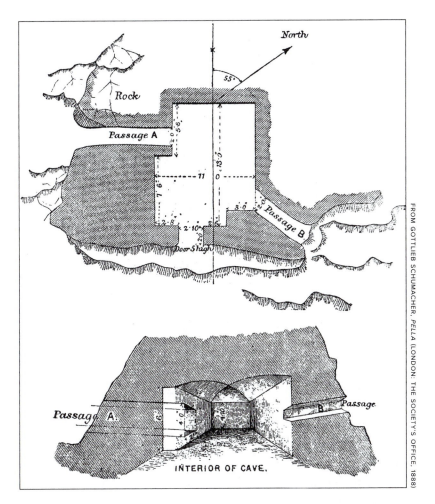

SCHUMACHER'S ANCHORITE CAVE. When German explorer Gottlieb Schumacher traveled to Pella in the 1880s, he investigated several of the site's caves, including one that had a rough-hewn, cross-vaulted ceiling and two narrow ventilation shafts (Passages A and B, shown in plan and in section in the drawing above). While he and other early researchers believed this and similar cave complexes could have been used by early Christian refugees, the Pella Hinterland Survey (PHS) found no clear evidence that the cave was in use during the first century.

small terrace, several feet above the terraced wadi floor. It is obscured by vegetation from below and totally invisible from above. It would be hard to find under most circumstances, but not impossible. This cave is located in a different area to the caves and tunnels discussed below, separated by an intervening side wadi.

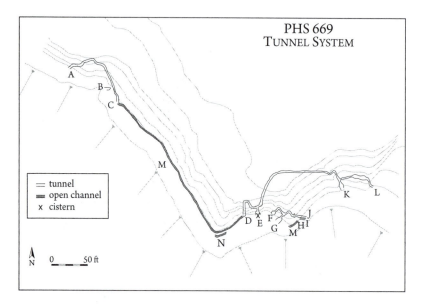

PHS 669
TUNNEL SYSTEM

= tunnel
= open channel
x cistern

0 _____ 50 ft

CHRISTIAN CAVES OR WATER SYSTEM? The PHS mapped a dozen interconnected tunnels and caves in the northern cliffs of the Wadi Jirm (labeled here A–L). While Schumacher believed these to be additional examples of caves and routes early Christians used while in hiding, the PHS found that they were actually part of a Roman-period water system that channeled the flow from a nearby spring into rock-hewn cisterns.

Tunnels and caves in the northern cliffs of the Wadi Jirm

Continuing southwest down the wadi another 500 feet or so, around a prominent bluff, the ground drops further away, the cliffs become taller and the wadi narrows. About halfway up from the valley floor (60–80 feet) the angle of slope changes to vertical, and at this level we found a series of tunnel entrances and caves, 12 in all, as described by Schumacher and Richmond (PHS site 669 A–L; see plan above). They were clearly manmade (having pick marks and lamp niches inside them), although natural tunnels in the tuffaceous limestone (formed by intense fluvial activity in the distant past) were utilized where available.[27] Some are now exposed as open-air channels due to subsequent collapse of the friable cliff face. Clearance, mapping and excavation revealed an associated cistern and channels in one of the tunnels and established the complex to be a system of water tunnels leading southwest through and around the cliff face from an upper spring (now dry). Richmond's plan of one segment of the tunnel series corresponds exactly with the PHS tunnels 669 D, E, F,

G, K and L.[28] The system was dated by the excavated pottery exclusively to the Roman period (first–third centuries C.E.). The archaeological evidence and interpretation of site 669 has been discussed elsewhere.[29] Schumacher's theory that these caves and tunnels were hidden refuges and escape routes associated with the flight of the Jerusalem church to Pella has now been disproved by a closer examination of the physical evidence, revealing a water system, although his chronology was serendipitously apt. However the story does not end there.

The upper-tier caves in the northern cliffs of the Wadi Jirm

Schumacher had continued his explorations westward down the wadi. He apparently didn't search the upper levels of the cliffs above the tunnel system. Although the cliffs are vertical, there is another tier 30–50 feet above the water system tunnels, which is accessible from above on the western side (by goats and agile humans) and which we explored in the Pella Hinterland Survey.[30] Along this natural ledge are numerous caves within the friable rock (including cave sites 666–668). As the surface is crumbly, and goat herders have made good use of their shelter through the ages, most of the caves appear to be natural. However the last cave before the first bluff toward the east was found to contain three substantial rock-cut niches of varying size in the walls (PHS site 666). It is large and open, measuring 13 feet wide by 11 feet deep. Further access around the east bluff is perilous but possible. Beyond is a 10-foot-wide ledge facing southwest, mounded with collapsed debris from the cliff above. The soil and rock debris mostly obscured a small opening about 8 inches high at the base of the cliff. It proved to be the beginning of another tunnel. Rectangular in section (about 3 feet high by 1.5–2.5 feet wide) and clearly rock-cut, the tunnel doglegs twice for a distance of nearly 30 feet, to open out into a large chamber, the first of multi-chambered cave PHS 667 (see plan on p. 84). This chamber (1) measures 16.5 by 20.5 feet and is distinguished by the presence of a rock-cut central pillar. Four more chambers open sequentially to the southeast, the last two obscured by massive roof collapse. The final chamber (5) has a large semicircular opening to the outside, set in a sheer and totally inaccessible cliff face looking southeast. This was the main source of light and air for the cave complex.

Unlike the other caves, the inaccessibility and obscurity of the site had kept it relatively undisturbed, and a large colony of bats flourished

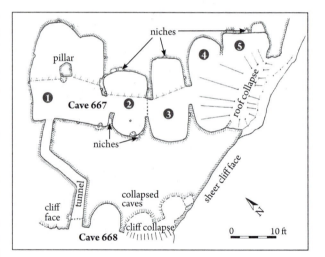

Courtesy P.M. Watson/Pella Hinterland Survey

PELLA'S CAVES OF REFUGE. About 30–50 feet above the entrance to the water system (cave and tunnel series 669), the PHS located another series of rock cavities (caves 666–668) (above; see plan right). The rock-hewn rooms, some measuring 15 x 15 feet, were impossible to date but were well equipped with lamp niches, a stone column and a porch-like gallery to create relatively comfortable living conditions. It is possible that this complex of chambers could have been used as a place of refuge for early Christians who had escaped to Pella.

inside. As a result the chambers were full of bat guano to a depth of more than 3 feet. In an attempt to record the cave system in the limited time available, only the southwest halves of the first three chambers were cleared of guano. Unfortunately there were no occupation deposits between the guano and the bedrock floor, and no artifacts were recovered. However, many features appeared during excavation, such as lamp niches for lighting

(22 in all), cupboard niches (nine) and cut floor depressions (three, and a cup hole), suitable for holding round-bottomed vessels. There was nothing to suggest that this multi-chambered complex was sepulchral, nor that it was for storage. The cleared dogleg tunnel is barely 3 feet high; its two angular turns were deliberately designed to make access difficult. The entrance is perilous to approach and easily hidden. Although its original exterior form is unknown due to the collapse of the cliff face onto the current ledge, it would be simple to hide it with brush or a boulder. Two mortises or slots in the interior walls on either side of the entrance suggest a blocking mechanism. The problem is that while the chambers have all the features suggesting human habitation, the first three chambers are also too low for a person to stand upright (measuring only 3.25–4.10 feet in height). It is probable that Chamber 5 and perhaps Chamber 4 were higher and more comfortable, but the amount of roof collapse makes this difficult to determine. Occupation in the first three chambers would not have been comfortable except for sleeping, but could have sufficed for a limited time. This consideration, along with the design of the access tunnel, would suggest that its purpose was not for permanent habitation, but for temporary occupation, as required in times of trouble.

There is another relatively open cave with at least one worked niche (PHS site 668) a few feet farther to the east from the entrance to PHS site 667. It is on the very edge of the bluff, but is now largely collapsed. It is feasible that all the caves on this upper cliff level were used for habitation, but erosion and collapse have removed the evidence.

PHS cave 667 is the only one that was deliberately hidden from view, set deep within the cliff and capable of holding numerous people. It can confidently be interpreted as a hidden cave of refuge.

Conclusion

There are no artifacts, no inscriptions and no decorations associated with the upper tier caves (PHS caves 666–668) to date their period of construction or use. Except for proximity, there is no apparent connection with the lower water tunnel system 669, except proximity. If the upper caves existed in the first centuries C.E., then the engineers and maintainers of the water tunnels would certainly have known about them. Pella has suffered many vicissitudes over thousands of years of occupation, wars and siege. The need for refuge was not necessarily limited to one catastrophe.

It would make a good tale to connect these caves, in particular the cave of refuge, with the first-century Christians, seeing them as seeking refuge in inaccessible and rigorous conditions. But there is nothing in the literary sources to indicate *how* they initially lived at Pella. If they did migrate and were received by the local population, they may just as well have lived in houses. The identification as anchorites was added by Schumacher to accommodate his interpretation of the caves and tunnels. He embellished the tradition by assuming the tunnels led into the plateau toward a later Christian sanctuary. R.H. Smith's interpretation of the sarcophagus beneath the West Church is sympathetic to Schumacher's (and later Richmond's) line of thought. In reality, it would have been a long and virtually impossible subterranean journey of nearly half a mile through friable bedrock. The lower series of tunnels (PHS 669) can now be seen as a more prosaic, but nevertheless interesting Roman water system probably associated with intense cultivation of the fertile valley floor. The "Schumacher anchorite cave" (PHS cave 750) and the previously undiscovered occupation caves (PHS caves 666, 667 and 668) must remain as a hypothetical scenario for early Christian presence at Pella. Nothing in the surviving evidence can relate them specifically to this period or to that group of people. Nevertheless it is ironic that Schumacher failed to find the one cave system that would have added weight to his argument, however shaky the premise.

The archaeology of Pella and its environs has revealed a functioning Hellenized settlement in the mid-first century C.E. capable of receiving refugees, whether within the existing urban fabric or more covertly in the immediate landscape. However, an earnest desire to establish a direct link with a potentially historical episode such as the flight of the early Christians can lead to assumptions and embellishments that are not warranted by the physical evidence when scrutinized. Archaeological investigations have yet to find anything that would confirm the presence of a specific population whose identity at this stage is more defined by their non-material belief systems than their material accoutrements. In fact, although their presence is not precluded,* neither Jews nor Christians have left any revelatory signature in the first-century C.E. cultural remains recovered to date at Pella.

*See Steven Bourke, "The Christian Flight to Pella: True or Tale?" *BAR*, May/June 2013.

5

Parting in Palestine

JOAN TAYLOR

THIS CHAPTER RECOUNTS THE "PARTING OF THE WAYS" IN JUDEA/
Palestine from the Roman destruction of Jerusalem and the Temple in
70 C.E. to the period following the Roman suppression of the Second
Jewish Revolt in 135 C.E. through the end of the third century.

It is often assumed that with the destruction of the Temple in 70 C.E.
Jewish life in Jerusalem and in the traditional heartland of Judea ceased. In
books, articles and courses, 70 C.E. is given as the end of "Second Temple
Judaism." However, neither our surviving literary sources nor archaeology
indicates that Jewish life in Jerusalem or Judea as a whole completely
ended in 70. Even without the Temple as a physical structure Judaism
persisted, with a continuing hope for the Temple's reconstruction. While
the Jewish population of Jerusalem was much reduced, it was not entirely
absent, and—despite its fame and supreme importance—Jerusalem was
only one of many Jewish towns and villages in Judea (see Josephus, *War*
3.51–52). The major cataclysm for the Jewish people appears instead to
have been a consequence of the Second Jewish Revolt (132–135 C.E.),
which was led by the revolutionary leader Simeon Bar-Kokhba (rightly bar
Kosba).[1] After the suppression of this revolt, the Roman emperor Hadrian
(see Plate 3) engaged in what can only be described as "ethnic cleansing"
in the area around Jerusalem. Jewish life in the heartland was shattered.
Hadrian renamed the country (until then officially "Judea" in Roman

nomenclature) as "Syria Palestina." A complete administrative reorganiza-
tion marked the end of Jewish law as the operational legal system.[2]

Josephus himself notes the continuing existence of the Jewish people in
Judea after the destruction of the Temple, with government and law intact.[3]
His *Antiquities of the Jews,* written in 93–94 C.E., more than two decades
after the destruction of the Temple, assumes that Jews and Judaism existed
as firmly as ever in Judea. Likewise, in his *Against Apion,* completed about 97
C.E., he simply assumes the vibrant existence of the Jewish people in Judea,
continually using the present tense to describe the practices and experiences
of Jews in their homeland. He begins *Apion* by explaining "how we came
to inhabit this country in which we live now" (1.1), a region he and/or his
sources call both "Judea"[4] and "Palestine."[5] Indeed, he assumes the continuing
authority of Jewish law in this land. The "government" or "jurisdiction"
(*politeuma, Antiquities* 1.5) is Jewish, with functioning law courts.[6]

After Josephus the historical evidence is quite patchy, but it can
be garnered from the works and epitomes (summaries) of the Roman
historian Dio Cassius (c. 230 C.E.), from historians preserved by Eusebius
of Caesarea (c. 320 C.E.), and from other Christian authors and later
encyclopedias.[7] In rabbinic literature, this is the period of the *tannaim*
(first to second centuries). There we can see the energy of Jewish legal
and theological discussion at this time.

Archaeology has also brought to light a wealth of Aramaic, Greek,
Nabatean and Hebrew papyri from the Judean desert caves close to
Ein Gedi, carried by doomed refugees from the bloody aftermath
of the second revolt, as well as from Masada and other sites.[*] These
provide secure evidence from the period just before as well as during the
revolt. They tell us not only about the Dead Sea area, but, more widely,
about Jewish administration, agriculture and law, and corroborate the
impression that Jewish law still continued, even in the heartland. We find,
for example, a Jewish re-marriage contract from Bethbassi in the toparchy
of Herodion dated to 124 C.E. (no. 291).[8] Interestingly, the papyrological
evidence includes letters from Bar-Kokhba himself. Fourteen of his letters
have been recovered.[9]

---

[*]See Roi Porat and Hanan Eshel, "Fleeing the Romans: Judean Refugees Hide in Caves,"
BAR, March/April 2006; Richard A. Freund and Rami Arav, "Return to the Cave of Letters:
What Still Lies Buried?" *BAR,* January/February 2001; Joseph Patrich, "Hideouts in the Judean
Wilderness," *BAR,* September/October 1989.

LETTER FROM BAR-KOKHBA. Among the scores of papyrus documents found in the Judean desert caves dating to the time of the Second Jewish Revolt was this letter—one of 14—written by Bar-Kokhba himself. Written in Hebrew, the letter chastises its recipient, Yeshua ben Galgula, regarding the "Galileans," possibly a group of Galilean fighters who were at his command.

Pottery from the period between the two Jewish revolts, especially the pottery dated by the nuanced work of Rachel Bar-Nathan at the salvage site of Shu'fat on the Ramallah road north of Jerusalem,[10] is now better understood. We also find a continuing use of vessels made of stone, which is not subject to impurity according to Jewish law. This reflects the fact that after the 70 C.E. destruction of Jerusalem, there were Jews in Judea concerned with Jewish purity laws.

Similarly, ritual bathing pools (*mikva'ot*) continued in use in many settlements to 135 C.E.[11] This, too, suggests that Jews were there, maintaining ritual purity practices. Ritual baths adjacent to the necropolis of Beth Shearim (second–third centuries) indicate that people were concerned about immersing after contact with the dead.[12]

This would also indicate that Jews felt the need to be cleansed of corpse impurity.[13] Traditionally this involved ashes from a red heifer, which had to be sacrificed and burnt "outside the camp," and in the Second Temple period this meant the Mount of Olives (Mishnah *Parah* 3:6–11). A person would be sprinkled with water mixed with these ashes on the third and seventh days and then be immersed in a *mikveh* and wait till sundown before being pure again (Numbers 19:1–21). The red heifer sacrifice was rare and ashes were stored for a long time—the Mishnah says there were only seven such sacrifices since the time of Ezra, the last one being by High Priest Ishmael ben Phiabi (*Parah* 3:5, cf. *Sota* 9:15; cf. Josephus, *Antiquities* 20.179, 194–196), which would have been around 59–60 C.E., furnishing enough ash for future generations. That this ceremony did not require a temple should be noted. This raises an issue about the continuation of elements of the Temple cult. The Temple had its conceptual origins in a *portable* tent of meeting (Exodus 25–31, 35–40), after all, and an alternative temple had a long history in Egypt at Leontopolis (Tell el-Yehoudieh) in the Heliopolis region (Josephus, *War* 7.421–436; *Antiquities* 13.62–73).[14] Curiously, Josephus, while always referring in the past tense to the Temple as a building, refers to the continuation of sacrifices in the present (e.g., *Apion* 2.193–198). Somehow, the concept of the Temple remained alive.

The Herodian dynasty also continued to rule a part of Judea post-70 C.E. (the Golan and Galilee), under governor Agrippa II.[15] Jerusalem, however, had been ruined after being burnt and razed. Josephus gives us a vivid picture of the horrors of the Roman siege, how all the forests and gardens 10 miles around were obliterated, and how the Temple, suburbs, city and walls were destroyed, with only the towers of the citadel and a small section of wall in the west remaining. Judean land that had been confiscated was sold off.[16]

The Roman Legion X Fretensis encamped in Jerusalem.* Archaeological excavations have recovered numerous roof tiles and drain pipes manufactured in the legion's pottery workshop. The workshop itself has been found in Binyanei Ha'uma, west of the city,[17] testifying to the fact that the legion engaged in building for the encampment and services. These terracotta tiles are stamped with the symbol of the legion—a wild boar and/or galley, with its abbreviation LEGXF or LXF. The top of a column extolling the emperor Titus (ruled 79–81 C.E.) has also been

*See Eilat Mazar, "Hadrian's Legion: Encamped on the Temple Mount," *BAR*, November/ December 2006.

TILE OF THE *LEGIO X FRETENSIS*. Following its destruction in 70 C.E., Jerusalem came under the watchful eye of the Tenth Roman Legion. Excavations throughout the city have found clear traces of the army's presence, including ceramic roof tiles stamped with the legion's initials (LEGXF) and emblems, a galley ship and the wild boar.

ZEV RADOVAN/WWW.BIBLELANDPICTURES.COM

found.[18] In 2010, a bathhouse serving the legion was discovered in the Jewish Quarter of present-day Jerusalem.

Who else lived in Jerusalem other than the Roman military? Clearly some other people, on the basis of archaeological evidence. The burial caves around Jerusalem indicate that there were still some Jewish ossuary burials there from 70 C.E. through to 135 C.E., in a period when the use of clay ossuaries began.[19] In terms of dating stone ossuaries, they are frequently assigned to the period prior to 70 C.E. on account of the assumption that Jews did not live in Jerusalem after the Temple's destruction, but it is clear that a more nuanced appraisal of associated grave goods is needed to test this dating more carefully.[20] Rabbinic references also indicate that Jews were in Jerusalem at this time. Rabbi Simeon ben Assai, who was active 100–130 C.E., refers to records in Jerusalem that he consulted (Mishnah *Yevamot* 4:13). Rabbi Akiva, who is associated with Bar-Kokhba, was among a group of four rabbis who visited Jerusalem.[21]

The important thing to note, however, is that the destroyed city of Jerusalem was not Judea as a whole. It is now clearer than ever that Jewish life continued elsewhere. In Galilee, the clay ossuaries associated with this period, and somewhat later, testify to practices of bone-collection brought by southern refugees.[22] These people came to unscathed pro-Roman Jewish cities such as Sepphoris, which in 67–68 C.E., after the revolt had begun in the north, issued coins in honor of Vespasian.[23] The city was renamed Diocaesarea during the reign of Trajan (c. 110 C.E.), to honor the emperor. Tiberias on the Sea of Galilee also continued to be loyal to Rome, and large numbers of coins were produced there.

These were safe places for Jews. They had Jewish city councils that administered Jewish law. A rich production of Galilean bronze coinage indicates thriving Jewish settlements in this area.[24]

Although Jewish government may be hard to distinguish in our few sources, it would be wrong to assume that it did not exist, especially when Josephus states that it did. Jurisdictions were city-based. In terms of a "lead" council for the Jewish nation, in rabbinic literature we have references to the esteemed council of sages in Jamnia (Yavneh), under Yoḥanan ben Zakkai.[25]

However, there is also mention of a "court of priests,"[26] apart from the sages, that may have continued in Jerusalem.[27] Judaism did not suddenly become uniformly rabbinic; rather, there appear to have been power struggles.[28] The rabbinic stories of Yoḥanan ben Zakkai are polemical. They reflect the view that the traditions of the sages are better than other schools of Jewish law.[29] The old notion that *the* Jerusalem council was transferred from Jerusalem to Jamnia after the destruction of the Temple, with the dawn of a new age of Rabbinic Judaism,[30] is no longer considered correct.[31]

Archaeological evidence from Jerusalem and elsewhere depicts Roman military oversight. The need for a heavy occupying force reflects the fact there was a substantial local population that the Romans wanted to control. Indeed, inscriptional evidence shows that after 117 C.E. two Roman legions were needed to control the population: The Tenth Legion remained in Jerusalem, while an additional Roman legion, *Legio* (*II Traiana Fortis*), was stationed in Galilee at Kfar Othnay.[32] While ultimate control lay with Rome, Roman military presence does not equate to martial law.

Jewish life in the heartland of central Judea was not crushed until 135 C.E., when the Romans quashed the Second Jewish Revolt. The main description of this is found in the surviving epitome by Dio Cassius, *Roman History* 69.12–14. Here we are told that when the Roman emperor Hadrian visited Judea en route from Egypt to Syria (in c. 129–130 C.E.), he ordered that a new temple to Jupiter Capitolinus should be constructed on the Temple Mount and that Jerusalem should be rebuilt as a Roman colony, Aelia Capitolina, Latin for "The City of the Capitoline Gods."[33] In reaction, there was revolt, with insurgents creating secret subterranean hideouts as bases to engage in attacks.

From coins, we learn that a Temple administration existed under a high priest named Eleazar.[34] Coins issued during the revolt served as an

ZEV RADOVAN/WWW.BIBLELANDPICTURES.COM

AELIA CAPITOLINA COIN. Minted in c. 131 C.E., this Roman coin depicts a temple to Jupiter, flanked by statues of Juno and Minerva, which the emperor Hadrian (shown on the coin's obverse) ordered to be built on Jerusalem's Temple Mount. Hadrian's order and his larger plan to transform Jewish Jerusalem into a Roman colony renamed Aelia Capitolina sparked the Second Jewish Revolt against Rome in 132 C.E. The new Roman name for the city is inscribed on this coin: COL(onia) AEL(ia) KAP(itolina).

instrument of propaganda, advertising the goal to liberate Jerusalem and rebuild the Jerusalem Temple.[35]

Dio Cassius states that Hadrian sent his best generals to put down the new revolt, with huge forces at their disposal.* Probably using official Roman military records, Dio Cassius is able to state with authority that 50 of the secret outposts of the rebels were destroyed and 985 towns and villages were razed to the ground. A total of 580,000 fighting men were killed in battle, he says, and the number of people who died as a result of starvation, disease and the burning of the towns and villages was impossible to reckon. As he writes, "So, almost all of Judea was turned into a wilderness."[36] Archaeology has confirmed this report, with the discovery now of more than 125 subterranean hiding settlement-complexes in the Shephelah, Hebron mountains and Bethel region, with archaeological evidence clearly indicating Jewish presence in some 330 settlements in Judea at this time.[†37] The level of destruction is widely evidenced.

From other sources we learn that there was a rebel center at Modi'in

*See Werner Eck, "Hadrian's Hard-Won Victory," *BAR*, September/October 2007.
†See the example of Horvat 'Ethri in Boaz Zissu, "Village Razed, Rebel Beheaded," *BAR*, September/October 2007.

COIN OF THE SECOND JEWISH REVOLT. "Year one of the redemption of Israel" is inscribed in Hebrew around a cluster of grapes on the reverse of this bronze coin from the first year of the Bar-Kokhba Revolt (132 C.E.). The obverse shows a palm tree with the inscription, "Eleazar the Priest," a reference to the otherwise-unattested high priest of the Temple administration, which was apparently still active despite the Temple's destruction.

and a final siege at Bethar. This was followed with a ban on Jews living in a large part of their former core homeland of Judea.[38] Judea was re-branded as "Syria Palestina." The renovation of Jerusalem as the *colonia* Aelia Capitolina went ahead, and with it Roman law.* In the new administrative zones of former Judea, the land was divided up into individual cities, with their own city jurisdictions.

Between 70 and 135 C.E., as Jews continued to live in Judea within a system of Jewish law, so did the group(s) we refer to as Jewish-Christians.[39] There is no reason to think that they were considered separate from Judaism, even if other Jews thought they erred in their belief in Jesus as Messiah.

To explore this a little further we can in fact turn to the New Testament and look to what it indicates not just in regard to the time it describes but the time in which it was written. The composite work of the Gospel of Luke and the Acts of the Apostles (Luke-Acts) is in my view now best dated from the first decades of the second century (c. 110–120 C.E.), just prior to the Bar-Kokhba Revolt.[40] Acts 1:1–15:21 is particularly concerned with identifying the early foundation of churches in wider

*See Hanan Eshel, "Aelia Capitolina: Jerusalem No More," *BAR*, November/December 1997.

COURTESY BOAZ ZISSU AND AMIR GANOR, ISRAEL ANTIQUITIES AUTHORITY

PLACE OF REFUGE DURING THE SECOND REVOLT. This underground complex located below the site of Horvat 'Ethri in the Judean Shephelah was one of more than a hundred such hiding places hewn out by Jewish villagers seeking refuge from the Roman legions sent to suppress the Bar-Kokhba Revolt. The Roman historian Dio Cassius writes that nearly 1,000 Judean towns were razed and that hundreds of thousands died in battle and even more from starvation and disease.

Judea-Palestine; Acts 15:22–28:31 ensures a line is drawn from Jerusalem to Rome, via Paul. It is not that the churches of Judea-Palestine have been replaced by Rome, any more than Antioch has been; but rather the validation of Rome—and the gentile mission—rests on the connectivity to the churches of Judea-Palestine. The gentile Christians are attached to those who "listen" (i.e., the Jewish-Christians) as an "also": "They will *also* listen" (Acts 28:28).[41]

According to Acts 15, Jewish-Christians (Nazarenes)[42] in Judea, which included "a large number of priests" (Acts 6:7) and Pharisees (Acts 15:5), kept to Jewish praxis—Sabbath laws, food laws, purity laws, circumcision, etc. But they could accept fellowship with non-Jews (Acts 15:19–21) within church communities on the basis of concepts that appear to define "righteous gentiles." The concept of righteous gentiles was based on the covenant with Noah for all humanity (i.e., the Noahide laws, from Genesis 9:4–6 and Jubilees 7:20–28).[43]

In Luke-Acts the Jewish-Christians in Judea are largely accepted by other Jews, despite attacks from the chief priestly authorities. The Pharisees are identified as the elite (Luke 7:36, 11:37,43, 14:1,7–11,12–14) who unwisely seek popular esteem,[44] but these Pharisees of Luke-Acts are also concerned with carefully defining the correct interpretation of Torah and function as circumspect teachers of the law (Luke 5:17, and see Gamaliel in Acts 5:34, 23:6,9). They warn Jesus respectfully to leave Galilee, as Herod Antipas wants to kill him (Luke 13:31), and caution him (addressing him as "teacher") that his disciples should not shout in loud voices as he arrives in Jerusalem (Luke 19:37–40). The Jerusalem population mourns when Jesus is driven out to Golgotha (Luke 23:27–31). On the other hand, the Sadducees are portrayed as linked with the hostile Temple hierarchy: the chief priests (as opposed to ordinary priests). In Acts 4:1 chief priests come with the captain of the Temple "and the Sadducees" to arrest Peter and John in the Temple, and in Acts 5:17 the high priest acts with "all his supporters from the school of the Sadducees" to arrest the apostles and put them in prison. This indicates an interesting differentiation between parties and divisions among Jews in Judea, and Acts ends with Jewish debate in Rome, in which some community leaders were persuaded by Paul and some not (Acts 28:25). This likewise reflects varieties of Jewish perspectives but no unified Jewish hostility to Jewish-Christians or Christians in general.

In this early period there are no definitive archaeological indicators of Jewish-Christian presence in Judea,[45] as with Christians overall, but the church historian Eusebius and other patristic authors testify to the continued presence of numbers of Jewish-Christians before Bar-Kokhba. Importantly, Eusebius cites a source with the names of 15 Jewish ("Hebrew") leaders of the Jerusalem church through to the end of the second revolt,[46] providing corroborating evidence that Jews, including Jewish-Christians, did continue to live in the damaged city of Jerusalem, despite the presence of the Legion X Fretensis, after a short interruption of residence there during the first revolt itself. Eusebius states that the church fled temporarily to the Decapolis city of Pella.[47] (See Chapter IV, "The Christian Flight to Pella? The Archaeological Picture," by Pamela Watson.) Somewhat later, and less reliably, in 392 C.E., Epiphanius records a tradition that when Hadrian arrived in Judea in 117 C.E. (actually 129/130 C.E.) he found Jerusalem quite ruined, but there was "a church of God that was small" and "seven synagogues" on Mount Zion, one of which survived structurally till the time of Constantine.*[48]

Eusebius's source for most of his information about the Jerusalem church between 70 and 132 C.E. was Hegesippus, who appears to have been ethnically Jewish and who wrote some "Memoirs" over five books around the year 150.[49] We have only occasional summaries and quotations from this work, but Eusebius quotes Hegesippus as stating:

> There were different judgments in respect to the [question of] circumcision, in respect to the children of Israelites, in regard to the tribe of Judah and [the tribe of] the Christ.
>
> (Eusebius, *Ecclesiastical History* 4.22)[50]

This is very important. Overall, the argument seems to be concerned with *identity*, so that the final point would be concerning whether the male children of the Christians ("the tribe of the Christ"[51]) were really part of Israel if they were circumcised. But this snippet of information and discussion is left hanging in Eusebius's history without the context it requires for its full understanding, since what was of interest to Eusebius was what Hegesippus said next about diverse groups within what he defined as Israel (Essenes, Samaritans, Sadducees, Pharisees and so on), not the subject of their dispute. The language nevertheless implies a careful and judicious assessment involving various parties, which reflects the rich variety of practices and opinions within Judaism in the period between the two revolts.

But in 132 C.E. things turned nasty. Justin Martyr, a native of Palestine from Neapolis (Nablus) in Samaria, notes that "Bar-Kokhba ordered Christians to be severely punished if they did not deny Jesus Christ and blaspheme him."[52] Eusebius states that the Christians refused to join his rebellion,[53] which may have been more of the core issue at stake; clearly Jewish-Christian reluctance to join in armed conflict against Rome would not have impressed Bar-Kokhba, whose tone in his extant letters against those who crossed him is severe. However, where Bar-Kokhba threatens Yeshua ben Galgula regarding some action concerning Galileans (Murabba'at 43; see p. 89), the identification of these as Christians is now thought unlikely.[54]

see p. 89

---

*See Kenneth G. Holum, "*Iter Principis*: Hadrian's Imperial Tour," *BAR*, November/December 1997; and Bargil Pixner, "Church of the Apostles Found on Mt. Zion," *BAR*, May/June 1990.

Given the exclusion from Jerusalem and the vicinity after 135 C.E. that afflicted all Jews, including Jewish-Christians, Eusebius appropriately notes that from the second revolt on the leaders of the church in Jerusalem were gentiles.[55] But continuity is assumed. The chair of James was preserved to the present by "the brothers each in turn,"[56] and certain traditions about sites are retained, in regard to Gethsemane and Golgotha, for example.*[57] This meant either that gentile Christians from churches in cities located on the coast or the Decapolis, which had mixed populations, moved to Jerusalem at this time, or else that Jewish-Christians abandoned Judaism. Perhaps both alternatives occurred.[58]

This leads to the question of how much of a definitive split between Judaism and Christianity might have been forced on Judea by the Romans. If Hadrian banned Jews (including Jewish-Christians) from living in Jerusalem and its vicinity, and gentile Christians maintained the church after 135 C.E., that is a powerful statement of difference with actual and symbolic resonances. To stay, the Christians in Jerusalem had to be accepted as non-Jews by the Roman administration; this recognition must have been staggering and resented by many within the Jewish community. We see this in what is said by Justin Martyr, a gentile convert to Christianity, writing c. 160 C.E., who would claim then that the praxis of Judaism was incompatible with true Christian belief.[59]

This is not to say that Christians were more favored by Romans than Jews, but only that as gentiles they were at least able to live within Jerusalem, with the magnificent offense of a temple to Venus obliterating the site of Jesus' tomb,[60] a temple commemorated in city coinage.[61] There are even some archaeological remains of this temple that have been found within the Church of the Holy Sepulchre.[62]

Hadrian's views on Christians, as evidenced by the rescript sent to the proconsul of Asia, Minucius Fundanus, c. 127 C.E.,[63] were pragmatic: Christians should be properly tried and found to be actually guilty of an illegality (atheism, treason, etc.), not simply convicted on profession of Christian belief.[64]

Nevertheless, the results of the Roman policy seem to have led to a worsening relationship between Jews and Christians in Judea. Jewish-Christians are likely associated with or placed within the general category

*See Joan E. Taylor, "The Garden of Gethsemane: Not the Place of Jesus' Arrest," *BAR*, July/August 1995.

of *minim* in rabbinic texts. *Minim* is a Hebrew term meaning (negatively) "sorts." In the *Birkat ha-Minim*—which was later associated with Rabbi Gamaliel II, who headed the Jamnia academy around 100 C.E.—*minim* are cursed.[65] Furthermore, the name *Notsrim* was added sometime before the fourth century, as evidenced by Jerome, who states that Jews curse Christians three times a day in synagogues;[66] overall *Notsrim* is the designation for Christians in the Babylonian Talmud[67] on the basis of Jesus being called *ha-Notsri*, a Hebrew word apparently designating "Nazarene" or "Nazoraean."[68] A Greek loan word approximating *Christianoi* (Acts 11:26) is never found in Mishnaic Hebrew.

Around 160 C.E., Justin Martyr understood that there was a Jewish curse against Christ and Christians (*Dialogue with Trypho* 96.2; cf. 16.4, 47.4, 93.4, 95.4, 108.3, 123.6, 133.6, 137.2) used in synagogues (16.4, 47.4, 96.2; cf. Tertullian, *Against Marcion* 4.8.1), which may indicate that the addition of the name *Notsrim* took place a little before this time, though most studies today prefer a late date.[69] A version of the *Birkat ha-Minim* with the name *Notsrim* has survived in two medieval Hebrew texts found in the Cairo Geniza, one of which runs:

> And for apostates let there be no hope, and may the insolent/ arrogant kingdom be uprooted speedily in our days. May the *Notsrim* and the *minim* perish instantly; and may they be removed from the Book of Life, and may they not be written together with the righteous. Blessed are you, Lord, who humbles the insolent/arrogant.[70]

What is striking here is the sense of a family feud. The notion that the *Notsrim* might have ever been in the Book of Life or written together with the righteous—requiring their removal or erasure—is perhaps the most interesting element here; it implies a previous inclusion. There is no significant differentiation between Jewish and gentile Christians. Both belong to a category that might once have been conceptually placed within or with Israel, in the Book of Life, as either Jews or righteous gentiles. But the sin of insolence required their removal.

Yaakov Teppler has argued that the curse was early, and that the term *minim* was largely meant to indicate Jewish-Christians anyway, without the inclusion of gentile Christians as would have been the case with the use of *Notsrim* alone.[71] Usually, however, the term *minim* is given a much wider scope, indicating "others" with whom the rabbis disagreed, with diverse referents. It is normally understood that the *Birkat ha-Minim* (in which Jewish-Christians were included within the category of *minim* but not specifically mentioned) was designed to bolster the rabbinic way against other interpretations of Judaism.[72] (See Chapter XI, "In Between: Jewish-Christians and the Curse of the Heretics," by Shaye J.D. Cohen.) While a key question has been to define when "*Notsrim*" were specifically added and defined, and there is no consensus on this, it does not actually matter for our purposes; it simply matters that there is evidence of cursing, in that Justin is clearly referring to *something*. He mentions there was a curse against Christ "after their prayers" (*Dialogue with Trypho* 137.6) when the *Birkat ha-Minim* is included within prayers,[73] so it may have been a different curse, but there may have been various statements against Jewish-Christians, all Christians and/or Christ either added to the *Birkat ha-Minim* or else separately said in some Jewish communities Justin knew, depending on the particular concerns of specific groups.[74] The limited point here is that these diverse curses are evidenced only *after* the Bar-Kokhba Revolt, at the very time that the struggle for rabbinic hegemony gained pace, and after the Roman ban on Jews living in central Judea when Christians would have had to choose whether or not to live as Jews if they also wanted to live in Jerusalem and the surrounding area, now Aelia Capitolina.[75]

There is no doubt that after the second revolt Jewish-Christianity in the heartland of Judea was damaged in the same way as the whole of Second Temple Judaism, in all its great variety. Celsus, writing c. 177 C.E., apparently wrote of Jews being "bowed down in some corner of Palestine."[76] Jewish life overall was concentrated in Galilee, in the main towns of Diocaesarea (Sepphoris) and Tiberias and Galilean villages,[77] in the Golan, in the south in the Idumean Negev (Daromas) and within increasingly cosmopolitan towns. The remarkable necropolis of Beth Shearim in the Galilean hills gives precious vignettes of the lives and beliefs of Jews in Palestine in the second and third centuries (see Plates 4, 5 and 6), a place where Greek, Aramaic and Hebrew inscriptions, attestations of the title "rabbi," representational and aniconic visual art using common Hellenistic motifs, the image of the menorah, and so on, indicate the hybrid cultural ambiance.*[78] Synagogues of the late second

*See "Beth She'arim," sidebar to Peter W. van der Horst, "Jewish Funerary Inscriptions—Most Are in Greek," *BAR*, September/October 1992.

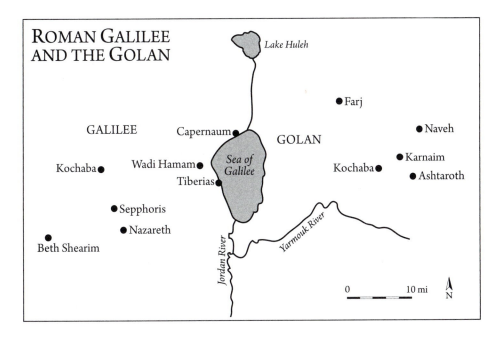

and early third centuries are, however, difficult to identify given the ongoing scholarly debate over their dating,[79] but may be represented by such recent finds as the synagogue at Wadi Hamam in Galilee.*[80] Like other Jews, Jewish-Christians would find locations of refuge, particularly in southern Syria and the Golan.[81] In the fourth century Jewish-Christians are said to have lived in villages called Kochaba, near Karnaim and Ashtaroth south of Naveh.[82] Jewish-Christians are also attested later as living in Choba, near Damascus.[83]

There may also be archaeological evidence to confirm their presence in this area. In 1888, Gottlieb Schumacher found a kind of cross-menorah at the site of Breikah (about 3 miles north of Farj). He also saw a menorah juxtaposed with a cross at nearby Khan Bandak-Ghadiriyeh.[84] W.F. Albright noted lintels with crosses and menorahs at Naveh in 1924.[85] In the 1980s Claudine Dauphin noted a number of inscriptions in Farj that may derive from Jewish-Christians.[86] These were scratched lightly into the hard black basalt stone of the region, on architectural fragments probably deriving from a church. When first scratched, these inscriptions would have stood out as white marks on the black background of the

*See Joey Corbett, "New Synagogue Excavations in Israel and Beyond," *BAR*, July/August 2011; see also photo on p. 141.

stone, but now they are barely visible to the naked eye and cannot easily be reproduced in photographs. The inscriptions combine the Jewish menorah with Christian symbolism such as the fish or the cross along with palm branch symbols that were used in both Jewish and Christian iconography. A drawing on the external face of a door lintel of the church (formerly a synagogue) in Farj shows a cross on the Rock of Calvary, which dates these inscriptions to the fourth century at the earliest, as it reflects the shrine in Jerusalem that dated to this time.[87]

The bars on the tops of the Farj inscriptions also date these typologically to the late fourth to sixth centuries.[88] The language of the inscriptions is Greek, not Hebrew or Aramaic. The use of the fish symbol confirms this, since the fish motif was used to express a Greek (and entirely universal) Christian message. The word "fish" in Greek was *ichthus*, the letters of which represented the assertion: I*esous* Ch*ristos* Th*eou* H*uios* S*oter*, "Jesus Christ, Son of God, Savior." Dauphin suggests that the archaeological evidence as a whole here indicates that Jews and Jewish-Christians lived side by side. This would tend to suggest that a parting of ways was not very deeply felt even here, from which we may extrapolate centuries of peaceful coexistence beforehand.

Beyond the Golan, in Jewish Galilee, there is as yet nothing that bears scrutiny in terms of archaeological evidence for Jewish-Christians in the second and third centuries, though this does not mean Jewish-Christians did not exist in Galilee at this time.[89] Epiphanius reports that a Jewish convert to Christianity, Joseph of Tiberias, built four churches in Jewish areas by the authority of the emperor Constantine in order to help convert Jews. These were built in Nazareth, Diocaesarea, Capernaum and Tiberias around the year 335 C.E.,[90] but these churches are not connected to existing Jewish-Christian communities. Rather, they were placed in the center of Jewish ones. In Tiberias the new church was apparently built in a corner of the ruined Hadrianeum, and in my view this is the church recently discovered in Tiberias by Moshe Hartal and Edna Amos in the center of town.[91] My own examinations also indicate that the archaeological remains attributed by the excavators to Jewish-Christians in Nazareth and Capernaum in the second and third centuries are actually the modest structures built by Joseph of Tiberias in the fourth.[92] If Jewish-Christians existed in Galilee itself through the second and third centuries, they may have had their own places of worship in villages, as evidenced later in the Golan, but these have not yet been found.

Elsewhere, the distinction between Judaism and Christianity is clear. The character of Christianity within Palestine as a whole became predominantly gentile by the time of Eusebius, in the early fourth century, as we see clearly in his work *The Martyrs of Palestine*, chronicling those who were killed following Diocletian's edict of 303 C.E., which required Christians to make sacrifices to pagan gods. Extant Greek and Syriac texts of *The Martyrs of Palestine* indicate that Christian centers existed in Caesarea and Gaza, as well as in Eleutheropolis (Beth Guvrin), Scythopolis (Beth Shean), Gadara, Batanea, Aelia and Jamnia (Yavneh), all of which sent bishops to Constantine's Council of Nicaea in 325 C.E.[93]

In 2005 a third-century prayer hall with a 54-meter-square mosaic dedicated to "god/divine Jesus Christ" (see p. 137) was found near Megiddo within the precincts of Legio (Maximianopolis), and indeed within the Roman military compound itself.* This fits nicely with the fact that a bishop from Legio (Maximianopolis) was sent to the Council of Nicaea in 325 C.E.;[94] Christians must have existed in this location at some point beforehand, though the mosaic had been purposely covered over, perhaps in the crisis of the persecution of 303 C.E.[95]

Conclusions

Overall we see in Judea-Palestine an evolving and patchy picture, with many holes due to lack of historical and archaeological evidence. Jews and Jewish-Christians (who were undoubtedly the most common type of Christians in Judea-Palestine initially) suffered severe blows together in both the first and second revolts, with the latter being completely devastating for all Jews in Judea. Persecution of Jewish-Christians by Jews in Judea is mentioned in relation to the second revolt, and then only in relation to Bar-Kokhba himself, whose severity against opposition is testified in the papyri found in the Judean desert caves. From 160 C.E. onward there is mention of curses against Christ or Christians made in synagogue contexts, which may reflect the development of the *Birkat ha-Minim*, which at some point before the fourth century and in some quarters was a dual curse against *minim* and *Notsrim*.

*See Vassilios Tzaferis, "Inscribed 'To God Jesus Christ': Early Christian Prayer Hall Found in Megiddo Prison," *BAR*, March/April 2007. Tzaferis, however, prefers an initial date for the structure in the latter part of the third century.

Archaeological evidence indicates that Jews and Jewish-Christians lived together in villages of the Golan in the fourth to sixth centuries, with different synagogues. Perhaps here and elsewhere this was also true at an earlier time, though there is currently no archaeological evidence for Jewish-Christianity in Galilee.

After the Second Jewish Revolt, Christianity became predominantly gentile in Palestine. The population as a whole was mainly Syro-Phoenician. The Syro-Phoenicians, with a Hellenistic culture, had for a long time lived as majorities in most of the coastal cities from Gaza in the southwest to Ptolemais (Akko) in the northwest and in the Decapolis from the territory of Hippos-Sussita in the northeast to Abila in the southeast. Hellenistic law codes operated in these cities and the Syro-Phoenicians worshiped within syncretistic cults. Samaritans lived in the city of Sebaste and in the area around Mount Gerizim and Shechem,[96] which became the city of Neapolis Flavia in 72/3 C.E. After the second revolt, both the Syro-Phoenicians and the Samaritans spread out into former Jewish areas in the heartland, around Jerusalem and traditional Judea.

Aelia Capitolina, formerly Jerusalem, was now a Roman colony. Only gentile Christians could live in the city; Jews were forbidden not only here but elsewhere in a wide area of their old homeland of central Judea.

This Roman initiative to differentiate between Jews and non-Jews would have entailed an insistence on definition; thus a radical break with Judaism was forced on Christians here and elsewhere in the exclusion zone, with wide symbolic and practical ramifications.

6

Christianity in Antioch: Partings in Roman Syria

ANNETTE YOSHIKO REED AND LILY VUONG

THE LOCAL CULTURES OF NORTHERN SYRIA PLAYED A PIVOTAL ROLE
in the partitioning of Christian identities from Jewish piety and
peoplehood.[1] A striking number of the sources cited as exemplary of the
"parting(s) of the way(s)" are from or about Syria. Not only is Paul's call
to be "apostle to the gentiles" situated on the road to Damascus, but both
Paul and Luke-Acts point to Antioch as the setting of an early controversy concerning the interactions between Jesus' Jewish and non-Jewish
followers.[2] Although the precise character of the "incident at Antioch"
remains debated,[3] it is clear that local controversies in Syria spurred
efforts to distinguish non-Jewish affiliation with the Jesus movement from
adherence or conversion to Judaism. Problems in Antioch prompted the
articulation of what became a distinctively Christian vision of biblically
based piety for gentiles.

Roman Syria was also a crucible for new approaches to conceptualizing identity and difference. At the end of the first century, the author
of Luke-Acts points to Antioch as the place where the name "Christians"

(Greek, *Christianoi*) originated as a distinguishing label for Jesus' disciples (Acts 11:26). In the same city, early in the second century, the bishop Ignatius coined the term *Christianismos*—the Greek word from which our concept and category of "Christianity" ultimately derive. Ignatius did so, moreover, through contrast with *Ioudaismos* (literally "Judaizing," "Judeanness" or "Jewishness").[4] Just as Paul and Luke-Acts reflect some of the social realities in Syria that shaped incipient ideas about "Christians" as a distinct group within or alongside "Jews," so Ignatius also points to this region's place in the development of the discourse of Jewish/Christian difference. In this, too, local Syrian dynamics had far-reaching consequences: Ignatius's notion of *Christianismos* spread westward throughout the Roman Empire, informing new notions of "religion" in late antiquity and beyond.[5]

Yet these snapshots of separation do not tell the whole story. Syrian sources also loom large in our evidence for the continued vitality of older and other models of conceptualizing belief in Jesus as complementary with Jewish peoplehood and practice. Evidence for third- and fourth-century Syria, in fact, is unique in preserving the other side of the story of how "Christian" identities came to be categorically distinguished from "Jewish" identities. The Syrian authors of works such as the fourth-century Pseudo-Clementine *Homilies* and *Epistle of Peter to James* appeal to the apostles Peter and James to define the piety, pedagogy and practice of Jesus' followers in radical *continuity* with Judaism.[6] These rare but important works—often labeled "Jewish-Christian"[7]—also defend some of the same practices condemned as "Judaizing" in other Syrian writings, such as the *Didascalia Apostolorum* and John Chrysostom's sermons *Against the Judaizers*. Taken together, these third- and fourth-century sources show that Syrian Christians continued to disagree about which parts of Judaism formed the church's heritage in Israel's history and scriptures, which parts might be too "Jewish" to be "Christian," and whether such distinctions even made sense.

In what follows, we survey some of the most important sources for understanding the partitioning of Christian identities from Jews and Judaism in Syria in the first four centuries C.E. Perhaps particularly in the case of Syria, the emergence of distinctively Christian identities cannot be understood apart from a sense of inner-Christian resistance to the severing of longstanding social and communal connections. Separatists like Ignatius did not immediately succeed in reshaping local lived realities in the image of their theological ideals.[8] To the degree that one can tell a

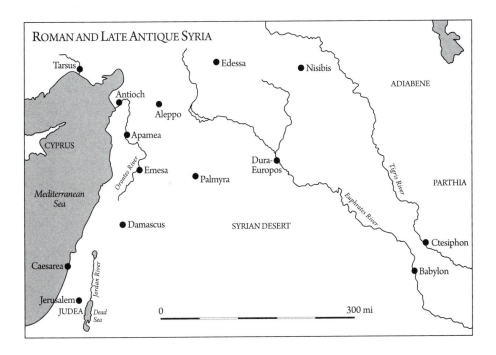

story about Christians and Jews "parting ways" in Roman Syria, it is the tale of a prolonged process, far more complex and contested than the proclamations of famous separatists convey.

For our purposes, "Roman Syria" can be defined as the region centered on Antioch and stretching from the eastern coast of the Mediterranean to the Roman Empire's eastern border.[9] As Han Drijvers notes, "Antioch and Edessa are the two poles of Syrian Christianity as it developed during the first centuries A.D. in the Roman province of Syria."[10] Accordingly, we here focus primarily on the area bounded by Antioch on the Orontes River in the west and by Edessa and Nisibis beyond the Euphrates in the east, including other cities along the Orontes, such as Apamea and Emesa, together with the Syrian Desert, stretching southward to Damascus.[11]

In the first four centuries C.E., the political and administrative boundaries of this region were unstable and shifting, due both (1) to the periodic remapping of the provinces of the Roman Near East; and (2) to Roman conflicts with its eastern imperial rivals (especially Parthia) in the border zone between the Euphrates and Tigris rivers. By virtue of the former, Judea and the Galilee were administered as part of "Syria" in some sense for much of the period here surveyed. By virtue of the latter,

Mesopotamian kingdoms like Edessa could maintain some measure of native rule even into the third century.[12]

In what follows, we distinguish between Roman Syria and Roman Palestine, following the longstanding notion of the distinctiveness of the land of Israel in Christian as well as Jewish writings.[13] Yet, as we shall see, proximity to Palestine shaped the experiences of Syrian Christians and Jews, not least due to overlaps in culture and language: Syria was thoroughly bilingual throughout the period surveyed below, with various Aramaic dialects (e.g., Syriac) flourishing alongside the Greek language used for Roman administration and elite education.[14] Partly as a result, Syrian Christians continued to engage Jews and Judaism, not only through biblical exegesis or New Testament polemics, but also with some awareness and engagement with Jewish practices and teachings current in their own times.

Flavius Josephus

Writing at the end of the first century C.E., the Jewish historian Flavius Josephus points to the large population of Jews in Syria and the widespread Syrian curiosity about Judaism (e.g., *War* 2.461–463; 7.43). He repeatedly draws attention to the antiquity and equality of the Jewish community within Antioch in particular.[15] In his *Antiquities of the Jews* (12.119), he states that Jews had equal civic status since the city's founding and that this status remained intact in his own time. Even after the Jewish revolt in 66–72 C.E., Vespasian and Titus both upheld the civic rights of Antiochene Jews as Antiochenes. In *Against Apion* (2.39), Josephus thus cites Antiochene Jews as exemplary of Jewish civic participation: "Our own people who reside in Antioch are called 'Antiochenes,' for the founder, Seleucus, gave them civic rights [Greek, *politea*]."[16]

In Josephus's *Jewish War*, similar statements are coupled with references to the grandeur of the city's synagogue and the degree of Syrian interest in Jewish festivals and practices:

> The Jewish/Judean *genos*, densely interspersed among the populations of every portion of the world, is particularly numerous in Syria, where intermingling is due to its proximity [i.e., to Judea]. But it was at Antioch that they specially congregated, partly owing to the greatness of that city, but mainly

because the successors of King Antiochus [i.e., Antiochus I Soter, ruled 280–261 B.C.E.] had enabled them to live there in security. For, although Antiochus surnamed Epiphanes [ruled 175–164 B.C.E.] sacked Jerusalem and plundered the Temple, his successors on the throne restored to the Jews of Antioch all such votive offerings as were made from brass, to be laid up in their synagogue, and moreover granted them civic rights on an equality with the Greeks. Continuing to receive similar treatments from later monarchs, they multiplied in number, and their richly designed and costly offerings formed a splendid ornament to their temple. Moreover, they were constantly attracting to their religious ceremonies multitudes of Greeks, and these they had in some measure incorporated with themselves.

(Josephus, *War* 7.43–45)[17]

Josephus's references to female proselytes in Damascus (*War* 2.559–561) and his account of the first-century "conversion" of the rulers of the Mesopotamian kingdom of Adiabene (*Antiquities* 20.34–48) similarly suggest that "pagan" interest in Judaism was not uncommon in the region.[18]

Apart from Josephus, there is little Jewish evidence for Syrian Jewry in the first three centuries C.E. "Despite its large size and relatively long history," Lee Levine notes, "the Jewish community of Syria generally, and of Antioch in particular, is only very partially known."[19] The general plausibility of Josephus's accounts, however, does find some support. An epigraph from Beth Shean attests the continued close connections of Antiochene Jews with Roman Palestine.[20] Posidonius and Numenius— two "pagan" authors from Apamea—offer some first-hand evidence for claims about Syrian interest in Judaism.[21] Likewise, discussions in the Mishnah and Tosefta about the applicability of laws concerning the land of Israel in Syria make most sense against the background of vibrant Jewish communities in the region.[22]

It seems plausible, as Josephus suggests (*War* 7.43), that the size of Antioch's Jewish community resulted from its proximity to Judea.[23] This proximity likely also fostered Syrian interest in Judaism, not least because Antioch and its environs received patronage from Herod the Great during his reign as patron king of Judea (37–4 B.C.E.; *War* 1.422–425). But Antioch's location—only 300 miles from Jerusalem—also meant that

ENGRAVED MENORAH FROM ANTIOCH. A menorah and the Greek letters *gamma, omicron, lambda* and *beta*—perhaps a Greek transliteration of a Hebrew name—are engraved on this now lost marble fragment found at Syrian Antioch in the 1930s. Despite numerous historical accounts of the importance and prosperity of Antioch's Jews, few physical traces of their presence remain. This engraving is one of the few objects that can be clearly associated with the city's ancient Jewish community.

local hostilities in Roman Palestine sometimes rippled into Syria during the reigns of Herod's heirs and especially during the First Jewish Revolt.[24] Even though the Roman leaders of these efforts confirmed the traditional civic rights of Antiochene Jews as Antiochenes, the revolt sparked popular anti-Jewish sentiment. At a time when the Greek term *Ioudaios* could mean "Judean" (in the geographical or "ethnic" sense) no less than "Jew" (in the "religious" sense), some Antiochene Jews seem to have felt the need to make clear that their loyalties lay *not* with the rebellious Judeans but rather with the now-Roman city that had long been their home.

Or, at least, this is the situation evoked by the continuation of the above-quoted passage from Josephus's *Jewish War*. Whereas his later writings invoke the harmoniously Jewish and Antiochene affiliation of Antiochene Jews, he here admits that the double affiliation was not without its problems, particularly "when the present war began, and Vespasian had newly landed at Syria, and hatred against Jews was everywhere at its height" (*War* 7.46). Josephus tells how a Jew named Antiochus, the son of "chief magistrate of the Jews in Antioch," betrayed his community, leading to violence against them by some of their fellow citizens. Antiochus is said to have signaled his rejection of Judaism "by sacrificing after the manner of the Greeks," encouraging violence against Antiochene Jews who would not do the same, and abandoning Sabbath observance for himself and his servants (*War* 7.47–53). As a result—according to Josephus—"the rest of the seventh day was dissolved not only at Antioch, but the same thing which had its origins there was done in other cities too, in like manner, for some small time" (*War* 7.53).

Josephus's tale of Antiochus the Antiochene Jew reads less like an accurate report and more like a folkloristic composite of local events and experiences. When considered together with his other comments about Syria, it may nevertheless help to contextualize what we know of the earliest Christians in the region. On the one hand, Josephus affirms the prominence and visibility of Jews in Antioch, as well as the longstanding curiosity about Jewish beliefs and practices among various "pagans" in both Roman Syria and neighboring Mesopotamia. His writings thus help to situate the quick spread of the Jesus movement into Antioch as well as the adoption of belief in Jesus alongside Jewish *kashrut* and purity practices even by those of non-Jewish lineage. On the other hand, Josephus attests a rise in Syrian hostility against Jews during the Jewish revolt, as seemingly answered by some Syrian Jews through identity-charged choices of ritual practice (Greek sacrifice vs. Jewish Sabbath observance).[25] As such, his writings also illumine early Christian efforts at "parting," as not solely a theological matter, but as also shaped by civic, social, military and political dynamics.

"Throughout antiquity," Tessa Rajak observes, "Antiochene Jewry—more than that of most other Greek-speaking Diaspora cities—seems to have been characterized by sharply contrasting fortunes: on the one hand, highly permeable religious boundaries, open to renegotiation and implying close interaction with neighbours, and on the other, the periodic production of situations of extreme conflict and of violent confrontation."[26] That a similar pattern may be found in Roman Syria, more broadly, is suggested by the case of Damascus. Josephus makes reference to the many Damascene women who were proselytes to Judaism but also to the massive slaughter of Damascene Jews during the Jewish revolt (*War* 2.559–561). As we shall see, ambivalence similarly marked Syrian Christian attitudes toward Jews and Judaism: Geographical and cultural proximity is matched by the intensity of potential hostility, particularly after 70 C.E.

The evidence from Josephus also offers an important caution, especially as we turn now to consider the New Testament and early Christian sources. Ancient writers only seldom mention the "ethnicity" of their authors, audience or enemies. It can be tempting to assume that Torah-observant Christians are of Jewish lineage or, conversely, that those Christians who argue against Torah observance must have been non-Jews.[27] From Josephus, however, we learn that some non-Jews in Syria embraced characteristically Jewish customs (and sometimes faced persecution for it), while some Syrian Jews chose to abandon such customs. Jewish evidence for Syria thus reminds us (1) that Jewish practices were attractive to non-Jews in Roman Syria and Mesopotamia long before the rise of Christianity; and (2) that Syrians of Jewish lineage could be among those who most forcibly rejected them, even apart from any belief in Jesus as messiah.

New Testament evidence for the earliest Syrian Christians

The Gospel of Matthew includes the claim that Jesus' teaching, preaching and healing in the Galilee caused his "fame to spread throughout all Syria" even within his lifetime—or at least in the areas "from the Galilee and the Decapolis and Jerusalem and Judea and from beyond the Jordan" (Matthew 4:23–24). Its early spread to Damascus is similarly suggested by the New Testament accounts of Paul's vision and commission.[28] If Luke-Acts' more expansive version is accurate, the earliest Damascene church included at least one prominent Torah-observant Jewish disciple of Jesus on good terms with the non-Christian Jewish population of the city (i.e., Ananius [Acts 22:12]).[29] That Syrian proselytes to Judaism were also among the first Christians is suggested by Luke-Acts' passing reference to "Nicolaus, a proselyte of Antioch" (Acts 6:5).

The author of Luke-Acts—possibly himself from Antioch (Eusebius, *Ecclesiastical History* 3.4.6)—reports that some of Jesus' followers left Jerusalem after the persecution of Stephen (Acts 7; i.e., 30s C.E.), traveling "as far as Phoenicia and Cyprus and Antioch" (Acts 11:19). These travelers spread the gospel to their fellow Jews.[30] "Men of Cyprus and Cyrene" then arrived in Antioch, preaching to non-Jews (Acts 11:19–20). Thereafter, the apostles sent Barnabas to the city, and he brought Paul; the two are said to have taught there for a year (Acts 11:21–26). It is in this context that Luke-Acts points to Antioch as the place where Jesus' disciples were first called *Christianoi*.[31] Even he, however, admits that the diversity of Christians in Antioch did not end with any "official" mission; Barnabas and Paul were

ST. PAUL'S GROTTO IN ANTIOCH. This monumental Crusader-era façade (11th century C.E.) built into a cliff face on the outskirts of ancient Antioch (modern Antakya) commemorates the cave where, according to tradition, the apostles Paul and Barnabas preached the gospel and established the first community of "Christians" (Acts 11:25–26).

followed by prophets from Jerusalem (Acts 11:27, 13:1).[32]

In short, the spread of the gospel to Syria was not a matter of the founding of a central community by a single apostle or mission. Travel between Jerusalem and Antioch was so commonplace that news of Jesus likely spread in *ad hoc* fashion. Just as Syrian proselytes went to Jerusalem, so Jewish followers of Jesus from Jerusalem, Tarsus, Cyprus and Cyrene came to Antioch. Even when Barnabas and Paul left Antioch to teach in other locales (Acts 13:2–3), they encountered Antiochenes.[33] Among the results was a striking degree of demographic diversity among even the earliest followers of Jesus in Antioch. These included Jewish disciples, teachers and prophets who came to the city from elsewhere; Syrian converts to Judaism who accepted Jesus; and perhaps also Syrian Jews, as well as non-Jewish believers in Jesus from elsewhere. Christian missionaries to the region would have encountered established communities of local Jews with synagogues frequented by interested non-Jews,[34] but also competing varieties and visions of Christianity.

In Paul's Epistle to the Galatians and in Acts 15, we glimpse some of the conflicts arising from such diversity. Both, as noted above, depict events in Antioch as catalyzing debates about which specific laws in the Torah/Pentateuch apply to those non-Jewish believers in Jesus who were not already Jewish proselytes. Paul's account is earlier in date and more explicit in describing conflict; it is, however, far less full in its description. Paul raises the topic in the context of his assertion to the Galatians of his own apostolic authority apart from the apostles in Jerusalem. Significantly for our purposes, Syria looms large in his argument—not just due to the Damascene setting of his call to serve as "apostle to the gentiles" (Galatians 1:15–17) but also due to his claim to have traveled throughout Syria before he was known by sight by the leaders of the Jerusalem church (1:20–21).[35] Paul argues for his own authority, in other words, in part by alluding to the autonomy of Syrian-Christian communities.

Paul's authority, in turn, buttresses his argument against those who insist on the circumcision of non-Jewish believers in Jesus. To persuade the Galatians, he appeals to a time when he himself was in Antioch and visited by Peter/Cephas (Galatians 2:11), who initially, according to Paul, joined him in sharing meals with non-Jews (Galatians 2:12). Paul accuses Peter and others of stopping this practice upon the arrival of men "from James" due to fear of "the circumcision faction" (Galatians 2:12–13). This prompts Paul to confront Peter publicly with a charge of hypocrisy: "If you are a Jew [*Ioudaios*] living life gentile-like [*ethnikôs*] and not Jewishly [*Ioudaikôs*], how can you compel the nations/gentiles [*ta ethna*] to Judaize [*ioudaizein*]?" (Galatians 2:14).

Paul's subsequent explanation—"We ourselves are by nature Jews and not sinners from the nations [*eks ethnôn*], knowing that a person is not set right from deeds of law, except through faith in Jesus Christ"

(Galatians 2:15–16)—has had a long afterlife in Christian discourse about Judaism and Jewish/Christian difference. The original sense of these lines, however, is less clear. What precise practices are encompassed by "works of the law," and how do they relate to "Judaizing" (i.e., affiliating with Jews/ Judeans or acting in a Jewish/Judean manner)? What did "Judaizing" even mean in an era prior to the standardization of practices of conversion— and at a time when the Greek term *Ioudaios* could still mean "Judean" no less than "Jew"?[36]

On the one hand, the focus on eating raises the possibility that issues of purity were at stake. Despite the limitation of ritual impurity to Israel in the laws of the Torah, did Paul's opponents deem non-Jewish followers of Jesus impure in some manner contagious to his Jewish followers or to the sanctity of the communal meal? Or, like Ezra-Nehemiah's arguments against intermarriage, were their suspicions about mixed eating based in some notion of non-Jews as inherently impure?[37] Or, as in some of the Dead Sea Scrolls (e.g., 1QS 6:13b–25), did they seek to regulate "pure food" as part of entrance into the community—whether on the model of the Temple's circles of sanctity or following more common Mediterranean cultural practices?[38] Paul does not explain.

The possibility that the problem might have been as much social as halakhic is raised by his usage of the term *Ioudaismos* earlier in his Epistle to the Galatians (1:13–14). There, the adoption of Judean/Jewish ways (i.e., *ioudaizein*, "Judaizing") is treated as a continuum of activity in which even Jews engage to differing degrees. Paul refers to "my way of life in the manner of Jewishness [*en tô Ioudaismô*]" prior to his commission as "apostle to the nations," and he explains his persecution of Christians as "advancing in the manner of Jewishness [*en tô Ioudaismô*] beyond many of my contemporaries among my people, by superfluously taking the initiative in zeal for my ancestral traditions." He depicts himself, in other words, as once too zealously "Jewish/Judean." In this regard, his usage recalls Josephus's references to variously "Judaizing" Syrians, only some of whom did so "all the way to circumcision" (*War* 2.454; cf. LXX Esther 8:17), as well as with his description of Jews in Antioch who "always drew to their religious ceremonies a great multitude of Greeks whom they made in some way a part of themselves" (*War* 7.45).[39] There, Jewishness is described, not by the metaphor of a bounded territory that one is either inside or outside, but rather as a matter of action and degree. By framing the "incident at Antioch" with reference to his own overzealous Jewishness, Paul deploys a similar sense of "Judaizing," evoking the tensions similarly caused by those who self-affiliated with Judean or Jewish peoplehood to the degree that they exclude non-Jews from their meals and community.[40]

The version of events in Acts 15 has been shaped by a later impulse to depict harmony between the apostles.[41] In this version, the trouble is said to have begun when unnamed followers of Jesus came to Antioch from Judea, teaching gentile followers of Jesus that "unless you are circumcised according to the custom of Moses, you cannot be saved" (Acts 15:1). In stark contrast to Paul's emphasis on his autonomy (Galatians 1:20–21), Luke-Acts describes the apostle as forestalling any decision until consultation with Peter and others in Jerusalem (Acts 15:2). From this retrospective purview, there is no conflict among Paul, James or Peter. All of the apostles and elders consult; Peter argues for the exemption of gentile believers from the full yoke of the Torah observance; and James comes to a decision:

> I have reached the decision that we should not trouble those gentiles who are turning to God, but we should write to them to abstain only from things polluted by idols and from *porneia* [i.e., improper sexual practices; cf. Hebrew, *zenut*] and from whatever has been strangled and from blood; for in every city, for generations past, Moses has had those who proclaim him, since he has been read aloud every Sabbath in the synagogues.
> (Acts 15:19–21)

This account is not simply shaped by the later aim of resolving apostolic conflict. James rules out circumcision as a requirement for worship of Israel's God and inclusion in the community of the saved (cf. Acts 16:1–3)—as logically follows from the precedent of a longstanding Jewish openness to non-Jews frequenting synagogues and learning about Moses and the Torah. Issues of eating, however, are not so easily resolved. James's ruling does not simply proclaim gentiles as exempt from *kashrut*; rather, it reflects exegetical engagement with the challenge of creating a biblically based gentile praxis from the laws of the Torah/Pentateuch itself.

Presumed in this "apostolic decree"—the prescriptions credited to James and repeated in the letter said to have been written to Syrian and other non-Jewish followers of Jesus (Acts 15:23)—is a reading of God's commandment to Noah to refrain from eating blood in Genesis (i.e., Genesis 9:4) as a model for biblically based gentile piety. Yet this ruling also builds on Leviticus' regulations concerning *gerim*, non-Israelites sojourning in the promised land. *Gerim*, for instance, are included with Israelites when Leviticus rules that the blood of animals slain for meat must be poured out and covered (Leviticus 17:10–14)—a regulation that rules out the consumption of meat from a strangled animal. The other guidelines credited to James entail avoidance of two of the three "abominations" that Leviticus depicts as polluting for the land of Israel and thus forbids for both Israelites and *gerim* who live there, namely idolatry and improper sexual practices (Leviticus 18:24–30, 19:31, 20:1–3; also Numbers 35:15).[42] The innovation is not the inclusion of non-Jews, but rather the inclusion of locales outside of the land of Israel. Biblical regulations for *gerim* in Israel are stretched to apply also to "believers from the nations in Antioch and Syria and Cilicia" (Acts 15:23). The resultant regulation of gentile Christian praxis finds some parallel in later rabbinic lists of the Noahide commandments binding on non-Jews (Tosefta *Avodah Zarah* 8.4; BT *Sanhedrin* 56a) but also tackles some of the same questions raised in rabbinic discussions about purity and eating, on the one hand, and the halakhic status of Syria, on the other.[43]

Antioch is not mentioned by name elsewhere in the New Testament. Worth noting, however, is its traditional association with the Gospel of Matthew, which most scholars posit as written by Christians of Jewish lineage in the decades after the destruction of the Jerusalem Temple.[44] Although the Gospel's provenance remains debated, scholars who support a Syrian provenance have pointed *both* to its use by Ignatius of Antioch *and* to its value in reconstructing Ignatius's "Christian-Jewish" or "Jewish-Christian" opponents.[45] Even if this gospel originated in the Galilee or elsewhere,[46] it had a particularly rich Syrian *Nachleben* and raises issues that resonate with the tensions in Antioch in particular. Most notable, for our purposes, is Matthew's combination of a portrait of Jesus as fulfilling the Sinaitic Torah in his teaching and Jewish messianic prophecies in his life, with a fierce polemic against Pharisees and other Jews. Whether these polemics arise from "inside" or "outside" Judaism depends largely on one's definition of "Judaism"—a category fluid and contested, even more so then than now. Does Matthew depict Jesus' followers as simply better Jews than (non-Christian) Pharisees?[47] Or does this gospel attest a

"Jewish branch within a Jesus movement that was not exclusively linked to a particular people"?[48] Or does it denigrate "the Jews" as a people as no longer heir to the Jewish scriptures and no longer worthy to stand in lineage with the prophets of the past? Just as in modern scholarship, so multiple possible interpretations were offered and debated in late antiquity—perhaps most intensively in Syrian locales.[49]

Ignatius of Antioch

Unequivocally explicit statements about the mutual exclusivity of "Christianity" and "Judaism" occur—first and most famously—in the letters of Ignatius of Antioch in the early second century. Most important, for our purposes, are his letters to the Philadelphians and the Magnesians. Even as Ignatius addresses problems in these locales, his articulation speaks to the continued diversity of Christianity—and Christian approaches to the Torah/Pentateuch—within his own Antiochene context. As Magnus Zetterholm stresses, "Ignatius' concept of the relation between Christians and Jews is no *ad hoc* solution, but emanated from the local situation in Antioch."[50]

As noted above, Ignatius was the first to use the term *Christianismos*, and he defined the new term through a contrast with *Ioudaismos*. It is perhaps telling, however, that Ignatius's attacks on "Judaizing" are all set in an *inner-Christian* context.[51] In his letter to the Philadelphians, for instance, he writes:

> But if anyone expounds *Ioudaismos* to you, do not listen to him; for it is better to hear *Christianismos* from a man who is circumcised than *Ioudaismos* from a man who is uncircumcised. Both of them, if they do not speak of Christ Jesus, are to me tombstones and graves of the dead on which nothing but the names of men are written.
>
> (Ignatius of Antioch, *Philadelphians* 6.1–2)[52]

Ignatius's reference to an uncircumcised man preaching Judaism most plausibly refers to those Christians whom he deems too dependent on Jewish scriptures—perhaps, as Paul Foster suggests, "Gentiles who held to a form of Christian faith that promoted Jewish observance without the necessity of circumcision."[53] Likewise, the circumcised Christianizer of whom he speaks could be either a Jewish follower of Jesus or a non-Jew.[54]

The contrast drawn here is less between Jews and non-Jews or Jews and Christians, and more among different followers of Jesus with differing interpretations of the prescriptions of the Torah/Pentateuch—all of which are now irrelevant, in Ignatius's estimation. Indeed, later in the same letter, he mocks those Christians who base their belief in Jewish scriptures and Jewish prophets: "I have heard some saying, 'Unless I find it in the archives, I do not believe in the gospel' ... But for me, the archives are Jesus Christ; the inviolable archives are his cross and his death and his resurrection and faith through him" (*Philadelphians* 8.1).[55]

In Ignatius's letter to the Magnesians, the juxtaposition of "Christianizing" and "Judaizing" forms part of an extended contrast between the old and the new. Ignatius here exalts "those who lived in old ways [and] came to newness of hope, no longer keeping Sabbath, but living in accordance with the Lord's day" (*Magnesians* 9.1). Similarly, he exhorts the Magnesians "not to be deceived by erroneous opinions, nor by old fables, which are useless; for if we continue to live until now according to *Ioudaismos*, we confess that we have not received grace" (*Magnesians* 8.1). The contrast is then explored in terms of the relationship between *Ioudaismos* and *Christianismos*:

> ... Therefore let us become his disciples and learn to live according to *Christianismos*; for one who is called by any name, other than this, is not of God. Set aside, then, the evil leaven, old and sour, and turn to the new leaven, which is Jesus Christ. Be salted with him to keep anyone among you from being spoiled, since you will be convicted by your odor. It is ridiculous to profess Jesus Christ and to Judaize; for *Christianismos* did not trust in *Ioudaismos*, but *Ioudaismos* in *Christianismos*, into which every tongue that has believed in God has been gathered together.
>
> (Ignatius of Antioch, *Magnesians* 10.1–3)

Both terms retain a sense of movement from one state to another. What Ignatius argues is that it is perverse to move from the new to the old.

In Ignatius's letters, we thus see some seeds of the later use of the categories of "Judaism" and "Christianity" to denote two stages in a single history; now that the new age has dawned, the old ways are no longer necessary or efficacious.[56] In the process, Ignatius also contributes to the re-orientation of debates over Torah observance. Luke-Acts' account of the apostolic decree reflects engagement with the challenges of deriving biblically based precepts of gentile piety and determining the post-sacrificial application of Torah law in the messianic age (Acts 15; see above). For Ignatius, however, Torah observance becomes a mark of a movement toward a Jewish affiliation (i.e., "Judaizing") now deemed inherently incompatible with a "Christianizing" movement toward grace. After the coming of Christ, in his view, those who do not bear the name Christians are "not of God." As Judith Lieu rightly stresses, "Ignatius opposes not *law* and grace, but *Judaism* and grace."[57]

After Ignatius: Resisting "parting(s) of the way(s)"

It can be tempting to treat Ignatius as the end of the story of Christianity's emergence as a "religion" distinct from Judaism; after all, he proclaims their mutual exclusivity in no uncertain terms.[58] To do so, however, is to miss a critical factor in the early Christian negotiation of the church's connections with Jews and Judaism—namely, the intra-Christian debates surrounding Marcion (flourished c. 140–160 C.E.). (See Chapter VIII, "Jews and Christians at Rome," by Margaret H. Williams.) Much of what became "orthodox" in Christian discussions of Judaism resulted from resistance to Marcionite assertions of Christianity's complete distinction from Judaism. Taking Ignatius's position to its logical extreme, Marcion sought to sever the church from the Jewish scriptures and Israel's God and history.[59] In response, proto-orthodox Christians throughout the Roman Empire (e.g., Justin Martyr, Irenaeus, Tertullian) celebrated what became enshrined as the church's "Old Testament" and defended Jewish monotheism, prophecy and history as essential elements of Christianity as well.[60]

In light of the intense anti-Jewish sentiments in Syria during the time of the First Jewish Revolt, it is perhaps not surprising that Marcion's ideas were popular in the region after the Bar-Kokhba Revolt (132–135 C.E.).[61] Yet, consistent with the longstanding pattern of Syrian sympathy and curiosity toward Judaism, there was also an especially sharp Syrian response to Marcionism.[62] Already in the second century, Theophilus composed a treatise against Marcion in Antioch, as did Bardaisan in Edessa; that Marcionism remained a defining issue for Christianity in Edessa well into the fourth century is clear from Ephrem the Syrian's polemics as well.[63]

Among both Antiochene and Edessene Christians, Marcionism

also inspired intensive reflection on the Jewish scriptures—as evident from sources ranging from Theophilus's engagement with Genesis in his *Apology to Autolycus,* to Tatian's defense of the Torah as "barbarian" wisdom in his *Oration Against the Greeks,* to the Peshitta, a translation of the Hebrew Bible into Syriac, the Aramaic dialect of Edessa.[64] Whether in interaction with Syrian Jews or mainly in reaction to Marcion,[65] early Syrian Christians embraced the Jewish scriptures as the core of a new Christian *paideia* (i.e., system of education and knowledge) created in contrast to the Greek *paideia* dominant among Roman elites. In works ranging from Tatian's *Diatessaron* to the *Protevangelium of James,* they also reclaimed and enhanced elements of the gospel tradition that Marcion had excised as Judaizing accretions.

In addition, the majority of sources that modern scholars call "Jewish-Christian" hail from late antique Syria and respond in some fashion to Marcionite ideas. Contrary to the assumption that Jewish varieties of Christianity should have declined after the failure of the First Jewish Revolt in 70 C.E., F. Stanley Jones has shown how "Jewish-Christianity" emerged as a vital strand of Christian tradition over a century later—as part of a continuum of local Syrian responses to the "direct and aggressive assault on the understanding of [the church's] Jewish heritage ... from Marcionite Christianity."[66] Far from an archaizing perspective silenced by the success of Paul's gentile mission, it was mobilized "into defensive and creative activity" by the encroachment of Marcionism into Syria with its "denial of the creator god, of the goodness of creation, and of the goodness of marriage and childbearing."[67]

To stop our story with Ignatius, thus, is also to miss much evidence for distinctively Syrian articulations of the religion of Jesus and his Jewish apostles—and their gentile converts—as part of Judaism. Third- and fourth-century sources from Syria are especially rich in data that shed doubt on the finality or decisiveness of any early "parting(s) of the way(s)." Far from signaling the establishment of clear-cut and mutually exclusive "Christian" and "Jewish" identities already in the first or second century, Syrian evidence suggests that early moments of separation were not so much pivot points as stages in a complex and prolonged process. At least in this region, differentiation was often predicated on proximity and entanglement, and separation met with some resistance.

In exploring evidence for convergence and contestation, we do not

mean to downplay the early evidence about Syria's place in the conceptu-
alization of "Christian" identities as distinct from Jewish peoplehood and
purity practices. Our aim, rather, is to contextualize these developments.
Syria, after all, offers unique data for inner-Christian resistance to the
separation of Jesus-centered visions of the true Israel from the scriptures,
practice and history of the Jews.

Behind these concepts, moreover, we may glimpse hints of local Syrian
cultures in which identities were partitioned in different ways than in their
western counterparts. Whereas Alexandrian Christians like Clement were
innovating a new threefold division of humankind into "Jew," "Greek" and
"Christian,"[68] older dichotomies like "Jew"/"Greek" and "barbarian"/"Greek"
persist in many Syrian sources—not least because of their resonance
with competing perspectives on proper *paideia*.[69] Hellenistic philosophy
flourished in Syria, especially in Apamea under Iamblichus. Yet, like their
"pagan" counterparts, even Syrian Christians steeped in Greek *paideia* often
embraced their "barbarian" identities; in the second century, for instance,
both Tatian and Lucian proudly proclaim themselves "Assyrians."[70] Like
Tatian, moreover, Theophilus of Antioch defends Christianity in part by
positing the superiority of the Jewish scriptures to the "pagan" mythology
and philosophy at the heart of Greek *paideia*.

In the century between the renewal of Roman campaigns against
Parthia by Trajan in 114–117 C.E. and the fall of Parthia to Sassanian
Persian forces in 225/6 C.E., Syria attracted much Roman imperial activity
and concern. It was during this period that the Mesopotamian cities of
Edessa and Nisibis were brought into the sphere of Roman governance—
in the case of Edessa, briefly at first under Trajan, but more firmly after
Septimius Severus's Parthian campaigns in 195–197 C.E., after which the
Roman province of Osrhoene was created.[71] The same century saw the
reign of the Roman emperor Elagabalus (ruled 218–222 C.E.)—a circumcised Syrian priest from Emesa who ruled from Antioch and who is said
to have attempted to spread Syrian monotheism westward to Rome.[72]

By the time northern Mesopotamia came under Roman rule, Christianity had already arrived there. Notwithstanding the later claims of the
Doctrina Addai, the origins of Christianity in Edessa remain uncertain,
and the possible role of Jews and Judaism much debated.[73] Due to lack
of evidence, the possible connection of Christianity in Nisibis with the
Jews of the city or the converts of Adiabene must remain in the realm

of speculation.[74]

What is important, for our purposes, is that the period after Ignatius sees Syrian Christianity increasingly shaped by Edessene thinkers. During the reign of Abgar the Great (ruled 177–212 C.E.)—the last native king of Edessa—a philosopher like Bardaisan could write in Syriac in the Edessene court and reach a readership that included his fellow Christians but also "pagans" like Porphyry.[75] In the century following the absorption of Edessa as a Roman colony (213 C.E.), it remained common for Syrian Christians to write in Greek. Yet third- and fourth-century writings like the *Didascalia Apostolorum* and Pseudo-Clementine *Homilies* and *Recognitions* were translated into Syriac soon after their composition. As we shall see, these sources speak to the local trajectories of ideas and debates discussed above, but they also attest a transitional age in Roman Syria, prior to the Christianization of the Roman Empire but also to the emergence of a distinctively Syriac tradition of Christian liturgy, literature and learning in the mid-fourth century and following.[76]

Didascalia Apostolorum

The third-century *Didascalia Apostolorum* adopts the narrative setting of the apostolic council in Acts 15 (*Didascalia Apostolorum* 1, 24), claiming to preserve the full contents of the letter sent in response to the "incident at Antioch" (Acts 15:23). Although its concerns are not limited to the questions of gentile purity and piety, it attests the continued relevance of such issues as well as the continued observance of biblical and other Jewish laws by other Syrian Christians.[77] Whereas the debate in Acts 15 focused on circumcision and *kashrut*, the practices here condemned include ritual ablutions with water and the keeping of menstrual purity, as well as vegetarianism and asceticism (*Didascalia Apostolorum* 23–24, 26).[78] Whereas Luke-Acts focuses on the problem of gentile Torah observance, the focus here falls on Jewish converts to Christianity. Against those who "have been converted from the People," the authors of the *Didascalia Apostolorum* stress that one must not "keep vain bonds: purifications and sprinklings and baptisms and distinction of meats" (*Didascalia Apostolorum* 26).[79]

The authors of the *Didascalia Apostolorum* do not simply cite Paul's contrast of law and faith or Ignatius's contrast of Judaism and grace. Rather, consistent with the precedent in Acts 15 and the affirmation of the Torah by Theophilus and others, they root their teachings in biblical exegesis.[80] What they posit is a distinction between two types of legislation within the Torah/Pentateuch: (1) the law (*nomos*) of Moses, as exemplified by the Ten Commandments and binding on all worshipers of the One God; and (2) the *deuterosis* or second law (Syriac, *tinyan nimosa*) given as punishment for Israel's worship of the golden calf and thus meant specifically for the Jewish people. Against those Jewish women who continue washing for menstrual purity even after Christian baptism, they thus rule that such washing is no longer needed—and may even negate baptism's power to exempt Jews from the bonds of the second law (*Didascalia Apostolorum* 26).[81]

The term *deuterôsis*, as Hillel Newman notes, "has no precedent in Greek as a term describing a form of tradition or instruction" but is a calque on "*Mishnah* ... a parochial term stemming from rabbinic circles."[82] Whether the authors of the *Didascalia Apostolorum* are the first to use the term or follow soon after Origen, its appearance here is thus significant. As William Horbury notes, the adoption of this term breaks from the earlier Christian tradition of discussing Pharisaic and other post-biblical Jewish tradition (e.g., *paradosis* in Matthew 15:1–20; Mark 7:1–32), signaling an "enlargement of the Christian vocabulary of Jewish tradition" most plausibly situated among "contacts between gentile Christians, Christian Jews and non-Christian Jews."[83]

Charlotte Fonrobert goes so far as to call the *Didascalia Apostolorum* a "counter-Mishnah," pointing to parallels with traditions found in contemporaneous rabbinic sources (i.e., Mishnah, Tosefta) to suggest that their understanding of Christian identity has been significantly shaped by contacts with Jews of their own time.[84] If she is correct, the *Didascalia Apostolorum* attests rabbinic influence on Syrian Jews as well as the continued importance of Judaism—both past and present—within Syrian Christianity.[85]

Pseudo-Clementine literature

The Pseudo-Clementine corpus consists of two fourth-century novels written in the name of Clement of Rome—the *Homilies* and the *Recognitions*—together with associated materials such as letters attributed to James and Clement.[86] These works preserve arguments for some of the positions countered by the *Didascalia Apostolurum*, including the

PSEUDO-CLEMENTINE MANUSCRIPT. The complexity of Syrian Christianity's relationship with Judaism is evidenced in two anonymous fourth-century writings—the *Homilies* and the *Recognitions*—written in the name of Clement, an early bishop of Rome. These works recount Clement's adventures with early church figures like Peter and Barnabas and stress the similarities and shared beliefs of Judaism and Christianity and the need for Christians to maintain Jewish purity laws. This Syriac translation of the *Homilies* and the *Recognitions*, dated to 411 C.E., was written in Edessa, a center of Syrian-Christian learning throughout late antiquity.

assertion of the necessity of menstrual purity for followers of Jesus.[87] Whereas the *Didascalia Apostolorum* extends Acts 15, the Pseudo-Clementine authors counter Luke-Acts' portrayal of Peter and James.[88] The following complaint, for instance, is there credited to Peter:

> Some from among the Gentiles have rejected my legal preaching [*nomimon … kerugma*], attaching themselves to certain lawless [*anomon*] and trifling preaching of the man who is my enemy [i.e., Paul]. Some [i.e., Luke] have attempted these things while I am still alive, to transform my words by certain intricate interpretations towards the dissolution of the Law—as though I myself were also of such a mind but did not freely proclaim it; God forbid!
>
> (*Epistle of Peter to James* 2.3–4)

Countering the "apostolic decree" in Acts 15, they also depict Peter as preaching the necessity of ritual purity regulations to non-Jews:

> And this is the service that He [i.e., God] has appointed: to worship Him only; and to trust only in the Prophet of Truth; and to be baptized for the remission of sins and thus by this pure baptism to be born again unto God by saving water; not to partake of the table of demons—that is, from food offered to idols, dead carcasses, strangled [animals], those caught by wild beasts, blood; not to live impurely; to wash after intercourse with women; for them [i.e., women], also to keep menstrual purity; for all, to be sober-minded; to act well; not to do injustice, looking for eternal life from the all-powerful God and asking with prayer and continual supplication that they may win it.
>
> (Pseudo-Clementine, *Homilies* 7.8.1–3)

In contrast to the *Didascalia Apostolorum*, the Pseudo-Clementine authors thus depict all the Torah's Levitical laws as equally binding on all who worship the God of Israel. In the Pseudo-Clementines, baptism is presented as the first step in purifying the defilement that accrues to non-Jews due to their idolatry, animal sacrifice and menstrual pollution. Yet all followers of Jesus must continue to maintain purity by immersing after sexual intercourse, by practicing menstrual separation, and by avoiding blood, carrion, food offered to idols and any meat that has been improperly slaughtered.[89] Together with pious acts, washing for purity is here said to cleanse the soul from sin and to protect against the demonic indwelling caused by idolatrous worship.

Different works and strata of the Pseudo-Clementines construe the relationship of Jews and Christians in slightly different ways.[90] Most relevant for our purposes is the *Homilies*—the version of the Pseudo-Clementine novel that most emphasizes the complementarity of Judaism and Christianity. The *Homilies* confirm the efficacy of Torah observance for Jews and depict the coming of Jesus as the opening of a parallel line of salvation for gentiles. Moses and Jesus, in fact, are said to have taught the same message, albeit to different audiences:

> ... Jesus is concealed from the Hebrews who have taken Moses as their teacher and Moses is hidden from those who have believed Jesus. For, since there is a single teaching by both, God accepts one who has believed either of these ... Neither, therefore, are the Hebrews condemned on account of their ignorance of Jesus, by reason of Him [i.e., God] who has concealed him—provided that they, doing the things commanded by Moses, do not hate him whom they do not know. Nor are those from among the Gentiles condemned, who do not know Moses on account of Him who has concealed him—provided that these also, doing the things spoken by Jesus, do not hate him whom they do not know.
> (Pseudo-Clementine, *Homilies* 8.6–7; cf. *Recognitions* 4.5–6)[91]

It is perhaps telling, then, that the terms "Christian" and "Christianity" are never used in the Pseudo-Clementine *Homilies*. The authors speak of Jews—and Pharisees in particular—as heirs to the teachings of the prophet Moses. Peter and Barnabas self-identify with Jews and Israel (e.g., *Homilies* 1.13; 3.4; 9.20). Yet even when referring to Clement and other gentile followers of Jesus, the *Homilies* refrain from distinguishing them as "Christians." Most often, they are called "Godfearers" (Greek, *theosebeis*)—a term that we find elsewhere applied to gentile sympathizers with Judaism.*[92] (See Chapter III, "The Godfearers: From the Gospels to Aphrodisias," by Bruce Chilton.)

In the Pseudo-Clementine *Homilies*, the term *Ioudaios* is even

*See Angelos Chaniotis, "Godfearers in the City of Love," *BAR*, May/June 2010.

redefined so as to include gentile followers of Jesus:

> If anyone acts impiously, he is not pious. In the same way, if a foreigner keeps the Law, he is a Jew [*Ioudaios*], while he who does not is a Greek [*Hellên*]. For the Jew, believing in God, keeps the Law [*nomon*].
>
> (Pseudo-Clementine, *Homilies* 11.16)

The category of "Jew" here denotes anyone who follows the law that God laid out for them. As a result, the category of "apostle" is not a subset or paradigm of "Christian"; in the *Homilies*, it marks adherence to the true religion proclaimed by Moses and Jesus—in contrast both to "pagan" polytheism and to the "heresies" that use Christ's name to promote false beliefs and impure practices.

If Christianity and Judaism appear to differ, the reader of the Pseudo-Clementine *Homilies* is assured that this is only because God chose to hide the prophet of one from the followers of the other (*Homilies* 8.6). Even as its authors acknowledge that most Jews and Christians are blind to Christianity's true nature as the divine disclosure of Judaism to other nations, they proclaim those who understand as specially blessed. Through the Jewish apostle Peter, they reveal that there are two paths to salvation, and the two paths are actually one; no one is wiser, however, than the few who embrace both (*Homilies* 8.7; cf. *Recognitions* 4.5).

This positive representation of Jewish tradition, moreover, seems to be matched by some knowledge and awareness of the Judaism of the authors' own time. By means of Peter, for instance, its authors reveal that Moses "gave the Law with the explanations" to the 70 elders (*Homilies* 2.38; cf. Numbers 11:16),[93] and they assert the importance of oral traditions from Moses in ensuring the continuance of proper leadership among the Jewish people:

> The Law of God was given, through Moses, without writing [*agraphôs*] to seventy wise men, to be handed down, so that the government might be carried on by succession.
>
> (Pseudo-Clementine, *Homilies* 3.47.1)

Such assertions recall the authority-claims made by rabbis in Roman Palestine around the same time that the *Homilies* was taking form in Syria. Early rabbis used common tropes of succession to trace their authority to Moses, most famously in Mishnah *Avot* (1–5).[94] By the fourth century, moreover, assertions of continuity had been extended into the distinctively rabbinic doctrine of the Oral Torah revealed to Moses at Mount Sinai.[95]

This confluence of ideas has led Albert Baumgarten to suggest that some Pseudo-Clementine authors knew and accepted rabbinic authority-claims.[96] Their own understanding of apostolic succession may even be shaped by an effort to emulate such claims.[97] Just as the *Homilies* compare the "seat of Moses" with the "chair of Christ,"[98] so the *Epistle of Peter to James* cites Jewish transmission of Moses' teachings as a model for trustworthy Christian transmission of the teachings of Jesus preserved by Peter:

> I beg and beseech you not to communicate to any of the Gentiles the books of my preachings that I sent to you nor to anyone of our own tribe before trial. But if anyone has been proved and found worthy, then to commit them to him, after the manner in which Moses delivered his books to the Seventy who succeeded to his seat [*tên kathedran*] ... For, his countrymen [i.e., the Jews] keep the same rule of monarchy and polity everywhere, being unable in any way to think otherwise or to be led out of the way of the much-indicating scriptures. According to the rule delivered to them, they endeavor to correct the discordances of the scriptures if anyone, not knowing the traditions [*paradoseis*], is confounded at the various utterances of the prophets. Therefore they charge no one to teach, unless he has first learned how the scriptures must be used. And thus they have amongst them one God, one Law, one hope.
>
> (*Epistle of Peter to James* 1–2)

It is unclear whether the Pseudo-Clementines preserve any first-century traditions that can be traced back to Peter himself, or even second-century traditions from or about Peter, James and the Jerusalem church.[99] From the parallels between the *Homilies* and the *Recognitions*, however, F. Stanley Jones has shown that elements of an earlier form of the novel can be recovered.[100] This novel, which Jones dates to 220 C.E., provides another important clue to Syrian-Christian self-definition.

Distinctively Syrian elements include an interest in questions of fate and astrology, and—most notably for our purposes—a concern to counter Marcionite perspectives. Throughout the *Homilies* and *Recognitions*, Peter's main enemy is Simon Magus*; although a conflate figure, Simon is often used as a mouthpiece for characteristically Marcionite positions, such as the attempt to "show from the Scriptures that [the deity] who made the heaven and the earth, and all things in them, is not the Supreme God, but that there is another, unknown and supreme" (*Homilies* 3.2).[101]

Also significant, for our purposes, is the possibility that the Pseudo-Clementine *Homilies* preserve and rework earlier Jewish traditions. This possibility has been raised most recently by James Carleton Paget in relation to a section of the work, which is unparalleled in the *Recognitions* and which presents Clement defending Judaism and condemning Hellenism in debates with Appion (*Homilies* 4–6).[102] If Carleton Paget is correct, this section of the *Homilies* provides overlooked evidence for a form of Judaism distinctive to Syria. Its integration into the *Homilies*, moreover, would reveal continuity between Syrian-Jewish resistance to Greek *paideia* and Syrian-Christian attempts to posit Jews and Christians as aligned in monotheism, purity and piety against "pagan" idolatry, polytheism and philosophy.[103]

At the very least, the Pseudo-Clementines offer a striking point of contrast with the anti-Judaism typically associated with fourth-century Christianity. The *Homilies*, in particular, present a surprisingly harmonious picture of Judaism and Christianity, conceived in terms of supplementarity rather than supersession. It also stands as a reminder that Syrian-Christian approaches to Judaism remained diverse and complex for centuries after Ignatius. In the same era that Syrian Christians like John Chrysostom were condemning some practices as too Jewish to be Christian, those like the Pseudo-Clementine authors were critiquing those whom they deemed too Greek to be Jesus' true heirs.[104]

As such, the Pseudo-Clementines help to contextualize Chrysostom as well.[105] The writings of this late-fourth-century bishop attest to the resonance of Ignatius's approach to defining *Christianismos* in contrast to *Ioudaismos*, not just among Latin authors like Tertullian and his heirs, but also among Christians writing in Greek in Syria.[106] Whereas many

*See David R. Cartlidge, "The Fall and Rise of Simon Magus," *BR*, Fall 2005.

of Chrysostom's contemporaries in the Latin West seem to have taken Jewish/Christian difference largely for granted, his sermons *Against the Judaizers* (386–387 C.E.) attest the continuing intertwining of "Christian" and "Jewish" identities in Antioch: Chrysostom lambasts the "Judaizing" practices of his flock in great detail, and his writings offer indirect evidence for Syrian Christians who frequented synagogues and participated in Jewish festivals and practices, well into the late fourth century.[107]

Chrysostom complains that "many of those within our ranks claim to think as we do, but some will approach the spectacle of the festivals [of the Jews], and others will even join them in celebrating and will share in their fasts" (*Against the Judaizers* 1.1). "What are you running to see in the synagogue of the Jews who fight against God?," he asks his fellow Christians, pleading, "Do not run to the synagogue!" (*Against the Judaizers* 4.7; 6.6–7; cf. 8.8). Just as his sermons suggest that the perspectives of the Pseudo-Clementines were not merely relics of an earlier age, so the Pseudo-Clementines show that Chrysostom's sermons are less about anti-Judaism and more about an inner-Christian conflict. Even at the dawn of the Christianization of the Roman Empire, decades after the Council of Nicaea, there remained a continuum of competing Syrian perspectives on the precise place of Jewish practice, purity and peoplehood in Christian identity.[108]

Conclusion

To the degree that we can speak about "Christianity" as "parting" from "Judaism" in Syria in the first four centuries C.E., differentiation remains predicated upon proximity. In the late fourth century and following, however, the Christianization of the Roman Empire and subsequent ecclesiastical councils introduced new local and imperial dynamics, particularly into Antioch.[109] At the same time, Edessa was emerging as a center of Christian liturgy, learning and literature in Syriac, due in part to an influx of new learning from Mesopotamia, brought by Christians like Ephrem who fled there after the sack of Nisibis by Sassanian Persians in 359 C.E.

Sidney Griffith notes how Sassanian incursions into the region, the Syriac language and Edessa's "frontier culture" resulted in a "cross-frontier community" of Syrian Christians straddling Roman and Sassanian empires.[110] This trans-imperial context also had an impact on Christian engagement with Jews and Judaism in the eastern half of Roman Syria—shaped less by proximity to the land of Israel and increasingly by a new shared cultural context. Just as the heart of Rabbinic Judaism was shifting from Roman Palestine to Sassanian Babylonia in the wake of the Christianization of the Roman Empire, so the center of Christian learning in Syriac was shifting as well. Especially after the condemnation of Nestorius at the Council of Ephesus in 431 C.E. and the closure of the "school of the Persians" in Edessa in 489 C.E., Edessene Christians settled in the Sassanian Persian empire, and the "school of Nisibis" emerged as a center for Syriac learning and literary production.[111] Under Sassanian rule in Mesopotamia, Jews and Christians engaged in a parallel culti-vation of biblically based pedagogy and Aramaic scholasticism under Zoroastrian rule.[112] Among the results was the spread of Syriac as the dominant language of Christian liturgy and learning outside of the Roman Empire, from Mesopotamia and Persia into regions with little or no Jewish presence, including Central, South and East Asia.[113]

Evidence from Roman Syria thus provides a powerful reminder that the history of Jewish/Christian relations is not a single story that can be abstracted *either* from the local cultures in which individuals lived and interacted *or* from the imperial and trans-imperial contexts that shaped them.[114] Nor is it simply a story about the spread of Christianity in the Roman Empire and its effects on Europe and the West. Rather, as we have seen, the literary and liturgical products of local dynamics in Syria came to be exported *both* westward *and* eastward, shaping visions of Christianity and its relationships to Judaism even beyond the Roman Empire.

7

Living Side by Side in Galilee

Eric M. Meyers

SCHOLARSHIP ON HOW AND WHEN JUDAISM AND CHRISTIANITY became two distinct religious traditions and went their separate ways is becoming increasingly nuanced. This is surely true of Judaism and Christianity in the Holy Land, and especially in Galilee, as a result of recent archaeological surveys and excavations. The older view that the split occurred early in the Roman period after the two Jewish revolts against Rome (66–70 C.E. and 132–135 C.E.) can no longer be maintained. The separation came much later.

Nineteenth-century scholarship viewed the break as coming on the heels of a Second Temple Judaism that was understood as increasingly narrow and legalistic and which Jesus had rejected. This view was primarily fostered in Protestant historical-critical scholarly circles.[1] The often-presumed aftermath of those events was that the two communities of Christians and Jews had only hostile relations from that time forward and evolved in relative isolation from one another.[2]

A subtext of this view has been the thesis that it was only with the Christianization of the Roman Empire in the Byzantine period that Judaism defined itself. According to this view, the previous centuries, after the two wars with Rome, had been a time when only "a very small number of [Jews]

133

... still insisted on the importance of Torah, of Judaism in their symbolic world."[3] Modern scholarship overwhelmingly rejects these views.

The years from the end of the Bar-Kokhba Revolt to Constantine (135 to c. 306–337 C.E.) were in fact formative in the development of the synagogue and in producing the tannaitic literature (exemplified by the Mishnah) and much of the Talmud of the land of Israel.

Turning to the material culture of the region—and the Galilee in particular: The evidence for Christianity in the Holy Land at this early time is very meager. The artifacts and/or places that can be positively identified as Christian before Constantine are relatively few. Capernaum and Megiddo (more specifically, Kfar Othnay) are the chief examples, with Nazareth not far behind.[4]

The Franciscan scholars who excavated at Capernaum have long argued that the Jesus movement, rather than having fled to Pella during the First Jewish Revolt against Rome (as some ancient sources claim—see further discussion in Chapter IV, "The Christian Flight to Pella? The Archaeological Picture," by Pamela Watson), went on to Galilee, where Jesus' ministry had focused years earlier.[5] They also turned to rabbinic literature about the *minim*, or Jewish-Christians, to support their view of a Christian presence in Galilee.

There is no doubt that the Jerusalem church was strong in the early Roman period; Eusebius provides a detailed list of bishops that stretched from James, the brother of Jesus, to the time of Bar-Kokhba (*Ecclesiastical History* 4.5; contradicting his claim that the followers of Jesus had all fled to Pella during or after 70 C.E.). Moreover, the church remained in Jerusalem after the Second Jewish Revolt (132–135 C.E.) and, in contrast to the earlier church, became predominantly gentile. By the third century, Caesarea Maritima emerged as a leading center of Christian learning; Origen moved there in 232 C.E., and Eusebius became bishop there a century later.[6] All this is to say that there can be no doubt about the existence of the nascent Christian community in the Holy Land during this period. Finding material remains of that community, however, especially in Galilee, is quite another matter.

In search of such evidence, scholars have turned to the city of Sepphoris in the time of Herod Antipas (4 B.C.E.–39 C.E.), suggesting that Jesus would have visited there, although Sepphoris is not even mentioned in the New Testament. The other major urban center in the north, Tiberias,

SEPPHORIS THEATER. Located about an hour's walk from Jesus' hometown of Nazareth, the city of Sepphoris, though not mentioned in the New Testament, was an important Galilean administrative center during the Roman period. By at least the second century, Sepphoris had many elements of a proper Roman city, including this 4,000-seat theater. Archaeologists continue to debate, however, whether the Sepphoris that Jesus knew was already a thoroughly Hellenized city, or a Galilean town that had largely retained its Jewish character.

ROMAN MILITARY BREAD STAMP. Excavations in 2008 at Kfar Othnay near Megiddo uncovered a third-century C.E. building complex. The facility served the local Roman legion, as evidenced by the discovery of two stone bread stamps. It was common for the Roman military to stamp its bread with the name of the soldier-baker and/ or the military unit for which it was made. This bread stamp from Kfar Othnay has three lines of text inscribed in reverse so that the impression on the bread would read: CAECIL, TER IUL, MAXIM, or "(Product of) Iulius Maximus, (century [company] of) Caecilius Tertius."

also rebuilt by Herod Antipas, is mentioned in John 6:1,23 and 21:1, but not as a place that Jesus visited. In the case of Sepphoris, which would have been a walk of only about an hour from his home in Nazareth, it is quite possible that Jesus visited there. But there is also good reason to think that Jesus would have avoided these cities, since he might have been offended at the high level of Hellenization or urbanization in both places. Or perhaps it was because of his distaste for the Herodian dynasty and the fate of John the Baptist at their hands.[7]

In any case, except for the possibility of Jewish-Christians at Sepphoris, we simply have no clear evidence for the existence of a Christian community in Galilee prior to Constantine except for: (1) the third-century Christian mosaic and possible meeting place for Christians at Kfar Othnay near Tel Megiddo and Legio, headquarters of the VI *Ferrata* legion; and (2) whatever sort of Jewish-Christian community may have existed at Capernaum.

Excavations at Kfar Othnay in 2005 uncovered a facility that served the nearby Roman legionary camp. It is clearly dated to the third century

MOSAIC FLOOR AT KFAR OTHNAY. A rectangular room in the western wing of the military complex contained a mosaic floor that identified it conclusively as a Christian gathering place. An inscription on one side of a geometric mosaic panel (left, bottom inscription) reads, "Akeptous the God-lover has offered this table to God Jesus Christ as a memorial," the earliest archaeological designation of Jesus in this way. The largest panel in the mosaic floor (right) bears a central medallion with two fish (a popular Christian symbol) surrounded by colorful geometric patterns and an inscription identifying the work's patron, "Gaianus, also called Porphyrius, centurion, our brother."

This third-century Christian gathering place in the midst of a Roman military encampment, at a time when Christians were being persecuted elsewhere in the Roman Empire, suggests that the community here felt secure identifying themselves as followers of Jesus.

C.E. by numismatic and ceramic evidence; it went out of use in the early fourth century. Some of the pottery suggests a domestic function; bread stamps indicate the presence of a bakery. The excavation of a rectangular room in the western wing of the unit conclusively points to a gathering place for Christians to worship and probably to partake of the Eucharist.*[8] The evidence for this comes from a mosaic floor that includes several important inscriptions. One reads, "Akeptous the God-lover has offered this table to God Jesus Christ as a memorial." The term for "God Jesus Christ" is a familiar Greek abbreviation for *nomina sacra* (sacred names). Another panel includes a central medallion with two fish and a Greek

*Vassilios Tzaferis, "Inscribed 'To God Jesus Christ': Early Christian Prayer Hall Found in Megiddo Prison," *BAR*, March/April 2007.

HOUSE OF PETER. The remains of a fifth-century octagonal memorial church (today covered by a modern glass-bottomed church) built over the ruins of a fourth-century house church that marks the spot of a first-century house believed to be St. Peter's home. Unusual plastering on the earliest structure suggests that its function shifted from a private domicile to a place for public gatherings at an early time.

inscription that identifies the mosaic's donor as "Gaianus, also known as Porphyrius, centurion, our brother." Four panels most likely supported the table given by Akeptous. Quite remarkably, this room clearly testifies to the presence of Christians among the Kfar Othnay and Leggio populations. Moreover, they were allowed to gather and worship in what was probably a public building. The images of fish may also be construed as Christian symbols. In a most unlikely place, near Tel Megiddo, where Roman soldiers were quartered in the third century C.E., we thus find the presence of Christians at a time when Christians were being persecuted elsewhere in the Roman Empire. Here, however, they were apparently quite secure in their religious identification.

At Capernaum the situation is more complicated. There the evidence is open to interpretation; it is not nearly as clear as we have seen at Kfar Othnay. The excavators of Capernaum, Virgilio Corbo and Stanislao

138

BYZANTINE SYNAGOGUE AT CAPERNAUM. This white limestone synagogue from the Byzantine period sits atop remains from an earlier period, perhaps an earlier synagogue. About 100 feet south is the so-called House of St. Peter (opposite) where Jesus is said to have stayed while in Capernaum.

Loffreda, identified a small domicile at the site as the "House of Peter" and thus a house that Jesus must have visited.* The Gospels all report that Jesus preached and taught and worked miracles at Capernaum, and some even report that it was his home (Mark 2:1; Matthew 4:13, 9:1). The site is traditionally regarded as the home of the apostles Peter, Andrew, James, John and Levi/Matthew (Matthew 4:13–22 and Matthew 9:9/Mark 2:14). The structure identified as Peter's house is situated a mere 100 feet (30 meters) south of the famous white limestone Byzantine-period synagogue. At the House of Peter, a modern glass-bottomed church has been built over the remains of a fifth-century octagonal church that is built over an even earlier fourth-century church (identified by the excavators as a *domus ecclesia*) with graffiti on its walls, which is built over the supposed House of Peter.

There is no doubt that the domicile dates back to early Roman times

*See James F. Strange and Hershel Shanks, "Has the House Where Jesus Stayed in Capernaum Been Found?" *BAR*, November/December 1982.

and was in use during the life of Jesus and Peter. The unusual plastering on the late first-century walls and ceiling suggests that the use of the building changed at that time from a domicile to a building with a public function. In the western part of the village, this appears to be the only house with such plastering. The dating of the plaster, however, has been questioned,[9] and the bulk of the graffiti comes from a later stage. Their readings have also been challenged.[10] Strange and Shanks concluded that the House of Peter "cannot be confirmed—certainly not by inscriptions referring to St. Peter. But a considerable body of circumstantial evidence does point to the identification as St. Peter's house."[11] Still, there is no consensus on this matter or on the identification of many of the earliest supposed Christian churches or prayer places in the Holy Land. Since the first Christians typically gathered in private houses, their domiciles may be indistinguishable from those of their neighbors. The case of Kfar Othnay is an exception; it offers tantalizing testimony to pre-Constantinian Christianity in a period of great change.

In a recent publication, Lee Levine asked an important question that is central: "Was there a crisis in Jewish settlement in the eastern Galilee of late antiquity?"[12] This issue has become a heated one in recent years due in no small measure to the enormous strides made in the archaeology of the region—both in survey and excavation. I would add an additional question to Levine's: How was the Jewish settlement of Galilee affected by Christian church building? Or to put it slightly differently: Did the Christianization of Galilee impact Jewish settlement in either eastern or western Galilee?

A major figure in this debate is Uzi Leibner, whose systematic survey of the region has come under strong attack by Jodi Magness.[13] Magness concludes, erroneously in my opinion, that Leibner's survey results cannot be accepted because several of the excavated sites that he mentions continued, in her view, well into the Byzantine period (Jalame, Meiron and Sepphoris). In addition, she calls into question the dating of some local Galilean pottery types—something about which I have disagreed with her in a number of places.[14] But as Levine points out, of the 120-or-so Galilean synagogues, "all but some half-dozen of these synagogues were built and functioned in the Late Roman and Byzantine periods."[15] I have challenged the notion that so few synagogues existed in the Roman period and maintain that position still.[16] The fact that there are so many Byzantine structures preserved means that the earlier,

WADI HAMAM SYNAGOGUE. While conducting an archaeological survey, Uzi Leibner uncovered this synagogue buried just below the surface at Wadi Hamam in the eastern Galilee. He dates the structure as early as the late third century C.E., which places it just before the Byzantine period, in the late Roman period. Most of the more than 120 ancient synagogues in Galilee date to the Byzantine period, but (as the Wadi Hamam synagogue suggests) many of them may have had earlier phases or predecessors in the Roman period. This indicates that Judaism was flourishing in Galilee before and during the spread of Christianity.

Roman-period phases have been badly disturbed and/or removed in the process of rebuilding or refurbishing. Also, the many mentions of synagogues and synagogue liturgy in the early rabbinic literature make it highly likely that some sort of earlier structures existed. The increasing number of early synagogues from the Second Temple period and even from between the two Jewish wars with Rome makes the idea that there were no Roman-period synagogues most unlikely.[17]

The question of whether there was a crisis from the second half of the third century to the mid-fourth century that affected Jewish settlement has to be put in the larger context of what was happening in the land during this period. The earlier part of the Roman era, from about 135 to about 250 C.E., is often described as the *Pax Romana*, the "Roman

Peace," which may be characterized as a time of significant building and the expansion of settlements. Such a positive assessment of that period in a way answers part of Levine's question: Jewish life was flourishing in this earlier period, associated with Rabbi Judah the Patriarch, even though we can identify only a handful of synagogue remains.[18] This is the period of the *tannaim* (sages), the redaction of the Mishnah and the emergence of the liturgy of the ancient synagogue. If we may accept that the tannaitic period was a very creative era in the history of Palestinian Jewry, there must have been a significant Jewish presence in Galilee despite the relatively elusive archaeological evidence.[19]

Let us turn to the fourth century in an attempt to understand the impact of the rise of Christianity on the Jewish population centers and village life in Galilee.

The conversion of Emperor Constantine to Christianity, as well as his gaining control of both halves of the Roman Empire and bringing Palestine into his domain in 324 C.E., constitutes a fundamental change in the history of the West. Because Palestine was the place where Jesus had lived and walked, it achieved the special status of "Holy Land." The visit of Constantine's mother, Helena, in the fourth century also lent special status to the holy places, and Constantine initiated a program of church construction to venerate them.* By the end of the Byzantine era in the seventh century, a period of approximately 300 years, more than 400 churches and chapels had been built in the land of the Bible.[20] In short, the landscape of the Holy Land was transformed.

One might suppose that a byproduct of this would be the diminution of the Jewish community. But that was not the case. Despite a decline in new Jewish settlement in the fourth century, the significant remains of ancient synagogues in Galilee, the Golan, and the many Jewish towns and villages suggest a strong Jewish community that thrived throughout the Byzantine period and even into the early Arab period.†

This does not mean that Jewish life arose in response to imperial Christianity, as some have suggested. A robust form of Jewish life was already there, as I have argued, in the Roman period and especially in the tannaitic period.[21]

*Yoram Tsafrir, "Ancient Churches in the Holy Land," *BAR*, September/October 1993.
†For an overview of the Golan's synagogue sites, see Chaim Ben-David, "Golan Gem: The Ancient Synagogue of Deir Aziz," *BAR*, November/December 2007.

Recent examination of the material culture of the nascent Christian community in the land of the Bible during the Byzantine period does provide important new insights, however, into how the two communities related in the important period after Constantine.

Despite all the church building and pilgrim traffic that was spawned by the adoption of Christianity as the official religion of the empire in the fourth century, the evidence for the adoption of Christianity in rural Palestine is very limited in the early Byzantine period. This evidence increases to a significant degree only in the middle of the fifth and sixth centuries.[22] This means that Constantine's building projects at the holy places represented a major gain for Christianity only in the urban areas: Jerusalem, Bethlehem, around the Sea of Galilee and in the Lower Galilee.[23] The impact of Christianity, which increased significantly in this period, did not extend to the rural population, however.[24] Even paganism continued to prevail in many places in the fifth and sixth centuries, indicating that Christianity's spread was neither uniform nor rapid.[25] At the same time "large areas of rural Palestine, such as Galilee and Samaria, had an absolute Jewish or Samaritan majority," as Doron Bar has pointed out.[26]

Motti Aviam's survey of western Galilee between 1980 and 1992 provides an especially important database.[27] It identifies 140 sites from the Byzantine period. Remains of churches and monasteries were found in 63 of them; 13 others had architectural remains with crosses on them.[28] This enabled Aviam to draw distinct boundaries between Christian areas, Jewish areas and pagan areas in Upper Galilee. The Jewish sites were in eastern Galilee, the Christian sites were in western Galilee. The line of demarcation begins at Fassuta in the north (near Ma'alot), which has a single church with 11 small sites nearby, all of which date to the Byzantine period (see map p. 144). The line continues south to er-Rama (near Karmiel, which is slightly southwest in the Beth Hakerem Valley), where the remains of both a church and a synagogue have been identified. The church no doubt represents a new population in the later Byzantine period that replaced the Jewish community there. East of this line, no remains of any churches have been found, though dozens of synagogues have been discovered.[29] The northern borderline between Jewish and Christian regions may be identified at Sasa in the west, extending to Baram, Qazyon and Yesod HaMa'alah in the east. North of these sites no Jewish synagogue remains have

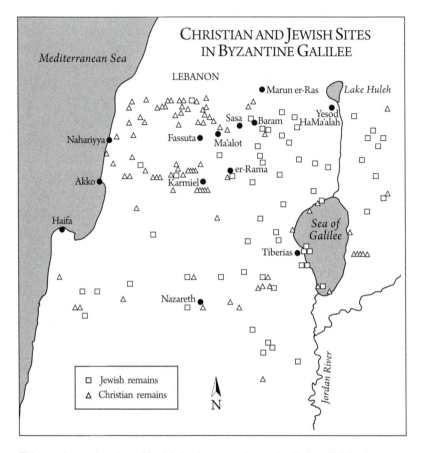

This map based largely on Motti Aviam's survey shows the distinct division between Christian and Jewish areas of the rural Upper Galilee in the Byzantine period. The Christian sites are mostly located in the west, having spread inland from coastal sites such as Akko and Nahariyya; the Jewish sites are in the east. The borderline runs from Fassuta in the north to er-Rama in the south. The more urban Lower Galilee did not have such clear segregation of its sites.

been identified; only churches have been identified north of this line in southern Lebanon (Yarun, Marun er-Ras).

In the pagan areas there were virtually no mixed communities; in several Jewish villages, however, there were also a few Christian families (e.g., Gush Halav), and in several Christian villages there were Jewish families (e.g., Kfar Yasif). In all of these cases, however, there were no sacred public buildings, a situation quite different from the urban setting.[30]

The sole example of Christian penetration into an area that was solidly

Jewish for centuries is Capernaum, a holy site where the House of Peter was converted into a *domus ecclesia* and later into an octagonal church, as described above.[31]

The situation in Lower Galilee is quite different: No border between Jews and Christians could be identified, even though many smaller settlements were scattered throughout the area. Churches and monasteries have been discovered close to Jewish villages and towns where Christian religious centers developed.[32] The extensive Christian population of western Galilee, largely unknown prior to these surveys and excavations, was divided among the dioceses of Tyre, Akko and Sepphoris. On the basis of the epigraphical remains, Aviam concludes that the population was largely of Semitic origin.[33] Moreover, he also concludes that the process of Christianization began with the conversion of pagans to Christianity along the coast; this continued later with the assistance of monks who lived in the monasteries and began converting the smaller, rural pagan communities. Only later did the monks attach themselves to monasteries in the larger Jewish communities such as Tiberias (Mount Berenice), and ultimately around the smaller Jewish communities in Upper Galilee later in the Byzantine period.[34] While the chronological situation is not entirely clear, that is, when precisely in the Byzantine period this change occurred, we can say with reasonable certainty that it did not occur in the fourth century and probably occurred in the latter part of the fifth and sixth centuries, what in archaeological terms we might call the Byzantine 2 period.

This chronology is the basis of Doron Bar's work, cited above, and is supported by both Aviam's and Leibner's surveys and excavations.[35] If they are correct, we can no longer accept the old view regarding the speed and effectiveness of the spread of Christianity in these areas during the fourth century. We must now view that process as having occurred over a much longer period, extending over the entire Byzantine period.[36] Of the 450 churches that have been identified in Byzantine Palestine, Bar notes that only 240 may be described as community churches and associated with rural Palestine. During the initial period of the Byzantine era, or Byzantine 1, until c. 450 C.E. or slightly later, the distribution of churches may be characterized as localized at the holy sites. Most financial resources were directed to the holy sites and urban areas in an attempt to convert what was a remote province of the Roman Empire into the "Christian Holy Land."[37]

These urban areas comprised the true locus where Christianity, Judaism and paganism met; it was in the urban centers (e.g., Sepphoris, Beth Shean/Scythopolis, Caesarea Maritima) where the intelligentsia resided. At Sepphoris, for example, two churches were erected in about 500 C.E.; each was twice the size of the local synagogue from this time. These churches were strategically situated along the two main arteries of the town, the *cardo* and the *decumanus*, the result of efforts by an enterprising bishop named Eutropius. The location of these churches in a town with a Jewish majority suggests a kind of ecumenism reflected also in the common artistic and visual representations that decorated both civic and religious spaces.[38] The civic space is best represented by the Nile Festival Building constructed in the early fifth century and decorated with many mosaics, both geometric and figural. One of the best-known mosaics features a huntress riding on a horse; another features a centaur leaping on his hind legs. Perhaps most striking of all is the depiction of the Nile itself as a half-naked woman who personifies Egypt and its fertility alongside a nilometer that measured the depth of the Nile (see Plate 9). The synagogue from this same era includes many figural scenes and inscriptions, but the zodiac panel is at the center, which is occupied by the sun (not Helios), riding on a chariot drawn by four horses.*[39] It was only during the latter part of the Byzantine period, Byzantine 2 until the Persian conquest of 614 C.E., that the church turned its attention to the rural areas after a measure of success in the urban areas had been achieved.[40]

This delay, as it were, in focusing on the rural areas, may well be a factor in the burst of synagogue building or rebuilding that led Levine and others to comment on the multiplicity of synagogue remains from a time when the church was growing stronger.[41] If there was no real attempt to convert the population in the hinterland in the early phase of the Byzantine period, there certainly would not have been much of an attempt to ban Jews from building or rebuilding synagogues despite the increasingly restrictive legislation that emerged within the church regarding the Jewish community.[42] We may add this to a growing list of reasons why there was a kind of floruit of Jewish life in Galilee in the early Byzantine period. In the Golan Heights, a similar burst in synagogue building occurred slightly later, in the fifth and sixth centuries.[43]

*Zeev Weiss, "The Sepphoris Synagogue Mosaic," *BAR*, September/October 2000.

SEPPHORIS ZODIAC MOSAIC. The Sepphoris synagogue features a zodiac circling the sun (rather than the face of Helios, as in a number of other synagogues) riding a chariot pulled by four horses. Surrounding this central scene are the 12 zodiac signs, several of which are damaged but still preserve details—and Hebrew inscriptions—that allow them to be identified. Each sign is also identified by the Hebrew month to which it corresponds.

The location of most of the rural churches on the outskirts of settlements, in the view of Doron Bar, is symptomatic of Christian insecurity even in the later part of the Byzantine period. When a church was located more centrally within a settlement, he argues, it reflects the strength of the Christian population's position in that community. This would seem to be at variance with Aviam's view, noted above, that it was the missionary activity of the monks and the presence of monasteries that indicated a more active posture with respect to conversion.[44] Bar argues that one of the main differences between the rural churches and synagogues in the Byzantine period is precisely their location: The synagogues were normally located in the center of villages because of their communal function as a house for prayer, community center, and a place for visitors to stay.[45] In terms of the demographics of the Byzantine period, however, there is no doubt that the Christian community was growing rapidly and became the largest ethnic-religious group within Palestine. This did not happen immediately after Constantine's conversion but only more gradually over the course of several centuries. Bar maintains that the conversion rate of pagans to Christianity in Palestine was similar to that of other places in the Roman Empire and that Jews and Samaritans maintained their identity much longer than usually assumed; only as a result of missionary activity was Christianity embraced.[46] A major inference is that paganism remained robust well into late antiquity and well into the Byzantine period, as did Jewish life.

The view that the Christianization process was much slower and less systematic than previously thought has gained much ground in recent years. In a 2001 monograph, Seth Schwartz doubted that the process could have been completed before the reign of Justinian (527–565 C.E.), if by then. He argued that the rebirth and redefinition of Judaism was much indebted to the process earlier in the Byzantine period that produced major rabbinic literature, as noted above.[47] Fergus Millar writes that the establishment of Christian communities and the presence of a bishop in no way meant the suppression of paganism, though the landscape of Palestine was truly altered after the process of Christianization had begun.[48] Adiel Schremer quotes Yaron Dan from a 1984 Hebrew monograph in support of such a view:

> The spread of Christianity in Eretz Israel was slow ... One could say that only during the late fifth century or early in the sixth century did the Christians become the chief population element in Palestine. Even so, this was true only from the perspective of the country as a whole, as this was not the case in Galilee or in the hills of Samaria.[49]

Schremer, in his own words, puts it this way:

> Moreover, although the intensive activity of the Roman emperors surely contributed to the Christianization of Palestine, it is clear that this was manifest primarily in places associated with Jesus' activity, such as Jerusalem, Bethlehem, and the like, but much less in the rest of the country.[50]

Conclusions

The parting of the ways between Jews and Christians in the Holy Land, and in particular in Galilee, is unfortunately a very complicated affair. While archaeology can tell us something about the pace of Christianization, it cannot tell us how Jews and Christians were getting along during the period under consideration. Before Constantine, we have very little material evidence for the existence of Christianity in the Holy Land. Demographics and literature of the rabbis and church fathers suggest, however, that a significant group of Christian believers, many of whom were gentile Christians, stayed in the land and were attracted to the liturgy of the synagogue. Many of them continued to observe circumcision, the Sabbath and the dietary laws.[51] Patristic sources often repeated testimony to the effect that Christians frequented synagogues "annoyingly often."[52] No doubt many were brought into the mainstream when Constantine made Christianity a recognized religion of the empire, to which he himself ultimately subscribed. But as archaeology has shown, conversion came slowly to many parts of Palestine, and while pilgrimage brought many Christians from abroad to the *loca sancta* of the church, large portions of the population remained attached and committed to their native traditions until the dawn of the Middle Ages, even after the Persian and Islamic conquests. That Judaism and Jews were somewhat immune to the spread of Christianity is evidenced by the explosion of synagogue (re)building, the boon in the literary composition of *piyyut* (poetry), the writing of midrash (biblical commentary), and the continued translation and retranslation of the Bible in the form of Aramaic Targums (with many expansions that were close to the genre of midrash). We could not have said this before the discovery of the Cairo Geniza more than 100 years ago.

Judging from the rather distinctive settlement patterns in the Byzantine period, Jews, Christians and pagans apparently lived peacefully alongside one another in the urban areas (e.g., Sepphoris, Beth Shean/ Scythopolis) and near the holy sites. In more rural areas, they tended to live in distinct regions. Aside from an exception here and there, Jews and Christians kept pretty much to themselves in the hinterland, though there must have been contact and trade along the borderlines. It is not at all clear from the material record to what extent we can then say that "good fences made good neighbors" or that one tradition or the other refrained from proselytizing the other.

Although in earlier periods Jews maintained purity laws in very visible ways, by building ritual baths (*mikva'ot*) and using tableware manufactured in Jewish pottery-making centers, those sorts of practices appear to be in decline in the Byzantine period,[53] which suggests that the rural borders were very porous and that contacts and interaction were regular features of everyday life. This would be especially so on borderlines, for example, between eastern and western Galilee and in the Golan, where clusters of Jews, Christians and pagans—although separated on the interior of those areas—could hardly avoid contact with the "other" in the normal course of time.[54]

The slow rise of Christianity in the rural areas indicates that Palestine was not so different from other parts of the empire where the new faith was also slow to catch on. Only the holy places distinguished the Holy Land and brought new money and wealth to the entire region as pilgrims came and went. A survey of the local inscriptions suggests that most of the converts to Christianity were local Semites or indigenes, as well as some Semitic newcomers to the Golan, whose ties were to be divided between the eastern traditions of the church and the newly expanding church of Rome.[55]

Given the sort of churches and synagogues these two communities left behind, with beautiful mosaics, chandeliers, pottery and great literatures, we would be making a great mistake if we were to think of Jews and Christians only as enemies. Insofar as they each participated in a common material culture imbued with a love of Greco-Roman culture that is preserved for all to see and lived alongside one another for nearly a millennium, and despite the rhetoric of much of the literature, I believe we must view the parting of the ways pretty much as a family affair. The gap between "the rhetoric of separation and the reality of fluid boundaries and intercredal interactions" pointed out by Annette Yoshiko Reed is surely supported by the evidence of material culture.[56] There is no doubt that the two religions went in different directions from an early time, but separation between Jews and Christians was more fluid, even in the Byzantine period. The unfortunate end of Jewish-Christian relations in the Holy Land must be associated more with the Crusades and events in modern history than with what we find in the Holy Land in late antiquity.

8

Jews and Christians at Rome: An Early Parting of the Ways

MARGARET H. WILLIAMS

To dispel the gossip [that he had ordered the burning down of Rome] Nero therefore found culprits on whom he inflicted the most exotic punishments. These were people hated [*invisos*] for their shameful offences [*flagitia*] whom the common people [*vulgus*] called Christians [*Christianos*]. The man who gave them their name, Christus, had been executed during the rule of [Emperor] Tiberius by the procurator Pontius Pilatus. The pernicious superstition [*exitiabilis superstitio*] had been temporarily suppressed, but it was starting to break out again, not just in Judea, the starting point of that curse, but in Rome, as well, where all that is abominable and shameful in the world flows together and gains popularity.

(Tacitus, *Annals* 15.44)[1]

Unlike most of the evidence to be considered in this chapter, the passage just cited can be dated with precision: It occurs just over half way through Tacitus's account of "the year of the consuls Gaius Laecanius and Marcus Licinius" and so can be pinned down exactly to the summer (July) of 64 C.E.[2] Thus little more than 30 years after the execution in Jerusalem of Jesus of Nazareth (Christus) by the Roman prefect of Judea, Pontius Pilate,[3] Jesus' followers in Rome, by now for the greater part gentile, had become sufficiently distinguished from the long-established Jewish community there for the commoners to have assigned them a nickname and the Roman authorities to have picked on them rather than the Jews as scapegoats of first choice.

Separation of Christians from Jews, then, must have started extremely early in the imperial capital, if within a generation of the death of Jesus of Nazareth neither the common people nor the authorities had any difficulty in distinguishing between the adherents of those two closely related "superstitions," as elite Roman writers disparagingly referred to them.[4] But how and why did that gulf open up so early and why did it become all but unbridgeable from around the end of the first century C.E.?

I. Early history of Jews and Christians at Rome

From the Late Republic to the Early Empire (139 B.C.E.–14 C.E.)

Jews first crop up in Rome in 139 B.C.E., when for reasons that remain unclear they were expelled from the city by the *praetor peregrinus*, the magistrate with responsibility for aliens. Nothing in the brief, late and confused evidence for this episode[5] suggests that they were permanent inhabitants of the city.[6] Indeed, it is not until well into the next century (59 B.C.E.) that an established Jewish community is attested at Rome.[7] When that community took root is not known. All we can say for certain is that from the early 50s B.C.E. onward Jews comprised an easily recognizable element of the Roman population, distinguished by, among other things, their enthusiastic, not to say rowdy, participation in public meetings,[8] their extravagant mourning behavior,[9] and other unusual cultural practices, most notably Sabbath observance, abstention from pork and circumcision.[10] Writers of the Augustan period (31 B.C.E.–14 C.E.) allude to the Jews and their distinctive customs quite frequently, their knowledge drawn presumably from either the ownership of Jewish slaves or observation of the capital's large and conspicuous Jewish community,[11] the bulk of it located at that time across the Tiber in Regio XIV (Trans-tiberinum).[12] Judging by references to this ethnic group, it would seem they were regarded more with amusement than with anything else: In Roman eyes, the practices arising out of the Jews' long-held "superstition" might be rather odd but there was nothing shameful or offensive, let alone threatening, about them.[13] Even the emperor Augustus himself was not above making the Jews' pork taboo the subject of a sly sally.[14]

The Jews under Tiberius (14–37 C.E.)

In the post-Augustan period, however, starting in the reign of Tiberius (14–37 C.E.), the first emperor of the Julio-Claudian dynasty that ruled Rome until 68 C.E., a different view of the Jews seems to have taken hold, at least in elite Roman circles. Instead of being regarded somewhat indulgently, time and again the Jews found themselves the object of hostile attention. In 19 C.E., for example, not only was the decision taken by the city fathers (i.e., the Senate) to expel them en masse from the city, but 4,000 young Jewish males "of suitable age" (*idonea aetate*) were rounded up and conscripted for military service in malaria-infested Sardinia.[15] Those who objected, presumably on the hitherto allowable grounds that observation of the Jewish law (the Torah) was not easily compatible with the demands of the Roman army life, were dealt with summarily (i.e., executed).[16] Further, if Philo is to be believed, Jews in Rome came under threat of yet more punishment just 12 years later. According to a passage in the *Embassy to Gaius*, Tiberius's chief henchman Aelius Sejanus was planning fresh measures against both Jews in general and those of the capital specifically at the time of his downfall in 31 C.E.[17] That there were any Jews in Rome in that year to be threatened with punishment may cause surprise after the events of 19 C.E. No expulsion from Rome, however, ever had much of a long-term impact, since the authorities tended to lose interest in groups they had targeted once the needs of the moment, usually political, had been satisfied. By 31 C.E. many of those who had been expelled in 19 C.E. may well have drifted back.[18]

Precisely why the government of Tiberius adopted such a hostile stance toward the Jews of Rome remains a matter of considerable scholarly dispute, into which we need not go here.[19] But what admits of no doubt is that during the reign of that emperor a distinct hardening of attitudes occurred. Clearly Jews had now been added to the list of suspect groups regarded by the authorities as convenient targets when a diversion was needed. Ease of attack in the Jews' case must have been facilitated by their unusually high visibility: Their numerous prayer houses in Trans-tiberinum, the focal points of their Torah and Temple-focused life, were a conspicuous element in the cityscape of early imperial Rome.[20]

From Tiberius to the accession of Claudius (31–41 C.E.)

From the fall of Sejanus (31 C.E.) to the unexpected accession to power of the emperor Claudius in 41 C.E.,[21] the history of the Jews in the capital is a blank. For us, that is a huge drawback, as it was probably during that decade that the Christian message, with all its potential for destabilizing and even splitting the Jewish community, was brought to Rome. Who first brought that message is unknown but the most likely people to have spread the word of the arrival of the long-awaited Messiah in the person of Jesus of Nazareth and the imminence of a new and better world order are Jews returning to the city from pilgrimage to Jerusalem. Though the account in Acts of the first Pentecost after the death of Jesus is clearly theologically driven, its inclusion of "visitors from Rome, both Jews and proselytes" (Acts 2:10) among the Diaspora Jews who gave ear to and were convinced by Peter's preaching on that occasion is not implausible. The Augustan Peace (*Pax Augusta*) had made travel throughout the Roman world a relatively trouble-free affair, and until the Temple was destroyed in 70 C.E., Jerusalem was "the pilgrimage site par excellence."[22]

The Jews of Rome under Claudius (41–54 C.E.)

The potential of the Christian message to disrupt Jewish community life at Rome, just noted, appears to have been realized there relatively early. For on the least strained interpretation of the meager surviving evidence, it would seem that by the end of the 40s C.E. it had become the catalyst for sustained turbulence among the Jews of the capital. The key piece of evidence here is the well-known sentence in Suetonius's *Life of the Deified Claudius* 25.4, written some 70 years or so after the event, which runs, "*Iudaeos impulsore Chresto assidue tumultuantes Roma expulit*" ("He [Claudius] expelled the Jews from Rome on account of their continuous, Chrestus-instigated rioting").

Among the various scholarly interpretations of this much-discussed passage, the one that sees in Chrestus a reference to Jesus Christ seems to me to be the most persuasive, since Chrestus is clearly attested as an alternative spelling of Christus and Suetonius rarely bothers to supply the names of the minor characters who occasionally feature in his works.[23] To be sure, this requires the assumption that Suetonius is being somewhat careless here: Obviously the cause of riots occurring c. 49 C.E. cannot have been Christ himself, as Suetonius's Latin implies; most probably the "riots" were caused by debates within the Jewish community about "the Christ" (i.e., the Messiah) that simply got out of hand.[24] However, Suetonius is not always the most careful of writers, as even his admirers are ready to concede.[25] As for the "tumults" themselves, these are best interpreted as analogues to those attested in several Diaspora communities in the eastern provinces during roughly the same period. In various places in Asia Minor and Macedonia in the late 40s C.E., attempts by Jews, most notably Paul, to disseminate the Christian message among their fellow Jews had resulted in ugly outbreaks of violence.[26]

Division within the Jewish community of Rome, then, can to some degree be attributed to internal dissensions between those who accepted the messiahship of Jesus of Nazareth and those who did not. But of far greater significance for the ultimate separation of Jews and Christians at Rome was the action taken on the occasion of the Chrestus/Christ-inspired disturbances by the Roman authorities. For the upshot of those riots was yet another expulsion of Jews from the capital. To understand why this particular Roman action, ordered personally by the emperor Claudius, was a major factor in the split between Christians and Jews at Rome, we need to consider briefly the likely composition of the many synagogal communities in the Roman world at that time.

The composition of early imperial synagogal communities

Synagogal congregations in general in the Roman world at that time were not exclusively composed of Jews. Frequently attested also in Sabbath congregations in the synagogue are gentiles, a minority of whom had even gone so far as to convert formally to Judaism. The best evidence for these interested gentiles (the so-called Godfearers) and converts (proselytes) relates to Diaspora communities in Rome's eastern provinces. (On the Godfearers, see Chapter III, "The Godfearers: From the Gospels to Aphrodisias," by Bruce Chilton.) There, people such as these often proved to be the most responsive to the Christian message and hence the most

ALBUM/ART RESOURCE, NY

ROMAN EMPEROR CLAUDIUS. It was during the reign of Emperor Claudius (41–54 C.E) that debates over Jesus' messiahship began to cause rifts within Rome's diverse Jewish community, made up of both ethnic Jews, gentile converts and Godfearers. As a result of increasingly violent and public feuds, Claudius expelled large numbers of Torah-observant Jews from the city, leaving early Jewish believers-in-Jesus free to develop an identity separate from those who continued to observe Jewish law.

fertile source of converts.[27] But the imperial capital, too, had its Godfearers and proselytes.[28] On the very reasonable assumption that they will have been no less responsive to the Christian message than their provincial counterparts, it follows that by the late 40s C.E. there must have been at Rome many non-Jews among the ranks of those convinced of the messiahship of Jesus and his ability to save them when the end time, now believed to be imminent, arrived.

These people would not, of course, have been affected by Claudius's targeting of the Jews c. 49 C.E. While the latter, who included Jewish-Christians such as Paul's friends, Aquila and Priscilla, were obliged to leave the city (Acts 18:2), these gentile Christians were free to stay. Moreover, now that the Torah and Temple-focused element of the community had been largely removed, crucially they were also more at liberty to strike out on their own and reconfigure their identity.

The impact of the Claudian expulsion
on Jewish-Christian relations at Rome

That many chose to do so is shown by Paul's Epistle to the Romans.[29] For the picture that emerges from this letter to the Christians of the capital, written probably c. 56/57 C.E., is of a community now dominated by confident gentiles, immensely proud of the Torah-lite lifestyle that they have developed for themselves. For these people, their sights set firmly on the new age that is about to dawn, the Temple, Sabbath observance and the food restrictions enjoined by the law of Moses are an irrelevance, and fellow Christians still in thrall to the Torah were almost beneath contempt. As for the latter, who by this time almost certainly will have included Jewish-Christians who had returned from their various places of exile,[30] they responded in kind: Contempt was met with contempt and the community split from top to bottom. Hence Paul's desperate attempt, as expressed in Romans, to heal the breach—"Do not," he implores his squabbling addressees, "ruin the work of God for the sake of food ... Each of us must consider his neighbor and think what is for his good and will build up the common life."[31] This plea for mutual forbearance, however, would appear to have fallen on deaf ears. The Judeo-Christian community remained hopelessly divided to the extent that by 64 C.E. at least some of its members could be identified even by total outsiders (viz. the Roman mob) as constituting a discrete sect. What caused these people, the *Christiani*, to be viewed as entirely different from mainstream Jews, now once again established in the capital, is not clear. Tacitus claims that it was the Christians' shameful offences (*flagitia*),[32] by which he is probably alluding to alleged practices such as cannibalism (a misrepresentation of the Eucharist) and incest (a misunderstanding, possibly, of the Christians' open talk about brotherly love).[33] Whatever it was, it was enough to demonstrate, at least to the satisfaction of fearful and hostile "pagans," that these two closely related Judean superstitions were significantly different.

II. Nero's persecution of the Christians (64 C.E.)

To return now to the event with which we opened this chapter—Nero's persecution of the Christians in 64 C.E. Why were these individuals pursued with such vigor and punished with such sadism (e.g., turned into living torches) by the Roman authorities? Why were the Jews, hitherto a regular government target, totally ignored?

Unfortunately our sources for this episode lack specificity on these points. However, from the allusions they contain and our knowledge of how such episodes at Rome, basically witch hunts, tended to unfold, it may reasonably be inferred that it was probably a series of tip-offs from the common people that directed official attention toward the

ANCIENT ART & ARCHITECTURE COLLECTION LTD/ALAMY

ROMAN EMPEROR NERO. Noted for his vanity and extravagance, Nero (54–68 C.E.) is thought to have caused the great fire of Rome in 64 C.E. to create space for his new capital. Looking for a scapegoat, Nero accused Rome's much-maligned Christians of the arson, as the sect was rumored to be obsessed with the imminent and fiery destruction of the Roman world order. The city's Jews, on the other hand, were held blameless, perhaps because many prominent Romans of the day, including the wife of Nero, held them in high regard.

hated (*invisos*) Christians.[34] Made aware perhaps through the latter's excited chatter about the imminent destruction of the current world order by an all-consuming fire,[35] these humble residents of Rome (Tacitus's *vulgus*) may well have concluded that the Christians were more than likely to have had a hand in starting the blaze. Once provided with such a convenient scapegoat, the authorities will have felt no need to look any further. Indeed, the obliging way in which the initial batch of Christians to be arrested first confessed[36] and then "through envy and jealousy"[37] denounced yet more Christians, and those in large numbers (*multitudo ingens*),[38] will have meant that the authorities quickly had enough culprits to satisfy the political needs of the moment—viz. diverting blame from Nero for the fire.

As for the overlooking of the Jews on this occasion, two reasons suggest themselves: (1) the Romans, accustomed to thinking of the Jews mainly in terms of Sabbath observance, abstention from pork and circumcision, may simply not have associated them with fire raising; or (2) the Jews may, temporarily, have become untouchable thanks to having friends in high places. The actor Alityrus, a favorite with Nero, was a Jew.[39] The empress herself, Poppaea Sabina, appears to have shared the fascination with Judaism common in elite female circles at that time.[40] Whatever motives the authorities had for discriminating so sharply between Jews and Christians in 64 C.E.,[41] manifestly they were well aware that Jews and Christians each had a different set of beliefs and practices.

III. The Flavian emperors (70–96 C.E.)
Likely impact of the First Jewish Revolt (66–73/4 C.E.)
The divisions between Jews and Christians at Rome, already sufficiently deep under Nero to be noticed by outsiders, can only have widened as a consequence of the First Jewish Revolt and its aftermath. Breaking out in 66 C.E., it lasted through the final years of Nero's reign (66–68 C.E.) and the Roman civil wars of 68–69 C.E., only to be brought to an end in the early years of the Flavian dynasty, the ruling family that replaced the Julio-Claudians from 70 C.E. With the destruction of the Temple in Jerusalem in that year by Titus, son of the first Flavian emperor Vespasian, the back of the revolt was effectively broken.[42] For political reasons it suited the new dynasty to exploit to the full the recent victory over the Jews. It was the family's only claim to fame[43] and thus its only justification for becoming rulers of the Roman world. And so a vigorous propaganda campaign was soon launched against the Jews, the main purpose of which was to enhance the Flavians' standing. This propaganda, not to mention the more concrete fiscal measures now taken against the Jews, can only have had the effect of widening the gap between Christians and Jews. Why would Christians not opt to distance themselves further from a group now being deliberately humiliated and financially disadvantaged?

The anti-Jewish program of
Vespasian-propaganda and penalization
Christians in Rome in the early 70s C.E. cannot have been unaware of the humiliations heaped upon the Jews by Vespasian. They must have witnessed the elaborate pageant devised to celebrate his family's "Capture of Judea,"[44] the first Roman triumphal parade ever to be held for the suppression of a provincial revolt rather than for adding territory to the empire.[45]

Nor can they have remained untouched by the Flavians' relentless propaganda campaign in respect of their Jewish victory: Coins displaying the legend *Iudaea Capta* (the Capture of Judea) with a variety of images of dejected Jewish prisoners were repeatedly issued, and in denominations

JUDEA CAPTA COIN. One of a series minted during the reign of the Roman emperor Vespasian (shown on obverse) to commemorate the fall of Jerusalem in 70 C.E., this coin proclaims "Iudaea Capta" and depicts Judea as a mourning woman and a bound male captive, both shown beneath a palm tree, a common symbol of Judea. Judea Capta coins were in wide circulation throughout Rome and proved to be a potent symbol of Jewish defeat and subservience.

small enough for even the poor to have had handled them.*[46]

The city itself began to be filled with monuments of the Jews' defeat.[47] On permanent display in the splendid new Forum of Peace† were those objects in which the new emperor took "especial pride," namely the cult vessels of gold, looted from the Temple by his son's troops.[48] Chief among them was the spectacular seven-branched candlestick, the menorah. The highlight of the triumphal parade,[49] from now on (75 C.E. onward) it was to become a must-see object for inhabitants of Rome and visitors alike.[50]

But as flamboyant as Vespasian's anti-Jewish propaganda was, what in the end had a far greater impact and is of much greater relevance to our subject—namely, the separation of Jews and Christians at Rome—was a mere administrative measure. For in 70 C.E., as part of his program to restore the battered finances of the state, Vespasian decided to impose upon the Jewish people a brand new tax. All members of the Jewish race (*gens*) henceforth were required to pay two drachmas per annum

*See Robert Deutsch, "Roman Coins Boast 'Judaea Capta,'" *BAR*, January/February 2010.
†See Steven Fine, "The Temple Menorah—Where Is It?" *BAR*, July/August 2005.

to the Roman state[51] and a special treasury was set up in Rome itself to receive these monies. Its name was the *fiscus Judaicus*—literally the "Jewish Basket."[52] For individual adult males, this penalty for rebellion will not have made any difference to their finances—the new Jewish tax was but a re-branding of the annual dues, the half-shekel Temple tax, that they had previously paid for the maintenance of their national cult center in Jerusalem.[53] But Jewish families, as a whole, will have been affected, some grievously, since the scope of the tax was now widened to include women and children from the age of three.[54] A reflection of their hardship is the appearance of abject poverty as a leitmotif in Roman literary allusions to the capital's Jews from now on.[55]

But the injury brought about by the tax was not just financial. Emotional distress would have been caused, too. Since the Jews were the only people in the empire forced to pay an ethnic levy, they must have found the imposition of such a discriminatory tax extremely hurtful, particularly those (most of the Diaspora) who had played no part whatsoever in the revolt of 66 C.E. And they must have found the arrangements made by Vespasian for the destination of this new tax deeply insulting. The Romans knew perfectly well that the Jews' sense of identity was grounded in their aniconic monotheism—i.e., their worship of the imageless Yahweh alone, from whom they had received via Moses the distinctive law that shaped every facet of their lives.[56] Vespasian's decision, then, to use the Jewish tax money, first, for rebuilding the temple of Jupiter Capitolinus at Rome and then for maintaining the restored cult there,[57] was a deliberate affront: Essentially the Jews were being compelled to bend the knee to the chief protecting god of their conquerors. The humiliating position now forced upon the Jews finds clear reflections in the court poetry of the age: Martial's epigrams, for instance, abound with nasty asides and tasteless jokes at the Jews' expense.[58]

The Jews of Rome in the later Flavian period (79–96 C.E.)

The humiliation did not stop with Vespasian's death in 79 C.E. Flavian government as a whole is marked by great continuity. Consequently, it is not surprising to see Vespasian's sons, Titus (79–81 C.E.) and Domitian (at least at the beginning of his reign), still exploiting to the full their family's conquest of Judea and enthusiastically carrying on their father's anti-Jewish measures. Consequently we see the cityscape of Rome embellished with yet more monuments celebrating the Jews' defeat, most notably the Colosseum, dedicated in 80 C.E.,*[59] and the Arch of Titus,[†] erected by Domitian in 81 C.E. in memory of his recently deceased brother.[60] While the former monument contained a series of prominent bronze inscriptions drawing attention to the fact that the amphitheatre had been built from the spoils of the Jewish war,[61] the latter was decorated with two impressively detailed reliefs, one depicting the main Temple treasures being carried in triumph at Rome by the Roman military,[62] the other showing Titus riding in his triumphal chariot and being crowned by a winged Victory.[63] Coins still poured from the Roman mint reminding the populace of the capture of Judea.[64]

Exaction of the two drachma Jewish tax, meanwhile, also continued. But in the mid-80s C.E. there was a change.[65] Driven by the desperate financial situation in which he now found himself, Domitian decided to tighten the collection of all taxes, but that of the Jewish tax more than any other.[66] The delators (professional informers), eager to please and eager to profit, thereupon embarked upon a campaign of widespread harassment of alleged evaders of the tax, the consequence of which was considerable distress not just for Jews but also for numerous non-Jews, some of them almost certainly gentile Christians. By the time of Domitian's assassination in 96 C.E., so numerous had these malicious (and successful) prosecutions become that the new emperor Nerva (96–98 C.E.) was forced immediately to instigate reform.[67] Through his rapid intervention, the abuses promptly stopped. But that was not the only consequence of Nerva's actions. Through his speedy cleansing operation he also managed to create the perfect conditions for Jews and Christians to go their separate ways. To get a better understanding of his reforms and their unwitting consequences, we must now take a closer look at the maladministration of the Jewish tax under Domitian.

Abuse of the fiscus Judaicus under Domitian

The prime source for the abusive administration of the Jewish tax under Domitian is a passage in Suetonius's *Life of Domitian*, which forms the climax of his short survey of the monstrous injustices brought about by that emperor's increasingly tyrannical rule and extreme rapacity.

*Louis H. Feldman, "Financing the Colosseum," *BAR*, July/August 2001.
†See Fine, "The Temple Menorah," *BAR*, July/August 2005.

© ERICH LESSING

ARCH OF TITUS. The Arch of Titus was erected in 81 C.E. by the emperor Domitian in honor of his recently deceased brother's capture of Jerusalem 11 years earlier. One of the arch's carved panels (see detail below) depicts a triumphal procession in which Roman soldiers carry the looted Temple treasure, including the menorah. Also located near the arch is the great Colosseum of Rome, dedicated in 80 C.E. and likely financed by spoils from the Jewish war.

© ERICH LESSING

So important is this extract for the present discussion that it must be cited in full:

> Besides other taxes, that on the Jews was levied with particular harshness, accusations were laid against those who were living as Jews, without admitting it [*improfessi*], as well as those who had concealed their Jewish origin [*dissimulata origine*] and not paid the tax that had been imposed upon their nation [*imposita genti tributa*]. I remember as a young man being present when an old man of ninety was inspected by the procurator in a very crowded court to see if he was circumcised.
>
> (Suetonius, *Life of Domitian* 12.2)

As usual, Suetonius is frustratingly brief. To be sure, he fleshes out his discussion here with a rare personal reminiscence. But still, a mere two sentences are devoted to a subject that was responsible for generating one of the biggest scandals of Domitian's reign.

Nonetheless, despite the brevity, the basic issue can easily be described—it is alleged tax evasion on the part of two categories of people, the first consisting of gentiles and the second of Jews.[68] As to the composition of these categories, the first, it is fair to surmise, will have consisted mainly of pagan Godfearers, such as those described earlier in this chapter, and gentile Christians, some of them perhaps former Godfearers.[69] The most likely members of the second category will have been apostates (i.e., Jews who had completely abandoned "the customs of their fathers"[70]), Jewish-Christians who had severed all links with the synagogue, and perhaps some proselytes.[71] But these were not the only types of people to be swept up in the witch hunt for evaders of the Jewish tax. Suetonius's reminiscence about the distasteful treatment of the nonagenarian alerts us to the fact that there probably was a third category of potential victims—people who, though neither Judaizers nor Jews, happened to have been circumcised. Such people did exist—for, contrary to what most Romans believed, circumcision at that time was not an exclusively Jewish practice.[72]

Of the people hounded by the informers and punished by the courts for evasion of the Jewish tax, some will have been guilty. Although apostates and Jewish-Christians who had severed all links with the synagogue may well have felt that their prosecution was unfair, nonetheless they were liable for the tax in that they were ethnically Jewish and the tax itself had been imposed upon the Jewish people (*imposita genti tributa*). But many of the people charged with evasion of the tax will have been targeted without justification—neither the pagans and gentile Christians in category 1 (the *improfessi*) nor the circumcised, non-Jewish males in category 3 should ever have been deemed liable. That many of them were not only maliciously accused (calumniated) but even severely punished (confiscation of property was the usual sentence) is deducible from the urgency with which Nerva dealt with the scandal. So what exactly did he do?

IV. Nerva's overhaul of the Jewish Tax (96 C.E.)

To put an end to the abuses of the Domitianic era, Nerva immediately enacted a number of reforms. First, he abolished the charge of "Jewish life" that had been maliciously used to entrap so many innocent individuals: "Moreover, he put to death all the slaves and freedmen who had conspired against their masters and allowed that class of individuals to lodge no complaint whatsoever against their masters; and no persons were permitted to accuse anybody of treason [*asebeia/maiestas*] or of adopting the Jewish mode of life [*Ioudaikos bios*]."[73] A restitution of assets was then ordered to those whose property had been unjustly confiscated, preceded presumably by the quashing of their sentences.[74] It is to this latter act that Nerva's magnificent bronze coins of early 96 C.E. bearing the legend *Fisci Ivdaici Calvmnia Svblata* (Removal of the Calumnies/False Accusations associated with the *fiscus Judaicus*) must surely refer.*[75] It was probably on this occasion also that liability for the Jewish tax was redefined—no longer was it to be an ethnic levy, "paid by all Jews wheresoever they lived";[76] henceforth only Jews who "continued to observe their ancestral customs" were required to pay, an arrangement still operative in Dio Cassius's own day, the early third century C.E.[77]

It should immediately be obvious why these measures will have facilitated the further loosening of ties between Jews and Christians. Before Nerva's reforms, there probably were many Jewish-Christians who would have liked, on account of their "faith position," to sever their

*Schlomo Moussaieff, "The 'New Cleopatra' and the Jewish Tax," *BAR*, January/February 2010.

COIN REFORMING THE *FISCUS JUDAICUS*. According to the legend on its reverse (right), this Roman coin issued during the reign of the emperor Nerva (96–98 C.E., who is depicted on the obverse) commemorates the "removal of the false accusations associated with the *fiscus Judaicus*." Nerva's predecessor, Domitian, had indiscriminately imposed the "Jewish tax" on any who might be considered Jewish, from ethnic Jews to apostates to gentile Christians and Godfearers. With Nerva's reforms, the tax was made applicable only to Jews who "continued to observe their ancestral customs," which may have led many Jewish-Christians to finally leave their synagogues for good.

links with the synagogue. However, because of their obligation to pay the Jewish tax, these Jewish-Christians may well have found it convenient to continue their synagogal membership—from 70 C.E. the synagogue almost certainly acted as both the registry for payers of the Jewish tax and the collection point for their contributions before the transfer of the latter to the *fiscus Judaicus*.[78] Nor would synagogal membership merely have been a convenience for these people. From the mid-80s C.E. it may well have been viewed by them as the best guarantee available against the unwanted attention of professional informers. However, with Nerva's restriction of the Jewish tax after 96 C.E. to those who "continued to observe their ancestral customs," the need for that guarantee would have become redundant. The result must have been that many of these now "liberated" Jewish-Christians either would have joined mixed congregations of the type that feature in the Epistle to the Romans or proceeded to set up their own Jewish-Christian assemblies.[79] Either way, their break with the synagogue would have been complete.

V. Jews and Christians in the second century C.E.

The testimony of Latin writers

The further distancing of Christians from Jews made possible by Nerva's reforms is reflected in the writings of all the major Latin authors from the first part of the second century C.E. whose works have survived.[80] The historian Tacitus, writing mainly under the emperor Trajan (98–117 C.E.), is in no doubt about the discrete natures of the Jewish and Christian "superstitions." While aware of their shared Judean origin,[81] he knows that they have now gone their separate ways. Suetonius, a contemporary of Tacitus but slightly younger, likewise has no difficulty in distinguishing between Jews and Christians. Unlike the historian, who does not bother to disguise the contempt and loathing he feels for both Jews[82] and Christians,[83] Suetonius is more discriminating: While Jews are referred to with a neutrality of tone almost unique in Latin writings on the Jews,[84] the Christians are dismissed in one short, contemptuous phrase—"*genus hominum superstitionis novae ac maleficae*" ("a class of men given to a new and wicked superstition").[85] With Suetonius, as with Romans generally, anything new was by definition bad.[86]

For Pliny the Younger, the senator sent from Rome to the province of Bithynia-Pontus c. 109 C.E. to sort out its many problems, the Christians likewise constitute a discrete (and noxious) sect.[87] His difficulties in dealing with its adherents, large numbers of whom were regularly being denounced to him, are the subject of the most famous section of his celebrated correspondence with the emperor Trajan—*Letters* 10.96 and 97. Uncertain though the interpretation of Pliny's own letter (10.96) is in many places, one fact emerges from it with startling clarity: Membership in the Christian sect is now an illegal activity, punishable by death. (Probably it had been made so by Nerva in 96 C.E.[88]) To be sure, those accused of being Christians could escape a death sentence from Pliny provided that they recanted in open court. The procedure they were required to follow involved prayers and offerings to the gods of Rome (the emperor included) and cursing Christ, "none of which things those who are truly Christian can be forced to do."[89] Those who refused to submit to these tests were automatically despatched for execution.

Pliny's letter is of course concerned with only one area, the province of Bithynia-Pontus. That the legal situation with regard to Christians was no different in other parts of the empire, including Rome itself, is shown by Trajan's terse reply. He states categorically that Christians are not to be sought out (*conquirendi non sunt*) but, if they are denounced to the authorities and subsequently found guilty, "they must be punished [*puniendi sunt*]."[90] Nothing could make clearer the dividing line now drawn between Jews and Christians. "Judaism" and "Christianity," at one time indistinguishable even to well-educated Romans (e.g., the Roman governor of Achaea in the early 50s C.E., L. Iunius Gallio[91]), now have been assigned entirely different statuses in Roman law: Jewish "ancestral practices" continue to be on the right side of it, the situation that had prevailed ever since the Jews first came under direct Roman rule; firmly placed on the other side, however, is now the Christians' "new and evil superstition."[92]

Christian sources

The extent to which these tidy legal distinctions impacted on Jews and Christians living in Rome is extremely difficult to document. There is no hard surviving historical evidence from Roman writers (i.e., pagan Latin authors) for Jewish-Christian relations at Rome during the reigns of Hadrian (117–138 C.E.) and the Antonine emperors, Antoninus Pius (138–161 C.E.) and Marcus Aurelius (161–180 C.E.).

Some light, however, can be shed on the subject by Christian sources. For in the middle decades of the century, several influential Christian teachers and writers were active in Rome, notwithstanding the illegal status of Christianity (*Christianismos*), as this offspring of Judaism had now come to be termed.[93] The most notable of these were Valentinus and Marcion, both of whom first came to the capital from the eastern provinces during Hadrian's reign, and Justin Martyr, who arrived there, also from the East, during the reign of Antoninus Pius.

Although the works of Valentinus and Marcion have not survived (basically because they were regarded as heretical and so suppressed by the established church), the views of these two important Christian teachers can be recovered to a large extent from the writings of their adversaries, most notably Tertullian.[94] For theological reasons too complicated to go into here, both Valentinus and Marcion rejected the Old Testament and its god—Marcion with particular violence.[95] Not only did he totally exclude the Old Testament from the list of works that he drew up for the edification of his numerous followers, but he thoroughly de-Judaized even such

Christian writings as he did admit to his canon.[96] How Marcion interacted with real, live Jews at Rome it is not possible to say. What admits of no doubt, however, is that his writings displayed an extraordinary hostility to Judaism—the Jewish god (Yahweh), the Jewish law (Torah) and all the symbols precious to Jewish life and faith were routinely and deeply denigrated.[97] With regard to the reasons for this extreme behavior, we can only speculate. However, given the fact that Marcion was operating in the immediate aftermath of the revolt of Bar-Kokhba (132–135 C.E.), the Second Jewish Revolt, it is entirely possible that he had absorbed more than a little of the all-pervading hatred of the Jews at that time.[98] In late Hadrianic/early Antonine Rome there existed a widespread and deep antipathy toward the Jews largely on account of the huge losses the Romans had incurred in the suppression of the Bar-Kokhba Revolt.[99] Gentile Christians in the city, such as Marcion, will have had an additional motive for loathing the Jews—namely Bar-Kokhba's vicious persecution of Jewish-Christians in Judea on account of their refusal to acknowledge his messiahship.[100] Hypothetical as the reasons for Marcion's hostility must remain, his core message is not in doubt: It was a strident call for the "radical dissociation" of Christianity and Judaism.[101] The proper object of Christian devotion, so Marcion preached, should be the new, superior deity that had appeared on earth in the form of Jesus of Nazareth, not the old, inferior god of the Jews as described in the Old Testament. Such teaching, which proved to be extremely popular both in Marcion's day and long afterward,[102] will hardly have helped to foster harmonious relations between the Jews and Christians of the capital.

Unlike Valentinus and Marcion, Justin Martyr can still communicate with us in his own words. Several of his works survive, the most pertinent of which for us is his *Dialogue with Trypho*, a monograph written at Rome probably between 155 and 160 C.E.[103] The work itself purports to be the record of a conversation between a Christian (Justin himself) and a Jew (Trypho) that occurred some 25 years earlier[104] and is said by Eusebius to have taken place in the city of Ephesus,[105] facts that might seem to render its testimony of dubious value for Antonine Rome. However, most scholars are of the opinion that, even if such a conversation did occur and is not just a literary fiction, Justin's work is unlikely to be a verbatim record of it. What the *Dialogue with Trypho* probably reflects, at least to some degree, is the contemporary situation in Rome and, more particularly, the issues preoccupying and dividing Jews and Christians there at that time.[106] As for those issues, the Jewish practice that clearly offends Justin most is the synagogal ritual involving the daily cursing of Christians. This was the so-called Benediction of the Minim (*Birkat ha-Minim*), which in reality was a prayer against heretics.[107] (See Chapter XI, "In Between: Jewish-Christians and the Curse of the Heretics," by Shaye J.D. Cohen.) Again and again Justin returns to this subject, roundly accusing Trypho with words such as these: "To the utmost of your power you dishonor and curse in your synagogues all those who believe in Christ,"[108] a charge that Trypho could hardly refute seeing that the malediction against heretics was an integral part of the synagogal liturgy.[109] Trypho, however, has his own issues, the most serious being the worship of Christ Jesus as divine. That, for him, is the most outrageous feature of the Christian cult and the ultimate blasphemy—in his view, no figure other than God (Yahweh) should be worshiped and that included his Messiah.[110] From this, one can see that the differences between Jews and "orthodox" Christians such as Justin are as great and as irreconcilable as those between Jews and the followers of the "heretics" Valentinus and Marcion. The gulf between Jews and Christians, no matter what form of *Christianismos* the latter espoused, has now become a chasm.

VI. The archaeological evidence

Nowhere is this chasm more clearly displayed than by the material evidence left behind by Jews and Christians—their underground communal cemeteries, known to us as catacombs.*[111] These were located along the major roads leading out of the capital, a legal necessity since it was against the law (except for emperors and their families) to be buried inside the city boundaries.[112] In terms of date, the Jewish catacombs preceded those of the Christians, recent radiocarbon analysis having established that the earliest part of the large Jewish burial complex northeast of the ancient city, now known as the Villa Torlonia catacomb, goes back to the first half of the first century C.E., if not earlier.[113] Although the other two principal Jewish underground cemeteries, the Vigna Randanini catacomb to the south of the city and Monteverde across the Tiber to the west,

*Letizia Pitigliani, "A Rare Look at the Jewish Catacombs of Rome," *BAR*, May/June 1980; Charles A. Kennedy, "Were Christians Buried in Roman Catacombs to Await the Second Coming?" *BAR*, May/June 1980.

PLATE 1. MACHAERUS. According to the first-century C.E. Jewish historian Josephus, the Herodian mountaintop fortress of Machaerus, perched high above the east coast of the Dead Sea (seen in the background) amid the rugged Transjordanian highlands, is where the eremitical prophet John the Baptist was imprisoned and ultimately beheaded. The Gospels claim that John was executed for declaring invalid Herod Antipas's marriage to his sister-in-law (Mark 6:17–29; Matthew 14:3–12), but John's eloquent preaching of the coming kingdom of God and the imminent downfall of the current order also attracted many followers, including Jesus of Nazareth, which made John a clear threat to Antipas's rule.

PLATE 2. THE HERODIAN PALACE AT MACHAERUS. Originally built as a fortified Hasmonean outpost in the early first century B.C.E., Machaerus was transformed into a luxurious palatial complex by Herod the Great. Like Herod's other fortified palaces discovered west of the Dead Sea, Machaerus included a courtyard with a royal garden, a Roman-style bath, a triclinium for fancy dining and a formal peristyle courtyard lined with porticoes.

PLATE 3. HADRIAN. The Roman emperor Hadrian (117–138 C.E.) appears as a fearless military hero in this bronze statue, found in a second-century Roman fort in the Jordan Valley. Hadrian may have triggered the Second Jewish Revolt (132–135/6 C.E.) when he announced he would erect a temple to Jupiter on the site of the ruined Jerusalem Temple and rebuild the city as a Roman colony named Aelia Capitolina, Latin for "City of the Capitoline Gods." After quashing the revolt with a massive show of force that shattered Jewish life in the land and saw hundreds of thousands of Judeans perish or sold into slavery, Hadrian incorporated Judea into the new Roman province of Syria Palestina in which the practice of Judaism was restricted and Jews could no longer enter Jerusalem.

PLATE 4. BETH SHEARIM NECROPOLIS. Three limestone arches frame the entrance to one of the more than two dozen catacombs of the remarkable necropolis of Beth Shearim in the Galilee. In the second, third and fourth centuries C.E., the cemetery served as the final resting place for both Palestinian and Diaspora Jews, including Rabbi Judah ha-Nasi, the rabbinic sage who famously compiled and edited the Mishnah in about 200 C.E.

PLATE 5. INSIDE THE BETH SHEARIM NECROPOLIS. Carved into the walls of the Beth Shearim catacombs are precious vignettes of the lives and beliefs of rabbinic-era Jews. Inscriptions written in Greek, Aramaic and Hebrew attest the diverse backgrounds of those buried here, as does the interesting combination of Jewish and Hellenistic imagery, like this depiction of a seven-branched menorah carved above the head of a man dressed in a Roman tunic.

PLATE 6. LEDA AND THE SWAN FROM BETH SHEARIM. With his great wings beating, Zeus in the form of a swan comes to Leda and leaves her with child in this carving from a third- or fourth-century C.E. sarcophagus recovered from Beth Shearim. Even into the rabbinic era, Greco-Roman artistic and mythological motifs continued to influence Palestine's Jewish community.

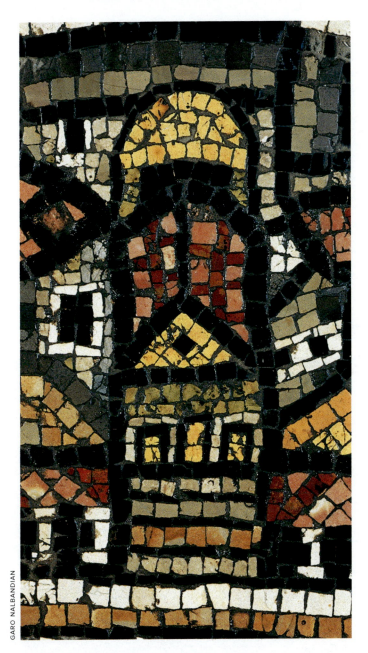

GARO NALBANDIAN

PLATE 7. CHURCH OF THE HOLY SEPULCHRE ON THE MADABA MAP. Following the legalization of Christianity in the early fourth century by the Roman emperor Constantine, his mother, Helena, visited Palestine to identify the landmarks from the stories about Jesus' life. Constantine then had churches built on a number of these holy sites, including the Church of the Holy Sepulchre in Jerusalem, which memorializes the location of Jesus' crucifixion and burial. The church is seen here as the centerpiece of the famous sixth-century Madaba Map in Jordan. The church sits on Jerusalem's main street, the Cardo, which is lined on each side with a portico. The triple-entry church is approached from the Cardo by steps. Like other churches on the map, it has a red roof. A golden dome at back sits over the Holy Sepulchre.

PLATE 8. MONA LISA OF THE GALILEE. This richly colored mosaic portrait of an unnamed woman was discovered among the ruins of a luxurious Roman villa at Sepphoris in the Galilee. The enchanting tilt of her head and near-smile earned her the nickname "Mona Lisa of the Galilee." The portrait is part of a much larger early-third-century mosaic carpet depicting scenes from the life of Dionysus, the Greek god of wine. The prevalence of such graven images suggests that by the third century, this traditionally Jewish town had become increasingly Hellenized and open to pagan influences.

PLATE 9. NILE FESTIVAL BUILDING MOSAIC. In this exquisite fifth-century mosaic carpet decorating the floor of the Nile Festival Building at Sepphoris, the reclining, half-nude woman at left personifies Egypt and its fertility. She is surrounded by wildlife and the bounty of nature and holds a cornucopia brimming with fruit. On the right is a nilometer, a tower-like pillar marked with numbered horizontal lines measuring the depth of the Nile. Depicted at the bottom of the scene is the Nile itself, its waters and banks teeming with fish and animals.

PLATE 10. VIGNA RANDANINI CATACOMB. While most Jewish catacombs in Rome feature typical symbols like the menorah and Torah ark (see below), a handful show elaborate figurative decoration, such as this elegantly painted tomb from Vigna Randanini. A garlanded circle gracefully adorns the tomb's ceiling and encloses a central medallion with a depiction of Victory crowning a naked youth. Surrounding the medallion and decorating the rest of the tomb are painted naturalistic scenes, including peacocks with feathers spread and birds flanking bouquets of flowers. Though rare, such decorations reflect just how thoroughly some Jews had assimilated Roman culture.

PLATE 11. VILLA TORLONIA CATACOMB. An array of ritual objects from the synagogue is depicted on the back wall of this beautifully painted arched niche tomb from the Jewish catacomb of Villa Torlonia. Two seven-branched menorahs with carefully articulated flames flank a cabinet (*aron*) where Torah scrolls are kept (the ends of two rolled scrolls are still visible inside the chest). Above the chest to the right, the sun peeks through the clouds, alongside a star and a moon. Painted beneath the menorahs are (from left to right) a citron (an *etrog*), a knife, a *shofar*, a vase, a pomegranate and a palm branch (*lulav*).

PLATE 12. THREE YOUTHS IN THE FIERY FURNACE. Scenes from well-known biblical stories about faithfulness and divine deliverance in the face of persecution often decorate Christian tombs in Rome. This painting from the Catacomb of Priscilla, for example, depicts the three Hebrew youths, Shadrach, Meshach and Abed-Nego, who were condemned to a fiery death by the Babylonian king Nebuchadnezzar but miraculously survived

unsinged (Daniel 3). Such stories would have resonated with Rome's Christians, who continued to be persecuted until Emperor Constantine issued the Edict of Toleration in 311 C.E.

PLATE 13. MURAL FROM THE DURA-EUROPOS SYNAGOGUE. The walls of the third-century synagogue of Dura-Europos in eastern Syria were covered with biblical scenes painted in al secco (dry fresco). The panel pictured below depicts Elijah's triumph over the priests of Baal in a sacrificial contest (1 Kings 18). In this scene, Elijah's white bull is immediately consumed by flames sent from God, while in the companion scene (not shown), the Canaanite offering remains untouched despite the priests' desperate pleas to Baal. The synagogue's elaborate paintings illustrate well-known stories from the Hebrew Bible and often convey a subtle polemic against pagan religions, but interestingly make no references to Christianity.

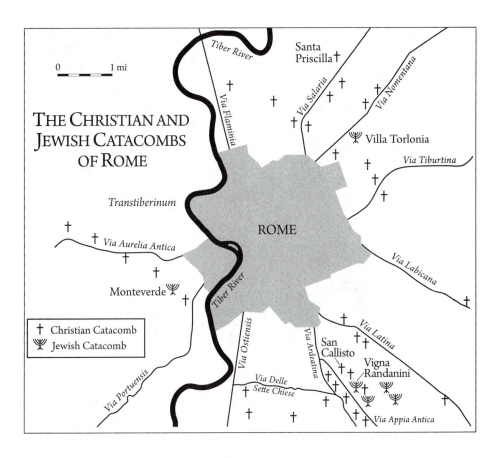

THE CHRISTIAN AND
JEWISH CATACOMBS
OF ROME

0   1 mi

Tiber River

Santa
Priscilla †

Via Salaria

Via Nomentana

Via Flaminia

🕎 Villa Torlonia

Via Tiburtina

Transtiberinum

ROME

Via Aurelia Antica

Via Labicana

Monteverde 🕎

Tiber River

†   Christian Catacomb
🕎   Jewish Catacomb

Via Ostiensis

Via Ardeatina

San
Callisto

Via Latina

Vigna
Randanini

Via Portuensis

*Via Delle
Sette Chiese*

Via Appia Antica

are probably to be dated somewhat later,[114] they are still earlier than the first Christian catacomb, the so-called Callisto, on the Via Appia. Its foundation can be assigned fairly precisely to the turn of the second/ third centuries C.E.[115] Whatever the foundation date of these catacombs, their peak use occurred in the third and fourth centuries C.E., the date generally given to all the material to be considered below.[116]

Common features of Jewish and Christian catacombs

In terms of overall appearance, Jewish and Christian catacombs are very much alike. Both types have the same two basic elements—an extensive network of narrow galleries, the latter cut sometimes on more than one level, and a small number of burial chambers (*cubicula*) leading off from those galleries at right angles. The grave-types, too, are for the most part the same,[117] as is the method for depositing the corpses. In both Jewish

THE BRIDGEMAN ART LIBRARY

CATACOMB OF PRISCILLA. Extensive underground cemeteries (known as catacombs) were the preferred burial places of both Jews and Christians in ancient Rome and have many features in common. The simplest tombs were niches in the catacomb walls, such as the ones shown here from the Catacomb of Priscilla, although wealthier families and high officials carved out larger private burial chambers. In both simple and elaborate burials, a horizontal slot would be cut into the wall for the body. Once the body was placed in the burial niche, or *loculus*, the opening would be sealed with a marble or terracotta slab bearing the name of the deceased and some kind of decoration.

and Christian catacombs the majority of the dead were laid to rest in rectangular, body-sized slots (*loculi*) cut into the gallery walls from floor to ceiling.[118] Once interment had occurred,[119] the *loculi* openings were filled with bricks and rubble and plastered over. In many (but not all) cases, these graves were then provided with some kind of identification—in the case of the poor and destitute, perhaps a fragment of glass, a coin or a shell embedded immediately in the wet plaster; for the better off, an inscribed marble memorial plaque was in due course prepared. A minority of both Jews and Christians, however, might have more costly burials—e.g., arched and frescoed niche tombs (*arcosolia*) holding one or two bodies[120] or elaborately carved marble sarcophagi.[121] Generally these types of grave tend to be found in the *cubicula,* which probably functioned as private family burial chambers, rather than in the galleries.

Differences between Jewish and Christian burials

Although Jewish and Christian catacombs may appear to be similar, closer examination of their contents reveals that the two socio-religious groups using them were very different. The inscriptional and iconographical evidence derived from them reveals that the Jews and Christians of third-to-fourth-century C.E. Rome inhabited entirely different thought worlds. While the Jews were mainly concerned with their conduct in *this* world, especially in relation to the law, the commandments and the synagogue, the principal focus of the Christians was on salvation and the world-to-come. A blissful life in that world was to be their reward for their faithfulness to Christ this side of the grave.

Jewish preoccupations

One striking feature of the approximately 600 surviving Jewish epitaphs from Rome is the comparatively large number of law-related words they contain.[122] The most frequent to occur is *hosios,* a common Greek adjective meaning "holy" but used by Jews as a translation for Hebrew *hesed,* a person notable for his/her exceptionally rigorous observance of the Torah.[123] But also found are several new words deliberately invented to compliment those whose lives had been focused on the law and commandments (in Greek, *nomos* and *entolai,* respectively,)—e.g., *philonomos* (lover of the law) and *philentolos* (lover of the command-ments).[124] Equally highly esteemed was expertise in Torah studies, whence the formulation of the entirely new funerary epithet *nomomathes,* learned in the law.[125] Among the few occupations deemed worthy of record by Rome's Jews were teacher of the law (*nomodidaskalos*)[126] and Torah scholar (*mathetes sophon,* pupil of the sages = *Talmid Hakam*).[127]

Also commanding considerable respect was service to the Jewish community, whether as an officeholder in the synagogue (e.g., *archisyna-gogos,* synagogue ruler) or as a community patron (i.e., mother or father of the synagogue).[128] Large numbers of Jewish males are remembered exclusively for such service and even women are occasionally celebrated in this way—e.g., the elderly, rich proselyte, Veturia Paulla, a convert to Judaism at the age of 70, who used her wealth to support the two Jewish synagogues of which she was the "mother."[129] To demonstrate that the community really appreciated the efforts of such people, another new funerary epithet was devised—*philosynagogos*, friend of the synagogue.[130]

Compared with this abundance of law and synagogue-related material, hard evidence for the Roman Jews' beliefs in respect to the world-to-come is exceedingly sparse. The common formula found at the end of scores of epitaphs, "In peace your sleep," may do no more than express the hope that the body of the deceased remain undisturbed.[131] The term "eternal home," which crops up occasionally as a term for the tomb, hardly suggests great expectations of renewed life in the world-to-come.[132] While it is entirely possible that large numbers of Rome's Jews did believe in resurrection (their fellow Jews at Beth Shearim certainly held such beliefs at that time),*[133] the only surviving evidence for this is the name Anastasios (*anastasis* is the Greek word for resurrection) but even that occurs only a handful of times in their catacomb texts.[134]

So much for the epigraphic evidence for the Jews. What about the iconographic? Given the close relationship that text and image generally enjoy when the two are found together,[135] it should come as no surprise to learn that the iconography of the Jewish catacombs reveals the same preoccupations as the epitaphs. Pictorially, the importance attached to the rigorous observance of the Mosaic law is displayed in the general avoidance of images of living things, as enjoined by the second commandment. The representation of the human figure was, for the most part, shunned. To my knowledge, the only surviving examples are the sculpted form of a young boy on a funerary couch found in the Monteverde catacomb,[136] and the totally unexpected depictions of Victory crowning a youth and Fortuna with her cornucopia on the ceilings of Painted Rooms I and II in the Vigna Randanini catacomb (see Plate 10).[137] Portraiture itself was totally avoided, as the sole surviving Jewish example of a Seasons sarcophagus shows: In the area of the front panel normally reserved for the portrait of the deceased, the Jewish specimen has a finely carved menorah instead.[138]

The centrality of the synagogue to Romano-Jewish identity is also well illustrated by the iconographical evidence. Here synagogal paraphernalia predominate, most commonly the menorah, the *aron* (cabinet for

---

*For Beth Shearim, see Peter Cooper, "The Necropolis of Beth She'arim," sidebar to Steven Fine, "Iconoclasm: Who Defeated This Jewish Art?" *BR*, October 2000.

MENORAH PLAQUE FROM VIGNA RANDANINI. Jewish tombs were typically adorned with murals and carvings depicting symbols from the synagogue and Temple, such as this delicately incised, 12-inch-tall marble plaque from the Vigna Randanini catacomb in Rome. An elegant seven-branched menorah is flanked by other common Jewish motifs, including a curved *shofar* (ram's horn) and *etrog* (citron) on the left and a *lulav* (palm branch), a ceremonial knife (or perhaps incense shovel) and a ritual oil vessel on the right. A now-faded inscription, which presumably gave the deceased's name, is carved within a *tabula ansata* frame above the flames of the candelabra.

the scrolls of the law), the *shofar* (ram's horn trumpet, blown at Rosh Hashanah, the New Year festival), and the *lulav* and *etrog* (the palm branch and citron used during Sukkot, the Feast of Tabernacles).[139] Of these, the menorah is by far the most common, occurring in every conceivable place in every single catacomb—e.g., on the ceilings and walls of *cubicula*; on the arches and back walls of *arcosolia*; on marble funerary plaques and even on otherwise unmarked loculus closures.[140] The forms vary widely (not all have seven branches)[141] and so does the standard of execution—while some are drawn so crudely as to defy definite identification,[142] others are exquisitely rendered, with even the flames from the lamps carefully articulated. While the finest painted examples are found in the Villa Torlonia complex (see Plate 11),[143] the best engraved specimen occurs on a marble plaque from the Vigna Randanini catacomb (see previous page).[144] Much has been written about the possible meanings of the menorah, a debate into which there is no room to enter here.[145] While in some cases it may well have an apotropaic or even an eschatological significance,[146] in many instances, most notably those where the menorah forms a group with other synagogal artifacts,[147] it probably should be seen as no more than that. There can be no doubt that at that period the synagogue was, as indeed it had always been,[148] a crucial element of Romano-Jewish identity.[149]

Christian concerns

When we turn to the epigraphic and iconographic evidence from the Christian catacombs of Rome, we are immediately aware of a different focus. Here what primarily concerns people is not this world but the next. Epigraphically, this is most clearly demonstrated by two things: (1) the immense popularity of the names Anastasios/Anastasia;[150] and (2) the practice of carefully recording the date of death, something that Roman Jews hardly ever did.[151] For Christians, the moment of death was when *real* life began, hence the care with which that critical piece of information was put into the public domain.

Iconographically, too, the Christians reveal their intense focus on the world-to-come in their magnificent frescoes, an art form that they exploited to a much greater extent and to far greater effect than the Jews.[152] Untrammelled by the need to rigorously observe the second commandment, they could illustrate at will Old and New Testament stories that offered clear confirmation of their most cherished beliefs. That the tales of Jonah and of Lazarus were among their favorites is hardly a surprise. Both were perfect illustrations of the virtual certainty of resurrection—Jonah because he had "lived again" after his "entombment" of three days in the belly of the whale,[153] and Lazarus because he had been miraculously restored by Jesus to life.[154]

Despite this emphasis on the world-to-come, the present world was not altogether neglected either pictorially or epigraphically. Until the

Edict of Toleration in 311 C.E., the world in which the Christians were compelled to spend their inferior, earthly life could be an unpredictable and, on occasion, a very frightening place, since refusing to deny the "name of Christian" (i.e., membership in the Christian sect) still remained a capital offense. Although persecution was generally sporadic and usually fairly localized,[155] nonetheless it remained a potential danger for those determined to maintain faith with the Lord Jesus Christ. It was surely the resulting feeling of insecurity that must largely account for the immense popularity with early Christian artists and their patrons of stories such as the Three Youths in the Fiery Furnace (see Plate 12) and Daniel in the Lions' Den. In both these tales, faith in God and resistance to idolatry even in the face of dire punishment from the secular authorities had been rewarded with deliverance.[156] The conviction that divine deliverance would be the ultimate reward of the faithful must, in its turn, account for the high incidence of the epithet *pistos* (faithful) in Christian epitaphs.[157] Just as *hosios* (devout) was the key virtue for Jews, so faithfulness was rated more highly than any other quality by Christians.

Conclusion

The parting of the ways, the separation of Christianity from Judaism, is a contentious issue in modern scholarship. There are scholars who deny that the ways ever parted at all.[158] Whatever happened in the various provinces of the Roman Empire, in Rome itself a separation definitely did take place, probably starting quite early, within 20 years or so of Jesus' death. Initially, the pressures that led to Christianity becoming a separate movement, cut off from its Jewish roots, all came from within the Jewish community itself, as Jew became divided from Jew over the messiahship of Jesus. Subsequently, however, the main drivers of the process were the Roman authorities. Claudius, the three Flavian emperors and Nerva can all be seen to have taken actions that had a significant and destructive impact on Jewish-Christian relations. To all intents and purposes, the break between Jews and Christians at Rome was complete by the early second century C.E., with subsequent events and developments (e.g., the Bar-Kokhba Revolt, the Marcionite rejection of the Old Testament and the evolution of the Christ-cult) only serving to confirm it. The consequence of that break can be seen quite clearly in the third–fourth-century C.E. evidence from the Jewish and Christian catacombs. Here we have two "faith communities" that appear, for all their shared roots, to have very little in common. While the material from the Jewish catacombs reveals remarkably little Christian influence,[159] such Jewish influence as can be seen in the Christian catacombs comes not from contemporary Jews but from Old Testament sources. That this material accurately reflects socio-religious realities cannot be doubted. It reveals two communities with substantially different values and practices—a situation that had come about because their ways had parted such a long time before.[160]

9

Christianity's Rise After Judaism's Demise in Early Egypt

ROBERT A. KRAFT AND ANNEMARIE LUIJENDIJK

VERY LITTLE IS KNOWN ABOUT THE BEGINNINGS OF THE JESUS movement in Egypt, but the separate existence of early Christianity as distinct from Judaism may have been in place from the early second century C.E.[1] This is at least in part because of political circumstances: The violent suppression of Jewish uprisings across Egypt and other parts of North Africa culminating around 117 C.E. led to the near disappearance of Jewish communities in many of these areas and especially in Egypt.[2] Evidence of a Jewish presence in Egypt does not reappear until the third and fourth centuries and beyond.[3] By that time, Christianity was viewed— and viewed itself—as completely independent of its historical parentage in Judaism. Roger Bagnall's 1993 review of the physical evidence, from *Egypt in Late Antiquity*, supports this picture:

A survey of the religious environment in which Christianity's rapid fourth-century growth took place would not be complete without some consideration of Judaism, its earliest matrix and then, as the process of distinction advanced, its rival. The large, active and visible Jewish community of Egypt had been crushed at the beginning of the reign of Hadrian [117–138 C.E.] after a bloody [Jewish] revolt, much if not all of its wealth confiscated. There is no way of estimating the extent of the slaughter and enslavement inflicted on the Jewish community by the Roman authorities, but it was decisive and permanent. Whatever remained is invisible in the documentation ...

Nothing ... suggests that the Jewish communities of Egypt ever recovered the numbers, visibility or Hellenic character by which they were marked before the great revolt [of the early second century C.E.], and from the fifth century on ... the very limited evidence from the cities of the Egyptian *chora* [hinterland, apart from Alexandria] indicates that the small numbers of Jews who lived in them managed to maintain their own community institutions, to keep up close contacts with Palestine, and yet to live routinely if not invisibly in an increasingly Christian civil society.[4]

Nevertheless, Christian traditions complicate the situation in various ways. For example, the extant works of the prolific Jewish author Philo of Alexandria, writing in Greek, who flourished in the mid-first century C.E., were preserved and transmitted *by Christians*, and not by surviving Judaism.[5] Indeed, according to the early-fourth-century Christian tradent, Eusebius of Caesarea, Christian monastics were already known to Philo, as described in Philo's treatment of the community of "Therapeutae" in northern Egypt.[6] Modern scholars have concluded that this identification is false, and that these Therapeutae were Jewish.[7] Eusebius also reports a tradition ("It is said") that Philo met with Peter in Rome, although to what effect relative to our present subject is not clear.[8] Eusebius does not explicitly claim that Philo became Christian or treat him as such.

Still another possibly relevant Christian claim concerns Barnabas, Paul's companion, according to Acts 13–15, and reputed author of the Epistle of Barnabas that is replete with quotations from Jewish scriptures and rife

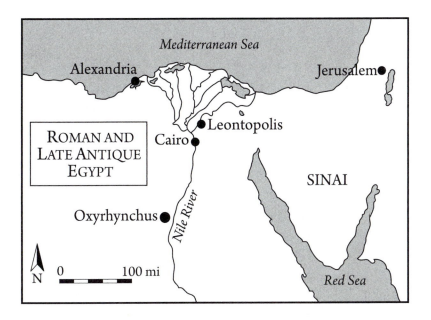

with animosity to Jewish cultic practices.[9] In some traditions, Barnabas is said to have preached in Alexandria[10] (others credit Mark with founding that church[11]). The epistle has sometimes been ascribed to an Alexandrian author and sometimes confused with the New Testament's "Hebrews."[12] If any of this were true, it would provide a strong Jewish background to the Barnabas-type of proto-orthodox Christianity, even if it is a Judaism that is inconsistent with what survived as "classical" Judaism.

It has also been argued that the fragmentary early Christian Gospel According to the Hebrews was a product of Alexandrian Christianity,[13] indicating that "Hebrews" was a self-designation in an early Egyptian *Christian* community.[14] If so, it is perhaps noteworthy that the gospel did not survive to be transmitted in "mainstream" Christian circles except in a few quotations.

Clement and Origen, "Gnosticism"

Knowledge of and sympathy for the sort of Judaism represented especially by Philo are reflected in two of our main early Christian sources firmly associated with Alexandria, namely Clement (c. 200 C.E.)[15] and his successor Origen (early third century). Whether these Christian savants acquired information and texts (e.g., of Philo) directly from Jews in northern Egypt is unknown, although even before Origen relocated to Caesarea on the Mediterranean coast of Roman Palestine, he learned some Hebrew and apparently had consultations with Jewish scholars as he began to prepare his massive edition(s) of the Greek Jewish scriptures and other Christian treatises and commentaries.[16] The presence of "Jewish" traditions in "Gnostic" materials discovered in Egypt may also be relevant to this discussion, but the current state of speculation provides little solid information.[17]

Jews expelled from Alexandria

In the year 414, violence between Jews and Christians in Alexandria led to the expulsion of Jews from that city by its newly appointed Christian bishop Cyril. The origins of the conflict are not clear; it appears that the Alexandrian Jewish community became caught in a power struggle between Cyril and the Roman prefect Orestes.[18] Whatever happened, from Cyril's exegetical writings it is clear that Cyril welcomed an opportunity to expel the Jewish population that by this time had again grown in influence and importance.[19] Already in his first festal epistle in 414 C.E., Cyril lashed out against the Jews, describing them as "being full of all malice ... and bringing forth in themselves every sort of impurity."[20] As the Christian historian Socrates reports, Cyril, in reaction to presumed Jewish violence, "accompanied by an immense crowd of people, going to their synagogues ... took them [the synagogues] away from them, and drove the Jews out of the city, permitting the multitude to plunder their goods. Thus the Jews who had inhabited the city from the time of Alexander the Macedonian were expelled from it, stripped of all they possessed, and dispersed, some in one direction and some in another."[21] The Jewish community of Alexandria never regained its importance or influence.[22]

Archaeological remains

Physical evidence of Jewish presence in Egypt, as earlier noted, is sparse for several generations after the Roman destruction of the Jerusalem Temple in 70 C.E. and especially after the Jewish uprising across North Africa in 117 C.E. Literary sources tell us that a Jewish "temple in exile" was established at Heliopolis (also known as Leontopolis) in Egypt, but it was closed by the Romans in 73 C.E. It is not clear what happened to its adherents and leaders (and library).[23] Similarly with the fate of the

"Jewish quarter" in Alexandria, the Therapeutae settlement along the nearby Mareotic Lake, or any remnants of Philo's family and students, etc. As Bagnall notes in the citation above, "Whatever remained is invisible in the documentation."

Papyrological evidence

Several papyri mention "Jews" or Jewish individuals in various pre-Christian Egyptian locations and connections,[24] and fragments of Jewish texts from pre-Christian times (especially copies of works later included in Greek Jewish scriptures) have survived in Egypt.[25] After the first century C.E., with the growing presence of Christianity in Egypt, it is difficult to know whether Jewish communities and institutions continued to produce "Jewish" materials or whether Christian communities preserved the originally Jewish texts that have survived. With regard to Jewish scriptures (the Christian "Old Testament"), the early adoption by Christians of the codex (book) format for their own special literature complicates matters. Did Jews use only scrolls for scripture, as is commonly supposed, or did Jews in the Roman period and in Egypt also produce scriptural codices? Partly because what became "classical" Judaism favored scrolls for scriptures, at least for liturgical use, Greek fragments of codex materials with Jewish content from the early period are usually assumed to be of Christian origin.[26]

Jews do re-emerge, however, in manuscripts from Egypt,[27] including some texts in Hebrew and/or Aramaic.[28] Some scholars have cited the use of "Jewish" names in the papyri as an indication of a Jewish presence, but as Bagnall and others have pointed out, this is a flawed criterion. "Biblical names" are well attested in Christian contexts quite early, and, on the other hand, it is clear that many Jews in Egypt used typically Greek names, as did Christians (and "pagans") as well.[29] The few instances in the papyri in which someone is identified as "a Jew" are the safest indicators. For instance, a papyrus from the year 400 found in Oxyrhynchus relates that a man named Aurelius Joses, son of Judas, a Jew (*Ioudaios*), leased a ground-floor room and cellar from two nuns, Aurelia Theodora and Aurelia Tauris, daughters of Silvanus.*[30] At least in some Egyptian cities, Jews and Christians continued to live close together—even in the same house.

*For more on Oxyrhynchus, see Stephen J. Patterson, "The Oxyrhynchus Papyri: The Remarkable Discovery You've Probably Never Heard Of," *BAR*, March/April 2011.

OXYRHYNCHUS PAPYRUS. Having largely disappeared from Egypt following the revolts of the early second century C.E., Jewish communities re-emerged along the Nile only centuries later, as evidenced by this papyrus document recovered from the site of Oxyrhynchus in Middle Egypt. Dated to about 400 C.E., the document is a lease in which a Jew named Aurelius Joses, son of Judas, rented a room from two Christian sisters and nuns named Aurelia Theodora and Aurelia Tauris, who owned and lived in the house.

COURTESY THE EGYPT EXPLORATION SOCIETY

The papyri may also indirectly attest Christian animosity to Jews, as expressed in an "anti-Jewish" dialogue scroll fragment from the late third century, according to the original editor, C.H. Roberts. In his view it is an original production (an "autograph"), thus reflecting local Egyptian Christian attitudes.[31] But the fragment's relevance for the present discussion is problematic. Is it actually an autograph from Oxyrhynchus? Is it imitative of a Christian literary trope (see Justin's second-century *Dialogue with Trypho* situated in Asia Minor), rather than reflecting a contemporary situation in Egypt? The answers are unclear.

Finally, the materials in the Cairo Geniza, a vast collection of Jewish documents preserved in a Cairo synagogue,* sometimes reveal tantalizing clues of some sort of relationship between Christians and Jews in

---

*See Molly Dewsnap Meinhardt, "The Twins and the Scholar," *BAR*, September/October 1996; and Raphael Levy, "First 'Dead Sea Scroll' Found in Egypt Fifty Years Before Qumran Discoveries," *BAR*, September/October 1982.

Egypt in late antiquity—e.g., fragments of Origen, Augustine and Syriac Christian materials were reused (palimpsests) for writing Hebrew texts.[32] Possibly when the church building was acquired by Jews and transformed into a synagogue in the ninth century, Christian materials were left in the building and were reused by the new Jewish owners, eventually to become items in the geniza.[33] Alternatively, the Christian texts may simply have been purchased on the Egyptian "used manuscript" market in late antiquity and repurposed by their new Jewish owners.[34] In either case, significant contact between Christians and Jews would be unlikely, and in any event would be much later than any hypothesized "parting of the ways" between them.

Conclusions and suspicions

There is no evidence that in Alexandria or in Egypt generally, "Christianity" gradually or suddenly emerged from a "Jewish" matrix at a particular time and established itself as separate and distinct, alongside a contemporaneous Jewish population. Indeed, the argument has been made that for all practical purposes, Judaism as a public, recognized feature disappeared from the Egyptian scene in the wake of the tensions with Rome that climaxed in the decimation of the Egyptian Jewish community in 117 C.E. While at the individual level such a total purging (through annihilation, enslavement, exile, immigration, assimilation or whatever) may be unlikely, especially outside the urban centers, it could certainly be true as a feature of public life and official Roman-Egyptian policy. By the time "Jews" re-emerge as a recognized group on the public scene in Egypt in the late third century and beyond there would seem to be no confusion of Jews with Christians. The "ways" have certainly "parted" by then, but without the more gradual separation processes that seem to have been present in some other locations.

10

Ebionites and Nazoraeans: Christians or Jews?

MATT A. JACKSON-MCCABE

TO UNDERSTAND HOW CHRISTIANITY AND JUDAISM "BECAME TWO,"
it is helpful to consider more generally the two different ways a new religious
movement might conceptualize its departure from existing options. On
one hand, a group might claim that it represents a better, truer version
of some already existing form of religious identity. Groups that conceive
of themselves in this way lay special claim to some desired name in what
amounts to a competition for an established and esteemed identity. In
such cases the most proximate and troubling "others" are those outside
the immediate group who also want to claim that name. Tensions often
run high, particularly if one or more parties assert an *exclusive* claim to the
name. What might otherwise be simple observations of difference between
competitors can become highly charged recriminations. From a sociological
perspective, group formations of this kind are typically called sects.[1]

   On the other hand, a new religious movement might eschew all
existing options and present itself as an altogether new identity. Social
tensions in movements of this kind can run just as high; societies, after

all, are often especially wary of new religions, as the popular connotations of the term "cult" well illustrate.[2] In this situation, however, the tensions are obviously not between claimants to the same form of cultural identity, but between groups engaged in what they perceive more broadly to be better and worse forms of analogous behaviors—what might be called different forms of religion, not different varieties of *a* religion. Groups of this kind generally compete for the title of the "true religion."

Approaching the historical "partings of the ways" between Christianity and Judaism from this perspective means we must distinguish "parting," on the one hand, in the sense of a group's efforts to limit social interaction with others, from "parting," on the other, as a group's strategy of achieving social differentiation by conceptualizing itself as a new and altogether different type of identity. As applied to the early followers of Jesus, asking "how Judaism and Christianity became two" is less a question of social interaction than of the invention of cultural identities. In what times and places did various Jesus groups come to consider not simply, say, Pharisees and Sadducees, but Jews as such to be an "other," and to substantiate that difference by creating an abstract distinction between "Christianity" and "Judaism"?

Viewing the matter in this light should caution us against looking to some particular moment in time, or even some specific belief or practice, as though it were itself decisive. Given the wide variety of both early Jewish groups and early Jesus groups, and particularly the ongoing tensions one finds among the Jesus groups regarding the question of "Jewishness," there is every reason to think that the creation of "Judaism" and "Christianity" as distinct religions took place unevenly; that even as some Jesus groups in some times and places understood themselves to be engaged in something different from what Jews did, others construed their alignment with Jesus itself to be a claim on Jewish identity.[3] The very self-described orthodox writers who asserted a fundamental and essential difference between "Christianity" and "Judaism" continued for centuries to decry others among them for whom that difference was apparently not so evident.

Two such groups are of particular interest: Ebionites and Nazoraeans. Unfortunately, virtually everything we know about them comes from hostile reports of early catholic writers who dismissed them as heresies. No archaeological evidence can be linked confidently to either group.

Even their literary remains are known only from fragmentary quotations provided by their critics.[4] While this makes recovery of their self-understanding difficult, the evidence strongly suggests that behind these reports lie groups who understood their claims on Jesus to be integral to Jewish identity, not distinct from it.

Ebionites

The nature of the sources

Toward the end of the second century, in his extensive treatise *Against Heresies*, Irenaeus of Lyons (second-century bishop; 130–200 C.E.) gives a brief account of a group he calls Ebionites.[5] After comparing (somewhat ambiguously) their Christological teaching with that of one Cerinthus, Irenaeus proceeds to describe a group with "a Jewish way of life."[6] Not only, he says, do they "practice circumcision [and] persevere in the customs which are according to the Law," but they "ador[e] Jerusalem as if it were the house of God." The group is said to use only the Gospel of Matthew, and to reject Paul as "an apostate from the Law."

Irenaeus's account of the Ebionites is the first among many in subsequent centuries. Where the authors of these reports got their information, however, is not often clear. The source of Irenaeus's knowledge is itself unknown.[7] The development of a rather standard heresiological construction of the group is apparent, based mainly on Irenaeus's account; most reports seem simply to be passing along that tradition—or worse, drawing their own creative inferences from it. Others, most notably church fathers Origen (in the first half of the third century) and Epiphanius (in the late fourth) do seem to provide genuinely independent information. If Origen's reports are generally consistent with Irenaeus's tradition, though, Epiphanius's elaborate account includes a number of elements that stand in uneasy tension with, if not outright contradiction to what had been previously reported. Epiphanius's description, then, represents a special problem, and must be distinguished from the earlier sources. All other reports seem to be more or less derivative of these three (i.e., Irenaeus, Origen and Epiphanius).[8]

Origins and history

One exception, however, concerns Ebion himself, the supposed founder of the group. Irenaeus names no such figure.[9] Origen, with one possible exception, likewise speaks consistently of "Ebionites" as a group rather than of Ebion as a particular teacher.[10] Eusebius, who depends on both Irenaeus and Origen, does the same.[11]

The identification of a founder called Ebion is first found in works that seem otherwise to depend on the tradition associated with Irenaeus, namely Tertullian (c. 160–c. 225[?] C.E.) and Hippolytus (c. 170–236[5?] C.E.).[12] Though this Ebion would eventually become a fixture in the tradition, it is all but certain that no such person ever existed. The notion of a founding teacher called Ebion was in all likelihood merely an extrapolation from the name "Ebionite"—which actually had a quite different derivation—in line with the established heresiological convention of naming competing sects after their supposed originators.[13] Within the rhetoric of heresiology, this convention serves to frame one's competitors as followers of someone *other than* Jesus and the apostles, whom the heresiologist inevitably wishes to claim exclusively for his own group.

It is quite easy to imagine Irenaeus's notice about the Ebionite rejection of Paul as a reflection of the Ebionites's own heresiological rhetoric: framing self-proclaimed orthodox Christian writers like Irenaeus to be merely followers of Paul *rather than* followers of Jesus and the apostles. By the second century, portraying one's own group as the neutral repository of some pristine apostolic tradition while simultaneously countering the analogous claims of one's rivals had become the name of the game.

For Epiphanius, who is our main source of "historical" information about the Ebionites, Ebion figures as a "many-headed" monster who borrowed liberally from all manner of other heretics, taking "any item of preaching from every sect if it was dreadful, lethal and disgusting ... and patterned himself after them all."[14] The origins of the group are traced not to Jesus but to yet another heretical sect, the Nazoraeans, which Epiphanius locates in the region around Pella after the fall of Jerusalem. Ebion is said to have come ("as far as I know," Epiphanius says) from a village in that area called Cocabe, but to have subsequently preached in Asia and Rome.[15]

What we are to make of all this is difficult to say. If Ebion did not exist, specific historical claims about him are obviously untrue as well. Epiphanius's location of the group in Pella, moreover, is apparently based on his knowledge of a story relayed by Eusebius, who mentions neither Ebionites nor Nazoraeans in this connection.[16] The whole story is likely legendary, perhaps developed by some group who sought to establish its own historical link to the original Jerusalem community, and thus assert its own apostolic *bona fides*. (For further discussion, see Chapter IV, "The Christian Flight to Pella? The Archaeological Picture," by Pamela Watson.) No doubt the Ebionites claimed to be apostolic; but whether they did so in the form of this particular story there is simply no way to know.[17] At most, we might take this report to reflect some traditional memory of this or some similar group's presence in the named regions at some time in the past, regardless of how and when they got there.[18]

Clearly the central point Epiphanius wishes to score is that Ebionite ideas derive from anywhere but Jesus and the apostles. Claims of historical derivation are grounded less in concrete information than in the convenience for his polemical agenda. Of particular relevance in the present context, the links drawn between "Ebion," Cerinthus and the Nazoraeans likely grew out of the juxtaposition of Ebionites and Cerinthus in the account of Irenaeus, who was simply comparing Christologies.[19] Epiphanius simply invented a history that linked these suspiciously "Jewish" groups together genealogically.[20] The notion that Ebion belonged to the Nazoraeans is all the more problematic in that no one prior to Epiphanius had ever identified a heresy by that name.[21]

Epiphanius's tendency to turn observations of similarity into claims of historical derivation should also make us quite wary of his reports about subsequent "post-Ebion" developments within the group. The depiction of Ebion as a "monstrosity with many shapes" turns out to be a quite apt characterization of the group more generally as Epiphanius presents it. At the close of his lengthy treatment, he notes that he has already pointed out

> how each one of [the Ebionites] makes a different suggestion about Christ. Ebion himself ... [said that Christ] originated as a mere man from sexual intercourse. But at other times the Ebionites who derive from him say that Christ has a heavenly power from God, "the Son," and that the Son dons Adam and doffs him when convenient.
>
> (Epiphanius, *Panarion* 30.34.6)[22]

Epiphanius observes a similar shift in the Ebionite position on marriage and sexuality, and could just as easily have done the same regarding their whole approach to the Jewish scriptures.[23] In any case, the new information he reports about a divergent Ebionite Christology seems to come not from any report about the Ebionites *per se*, but from texts that Epiphanius himself has decided, for reasons that are not altogether clear, to assign to them. While it is possible that he did so because these were in fact Ebionite texts, it is equally possible that the whole idea of a many-headed heresy, full of internal contradictions that call for speculative historical explanations, is simply a function of Epiphanius's building a portrait of Ebionite doctrine out of texts that were not in fact theirs.[24]

In the end, we must admit that we know next to nothing of the historical circumstances surrounding either the formation of the Ebionite group or their continued evolution and eventual disappearance. If it is tempting to speculate on these matters, speculation, in the final analysis, is really all we have.[25]

Self-understanding

Whatever the group's actual historical origins and development, there can be no doubt that they claimed the same sort of fundamental and ongoing continuity with Jesus and the apostles that writers like Irenaeus and Epiphanius also claimed. A variety of sources indicate that the Ebionites explained their Torah observance in particular by appealing to the example of Jesus.[26] Similarly, the assumption that Torah observance had apostolic authority is implicit in the group's rejection of Paul's apostleship.[27]

But how did such claims translate into the group identity of the Ebionites? Did they, like their catholic rivals, understand their alignment with Jesus and the apostles to mean that they were involved in something other than Jewish piety? How did the group view itself in relation to other forms of collective identity current in its environment, particularly Christian and Jewish ones?

Here again we face a problem similar to and in fact closely related to the one we encountered in connection with the group's historical emergence and evolution: the crucial role played by naming in heresiological rhetoric. A key strategy employed by heresiologists is assigning names to rivals that the rivals themselves do not want. The most obvious example of this is the generic term "heresy." But it also frequently involves assigning them more specific, sectarian names intended to highlight their derivation from someone or something other than Jesus and the apostles.[28] Epiphanius, for example, says that Ebion "is a Samaritan" even while reporting that Ebion "rejects the name with disgust."[29] Conversely, one might also deny to one's rivals a name they *do* want, or one that is at any rate held as a name of esteem by one's own group. "Even today," Epiphanius says elsewhere:

> People call all the sects [*haireseis*], I mean Manichaeans, Marcionites, Gnostics and others, by the common name of "Christians," though they are not Christians. However, although each sect [*hairesis*] has another name, it still allows this one with pleasure, since it is honored by the name.
>
> (Epiphanius, *Panarion* 29.6.6)

Another strategy, finally, is to deny the group any name—and thus any independent significance—at all. Thus again Epiphanius on the many-headed Ebionites: "Since [Ebion] is practically midway between all the sects, he is nothing."[30]

The complex dynamics underlying the heresiological rhetoric of naming significantly complicates recovery of the self-understanding of groups like the Ebionites. From their classification as "heresy," it is clear that our hostile reporters would deny Ebionites the name "Christians." But did the Ebionites even want that name for themselves? Several writers imply that they did. Epiphanius, for example, running through the various traits that "Ebion" shared with other groups says that Ebion "has the Christians' name alone" (and "most certainly not," he hastens to add, "their behaviour, viewpoint and knowledge, and the Gospels' and apostles' agreement as to faith!").[31] Whether this was done simply as a pretense for denying them the name is not entirely clear; but there is no reason to think that the Ebionites rejected the name "Christian" on principle.

What is reasonably clear is that the name "Ebionite" reflects a term of self-identity used by the group. To be sure, the sources are not univocal on the matter. Eusebius presents this as a name of derision given to the group by "the first Christians ... because [the Ebionites] had poor and mean opinions concerning Christ."[32] This account reflects awareness of both the etymological derivation of the name from the Hebrew *ebion*, "poor" or "needy," and the apparently common tradition of mocking that name by giving it a demeaning interpretation.[33] By giving it a demeaning interpretation Eusebius uses one more "naming" strategy in the heresiological arsenal; and the derogation would be all the more effective if the name were actually used by the group.

Epiphanius appears to provide at least one interpretation of the designation offered by the group itself:

> But their boastful claim, if you please, is that they are poor because they sold their possessions in the apostles' time and laid them at the apostles' feet, and have gone over to poverty and renunciation; and thus, they say, they are called "poor" by everyone.
>
> (Epiphanius, *Panarion* 30.17.2)[34]

The fact that Epiphanius feels the need to deny this claim, countering that the name is really derived from their founder Ebion, indicates that it was actually made by the group.[35] Certainly their rivals would have had little reason to supply the group with such a convenient link to the apostles.

A self-designation as the "poor ones," moreover, is anything but surprising for a group with strong ties to Jewish culture. This is a highly charged term in Jewish scriptures, where it is used frequently and in a variety of texts to refer "to those within Israel who are suppressed and oppressed by other Israelites—those who have their legitimate rights taken away from them by the rich and powerful," but who can also, for precisely this reason, expect divine vindication.[36] The term was thus ripe for the picking by dissident Jewish groups who wished to define themselves over-against their more powerful rivals. (The Dead Sea sect did precisely that, identifying themselves as both "the meek" who will "inherit the land" and "the congregation of the poor" [*edat ha-ebionim*] in their commentary on Psalm 37.[37]) Whether or not the first-generation Jesus group in Jerusalem did the same (cf. Galatians 2:10),[38] the complex of ideas was clearly picked up in circles of Jesus' followers, including most notably in texts that arguably reflect a sectarian Jewish outlook.[39]

How then did the Ebionites view themselves in relation to Jews? Whatever their take on the name "Christian"—whether they considered it an honorable self-designation or a tolerable but not preferable term used by outsiders—did they consider their alignment with Jesus and the apostles to be in any way distinct from or extraneous to a Jewish self-understanding? More pointedly, did Jews *per se* represent—as they surely did, say, for Epiphanius—an "other" from the viewpoint of the Ebionites? Or did calling themselves the "poor ones" imply much the same for them as it did for the Dead Sea sect; namely, that they, despite their current lack of power, were in fact the elect of Israel?

We must be wary of reading our sources too naïvely. The uncomfortable fact is that terms like "Jew" and "Jewish" are sometimes intended as slurs in heresiological literature, names with which one saddles opponents in order to demote them.[40] Thus when Pseudo-Tertullian says that Ebion "brings to the fore ... the Law, of course for the purpose of excluding the gospel and vindicating Judaism," we are dealing first and foremost with the heresiologist's own terminology; the extent to which we are also glimpsing language used by the Ebionites themselves is far from clear.[41]

Nonetheless a few pertinent observations can be made. While Irenaeus characterizes the Ebionites somewhat ambiguously with reference to Jewish practices ("a Jewish way of life"), other sources more clearly frame them with reference to Jewish identity. Origen repeatedly uses "Ebionite" as a virtual synonym for "those of the Jews who accepted Jesus as Christ."[42] The same can be said of Eusebius, who equates Ebionites with "those of the Hebrews who believed in Christ."[43]

Moreover, such statements of Jewish identity do not seem to have been applied to the group merely from the outside. Indeed, Epiphanius has Ebion positively "professing to be a Jew." Epiphanius, ever the contrarian, nevertheless feels compelled to deny the group this name—to the point of pronouncing Ebionites as "the opposite of Jews." This suggests strongly that the group did in fact use a "Jewish" designation for themselves.[44] Finally, this does not seem to have been simply a matter of specifying an ethnic derivation as if in some distinction to a pietistic orientation. Origen faults the Ebionites for an all-too "fleshly" interpretation of the Jesus saying, "I was sent only to the lost sheep of the house of Israel" (Matthew 15:24; cf. 10:5–6), complaining (à la Paul) that they fail to recognize that "the children of the flesh are not the children of God."[45] If this is so, one can scarcely imagine that the Ebionites understood Jesus and the apostles to have initiated a movement that was anything other than Jewish. Indeed, if Epiphanius is to be trusted on the point, the Ebionite rejection of Paul included the charge that he was not himself really Jewish, but a Greek— the ultimate "othering" from this perspective.[46]

Taken as a whole, the evidence strongly suggests that these self-described "poor ones," like those at Qumran, represented a dissident Jewish movement, not tradents of a "new religion." Far from an external "add on," their claim on Jesus and the apostles was inextricably bound up with their claim on Jewish identity. If their non-Jewish rivals said that they were followers of Ebion rather than of Jesus, the Ebionites no doubt returned the favor, dismissing these self-proclaimed orthodox Christians as followers not of Jesus and the apostles, but of Paul.

Practice and belief

The practice and discourse emphasized by the Ebionites to differentiate themselves from other Jewish groups are, unfortunately, difficult to reconstruct. The heresiologists on whom we are dependent treat the group with limited knowledge and equally limited interest. To be sure, if one accepts as Ebionite the various texts Epiphanius assigns to the group, our knowledge would expand dramatically, particularly if we took the further step of attributing portions of the extant and extensive Pseudo-Clementine corpus to the group.[47] This is a rather shaky proposition, however, and one that requires the further (albeit not in itself implausible) assumption that the group changed rather dramatically over time. Given this uncertainty (and the constraints of space), I will limit myself in what follows primarily to what can be determined apart from the literature assigned to the group by Epiphanius.

To be sure, what most sticks out about the Ebionites from the heresiologists' viewpoint is their observance of Jewish law and custom[48]—circumcision, dietary restrictions, observance of the Sabbath and other Jewish holidays, as well as special reverence for Jerusalem.[49] None of this is remarkable for a Jewish group seeking to differentiate itself from other Jewish groups. While we might reasonably assume that the Ebionites, like other Jewish groups, instantiated their distinctiveness in particular interpretations of the practices enjoined by the Torah, we can say virtually nothing about what these might have been, as the heresiologists have little interest in nuancing the matter further from a Jewish viewpoint.[50] Eusebius's assertion that the group, in addition to observing the Sabbath, also "on Sundays celebrated rites like ours in commemoration of the Saviour's resurrection"[51] is perhaps more revealing. It is tempting to pair this report with Irenaeus's contrast between his own group's Eucharistic rite and an apparently equivalent Ebionite rite involving only water, not water mixed with wine.[52] The additional observance of a weekly rite commemorating their executed founder's transcendence of death would certainly have served as a regular reinforcement of the group's sense of its difference from other Jews, and perhaps especially their status as the presently powerless and yet inevitably-to-be-vindicated "poor ones."

The other thing about the Ebionites that jumps out at the heresiologists was their appeal to Jesus. Origen, in *Against Celsus*, divides Ebionites into two categories: those who confess "that Jesus was born of a virgin as we do and others who deny this but say that he was born like the other people."[53] In other works Origen simply presents the latter view (that Jesus was born like other people) as the Ebionite one, even explaining their name with reference to the "poverty" of their beliefs about Jesus.[54] Whatever one makes of this claim about two kinds of Ebionites,[55] it is the latter belief that is typically presented without further ado as Ebionite Christology in the early sources. Jesus was said by the Ebionites to be a man like everyone else: not only not divine, but in particular not born to a virgin; Joseph was his actual father.[56] Competing views from rival Jesus groups on this latter point in particular seem to have prompted an argument from the Ebionites regarding the famous passage from Isaiah 7:14 that either appealed to the Hebrew text or at least to a different Greek translation of it in order to show that it doesn't actually refer to a "virgin," but simply to a young woman.[57]

The assertion of the ordinary birth and humanity of Jesus implies that the Ebionites emphasized Jesus' baptism by John as the decisive moment when he came to represent an authority that was distinctly more than human.[58] Beyond this, however, there is little that we can say with confidence.[59] Hippolytus reports a view that Jesus was named "the Christ of God" as a result of the fact that he alone had observed the Torah.[60] Indications that the Ebionites asserted Jesus' Davidic lineage (specifically through Joseph) would seem to confirm that they interpreted him messianically; but what exactly that meant to them is unknown.[61] It is tempting to put this together with the idea of spirit possession occurring at his baptism[62] and suggest that he was viewed as a sort of prophet-king.[63] Even if this is so, how we might fill in that picture, and what sense the Ebionites made of his violent end, is unfortunately unknown. Apart from Irenaeus's notice that the Ebionites considered the world to have been created by the God of Israel, the church fathers have nothing more to say about their view of the world, its history or the human condition in which the Ebionite messiah functioned.[64]

Nazoraeans

The problem of the Nazoraeans

As we have seen, Epiphanius portrays the Ebionites as having grown out of another heretical group called the Nazoraeans. According to Epiphanius, the Nazoraeans seceded from the apostolic community in the days of Mark the Evangelist. Epiphanius says they "were Jewish, were attached to the Law, and had circumcision," differing from (other) Jews only insofar as they had "come to faith in Christ."[65] Epiphanius also emphasizes their use of Hebrew (with respect both to the Jewish scriptures and to their version of the Gospel of Matthew), and locates their contemporary communities "in Beroea near Coelesyria, in the Decapolis near Pella, and in Bashanitis at the place called Cocabe."[66]

No heresiologist before Epiphanius, however, had ever identified a heresy by this name. Jerome, on the other hand, who was personally acquainted with Epiphanius, subsequently makes a number of references to these Nazoraeans.[67] In one passage Jerome closely connects them to the Ebionites—indeed, apparently treating the two names interchangeably.[68] Like Epiphanius, he characterizes them as heretics "who accept Christ in such a way that they do not cease to observe the old Law,"[69] and emphasizes their use of Hebrew, citing several texts (again including a Hebrew version of Matthew) said to be theirs.[70] In contrast to Epiphanius, though, Jerome portrays this "heresy" as being much more widespread. Rather than being limited to a few towns, it is "until now ... to be found in all parts of the East where Jews have their synagogues." Nonetheless, Jerome elsewhere speaks specifically, as Epiphanius had, of a Nazoraean group in Beroea in particular—a fact that is all the more interesting since Jerome had spent some time in that region.[71]

Why references to a Nazoraean "heresy" that had supposedly existed since the first century suddenly appear only in these late-fourth-century works is a question. There is no good reason to think that Epiphanius had any direct knowledge of the group. His report about them is remarkably short on details and at times stereotypical. As in his account of the Ebionites, he makes a number of claims that appear to be little more than his own imaginative attempts to create historical connections where there are none.[72]

The source of Jerome's information, too, is unclear. On the face of it there would seem to be every reason to assume he had some firsthand acquaintance with the group during his stay in Beroea; at least this is the impression he wishes to create. Nonetheless, Jerome shows himself to be if anything even more prone to fabrication than Epiphanius; the various claims he makes have long been received with skepticism.[73] In the end it seems equally if not more likely that whatever knowledge either Jerome or Epiphanius had about a group called Nazoraeans is essentially secondhand.[74]

And, in fact, neither Epiphanius nor Jerome has much to report about the beliefs and practices of these Nazoraeans. Epiphanius speaks generally of their belief that Christ was a "child" or perhaps "servant" (*pais*) of the One God, but is remarkably forthright in confessing that he simply "cannot say" beyond that what sort of Christology they have—including, specifically, whether they share the same view of Jesus as "mere man" that characterizes the other "too Jewish" groups he criticizes.[75] Beyond this he cites only several items that support his claim that "they have no different ideas" than what Jews generally teach, namely resurrection of the dead, "the divine creation of all things" and the oneness of God.[76] Jerome, on the other hand, asserts quite explicitly that the Nazoraeans have a Christology much like his own: "They believe in Christ, the Son of God born of Mary the virgin, and they say about him that he suffered and rose again under Pontius Pilate, in whom we also believe."[77]

As has often been noted, the end result is a "heresy" about which Epiphanius and Jerome have little to critique beyond its observance of Jewish law. Even here, however, neither seems to have much real knowledge of what such adherence might mean in practice. Epiphanius gives no specifics beyond a rather stereotyped reference to "circumcision, Sabbath, and the rest."[78] Jerome doesn't even tell us this much. It is clear that the Isaiah commentary Jerome attributes to Nazoraeans utterly rejects rabbinic *halakhah* (see below); but the specific legal interpretations it advocates as an alternative, unfortunately, receive no mention.[79] The fact that this commentary explicitly endorses Paul and his mission, moreover, suggests that gentile members of the movement were accepted as such, and not considered subject to the law in any case.[80]

Complicating matters further, both Epiphanius and Jerome sometimes conflate equivalents of the term "Nazoraean" used of followers of Jesus generally in Syriac- and Aramaic-speaking regions with the name of a distinct "heresy." The more general usage, as both Epiphanius and Jerome are well aware, is reflected as early as Luke-Acts (Acts 24:5),[81] and it is also assumed by Jerome to be a current Jewish usage of the term based on the *Birkat ha-Minim*: "Until today in their synagogues they blaspheme the Christian people under the name Nazoraeans."[82] Epiphanius, on the other hand, interprets the *Birkat ha-Minim* with specific reference to a "Nazoraean" heresy.[83] When Jerome, then, in another passage, alludes to the *Birkat ha-Minim* while claiming that the Nazoraean heresy is found "in all parts of the East where Jews have their synagogues," it seems likely that the more general usage is once again being conflated with the name of a supposed heresy.[84]

What are we to make of all this? One possibility is that Jerome, having concrete knowledge of a distinct, localized (Beroean?) sect called Nazoraeans, infers from the *Birkat ha-Minim* that they are actually to be found all over the East, wherever there are synagogues. The other possibility is that the whole notion of a well-defined sect of "Nazoraeans" is ultimately the product of Epiphanius's—and, subsequently, Jerome's—heresiological imagination. Finding the language and culture of Jesus groups in the East suspiciously "Jewish," and aware that "Nazoraean" was a common usage there, Epiphanius and Jerome may have creatively combined disparate bits of information—the first-generation use of the term in Acts; reports of the *Birkat ha-Minim*; the existence of another "too Jewish" group called Ebionites—in order to effectively conjure into existence a Nazoraean "heresy" that allowed them to more clearly demarcate their own "orthodox" Christianity from Judaism.[85]

"Nazoraean" self-understanding?

The preceding considerations complicate the question of Nazoraean self-understanding. If in fact there is no good reason to assume that "a more or less organized faction with borders defined by characteristically 'Nazarene' doctrines, practices or self-understanding, distinct from other Syriac/Aramaic-speaking Christians" lies behind these reports,[86] the question of "Nazoraean" self-understanding is simply another way of asking about the various constructions of identity found among followers of Jesus in the East in late antiquity. (For further discussion, see Chapter VI, "Christianity in Antioch: Partings in Roman Syria," by Annette Yoshiko Reed and Lily Vuong.)

Even if we do assume the existence of a distinct (Beroean?) group of

Nazoraeans, though, the names used by Epiphanius and Jerome to label it are so bound up in their own apologetic rhetoric as to be all but useless for reconstructing the group's self-understanding. Jerome, for example, says that "since [the Nazoraeans] want to be both Jews and Christians, they are neither Jews nor Christians."[87] While this might seem to suggest that the group laid claim to both names, the main thing we learn from this passage is what *Jerome* thinks—that "Jew" and "Christian" are incompatible categories; and that groups, like the Nazoraeans, who can't be placed neatly into his taxonomy are in effect nothing at all.[88]

Epiphanius creates a rather different impression of the group's self-understanding:

> [T]hese sectarians [Nazoraeans] whom I am now sketching disregarded the name of Jesus, and did not call themselves Jessaeans, keep the name of Jews, or term themselves Christians—but "Nazoraeans," from the place name, "Nazareth," if you please!
>
> (Epiphanius, *Panarion* 29.7.1)[89]

The implication here is that the group chose the name "Nazoraean" in deliberate contrast to both "Jew" and "Christian." Once again, if this might seem at first glance to provide clear evidence for their self-definition, none of it can be taken at face value. The point of emphasizing their deliberate choice of the name "Nazoraean" over "Christian" is precisely to draw a historical wedge between this "heresy" and the apostolic community that, according to Acts, was at one time called by the same name (Nazarenes)—an apostolic community whose legacy Epiphanius wishes to claim exclusively for his own group. Before becoming known as Christians, he tells us, the apostles preferred to call themselves "disciples of Jesus ... as indeed they were," while merely tolerating the name "Nazoraean" when called this by outsiders (here alluding to Acts 24:5). In contrast, the "heretical" group, which he portrays as having "seceded" from the apostolic community, deliberately chose the name "Nazoraean" in blatant disregard for the name of Jesus![90]

A different dynamic is brought to bear when Epiphanius uses the designation "Jew." Here the strategy is to classify the group with a term they presumably do not want. According to Epiphanius, even if the group prefers to call themselves Nazoraeans, "they are simply complete

Jews"—which is to say, for him, *not* Christians.[91] Almost everything Epiphanius tells us about Nazoraean beliefs and practices follows directly on this claim, and is designed precisely to support it:

> They [the Nazoraeans] use not only the New Testament but the Old Testament as well, as the Jews do ... They have no different ideas, but confess everything exactly as the Law proclaims it and in the Jewish fashion—except for their belief in Christ, if you please! For they acknowledge both the resurrection of the dead and the divine creation of all things, and declare that God is one ... [The Jewish scriptures] are read in Hebrew, as they surely are by Jews ...
>
> (Epiphanius, *Panarion* 29.7.2–4)[92]

In short, where Jerome treats "Jew" as a name to which the group laid claim in order to deny it to them, Epiphanius frames it as a name they didn't want in order to saddle them with it.

More potentially productive are the fragments of "Nazoraean" works cited by Jerome. Jerome's quotations from an exegetical work on Isaiah preserved in his commentary on the same are particularly illuminating.[93] The text, composed in Hebrew or Aramaic, was apparently produced no earlier than the late second century.[94] Whether actually representative of a distinctly "Nazoraean" sect or not, the fragments provide a more direct glimpse of the self-understanding of the kind of group Jerome had in mind when writing about Nazoraeans.[95]

Most important in this respect is the fragments' running polemic against the rabbis, who are styled "the Scribes and Pharisees."[96] An interpretation of Isaiah 8:11–15 identifies Shammai and Hillel as the founders of these "Scribes and Pharisees." Derisive Hebrew puns on their names portray them as a "scatterer" and an "unholy" one, whose invented "traditions and *deuterôseis*"[97] "scattered and defiled the prescripts of the Law."[98] In what amounts to its own heresiological genealogy, the text proceeds to construct a (confused) line of descent from Hillel and Shammai to, among others, Yoḥanan ben Zakkai, Rabbi Akiva and Rabbi Meir in order to frame the rabbis as the present-day legatees of deviant, perverting traditions that the text elsewhere equates with magic and idolatry.[99]

Not surprisingly, the significance of Jesus is correlated directly with the traditions of Shammai and Hillel—whom, it is noted, "were born not long before the Lord."[100] Isaiah 9:1–4 is interpreted with reference to the coming of Christ precisely to free "Zebulon and Naphtali"—here, apparently, taken to represent the land of Israel more generally—"from the errors of the Scribes and Pharisees."[101] This is understood to represent the first step in what is ultimately a program to liberate the entire world from idolatry—a program, according to the text, that was carried forward by Paul in particular:

> Later ... the preaching was multiplied, through the Gospel of the apostle Paul ... And the Gospel of Christ shone to the most distant tribes ... Finally the whole world, which earlier walked or sat in darkness and was imprisoned in the bonds of idolatry and death, has seen the clear light of the Gospel.
>
> (Jerome, *Commentary on Isaiah* 9.1)

Here the "othering" of the rabbis is accomplished by a quite remarkable correlation of their traditions with gentile practices under the broad heading of idolatry.

It is clear from this passage that the "Nazoraeans" of these fragments aligned themselves with the larger Jesus movement that extended beyond Jewish society and indeed throughout "the whole world." But did these fragments view this movement as a "new religion"? Or did it simply think that gentiles, at last, were turning to the God of Israel as the prophets had long predicted?

There is only one passage that might suggest that these "Nazoraeans," like Epiphanius and Jerome, understood themselves to be involved in something other than Judaism. Jerome's rendering of the fragment on Isaiah 9:1 equates "the errors of the Scribes and Pharisees" with "the very heavy yoke of the Jewish traditions [*grauissimum traditionum Iudaicarum iugum*]." This equation suggests at minimum a certain ambivalence about the term "Jewish," if not an outright disavowal of it. Such usage, however, is entirely peculiar in the fragments, which otherwise consistently identify their primary "other" specifically as "Scribes and Pharisees," not Jews as such. One cannot help but wonder, then, whether this singular use of the term "Jewish" might not represent Jerome's interpretive Latin rendering rather than the actual wording of the source.

In fact it is otherwise clear that it is not "the Jews" as a whole but the rabbinic leaders in particular who represent most the proximate, and for that reason most distressing, "other" from the point of view of the fragments. If Christ came first to liberate Israel from the traditions of these "Scribes and Pharisees," Hillel and Shammai—their founders, as the text understands it—are identified explicitly as the specific "two houses [cf. Isaiah 8:14] that did not accept the Savior."[102] Subsequently, the "Scribes and Pharisees" are those "who earlier deceived the people ... [who] watch[ed] day and night to deceive the simple ones, who made men sin against the Word of God in order that they should deny that Christ was the Son of God."[103] This is not merely some decisive parting in the distant past, but an ongoing, immediate problem in the here and now: "*When the Scribes and Pharisees tell you to listen to them*," one fragment says, "you must answer them like this: 'It is not strange if you follow your traditions since every tribe consults its own idol.'"[104] The group saw itself in continued competition with the rabbis for the hearts and minds of those "simple ones" of "the people":

> O Sons of Israel, who deny the Son of God with a most vicious opinion, turn to him and his apostles. For if you do this, you will reject all idols which to you were the cause of sin in the past, and the devil will fall before you.
>
> (Jerome, *Commentary on Isaiah* 31.6–9; cf. 29.17–21)

The impression of the "Nazoraeans" we get from their interpretation of Isaiah is thus of a minority group attempting to resist rabbinic claims of authority within a Jewish social setting. The fragments construct a genealogy of the Scribes and Pharisees that functions as a *Jewish* heresiology. Rabbinic traditions are traced back to corrupting deviations by a pair of teachers (Hillel and Shammai) whose practices are said to have diverted the people from the true, original demands of the law. The implicit claim is that the teaching of Jesus—and more to the point, of the group insofar as it stands in continuity with him—represents that supposed true original from which the rabbis deviated. The "Nazoraeans'" own minority status among "the people" is explained by appealing to the rabbis' ongoing efforts to deceive "the simple," and the group holds out hope that it may yet prevail. In sum, what we seem to have here is not the rhetoric of a "new religion," but of a Jewish sect—albeit one that accepted Paul's spread of Jesus-veneration into the gentile world as a positive development.

Conclusion

Long after the first followers of Jesus came to believe that their crucified leader had been brought back to life; after Paul of Tarsus and others began to create gentile Jesus groups that did not think of themselves as Jews; after the Roman destruction of the Temple in 70 C.E. and the Bar-Kokhba rebellion (the Second Jewish Revolt, 132–135 C.E.); after many Jesus groups had effectively created a new religion by asserting an identity for themselves, "Christianity," that they said was essentially different from all other existing options in their world and from "Judaism" in particular; after all this, still other Jesus groups understood their alignment with Jesus and the apostles to be integral to their Jewish identity, not distinct from it. The historical and social realities underlying the heresiological reports about Ebionites and Nazoraeans are unfortunately largely lost to view. Like all Jesus groups, both undoubtedly drew a direct, unbroken line between themselves and Jesus—and denied this claim of their rivals. Whatever they may have made of the ever-expanding gentile Jesus movement and its discourse about "Christianity," neither the Ebionites nor the group behind the "Nazoraean" interpretation of Isaiah seem to have understood themselves to have been engaged in anything other than Jewish piety. However much the very real tensions between themselves and other Jews may have limited social interaction, the Ebionites and "Nazoraeans" did not interpret these tensions as a clash of different religions so much as one between better and worse forms of leadership within the Jewish community.

The presence of such groups throughout antiquity underscores the fact that Judaism and Christianity became two neither as a consequence of some single, finally decisive event, nor as the inevitable result of inexorable inner forces of essentially different religions. Indeed, the interpretation of historical events and the very notion that there are such essential, static realities underlying the terms "Judaism" and "Christianity" are themselves part of the ongoing rhetoric of Jewish and Christian identity. "Religions" do not part ways with each other as much as particular groups of people do.

11

In Between: Jewish-Christians and the Curse of the Heretics

SHAYE J.D. COHEN

JESUS WAS A JEW, BORN IN GALILEE. LIKE MOST OF THE OTHER inhabitants of the Roman province of Judea, he worshiped the God whose temple was in Jerusalem. Not only was Jesus a Jew, but so were all of his disciples ("apostles"), all those who gathered to witness his miracles or hear his words ("crowds"), and so were almost all those who benefited from his miraculous cures. As "king of the Jews" (perhaps "king of the Judeans" would be better), he was sentenced to death by the Romans. After his death his followers, all of whom were Jews like Jesus himself, constituted a Jewish movement, perhaps a sect, meeting and praying regularly in the Temple of Jerusalem and interacting with other Jewish worshipers. (At least this is the story in the opening chapters of the New Testament's Book of Acts.) And yet before very long the Jesus movement was no longer Jewish; it became something different, a social phenomenon of its own. This division, often called "the separation of Christianity from Judaism," or "the parting of the ways,"[1] my subject here, is the period from about 100 to 150 C.E. I do not discuss the first century C.E. or the period of the New Testament, discussed elsewhere in this volume.

First, let me be explicit about the methodological foundations on which this discussion rests. Some of these foundations are contested by scholars, as indicated in the notes.

• The parting of the ways is about people, societies and institutions, not about disembodied truth claims or the abstractions "Judaism" and "Christianity."[2]

• No doubt arguments between Jews and Christians about theological topics, such as the oneness of God, the place of angels and other intermediaries in the cosmic order, the nature of the Messiah, and the like, contributed to the social separation of the two groups, but the conflicting views in and of themselves have no necessary connection with the parting of the ways, unless we can demonstrate that such social separation was caused by a particular theological dispute.[3]

• The parting of the ways involves people whom we call "Jews" and "Christians," even if our ancient sources do not always use these labels. Rabbinic texts, for example, never use the term "Judaism" and never refer to the collectivity of Israel as "Jews." Justin Martyr's *Dialogue with Trypho* never uses the term "Christianity." Nevertheless, for the sake of convenience and clarity I shall continue to use these terms.

• The notion of "the parting of the ways" does not in the least suggest that Jews and Christians stopped speaking with each other, arguing with each other and influencing each other. Christian literature of the first centuries C.E. bears many signs of reaction to Jewish truth claims, and, if we believe modern scholarship, Jewish (rabbinic) literature of the first centuries C.E. bears many signs of reaction to Christian truth claims, but such reactions in and of themselves neither prove nor disprove a parting of the ways. They prove only that Jews and Christians continued to speak with each other.[4]

• There was no parting of the ways between gentile Christians and non-Christian Jews for the simple reason that their ways had never been united. Even the most Hellenized of Jews (e.g., Philo of Alexandria) belonged to Jewish communities that were socially distinct from "the Greeks," no matter how well these Jews spoke Greek, knew Greek literature, and assimilated Greek culture high and low. "God-fearing" gentiles may have associated themselves in some way with synagogues and other Jewish communal institutions, but unless they became proselytes ("converts") they were not members.*[5] A non-Christian Jewish community that admitted Jews and non-Jews alike, without prejudice and (in the case of males) without circumcision, is nowhere attested in antiquity.[6] So, for gentiles who believed in Christ and for Jews who did not, there was no need for a parting of the ways, even if there was a need on occasion for polemic, apologetic and recrimination. As we shall see, both the Romans and the gentile Christians of the early second century C.E., if not earlier, knew that the social space of Christians was separate from that of Jews. In spite of all this, I shall continue to use the phrase "parting of the ways" as a convenient shorthand to refer to the attitudes, institutions, beliefs and practices that attest the separateness of Jewish and Christian identities.

• Jewish believers-in-Christ had a choice: They could join the emerging Christian communities that were being populated more and more by gentile Christians; or they could try to maintain their place within Jewish society, a stance that would become harder and harder to maintain as the decades went by; or, if they were uncomfortable among non-Jewish Christians and non-Christian Jews, they could try to maintain their own communities, separate from each of the others. In various passages, the New Testament shows that in the first century C.E. the first of these possibilities was the norm; Jewish-Christians and gentile Christians were alike members of the newly created Christian communities. But as these communities became more and more gentile, and more and more hostile to non-Christian Jews (see below), their ethnically Jewish members had to decide if they were prepared to remain, at the cost of their Jewish identity, or if they preferred to maintain their position within the Jewish community,

---

*The distinction is apparent in the famous Aphrodisias inscription (see Angelos Chaniotis, "Godfearers in the City of Love," *BAR*, May/June 2010). This inscription (see p. 67) was set up long after the period under review in this essay (mid- to late fourth century), but I would argue that the social situation assumed by the text obtained centuries earlier as well.

or, if that was now impossible, to occupy a separate and interstitial space between gentile Christians and non-Christian Jews. Here, then, was a real parting of the ways, as Jewish-Christians had to negotiate their way between Jewish and Christian communities. Unfortunately many aspects of this story are hidden from us; the facts are few and far between, and the scholarly conjectures are many.[7] I shall discuss here the earliest rabbinic evidence on the relations between the rabbinic Jewish community and Jewish believers-in-Jesus.

• The parting of the ways between Jews and Christians also involves a third party, the Romans, with whom I begin my survey of the evidence.

Romans

By the early second century C.E. and consistently thereafter the Romans regarded Christians as not-Jews and Jews as not-Christians. This is seen most clearly in the persecutions. Throughout the second and third centuries C.E. the Romans persecuted Christians. Many Christians were arrested and tried; some were released after negotiating an arrangement with the prosecutor, but others were condemned and martyred. For the most part these were local persecutions, affecting the Christians of specific times and places; the persecutions under the emperor Decius in the middle of the third century and under Diocletian at the beginning of the fourth century were the only sustained empire-wide assaults on Christianity mounted by the Romans. The story of Christian martyrs has been told many times.[8] What is important for our purposes is the fact that the persecutions did not affect the Jews. Christians were arrested, not Jews. Christians were tried, not Jews. Christians were martyred, not Jews. In fact, by the middle of the second century C.E. Christian writers regularly accuse the Jews of assisting, or even goading, the Romans in their persecutorial activities.[9] At least one case is attested of a Christian converting to Judaism in order to escape persecution.[10] In other words, in the eyes of the Romans, Christians were not Jews, and Jews were not Christians. The two communities were separate.

This is confirmed, too, by the opposite case: When the Roman Empire persecuted Jews it ignored Christians. Simeon Bar-Kokhba (bar Kosba or bar Koziva) led a rebellion against the Romans in Judea in 132–135 C.E.; as either cause of, or response to, the rebellion, the Romans launched a persecution against Jewish observances. There is substantial scholarly debate about this persecution, some maximizing, others minimizing, its course and extent.[11] In any case, whatever the details may be, in connection with this war rabbinic literature records the martyrdom of a number of distinguished sages, the most famous being Rabbi Akiva. Christian texts accuse Bar-Kokhba of persecuting the (Jewish) Christians of Judea; since Bar-Kokhba had messianic pretensions, he could not abide the messianic claims of another.[12] In any event, the Romans paid no attention to the Christians in this war. In the eyes of the Romans, Jews and Christians constituted separate communities.[13]

In a recent book, Marius Heemstra argues that the Roman administration of the *fiscus Judaicus* played an important role in the parting of the ways.*[14] The *fiscus Judaicus* was a tax imposed on the Jews of the Roman Empire by the emperor Vespasian in the early 70s C.E. (For further discussion, see Chapter VIII, "Jews and Christians at Rome: An Early Parting of the Ways," by Margaret H. Williams.) Whereas formerly the Jews had sent a half-shekel (two drachmas) annually to the Temple of Jerusalem, now, after the destruction of that temple, they were required to send that same amount to the temple of Jupiter Capitolinus in Rome, which had been badly damaged by fire and was in need of repair and restoration. Vespasian did not concern himself about which Jews exactly would be liable for the new tax. His son Domitian (ruled 81–96 C.E.), however, administered the tax "harshly," trying to impose it upon two classes of individuals who had escaped the tax up to that point: those who lived a Jewish life without publicly acknowledging the fact, and those who concealed their Jewish origins. These two groups, says Suetonius, the famous biographer of the emperors and our main source, were now expected to pay the Jewish tax.[15] There has been much scholarly debate about the interpretation of these two categories. Heemstra argues that the first category includes gentile Christians (who lived a Jewish life without publicly acknowledging the fact) and the second includes Jewish-Christians (ethnic Jews who concealed their Jewish origins). In other words, under Domitian the Romans regarded both gentile Christianity and Jewish-Christianity as forms of Judaism; hence both gentile Christians and Jewish-Christians were liable for the tax.

*See my review, "Persecuting Jews and Christians," *BAR*, November/December 2012.

Domitian's exactions were unpopular in Rome. In 96 C.E. his successor Nerva immediately set about reforming the administration of the *fiscus Judaicus*, even issuing a coin celebrating this reform (see p. 166).* The essential part of the reform was to redefine Judaism as a religion; in the words of a Roman historian of the early third century C.E., only those "Jews who continued to observe their ancestral customs" would be liable to the tax. Christianity was now seen by the Romans as not-Judaism; the *fiscus Judaicus* applied to neither gentile Christians nor Jewish-Christians. One consequence of this fateful step is that Christians lost the legal protections that Jews had enjoyed for decades under Roman rule.

There are many uncertainties and debatable points in this reconstruction but at least it confirms the basic point that by the early second century C.E., Christianity—even Jewish-Christianity—became in Roman eyes a new thing separate from Judaism. Whether Roman perception in turn affected Jewish and/or Christian self-definition, or whether Jewish and/or Christian self-definition helped shape the Roman perception—these possibilities still require scholarly investigation.

Christians

Christian literature from c. 100 to 150 C.E. is uniformly hostile to Jews and Judaism.[16] Here is a brief survey of the main references.[17] The *Didache* (c. 100 C.E.) contains much material of Jewish origin, but the only time that the author alludes to Jews is the passage in which he calls them "hypocrites" and encourages his audience, "Do not let your fasts coincide with those of the hypocrites. They fast on Monday and Thursday, so you must fast on Wednesday and Friday" (*Didache* 8). Ignatius writes (c. 110–120 C.E.) that "if we continue to live in accordance with Judaism, we admit that we have not received grace" (*Magnesians* 8:1), and "it is absurd to profess Jesus Christ and to Judaize" (*Magnesians* 10:3), and "if anyone expounds Judaism to you, do not listen to him" (*Philadelphians* 6:1). For Ignatius, "Christianity" (a term that appears here for the first time) contrasts with "Judaism" (*Magnesians* 10:3; *Philadelphians* 6:1).[18] The Epistle of Barnabas (c. 130 C.E.) argues that Christians properly understand the Hebrew scriptures, especially the laws of the Torah, while "they" do not (2:7, 3:6, 8:7, 10:12). "They" are the Jews, also called "the

---

*See Schlomo Moussaieff, "The 'New Cleopatra' and the Jewish Tax," *BAR*, January/February 2010.

former people," in contrast with Christians who are "this people" (13:1); "they" received the covenant but were not worthy, therefore "we" have received it (14:1,4,5). The *Martyrdom of Polycarp* (c. 160 C.E.) posits that Jews aid the Romans in persecuting Christians.[19] According to the Epistle to Diognetus (c. 190 C.E., perhaps earlier), "Christians are right to keep their distance from the common silliness and deception and fussiness and pride of the Jews" (4:6); the Jews fault the Christians as "gentiles" (5:17, literally "of a different stock").

The two main anti-Jewish texts of the second century are the *Dialogue with Trypho* by Justin Martyr (c. 160 C.E., set in Ephesus, perhaps written in Rome), and *On the Pascha* by Melito of Sardis (c. 170 C.E.). These works are too long and too rich to be discussed here in any detail so I merely touch upon the highlights. The main argument of the *Dialogue with Trypho* is that the Bible (Justin is referring to the Hebrew Bible, the Old Testament, as there is no New Testament yet) belongs to us Christians, not the Jews, because we read it and understand it, while the Jews read it and do not understand it. Barnabas makes the same point, but Justin is much longer and much more detailed. The argument is developed around three themes: Christ is the new law, replacing the old law of the Jews that need not be observed; Christ is the promised Messiah, fulfilling the biblical prophecies; Christians are the new Israel, taking the place of the Jews, the old Israel.[20]

Melito's *On the Pascha* is a different sort of work entirely. Probably a sermon delivered to a Christian congregation in the Paschal (Easter) season, it develops the idea (first attested in Paul and the Gospel of John) that Christ is the Paschal lamb. By happy coincidence the Greek word *pascha*, "suffering," sounds like *pesah*, the Hebrew word for Passover. Christ is the slaughtered lamb who suffers, whose death brings about forgiveness and salvation for his people. For Melito, Christ the slaughtered Paschal lamb is also God and Lord. Melito draws the logical conclusion: The Jews (whom Melito calls "Israel") have murdered God, with the result that Israel itself now "lies dead," rejected by God. Melito has been called "the poet of deicide," since his is the earliest work to develop this theme.[21] Melito was probably a Quartodeciman, that is, a Christian who celebrates Easter (Pascha) on the 14th of the first lunar month of the spring, precisely when the Jews begin their celebration of Passover (Pesah). For other Christians, Easter is celebrated on Sunday, marking

Christ's resurrection; for the Quartodecimans, the Pascha is celebrated on whatever day of the week is the 14th of the month, marking Christ's redemptive suffering on the cross. Even though, or perhaps because, the practice of the Quartodecimans is close to Jewish usage, they were hardly close to Jews or Judaism, as Melito's invective shows.*

Scholars have long debated whether the anti-Judaism of these texts is the result of social competition between Jews and Christians, each side eagerly trying to win over converts, or whether it is a function of internal Christian self-definition, as the Christians of the second century C.E. tried to sort out exactly what Christianity was and what Christianity was not. Thus, for example, the intended audience of Justin's *Dialogue with Trypho* has been much discussed. At first glance, the book appears to be directed to a Jewish audience, as Justin tries to win over Trypho the Jew, and with him all Jewish readers. But the text also contains many signs that its primary function is to establish the proper limits of Christianity, to teach its readers how Christianity differs from Judaism. And some scholars have argued that Justin's target audience consists of Greeks who are thinking about converting to Judaism and becoming "proselytes." Justin is trying hard to convince them that Christianity, not Judaism, is the true fulfillment of the Hebrew scriptures, and that they should therefore convert to Christianity, not Judaism.[22] In any case, no matter how this question is answered, the anti-Jewish stance of virtually all early Christian texts shows that these authors understand Christianity to be not-Judaism. These authors assume that Jews and Christians inhabit separate communities. The texts regularly assert that Christians constitute a new people alongside pagans ("Greeks") and Jews, a people that is both old and new, old in that it fulfills the prophecies of scripture and new in that it replaces the old Israel.[23] There is no evidence in any of these texts—or anywhere else in antiquity, for that matter—for the existence of a community, whether Jewish or Christian, that included on equal terms gentile believers-in-Christ, Jewish believers-in-Christ and Jewish non-believers-in-Christ. In other words, these texts assume that Jews and Christians inhabit separate social spaces, each with its own leadership and membership.[24]

Justin adds more. He claims to know the reaction of the Jewish community to the spread of Christianity:

*See Samuele Bacchiocchi, "How It Came About: From Saturday to Sunday," *BAR*, September/October 1978.

> You [Jews] not only refused to repent after you learned that he [Jesus] arose from the dead, but, as I stated above, you chose certain men by vote and sent them throughout the whole civilized world, proclaiming that "a godless and lawless sect had been started by a deceiver, one Jesus of Galilee, whom we nailed to the cross, but whose body, after it was taken from the cross, was stolen at night from the tomb by his disciples, who now deceive men by affirming that he has risen from the dead and ascended into heaven"; and accusing him of having taught those godless, lawless and unholy things, of which to every nation you accuse all those who acknowledge him as their Christ, their Teacher and the Son of God. And, in addition to this, even now, after your city has been seized and your whole country ravaged, you not only refuse to repent, but you defiantly curse him and all those who believe in him.
>
> (Justin Martyr, *Dialogue with Trypho* 108.2–3)[25]

Justin here makes two claims. First, shortly after Jesus died, the authorities of Jerusalem[26] selected emissaries to travel throughout the civilized world to make known to Jews[27] the falsehood of Christianity, specifically, the falsehood of the story of Jesus' resurrection. The messengers accuse Jesus of having been a "deceiver,"[28] whose ultimate act of deception was carried out by his disciples. They stole his body and then spread the false story of his resurrection. Matthew (27:62–66, 28:11–15) knows the stolen-body story and attributes it to the chief priests, Pharisees and elders; Justin adds the universal messengers, the reference to the "godless and lawless sect," the accusation of obscene behavior ("godless, lawless and unholy things"), and the acknowledgment that "we" Jews (without any mention of the Romans!) crucified Jesus.[29] Second, even now, Justin says, after the city has been seized and the land ravaged in the war of Bar-Kokhba (132–135 C.E.), the Jews persist in cursing him and all those who believe in him.

Scholars debate the reliability of these two claims. Justin's claim that the Judean authorities sent out anti-Christian messengers throughout the Roman Empire is of a piece with the claim in the Book of Acts (9:1–2, 22:5) that the high priest commissioned Paul (via "epistles") to travel from Jerusalem to Damascus and to arrest there any followers of Jesus.[30]

Some scholars accept the fundamental historicity of these reports, but I (and many others) do not, because I find it impossible to believe that the office of the Jerusalem high priest commanded sufficient support and exerted sufficient authority so as to be able to control, or even attempt to control, Jewish religious life in the Diaspora. The high priest could not control Jewish religious life in Judea, so how could he control Jewish religious life in the Diaspora? It is more likely that Justin's report of the anti-Christian messengers (I leave aside the report of Acts) is a Christian invention, spun out from the Christian interpretation of various biblical verses that highlight the Jewish rejection of Jesus.[31] The claim that the Jews "even now" curse Christ and Christians recurs several times in the *Dialogue with Trypho*, and again there is scholarly debate about the meaning and reliability of this claim. Many scholars connect this anti-Christian cursing with the rabbinic *Birkat ha-Minim*, to be discussed below, but the *Birkat ha-Minim* does not curse Christ and did not in its earliest stages mention Christians at all. Furthermore, Justin does not always locate this cursing in the synagogue.[32] So Justin's report stands uncorroborated. Uncorroborated, of course, does not mean untrue; it means that we are not sure what to do with it.[33]

What is important for our purposes is that Justin, an important witness to Christianity in the mid-second century C.E., thinks that there is an unbridgeable divide between Jews who do not believe in Christ and gentiles (like Justin) who do. They speak with each other, as Justin does with Trypho, but the communities are unambiguously separate.[34] This is not particularly surprising: As I remarked above, Jews and gentiles had occupied separate social spaces long before Christians entered the mix.

Jews

If the advent of Christianity did not change the social separation of Jews and gentiles, it did introduce a new complication to Jewish communal life, since now there were two sorts of Jews, those who believed in Christ and those who did not. The Tosefta shows that the former (Jews who believe in Jesus) could be included by the latter (Jews who do not believe in Jesus) in the category of *minim*, conventionally translated "heretics." The meaning of this category and the identity of the people so labeled are much-discussed problems.

Since I am primarily interested here in the second century C.E., I shall focus first on the Mishnah and the Tosefta. Perhaps a brief word of introduction is in order. The Mishnah is the first rabbinic book; that is, the earliest rabbinic work to achieve closure. Over the centuries the text was added to here and there, to be sure, but we may assume that the Mishnah as we have it is substantially the Mishnah that emerged in the early or mid-third century C.E. A large work, written in Hebrew in the land of Israel, and devoted almost entirely to matters of practice, custom and law, it is remarkably uninterested in contemporary affairs. It is far more interested in the rituals of the Temple (which had been destroyed in 70 C.E.) than in the rituals of the synagogue, about which it says very little; it has far more to say about priests than about rabbis, about purity laws (which in the absence of the Temple were on their way to desuetude) and sacrifices than about atonement and prayer. It is not interested in establishing "orthodoxy" or delineating communal boundaries; it has far more to say about goring oxen than about heretics and heresy, far more about menstruating women than about the core beliefs of Judaism.

The Tosefta is similar to the Mishnah, only larger. It contains more anecdotes, more scriptural exegesis, more ruminations about nonlegal topics than does the Mishnah, but otherwise is very close to the Mishnah in arrangement and language. There is a complex synoptic relationship between the Tosefta and the Mishnah; on the one hand, the Tosefta regularly quotes or paraphrases the Mishnah, or assumes the existence of the Mishnah, but, on the other hand, the Tosefta also contains passages that seem to constitute the stuff out of which the Mishnah was created. In other words, the Tosefta appears to be both earlier and later than the Mishnah. Fortunately for us, this problem is not our problem.

I begin with the Mishnah. Here in translation is the text of all Mishnaic references to *min* ("heretic"), *minim* ("heretics") and *minut* ("heresy"). The translations are by Herbert Danby, slightly edited.[35]

(1) Mishnah *Berakhot* 9:5: At the close of every benediction in the Temple they used to say, "to everlasting"; but after the heretics [*minim*][36] had taught corruptly and said that there is but one world, it was ordained that they should say, "From everlasting to everlasting."

(2) Mishnah *Rosh Hashanah* 2:1: At first they would admit evidence about the new moon from any person, but after the evil doings of the heretics

[*minim*] they enacted that evidence should be admitted only from people that they knew.

(3) Mishnah *Megillah* 4:8: If one said, "I will not go before the ark in colored clothing," he may not go before it even in white clothing.

[If one said,] "I will not go before it in sandals," he may not go before it even barefoot.

If one makes his phylactery round—it is a danger [to him] and is not a fulfillment of the commandment. If one put them on the forehead or on the palm of his hand—this is the way of heresy [*minut*]. If one overlaid them with gold or put them over his sleeve—this is the way of outsiders [*hitzonim*].

(4) Mishnah *Megillah* 4:9: If one said [in his prayer], "May the good [pl.] bless you!"—this is the way of heresy [*minut*].

If one said, "May your mercies extend even to a bird's nest," or "May your name be remembered for good [occasions]" or "We give thanks, we give thanks!"—they silence him.

If one reads the laws of the forbidden degrees of sexual union [Leviticus 18] non-literally—they silence him.

If one says that *And you shall not give any of your seed to make them pass through [the fire] to Molech* [Leviticus 18:21] means "and you shall not give of your seed to make it pass to [or: to impregnate] an Aramaean woman"[37]—they silence him with a rebuke.

(5) Mishnah *Sotah* 9:15: ... and the kingdom shall convert to heresy [*minut*].

(6) Mishnah *Sanhedrin* 4:5: Adam was created alone ... for the sake of peace among mankind, that none should say to his fellow, "My father was greater than your father"; also that the heretics [*minim*] should not say, "There are many ruling powers in heaven."

(7) Mishnah *Hulin* 2:9: No one may slaughter [an animal in such a way that the blood fall] into a hole of any sort, but one may make a hole in his house for the blood to flow into; one may not, however, do so in the marketplace so that he not imitate the heretics [*minim*] ...

(8) Mishnah *Parah* 3:3: At the entrance to the Temple Court was set

ready a jar of the [ashes of the] sin-offering. They brought a male from among the sheep, tied a rope between its horns, and tied a stick and wound it about with the [other] end of the rope, and threw it into the jar. The sheep was struck so that it was startled backward [and spilled the ashes], and [a child] took of the ashes and mixed enough to be visible on the water. R. Yosi says: Do not give the heretics[38] an opportunity to lord it [over us]![39] but, rather, one [of the children] took [the ashes directly] from the jar and mixed them.

(9) Mishnah *Yadayim* 4:8: A Galilean heretic[40] said, "I cry out against you Pharisees, for you write in a bill of divorce the name of the ruler together with the name of Moses." The Pharisees said, "We cry out against you Galilean heretic, for you write the name of the ruler together with the name [of God] on the [same] page, and, moreover, you write the name of the ruler above, and the name [of God] below."

I cannot discuss these nine passages here in detail. Instead here are four comments.

First, note how small is the corpus. The nine passages taken together barely equal in length one typical Mishnah chapter. The Mishnah has 523 chapters.[41] The corpus is actually smaller than it seems because text no. 5, which states that in the end of days the "kingdom [the Roman Empire] will convert to *minut* [Christianity]," is obviously a post-Mishnaic addition, not earlier than the fourth century C.E.[42] So our corpus is even smaller than it first appears.

Second, the Mishnah's *minim* are a diverse lot. From the meager details the Mishnah provides we can see that some *minim* were active when the Temple still stood (nos. 1, 8,[43] and perhaps 2); some *minim* are characterized by their liturgical practice, whether in the Temple or the synagogue (nos. 1, 3, 4); some *minim* are characterized by other, nonliturgical practices (nos. 2, 7, 9) or by theology (nos. 1, 6, and perhaps 4). The *minim* are a varied lot.[44]

Third, the Mishnah alludes to the proscribed practices or beliefs of the *minim*, but does not define the groups or the individuals involved. It provides no details on who they are or how they fit (or don't fit) into rabbinic society, or what they otherwise believe or don't believe, do or don't do. The absence of clear definition of *minim* and *minut* is part and parcel with the Mishnah's lack of interest in defining orthodoxy and ecclesiology. That is, at no point does the Mishnah define correct Jewish belief, or set out criteria for membership in the Jewish community, or explain whether *minim* share those beliefs or meet those criteria. On all this the Mishnah is silent.

Fourth, the absence of *minim* from the opening paragraph of chapter 10 of Mishnah *Sanhedrin* is particularly remarkable. This Mishnah sets out three theological errors the proponents of which are punished by God with the loss of their share in the world to come:

> The following have no share in the world to come: one who denies the resurrection of the dead;[45] one who denies that the Torah is from Heaven; and an Epicurean.
>
> (Mishnah *Sanhedrin* 10.1)[46]

This is the only paragraph of the Mishnah that outlines, even if only by negation, some core doctrines of Rabbinic Judaism. These doctrines are: the resurrection of the dead; the divine origin of the Torah; and divine providence (God's supervision of human affairs, in particular the rewarding of the righteous and the punishing of the wicked, a doctrine denied by the Epicureans). Which ancient Jews denied, or at least were reputed to deny, these doctrines? The answer is, as many scholars have noted, the Sadducees as described by Josephus and the New Testament. The Sadducees denied the resurrection of the dead; denied the binding authority of the "tradition of the elders" of the Pharisees;[47] and maximized the role of free-will in human affairs.[48] Whether such Sadducees still existed in Mishnaic times is a difficult question that need not be treated here.[49] In any event, in this passage, the Sadducees are unnamed and *minim* are not mentioned.[50] Furthermore, in this Mishnah those who maintain these theological errors are punished by God, not by any human agency. The miscreants are not cursed; they are not threatened with excommunication or any other form of communal discipline. God will deal with them when they present themselves in the hereafter. In this world we do nothing to them except express our disapproval. I conclude that the Mishnah does not establish strong boundaries around its community; it is not interested in defining orthodoxy, suppressing deviance, or establishing the limits of dissent.[51]

So, to return to our topic: Where does that leave Christians, whether

Jewish or gentile? Nowhere. They are invisible in the Mishnah. The Mishnah's *minim* are not Christians (except in the interpolated passage no. 5), nor is there any sign of Christians anywhere else in the Mishnah. The editors of the Mishnah have little interest in *minim*, no interest in heresy, and no interest in Christians.

The Tosefta contains many additional references to *minim;* among these are two passages that apply the category of *minim* to Jewish-Christians and one passage that does not use the word *minim* but which refers to Jewish-Christians.[52] I shall present and discuss all three. Here is the first.

Mishnah *Shabbat* rules that "any of the Holy Scriptures may be saved from a fire [on the Sabbath]," even if the act of rescue entails the violation of the Sabbath. On this Mishnah, the Tosefta comments as follows:

> The parchment sheets[53] and the [Torah] scrolls[54] of *minim* may not be saved from a fire [on the Sabbath], but are allowed to burn where they are, they and their divine names.
>
> R. Yosi the Galilean says: On weekdays one cuts out [pierces] their divine names and hides them away, and burns the rest.
>
> R. Tarfon said: I swear by the lives of my children ["may I strike my children" or "may I twist my children"] that if these scrolls were to come into my hands I would burn them and their divine names. Even if a murderer ["pursuer"] were pursuing me, I would enter a house of idolatry rather than enter ["but I would not enter"] a house of theirs, for the worshipers of idolatry do not recognize him [God] and deny him, but these [*minim*] recognize God but deny him ...
>
> R. Yishmael said: If, in order to bring peace between husband and wife, the Omnipresent said that the holy writing on a scroll ["a scroll written in holiness"] is to be scraped off into water [Numbers 5:23], all the more so should the scrolls of the *minim*, which bring enmity between Israel and their father in heaven, be erased, they and their divine names! ...
>
> Just as they [the scrolls of the *minim*] are not to be saved from a fire, they are not to be saved from a landslide [or "cave-in"] or a flood, or anything else that would destroy them.
> (Mishnah *Shabbat* 16:1; Tosefta *Shabbat* 13:5)[55]

Who are these *minim*, who recognize God but deny him, who bring enmity between the people of Israel and God in heaven, whose houses are to be avoided even more than the houses of idolatry, whose scrolls are not to be rescued from a fire on the Sabbath, whose scrolls on a weekday are to have their divine names removed and the remainder consigned to the flames? Surely[56] these are Christians or, to be more accurate, Jewish-Christians. Their Jewishness is evident from the fact that they arouse divine wrath against the people of Israel, and from the fact that their Torah scrolls are written in Hebrew and contain the divine name in Hebrew. Their Christianness is evident from the first word of the excerpt, *ha gilyonim*, translated above "the parchment sheets," which seems to be a deliberate pun on the Christian name for the gospels (*evangelia*). We should like to know more about these gospels and scrolls.[57] In any case, the point of the passage is that Christian scrolls are not sacred although they contain the name of God; in fact, they should be actively destroyed (once their divine names have been removed). Surely[58] the passage also implies that God-fearing rabbinic Jews should distance themselves from the owners and purveyors of such texts.

The Tosefta contains two remarkable stories about the interaction of Jewish-Christians with rabbinic sages. The context is a discussion about *minim* prompted by Mishnah *Hulin* 2:9 (see above, Mishnah text no. 7). The Tosefta harshly condemns *minim* ("... their wine is the wine of idolatrous libations, their scrolls are scrolls of magicians, their children are *mamzerim*"[59]), even if their identity is no clearer in the Tosefta than in the Mishnah.[60]

The Tosefta then tells the following two stories:[61]

Story 1

It once happened that R. Eleazar ben Damah was bitten by a snake, and Jacob of Kfar Samah came to heal him in the name of Yeshua/Yeshu ben Pantira.

But R. Yishmael did not permit him.[62]

He[63] [R. Yishmael] said to him: You may not do so, ben Damah.

He [R. Eleazar] said to him: I will bring you a proof [from scripture] that he may heal me. But he did not have a chance to bring the proof before he died.

R. Yishmael said: Fortunate are you, Ben Damah, for you have expired in peace, and did not breach the fence [erected by] the sages.

Because anyone who breaches the fence [erected by] the sages—in the end punishment comes upon him,

As it is written, *he who breaches a fence—a snake shall bite him* [Ecclesiastes 10:8].

Story 2

It once happened that R. Eliezer was arrested on account of *minut*, and they brought him up to the platform to be tried.

The governor asked him: Should an elder like you engage in these things?

He answered: I consider the Judge trustworthy.

Now the governor thought that he had referred to him—though he referred only to his Father in Heaven—and so he said to him: Since you have deemed me trustworthy, I also said to myself, would these grey hairs[64] err in these matters? [Surely not!] Dismissed! You are released.

When he left the platform, he was distressed to have been arrested on account of *minut*. His disciples came to console him, but he refused to accept [their consolation].

R. Akiva came and said to him: Rabbi, may I say something to you, so that perhaps you will not be distressed?

He said: Speak.

He said to him: Perhaps one of the *minim* told you a matter of *minut* which pleased you?

He said to him: By Heaven! You have reminded me. Once I was strolling on the main street of Sepphoris when I met Jacob of Kfar Sikhnin who told me a matter of *minut* in the name of Yeshua ben Pantira and it pleased me. Therefore I was arrested on account of *minut*, for I transgressed the words of the Torah. *Keep your way far from her and do not go near the door of her house* [Proverbs 5:8].

For R. Eliezer taught: One should always flee from what is ugly and from whatever appears to be ugly.

Both of these wonderful stories are too rich to be discussed in full here. My interest is not in the stories' facticity, which is debatable at best and unrecoverable in any case, but in their construction of reality. That is, we do not know and have no way of knowing whether a man named Eleazar ben Damah, having been bitten by a poisonous snake, had a significant conversation with a Jewish-Christian named Jacob and an even more significant conversation with a rabbinic sage named R. Yishmael (whose floruit is customarily dated to the period 100–120 C.E.). We do not know and have no way of knowing whether a rabbinic sage named R. Eliezer ben Hyrcanus (whose floruit is also customarily dated to 100–120 C.E.) was once arrested by the Romans on the suspicion of being a Christian, and whether he afterward attributed his ordeal to the fact that he once had a conversation with a Jewish-Christian named Jacob.[65] I focus instead on how these stories imagine the relationship of rabbinic society and rabbinic sages with Jewish-Christian *minim*. I shall first discuss each story separately and then treat the two together.

But first a brief note on Yeshu (or Yeshua) ben Pantira. As scholars have long noted, this is a Jewish anti-Christian way of referring to Jesus. In response to the story in Matthew and Luke of Jesus' miraculous birth, Jews told a story of his sordid origins. Jesus, they said, was the product of an adulterous union of Mary with a Roman soldier named Panthera. The Jewish story was known already to Origen (writing c. 248 C.E.), citing the work of Celsus (c. 180 C.E.). From antiquity through the Middle Ages, Yeshu ben Pantira (or Pandira) is a standard Jewish appellation for Jesus of Nazareth.[66]

No one in the first story, neither R. Eleazar ben Damah nor R. Yishmael nor the narrator, doubts that Jacob of Kfar Samah is a potent healer. His power, which derives from the name of Yeshu ben Pantira, is such that he could have healed R. Eleazar ben Damah from his fatal snake bite. Why R. Yishmael objects so to a healing in the name of Yeshu is not explained. Nor are we told how R. Eleazar and Jacob came to know each other. R. Eleazar was about to try to convince R. Yishmael that in this case, in which his life was at stake, an exception should be made to the policy of keeping a safe distance from the name of Yeshu ben Pantira. We may assume that he was going to argue that danger to life overrides all sorts of prohibitions. But, alas, before he can make his case, he dies. Rather than lament or feel guilt over his death, R. Yishmael instead lauds

R. Eleazar's steadfast piety, for he did not breach the hedge of rabbinic discipline; R. Yishmael instructed him not to be healed by Jacob of Kfar Samah, and R. Eleazar followed those instructions, even at the cost of his life. The story ends with a brilliant stroke. In his brief but powerful epitaph, R. Yishmael cites the verse *he who breaches a fence—a snake shall bite him*. But, as the Babylonian Talmud perspicaciously observes, a snake did bite R. Eleazar! And R. Eleazar is innocent—he did not breach the rabbinic fence! The irony of course is intentional. Surely we are meant to understand that the verse is metaphorical: He who breaches the rabbinic fence, that is, he who does not follow the dictates and prohibitions of the sages, a snake will bite him, that is, he will suffer in the world to come. The snake that bit R. Eleazar in this world was not a metaphorical snake; but by acceding to the instructions of R. Yishmael, R. Eleazar guaranteed himself a share in the world to come. "Fortunate are you, Ben Damah, for you have expired in peace."[67] This story does not use the word *min*, but its placement as commentary on Mishnah *Hulin* 2:9, as extension of a Toseftan polemic against *minim*, and as an introduction to a second story about Jewish-Christian *minim*, strongly suggests that this story, too, is about people whom the narrator would characterize as *minim*.

The second story also features a Jewish-Christian named Jacob, presumably not the same one as in the first story. Here we have one story, R. Eliezer ben Hyrcanus on trial, and a story within the story, R. Eliezer interacting with a *min*. First is a trial scene: The Romans suspect R. Eliezer of being a *min*, that is, a Christian, and put him on trial.[68] With a clever double-entendre, R. Eliezer so impresses the judge that he is released. When R. Eliezer returns to his disciples, he is distraught: Why did God punish him thus? True, he was released unharmed, but why this trial and travail? When he is reminded of an incident, an accidental encounter with a Jewish-Christian *min* in Sepphoris, he is comforted; the ways of God are just.[69] The narrator, alas, does not reveal the content of the discussion between R. Eliezer and Jacob of Kfar Sikhnin, a gap that is filled in by the later version in the Babylonian Talmud. No matter the content of the conversation, what got R. Eliezer in trouble was the very fact of a conversation. Once, quite by chance, R. Eliezer chatted with a *min*, and that fact alone suffices to explain why God punished him by having him arrested for *minut*.

The two stories are juxtaposed in Tosefta *Hulin* and indeed their moral is the same: Pious rabbinic Jews are to stay away from Jewish-Christian *minim*, the disciples of Yeshu ben Pantira. This social barrier is defined in the first story as a hedge erected by sages, in the second story as a prohibition of the Torah (supported by a verse from Proverbs!). The encounters with Jewish-Christian *minim* depicted here are not dialogues about theology or philosophy. Neither encounter has anything to with "identity formation." Jacob of Kfar Samah intended to demonstrate the power of Yeshu ben Pantira by performing a healing in his name; Jacob of Kfar Sikhnin communicated some teaching in the name of Yeshu ben Pantira. Those modern scholars who argue that Christian truth claims in general, or Jewish-Christian truth claims in particular, had an important formative effect on the shaping of rabbinic truth claims will find little support here for their argument. The Jewish-Christian *minim* depicted here are not part of rabbinic society; they rub shoulders with rabbis but only occasionally and only desultorily. They are not rabbis and are not depicted as rabbis; no one mistakes them for rabbis. They are outsiders. R. Eliezer knows that Jacob of Kfar Sikhnin is a *min*; R. Eleazar ben Damah does not dispute R. Ishmael's characterization that healing in the name of Yeshu ben Pantira is wrong in principle. The message of the stories is: "Stay away!"; "Danger!"

In sum, from the rabbinic evidence surveyed so far, it is hard to know if there was a parting of the ways between rabbinic Jews and Jewish-Christians, not because there was so much intermingling between these communities but because there was so little. The Mishnah ignores them. The Tosefta has two—only two!—relevant stories set in the early decades of the second century C.E., but we have no way of assessing the historicity of either story or of determining whether the stories are evidence for the period in which they are set or for the period in which they were produced (probably third century C.E.). The stories imply that there is, and ought to be, avoidance of Jewish-Christians by rabbinic Jews. The same point emerges from the polemic in Tosefta *Shabbat* against the books of the *minim*, that is, Jewish-Christians. Perhaps the vitriolic denunciation of the *minim* in Tosefta *Hulin* also refers to Jewish-Christians; we can't be sure.

The meagerness of the data, and the pointedness of the data, strongly suggest that the rabbinic community and the Jewish-Christian community did not have much to do with each other. We may freely assume that rabbis and Jewish-Christians occasionally bumped into each other, as R. Eliezer and Jacob of Kfar Sikhnin did one day in downtown Sepphoris; we may even assume that they might have engaged from time to time in serious theological debates. But the evidence for these interchanges is meager (nonexistent in the Mishnah and Tosefta). The Tosefta regards Jewish-Christians (and others) as *minim*, which might suggest that Jewish-Christians were "inside" rabbinic society, but the evidence is sparse; there certainly is no sign that the sage editors of the Tosefta were more perturbed by the Jewish-Christian expression of *minut* than by other, no less noxious, expressions of *minut*.

I turn now to the *Birkat ha-Minim*, the liturgical expression of the rabbinic disdain for *minim*. *Birkat ha-Minim* literally translates as "the benediction concerning the *minim*" or, more fully, "the benediction of God, the destroyer of the *minim*." This prayer has had a long and tortuous history; by the fourth century C.E. it had become an anti-Christian prayer, but it did not begin as one. Let us look at the evidence. For the sake of completeness we shall look beyond the Mishnah and Tosefta to the Yerushalmi (the Talmud of the land of Israel) and the Bavli (the Babylonian Talmud) as well.[70]

The Mishnah says nothing about the *Birkat ha-Minim*. The Tosefta has one reference to *Birkat ha-Minim*, as follows:

> The Eighteen Benedictions of which the sages speak correspond to the eighteen appearances of the divine name in *Ascribe to the Lord, O divine beings* [Psalm 29]. [When reciting the Eighteen Benedictions] one should include the benediction about *minim* in the benediction about separatists [*perushim*[71]], the benediction about proselytes in the benediction about elders, the benediction about David in the benediction *who (re)builds Jerusalem*. If one recited each of these separately, he has [nevertheless] fulfilled his obligation.
>
> (Tosefta *Berakhot* 3:25)[72]

The heart of the rabbinic daily liturgy is a prayer consisting of 18 paragraphs, each paragraph devoted to a specific theme and concluding with a benediction of God ("Blessed are you, O God, who ..."). The history of this prayer is much debated. It seems that in early rabbinic times the themes, the number of themes, and the precise wording of each thematic paragraph were not yet fixed; at some point the number of benedictions was fixed at 18 (hence the prayer became known as "the Eighteen") and the specific themes were established. Fixed wording was not established until the early Islamic period. The quoted Tosefta passage attests some of these developments. The opening sentence tries to find a basis in scripture for the number 18; why the number of appearances of the divine name in Psalm 29 should have anything to do with the number of benedictions in the central prayer of the daily liturgy is not explained. Indeed, the Talmudim adduce other "proofs," most just as fanciful as this.[73] The Tosefta then explains that certain themes should be paired: *minim* should be paired with separatists (*perushim*); proselytes should be paired with elders; and King David should be paired with Jerusalem in the benediction *who (re)builds Jerusalem*. The purpose of these pairings is to allow the maximum number of themes to be treated without exceeding the 18-benediction limit. The Tosefta clearly implies that each of these themes is the subject of an already existing benediction.

The first of these pairs is our concern. The Tosefta says that the benediction concerning separatists (*perushim*) should be combined with the benediction concerning *minim*. The Tosefta does not explain the content of either benediction, but we may safely assume that the former benediction invokes God's power in destroying or otherwise harassing the separatists, while the latter does the same for the *minim*. Who are these separatists, and what is their relationship with *minim*? The Tosefta does not explain. Modern scholars have suggested that the "separatists" were those who abandoned the Jews of Judea in their struggles against the Romans or who otherwise separated themselves from the Jewish community. *Minim*, in contrast, as we have seen, are Jews whose theology and/or religious practice were "incorrect." By melding the two the Tosefta conflates political/social deviance with religious deviance ("deviance," of course, from the perspective of the group doing the defining, in this case the rabbinic sages).[74]

The Yerushalmi provides three important bits of additional information. First, it claims that the benediction about *minim* was instituted at the rabbinic conclave at Yavneh (the gathering of sages in the decades after the destruction of the Temple in 70 C.E.), although it is not clear whether the Yerushalmi means the original separate benediction about *minim* or the merged benediction about *minim* and separatists.[75] The Yerushalmi probably deduced this information from Mishnah *Berakhot* 4:3, which has Rabban Gamliel, a prominent sage of the Yavnean period, declare that a person should pray "Eighteen" every day. Second, the Yerushalmi provides an alternative version of the Tosefta's statement regarding the pairing of separatists with *minim*. Here is the Yerushalmi: "[When reciting the Eighteen Benedictions] one should include the benediction about *minim* and sinners in the benediction 'who lays low the arrogant.'" If we may assume that "who lays low the arrogant" (*makhniʿa zedim*) is the concluding phrase of the benediction against separatists, then we may conclude that the Yerushalmi agrees with the Tosefta: The benediction concerning *minim* (and sinners, too[76]) is to be combined with the benediction concerning separatists.[77] Third, the Yerushalmi states that if a prayer leader omits any of the Eighteen Benedictions, he is not compelled to go back to recite it at its proper place, unless he skips one of the following three benedictions, in which case he is compelled to go back to recite it. Why? Because "I suspect that he might be a *min*." The three benedictions are "who revives the dead," "who lays low the arrogant" and "who (re)builds Jerusalem." Omission of the benediction "who revives the dead" naturally raises the suspicion of unbelief in the resurrection of the dead.[78] Omission of the benediction "who lays low the arrogant" naturally raises the suspicion of *minut*, because the benediction calls for the destruction of separatists and *minim*. Omission of the benediction "who (re)builds Jerusalem" naturally raises the suspicion of unbelief in the Davidic Messiah. The Yerushalmi then reports a story about Samuel the Small who once, while leading the prayers, omitted the benediction "who lays low the arrogant," but was not compelled to go back, because no one suspected him of being a *min*. Why Samuel the Small omitted the benediction is not explained.[79]

The Bavli has a somewhat different version of all three of the Yerushalmi's points. It attributes the authorship of the benediction about *minim* to Samuel the Small, which the Yerushalmi does not do. It agrees with the Yerushalmi that the benediction was established at Yavneh, but claims that it was formulated at the specific request of R. Gamaliel. It agrees with the Yerushalmi that if a prayer leader omits the benediction about *minim* he is to be called to account, except that in the Yerushalmi he is made to go back and recite the benediction, while in the Bavli he is to be removed from his position. The story about Samuel the Small is told in somewhat different form, as is the ruling that the benediction concerning the *minim* is to be combined with another thematically related benediction.[80]

How to make sense of these conflicting and inconsistent traditions, and how to sort out their inter-relationship? These questions have been discussed many times in modern scholarship and cannot be treated here in any detail. In particular, scholars have long debated the historicity of the Bavli's claim that the *Birkat ha-Minim* was formulated at the request of R. Gamaliel. For our purposes the following points are important:

All three sources agree that the benediction had its own history before being incorporated into the Eighteen Benedictions.

The Yerushalmi and Bavli claim that the benediction was formulated in the period of Yavneh, the formative period of the Mishnah. This claim is unknown to the Tosefta.

The *Birkat ha-Minim* does not refer by name to specific groups. If we may take together all the categories named in the Tosefta and the Yerushalmi, we have separatists (*perushim*), sinners (*posh'im*), arrogant ones (*zedim*), as well as *minim*. These broad categories would seem to refer to classes of people, not specific groups.

None of the texts explains the purpose of the *Birkat ha-Minim*. Why do we praise God for destroying or laying low separatists and heretics? Both the Yerushalmi and the Bavli describe the negative social consequences that befall the prayer leader who omits or mangles the benediction; he needs to recite the prayer over again (Yerushalmi) or is removed from his post (Bavli). Many scholars have assumed that this indeed was the purpose of the benediction: to "smoke out" separatists and heretics who, we may presume, would not want to praise God for bringing about their own destruction. But even if the unmasking of heretics may have been an effect of the institution of this benediction,[81] we cannot be sure that it was its purpose. There are all sorts of reasons why we may wish to curse those whom we regard as our enemies;[82] the Yerushalmi and Bavli do not explain.

It is not impossible that the *minim* of the benediction are, or at least include, Christians. As we have seen, in two passages the Tosefta calls Christians *minim*, so it may be doing so here as well. However, the Tosefta uses the same label also for non-Christian heretics, so, absent additional evidence, the Christian connection is just a possibility, nothing more.

Furthermore, even if the *minim* here are or include "Christians," they are not Christians *tout court*. As we have seen, the Christians with whom the Tosefta is familiar are Jewish-Christians, ethnic Jews who believe in Jesus and stand in some relationship with the Jewish community. The *Birkat ha-Minim* says nothing about gentile Christians or Christianity at large.

Hence it is most unlikely that the benediction about *minim* has anything to do with Justin Martyr's statement, cited above, that the Jews daily curse Christ and Christians. The *Birkat ha-Minim* mentions neither Christ nor gentile Christians (like Justin). The *Birkat ha-Minim* is unknown outside the land of Israel and Babylonia; Justin's *Dialogue with Trypho* was set in Ephesus, and written (perhaps) in Rome.[83] In the late fourth century C.E., two church writers active in Byzantine Palestina, Epiphanius and Jerome, refer to the *Birkat ha-Minim*. Three times a day, they say, the Jews curse the Nazoraeans/Nazarenes, Jewish believers-in-Christ; Jerome even knows that the Jews call them *minim*. There can be little doubt that Epiphanius and Jerome are referring to the *Birkat ha-Minim*, which by the late fourth century C.E. had become explicitly anti-Christian (that is, anti-Jewish-Christian) and sufficiently well known to attract the attention of gentile Christian outsiders in Roman Palestina; in contrast, in the second century C.E. in Rome, Justin could not have known the *Birkat ha-Minim*.[84]

Some scholars have argued for a connection between the *Birkat ha-Minim* and three passages in the Gospel of John. The argument goes as follows. In three passages John says that the Jews (in one passage, the Pharisees) have put (or will put) "out of the synagogue" those who believe in Christ.[85] In this strand of the Gospel of John, being put out of the synagogue is a bad thing; Christian believers want to be in the synagogue, not outside it. Where else do we have evidence that Jews (Pharisees) are expelling (Jewish) Christians from synagogues? The *Birkat ha-Minim*, instituted at Yavneh and thus contemporary with the Gospel of John (c. 100 C.E.), is an ideal candidate. The *Birkat ha-Minim*, by providing a liturgical litmus test for heresy, expelled Jewish-Christians from the synagogue, precisely the setting for this strand of the Gospel of John.[86]

There is much to admire in this reconstruction even if in the final analysis it fails to convince.[87] The relationship of the Gospel of John to Jews and Judaism is much debated. If the Gospel was composed in Asia Minor or Syria, as is usually believed, it is most unlikely that anyone in either place would have ever heard of *Birkat ha-Minim* c. 100 C.E., since the reach of Rabbinic Judaism then fell far short of such distant locales. The *Birkat ha-Minim* is attested only in Israel and Babylonia. Furthermore, as I commented above, it is not clear that the intent of the *Birkat ha-Minim* was to expel *minim* from the synagogue community. Indeed, if it did so, it did so only indirectly. If the rabbis wanted to expel the *minim*, one wonders why they didn't just expel the *minim*. If the rabbis wanted to expel the Jewish-Christians, one wonders why they didn't just expel the Jewish-Christians. If the rabbis wanted to invoke a curse upon Jewish-Christians, one wonders why they didn't just curse them, as they would be doing by the fourth century. There are too many riddles and uncertainties here for a convincing case to be made.

In sum, the *Birkat ha-Minim* is important evidence for the limits of rabbinic pluralism; even in the coalition-building atmosphere of Yavneh—if indeed the attribution of *Birkat ha-Minim* to Yavneh be reliable—the rabbis had limits. *Minim* and separatists, sinners and arrogant ones, were beyond the pale. The identity of these social malcontents, the actions of these reprobates, the thoughts of these ne'er-do-wells were not important to the sages who framed this benediction. They were trying to be inclusive ...

Conclusions

The evidence surveyed here supports the view, once regnant among scholars but now unaccountably out of fashion, that by the early second century C.E. Jews (that is, ethnic Jews who did not believe in Christ) and Christians (that is, ethnic gentiles who did believe in Christ) constituted separate communities, each with its own identity, rituals, institutions, authority figures and literature. To be sure we may assume that there were Jewish communities of various sorts, for example, rabbinic and non-rabbinic, Hebrew-reading and non-Hebrew reading, and we may assume that there were Christian communities of various sorts, for example, proto-orthodox and "Gnostic," so generalizations are hazardous. But all the extant evidence points in the same direction. There were no mixed communities of Jews and Christians, except of course for Christian communities that numbered among their members Jews who had converted to Christianity, and except for Jewish communities that numbered among their members Christians who had converted to Judaism. But absent conversion, the boundaries between the Jewish and the Christian communities were clear enough and stable enough. As the century proceeded, the boundary would become ever clearer and ever more stable.

The evidence for all this, especially on the Christian side and from the perspective of the Romans, is abundant and consistent, and has been surveyed briefly above. Here are some additional considerations, not yet mentioned. A large stock of Judeo-Greek literature migrated with Christians in their journey out of Judaism; hence the Greek versions of the Hebrew Bible became Christian scriptures, just as they are Jewish. The works of Philo owe their preservation to this migration. The works of Josephus (which were completed around the year 100 C.E.) mark the end of this literary migration; Judeo-Greek writings composed after around 100 C.E. were not preserved by Christians and as a result have disappeared (aside from a few small exceptions).[88] The simplest explanation for this phenomenon is that after around 100 C.E. Christian communities were distinct from Jewish communities, not only the Hebrew-writing sages of Roman Palestina but also the Greek-writing Jewish communities of the Diaspora.

Justin (writing around 160 C.E.) states boldly and forthrightly that gentile Christ-believers are God's holy people, God's chosen people, the true children of God and the true people of Israel.[89] By the end of the second century, Christians are producing their own scriptures, which were distinguished from Jewish scriptures not only in content but also in form: They were written in codices (books) instead of scrolls, and they employed a distinctive system for abbreviating the names of God and Christ (Jewish scrolls had no such system).[90] By the end of the second century C.E., we have our earliest description (in Rome) of parallel and separate religious congregations, one a church (as we would call it) and one a synagogue.[91] By the third century if not earlier, we have evidence for separate burials; Jews and Christians were separated in death, as in life.[92]

The Christian evidence also shows that through the centuries, from the second century on, some Christians thought that other Christians associated with Jews too much, observed too many Jewish practices, attended Jewish synagogues too often, had a theology of Christ that was too low, or otherwise seemed "too Jewish." While these accusations of "Judaizing" are good evidence for intra-Christian disputes about proper practice and belief, they do not necessarily reveal anything about the interactions of Christians with Jews. The accusation of "Judaizing" is one Christian accusing another of doctrinal or ritual or attitudinal error; the accusation assumes that Judaism is not-Christianity and that Christianity is not-Judaism. Clearly the accused's sense of the relationship of Judaism to Christianity was more nuanced than that of the accuser, but we have no reason to believe the accuser's assertion that the accused was confused about the location of the boundary between Judaism and Christianity, or, what is more important for our purposes, the location of the boundary between Jews and Christians.[93] Thus, to pick one much-cited example, in the 380s C.E. some of the good Christians of Antioch attended synagogue on the Jewish New Year because they wished to hear the *shofar* being blown. This was but one of the many ways by which they showed reverence for the synagogue. Bishop John Chrysostom reproved them for being traitors to Christianity and for consorting with the enemies of Christ. The bishop believed that these Christians had effaced the boundary between Judaism and Christianity, but apparently these Christians disagreed. They were Christians whose Christianity did not prevent them from respecting Judaism and its rituals and from consorting with Jews. The fulminations of the bishop aside, there is no evidence that these Christians believed that they were violating their communal boundaries or indeed that they were uncertain about the location of those boundaries. The Christian community did not include Jews, and the Jewish community did not include Christians, even if some Christians wandered over to the synagogue from time to time. The accusation of "Judaizing" is not evidence for the un-parting of the ways.[94]

On the Jewish side virtually all of our evidence about Judaism post-100 C.E. is from the group known as rabbis or sages. We may be sure that there were non-rabbinic Jewish communities in Roman Palestina, Parthian/Sassanian Babylonia and the Roman Diaspora, but we do not have their texts (we cannot even be sure that they wrote any texts) and we have little information about their communal boundaries.[95] Hence, our discussion about Jewish evidence is basically a discussion about rabbinic evidence.

The most striking feature of the rabbinic evidence is its paucity. Given the enormous bulk of rabbinic literature, the paucity of explicit references to Jesus, Christianity and Christians is striking. The rabbis were basically not interested. Contrast, for example, the rabbinic discussion of idolatry, which occupies an entire tractate in the Mishnah, Tosefta, Yerushalmi and Bavli, which pops up in numerous other tractates as well, and which treats both the nature of idolatry (What is it? Where does it come from? Why does God allow it to persist?) and the degree to which Jews must distance themselves from it. In contrast, the sages are simply not interested in Christianity and Christians.

This is not to say that the rabbis did not have contacts with Christians; of course they did. In addition to the (relatively few) stories about encounters between sages and Christians—the two earliest such stories are discussed above—rabbinic literature contains various passages, usually to be found in works of scriptural exegesis (*midrash*), which seem to reflect rabbinic responses to Christian theological claims based on problematic scriptural verses. These passages are interesting and important to be sure and have received much attention in recent scholarship,[96] but do not affect the overall picture. The sages paid little attention to Christianity and its truth claims, and there is no sign that rabbinic identity formation was shaped by the need to respond to Christians. The communal boundaries were clearly delineated, even if doctrinal points and scriptural passages were occasionally open to debate.

In any case, when the sages do encounter Christians, and when they debate Christians about Christian truth claims and scriptural exegesis, their Christian interlocutors are Jewish-Christians, not gentile Christians. No surprise here, since we may assume that the rabbis kept their distance from gentile Christians just as they kept their distance from gentile polytheists. The Jewish-Christians whom the rabbis met seem to have lived on the margins of rabbinic society and on the margins of gentile Christian society. By the second century C.E., these Jewish-Christians did not fit in anywhere.

This brings us to the rabbinic neologism *min/minim*, conventionally translated "heretic/heretics." The term seems to have been a grab-bag or catch-all for various people (groups?) who upheld beliefs and/or practices that the rabbis did not like. The rabbis have other rhetorical means to indicate disapproval, but labeling a person as a *min* or a practice as *minut* was perhaps the most pointed, as is made evident by the *Birkat ha-Minim*. This was a paragraph incorporated into the daily liturgy praising God for destroying or otherwise discomfiting the *minim*. The Mishnah knows the category *min/minim/minut* but not the *Birkat ha-Minim*, which is first attested in the Tosefta. The social consequences of being labeled a *min* are never spelled out, just as the social consequences of the recitation of the *Birkat ha-Minim* are never spelled out. The category *minim* certainly can include, and in two Tosefta passages does include, Jewish-Christians, but the category is broader than just Jewish-Christians. Many modern scholars have argued that the institution of the *Birkat ha-Minim* played an important role in the parting of the ways between (rabbinic) Jews and (Jewish) Christians, but in recent years the pendulum has swung in the opposite direction and now there is an equally vociferous chorus on the other side, arguing that the *Birkat ha-Minim* had little or nothing to do with the emergence of two communities, one Jewish and the other Christian. In this chapter I have argued in favor of the latter view.

The Christian evidence and the rabbinic are disconnected. Christian texts (like Justin's *Dialogue with Trypho*) emphasize that Christianity is right and that Judaism is wrong, because Christians, not Jews, properly understand the Hebrew scriptures. There certainly is a parting of the ways here, at least in the reality as constructed by these texts. In contrast, rabbinic texts completely ignore gentile Christians, basically ignore Christian truth claims, and provide limited evidence for meaningful contact between sages and Jewish-Christians. Here the parting of the ways is expressed through avoidance and neglect. But it is a parting just the same.

12

The Complexities of Rejection and Attraction, Herein of Love and Hate

STEVEN FINE

MY GRANDPARENTS—REFUGEES FROM CZARIST RUSSIA—RAISED their family in Rochester, New York, in a working class neighborhood that included all kinds of European immigrants, all of whom were working hard to "make it" in America. Their next-door neighbors were an Italian family. At the center of the small, well-cared-for flowerbed kept by these neighbors was a large cement arch enclosing a statue of the Virgin Mary, often with fresh-cut flowers set before her. Expressing her discomfort with this sculpture—and particularly with its veneration, my grandmother referred to it as *the tsaylem*, "the idol." My mother, a child of the Great Depression, was convinced that the father next door was named *Kelev*, an epithet that my grandfather muttered each time he greeted his neighbor. *Kelev*, she later learned, is Hebrew (and thus Yiddish) for "dog." My grandparents thought of the "people next door" as good and friendly neighbors.

Years later, this time in Baltimore, I heard of a young boy from another Jewish family living in a similar kind of neighborhood in the 1920s who also had Roman Catholic neighbors, immigrants from Italy. Relations were warm between the two families, particularly among the children. One winter the parents of the Italian family were sick, and the Jewish boy was sent next door to deliver a home-cooked meal. Delighted, the Italian mother pinched his cheek, and said "You are such a good little *ammazza Cristi*," that is, "Christ-killer."[1] Expressed with love in her eyes, this immigrant spoke out of habit, clearly not fully cognizant of the implication of her words.

These stories of immigrant culture highlight the complexities of relationships between these communities over the centuries, complexities that thankfully were beginning to dissolve in this corner of the New World. But these attitudes have a very long history. Jews through the centuries mostly thought of Christians as gentile "idolaters."[2] And the charge of deicide—that Jews were (and continue to be) Christ-killers—has met with receptive ears since the second century.

That said, from the first century through the time of the emperor Constantine in the mid-fourth, the overarching Roman Empire—not particularly fond and often antagonistic toward both groups—provided a framework that supported a somewhat benign enmity between these communities. This balance changed with Constantine's new support of and ultimate conversion to Christianity. In the centuries that followed, Jews developed as a pressured minority, and orthodox Christianity became a totalizing and deeply intolerant imperial power.

For much of the past century, scholars discussed the relationship between Judaism and Christianity during these early centuries as a "parting of the ways."[3] This approach suggests that beginning during the first century, Judaism and Christianity had become completely separate competing religions, in enmity with each other. The Christianization of the Roman Empire left Jews precariously open to the kinds of religious pressures, if not persecution, experienced by all the traditional religions of the Roman Empire—not to mention "heretical" Christians.

Recent decades, however, have seen an opposite trend in scholarship, a search for the ways that these communities did not part at all. This approach asserts that Jewish and Christian communities remained intertwined for centuries, with deeply porous borders both dividing and connecting them.[4] While the former trend well fits the Europe left behind by my grandparents and their neighbors, the latter projects the lives of many contemporary Jews and Christians—especially the thoroughly Americanized grandchildren and great-grandchildren—to find a "pre-history" for a new kind of integration under the umbrella of American exceptionalism. This closeness is expressed most starkly by current high marriage rates between liberal Christians and Jews, but can be found in subtle ways even among the most "traditional" elements of each community.[5]

Both of these approaches have considerable merit in sensitizing us to the complexities of the relationship in late antiquity—a period in which Christianity took off from Judaism and each developed out of the heritage of Second Temple period Judaism in distinct ways, followed by centuries of pressured existence for the Jewish minority under antagonistic orthodox Christian imperialism. Jews were transformed incrementally from a licit and, in the third, fourth and even fifth centuries, often highly desirable, religious community to (like polytheism and non-orthodox Christian communities) a pressured and sometimes persecuted "superstition." At best, Jews came to be treated as a remnant of an earlier phase in God's plan under the triumphant Christian empire. It is no wonder, then, that Jewish literature expresses audible relief when the Sassanian Persians invaded Palestine in 614 C.E. When the Christians recovered their territory, renewed Byzantine persecution followed and gave way only with the Muslim conquest of Palestine in 636 C.E. From all indications, Jews received Mohammad's legions as messianic redeemers. For most of the ensuing centuries, it was preferable for Jews to be second-class, sometimes despised and often humiliated, "people of the book"—*dhimmis*—under Muslim rule than to be harshly tolerated "Christ-killers" as they had been under the Christians.

Both literary and archaeological sources reflect this ongoing relationship between Jews and Christians, and allow for a textured view of its complexities. Jewish literary sources include most prominently though not exclusively, the Cairo Geniza, that great repository of Jewish writings dating from antiquity through the early modern period.*[6] Patristic

---

*See Molly Dewsnap Meinhardt, "The Twins and the Scholar," *BAR*, September/October 1996; and Raphael Levy, "First 'Dead Sea Scroll' Found in Egypt Fifty Years Before Qumran Discoveries," *BAR*, September/October 1982.

sources tell us much more about the relationship, reflecting both the far greater interest that Christians have had in distinguishing themselves from Jews than Jews have had in Christian theology. Sources preserved by the Christian churches include Roman and Byzantine legal corpora and homilies by the fathers of the church. Legal corpora range from the great compendium promulgated under Emperor Theodosius II in 438 C.E., and the laws of the Visigoths from the lands that are now Spain and southern France in the seventh century. Churchmen who wrote about Jews include the greats of the church, from Ambrose and Augustine in the West to John Chrysostom in Asia Minor and Aphrahat in the East.

Over the past century or so, numerous archaeological sources have also been recovered that reflect this relationship, whether directly or through comparison between Jewish and Christian remains.[7] Together, archaeological and literary sources are largely in sync in describing a relationship of complexity, a "parting of the ways" more akin to an acrimonious traffic jam than to a happy fork in the road.

Constantine's decision during his lifetime to legalize and favor Christianity had deep implications for Jews. In previous centuries Jews seem to have pretty much ignored Christians—a situation expressed in a wide variety of rabbinic sources.[8] (See Chapter XI, "In Between: Jewish-Christians and the Curse of the Heretics," by Shaye J.D. Cohen.) While they appear occasionally, believers-in-Jesus were far less of a concern to the rabbis than Samaritans, Persian magicians, or Roman magistrates, soldiers, philosophers and thinkers.

At Dura-Europos, a small city on the Euphrates River on the Persian/ Roman border,* Jews purchased a housing complex near the city wall and converted it into a "house synagogue" in the third century. The walls of the main meeting room were covered with wall paintings illustrating scenes from the Hebrew Bible, read through the lens of Jewish lore that is also known from rabbinic sources; 60 percent of these wall paintings survive.

The decorative program of the synagogue was far more elaborate than that of the nearby and much smaller third-century Christian house church, in both the lavishness and sophistication of its wall paintings. A subtle polemic against the Palmyrene gods (who also had a temple at Dura) is expressed in a painting in the synagogue showing the damage

*See Stephen Goranson, "7 vs 8: The Battle Over the Holy Day at Dura-Europos," *BR*, August 1996.

done by the Ark of the Covenant to the temple of the Philistine god Dagon (including a broken "idol" of Dagon himself; see 1 Samuel 5–6). Another of the painted panels features Elijah's vanquishing the priests of Baal on Mount Carmel (1 Kings 18), here presented in ways typical of Roman religion (see Plate 13). Christianity is in no way referenced in the synagogue paintings.[9]

The paintings of the Dura church, on the other hand, reflect a far more complex relationship.[10] While Jews did not reference Christians, Christians (the "new Israel") illustrated their baptistery with both Old Testament and New Testament subjects. Thus, themes that all knew were derived from "Jewish" biblical sources were of vital importance to Christians, but the painters of the Dura synagogue paid no attention to Christian claims. As the current volume amply illustrates, Christian literature, beginning with the letters of Paul and the Gospels, was differentiating itself from Judaism. One early patristic source, the second-century father Melito, writing in Sardis in Asia Minor, presented a homily for Easter in which he both asserts the significance of celebrating Easter on the same day as Passover (the 14th day of the month of Nisan) to coincide with gospel accounts of the crucifixion, and developed, for the first time, the claim of deicide—that by not believing in Jesus, Jews continually kill the Savior.

A large Jewish community had resided in Sardis since the second century B.C.E. A magnificent synagogue from the fourth or fifth century C.E. has been excavated at the urban center of Sardis. It is the largest synagogue ever discovered; its members were prominent in the governance of the city. In a sense, Melito, with his venomous diatribe, represented "the mouse that roars," the small—probably beleaguered—Christian community of the second century, making up for its weakness with hyperbolic malice.[11] With the Christianization of the empire after Constantine, such voices were no longer benign, and the long-term effect of their words has been tragic. From the fourth century on, "house churches" like the one earlier at Dura-Europos, or the likely center of Melito's community in Sardis, were replaced with large public basilicas, paid for from public funds, throughout the Roman Empire. This was particularly the case in Palestine, where a construction boom of Christian sacred architecture created a Christian "Holy Land"—a process best reflected in a thoroughly Christian Palestine presented in the famous

DURA-EUROPOS BAPTISTERY. The murals from the baptistery in the third-century C.E. house church at Dura-Europos in eastern Syria (now installed in the Yale University Art Gallery) were illustrated with subjects from both the Old and New Testaments. Adorning the baptistery's eastern wall (seen in the right of the photo above) is a depiction of a solemn procession, led by two women, to Jesus' large, gabled tomb. To the left, above the baptismal font of the arched niche, is a badly deteriorated painting that depicts both Jesus as "the good shepherd" and Adam and Eve taking the fruit from the tree of knowledge (see reconstructed drawing, bottom).

SARDIS SYNAGOGUE. This synagogue uncovered at Sardis in modern Turkey—the largest ever discovered—was originally a Roman municipal building constructed adjacent to the city's main square. Sardis's large and influential Jewish community acquired the more than 100-yard-long building in the late second century and gradually converted it into an opulent synagogue that could hold more than 1,000 people.

sixth-century Madaba Map, with its many churches celebrating both Old Testament and New Testament history.*

Roman legal tradition, when read together with patristic sources and archaeology, provides a window into the relationship between the church and the Jewish community. Roman imperial legislation preserves a series of documents that reflect an increasingly hostile environment toward the Jewish community.[12] Of particular interest is the way that traditional Roman respect for Judaism as a "licit religion" was renegotiated by a legal bureaucracy that was committed to legal precedent and due process, whose protection of Judaism was weakening under the increasingly strident demands of the church. The Roman jurists now adjudicated the Christian destruction of synagogues—the architectural "footprints" of Jewish communities across the empire. For example, a ruling promulgated on February 15, 423, reads:

> It seems right that in the future none of the synagogues of the Jews shall either be indiscriminately seized or put on fire. If

*See Yoram Tsafrir, "Ancient Churches in the Holy Land," *BAR*, September/October 1993.

there are some synagogues that were seized or vindicated to churches or indeed consecrated to the venerable mysteries in a recent undertaking and after the law was passed, they shall be given in exchange new places, on which they could build, that is, to the measure of the synagogue taken ... No synagogue shall be constructed from now on, and the old ones shall remain in their state.

(Codex Theodosianus 16.8.25)[13]

Archaeological evidence of Christian destruction of synagogues is relatively sparse, yet it is not inconsequential. A synagogue at Ilici (modern Elche) in Spain was razed, and a church built over it. The same fate met the

MADABA MAP OF JERUSALEM. The sixth-century mosaic map discovered on the floor of a church in Madaba, Jordan, provided Christian pilgrims with an illustrated guide to the many churches and shrines built across the Holy Land to commemorate events from both the Old and New Testaments. The map's centerpiece is this oval-shaped rendering of Jerusalem featuring schematic depictions of the city's major thoroughfares and monuments as well as its famed churches, including the Nea Church, the church on Mount Zion and the golden-domed Church of the Holy Sepulchre at its center (see detail on Plate 7).

synagogue at Stobi, in Serbia and at Gerasa (Jerash) in Jordan, its beautiful mosaic floor buried beneath a larger church building.[14] In Palestine, the destruction of synagogues by fire at Ein Gedi and perhaps Caesarea Maritima and Huseifa on Mount Carmel, has been ascribed to Christians.[15]

A Hebrew liturgical poem of late antiquity, preserved in the Cairo Geniza, bemoans the destruction of synagogues in the Holy Land, which the poet absorbed into the mourning for the lost Temple of Jerusalem on the Ninth of Av.[16] It mentions the malicious destruction of synagogues in Kfar Hevrona, Lod, Jaffa, Huseifa and Haifa, and possibly a rabbinic study house (*beth midrash*) in Ono (on the Judean coastal plain).[17] The poet remembers and prays, "Remember, O Lord, the enslavement of Huseifa. Elders were slaughtered and my soul cried, tears clutched me at the destruction of Haifa."

Considerable evidence of destroyed synagogues has been discovered in the Aegean basin, including a capital with three menorahs and a partial inscription that reads "synagogue of the Hebrews" in Greek, both reused in the fill of a theater at Corinth.[18] At Nicaea (modern Iznik) in Asia Minor, an ashlar with a large menorah and a citation from Aquila's translation of Psalm 136:25 (LXX 135) was reused in the main wall of the Byzantine city (and later in a baptismal pool).[19] In Priene a large menorah plaque was turned upside down and reused as a paving stone in the cathedral floor.[20]

Perhaps the most evocative evidence of the violent process by which some Christians "parted ways" from Jews is from Laodicea in Asia Minor, earlier one of the "seven churches" of the Book of Revelation (3:14–22). There a column drum was decorated with a seven-branched menorah, flanked by a palm frond (*lulav*) and a *shofar*—clearly Jewish symbols.[21] Sometime during late antiquity, a large cross was haphazardly carved over the menorah—a common procedure by which Christians marked non-Christian sites as their own, "pagan" and now Jewish sites alike.

Jewish response to the Christianization of the empire beyond the writings of learned rabbis and occasional reports by church fathers is hard to gauge. It is likely that many Jews converted to Christianity with imperial support, as did their pagan and Samaritan neighbors. We hear something of Christian rage at any Jewish attempts to stop this conversion to Christianity in a law promulgated by the emperor (October 18, 329):

We want the Jews, their elders [*maioribus*] and their patriarchs informed that if anyone—once this law has been given—dare attack by stoning or by other kind of fury one escaping from their deadly sect and raising his eyes to God's cult [that is, becoming Christian], when as we have learned is being done now, he shall be delivered immediately to the flames and burnt with all his associates.

(*Codex Theodosianus* 16.8.1)[22]

Among the most famous Jewish converts to Christianity was Romanos the Melodist (sixth century), a Syrian Jew whose Greek liturgical poetry was quite renowned, especially a poem for the dedication of Hagia Sophia, the magnificent church in Constantinople. His church poetry has been associated with Jewish liturgical poetry of his time.[23]

REUSED ASHLAR FROM NICAEA. Evidence of Jewish synagogues and monuments appropriated or even destroyed by Christians can be found at numerous fifth- and sixth-century sites throughout the Mediterranean world. At Nicaea in Asia Minor, this ashlar with a beautifully carved menorah (underside) placed above Aquila's Greek translation of Psalm 136:25 (also underside) was no doubt originally part of a synagogue. It was reused in a later Byzantine city wall. The ashlar's adjacent face features the pronounced, deeply carved inscription of the emperor who dedicated the new wall.

MARVIN LABINGER, COURTESY STEVEN FINE

Jews, a colonized minority in late antique Palestine, benefited materially from Christianization, building large basilical synagogues in the styles of contemporary churches (despite legal restrictions), and adopting such customs from the Christian majority as women wearing marriage rings.[24] Naturally, Jews took on forms and ideas from the larger context, even imaging the divine throne as a heavenly version of the Byzantine royal court.[25]

Jewish liturgical poetry of late antiquity reinforces the line separating Jews from Christians, and rhetorically asserts superiority over the imperial power in an attempt to subvert the power disparity. In the "safety" of the Hebrew language (which few Christians knew), Yannai, a sixth-century synagogue poet, likely from Galilee, rails against the Christians. Yannai characterizes the colonialist Christians as those

> Who chose the disgustingly repulsive,
> Who rejoice in statues of human figures,

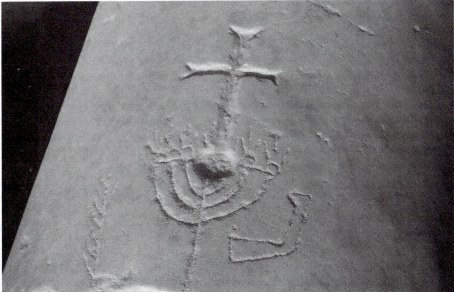

INSCRIBED COLUMN FROM LAODICEA. Another sign of Christian supercessionism is found on this column drum carved with Jewish and Christian graffiti from the site of Laodicea in Asia Minor. A deeply inscribed Byzantine cross has been carved through the branches of an earlier seven-branched menorah flanked by other clearly Jewish symbols, the palm frond and the *shofar*.

Who cleave to the dead over the living,
Who prostrate and pray to a bush.

* * * *

Who burn those who see their mystery,
Who arrange a sacrifice [*minhah*] of pig's blood,
Who, by their very nature, explode with illegitimate children,
Who fast and afflict themselves for emptiness,
Who acquire assemblages of bone.[26]

Yannai knew the claims of Christianity well and assumed that his synagogue audience knew them, too. Note particularly his charge that they "rejoice in statues of human figures" and "prostrate and pray to a bush" (that is, the cross) and, most tellingly, pray to relics ("assemblages of bone"). Other Jewish liturgical texts curse Christians and Jews as "heretics" who serve as "informers" to the gentiles.[27] Still other Jewish texts mock Christian claims—again in the safety of Jewish languages[28]—as a way of reinforcing Jewish resilience against steadily intensifying Christian colonial rule and the pressure for conversion.

In one rather bawdy text called *Toldot Yeshu* (*The Life Story of Jesus*), Mary is said to have conceived Jesus with a Roman centurion (a jab at the doctrine of virginal conception) and Jesus was crucified on a cabbage—after all, self-respecting trees refused to have their wood used for this purpose (mocking Christian fascination with the wood of the "true cross")![29]

Jews in the empire were, in fact, better off than other non-Christian orthodox communities. "Pagan" sites—places of traditional Roman culture—were destroyed in what was the largest wholesale cultural genocide before the arrival of the Spaniards in the New World.[30] "Encouraged" to embrace Christianity—as many did—Jews were allowed to survive as communities. For some Christian thinkers, continued Jewish existence served witness to the truth of Christianity. By the fifth and sixth centuries, Jews in Palestine were treated—like the archetypical placated "Indians" on an American "reservation"—as tamed historical curiosities of a long-past, in this case biblical, history.[31]

A second, less official conversation was occurring at around the same time: Non-Jews had long been attracted to Judaism, with considerable evidence of converts in the Second Temple period, especially from Jerusalem. Rabbinic literature also provides evidence of proselytes to

Judaism, perhaps the most famous being Aquila, who is said to have translated scripture into Greek, following the examples of his second-century teacher Akiva son of Joseph.[32] No proselytes are mentioned by name in rabbinic sources that reflect the third through fifth centuries, though patristic sources mention converts to Judaism in Byzantine Palestine.[33]

In addition to full-fledged proselytes, there were people known from Jewish and Christian sources as "Godfearers"—gentiles who did not convert to Judaism, but were sympathizers and supporters of the Jewish community. (See Chapter III, "The Godfearers: From the Gospels to Aphrodisias," by Bruce Chilton.) Sources as early as the Acts of the Apostles (e.g., Cornelius the Centurion of Acts 10), followed by fourth-century rabbinic sources, mention these "Godfearers." Considerable evidence for "Godfearers" comes from Asia Minor. For example, these *theosebeis* appear as donors of a large portion of mosaic, as well as a menorah, in the Sardis synagogue. We know this from inscriptions, discovered in the synagogue. Nor was this an isolated incident. "Godfearers" are well known particularly in fourth- and fifth-century inscriptions from Asia Minor—in Miletus, Aphrodisias and elsewhere. A Greek inscription on a theater bench at Miletus reads "place of the Jews and the Godfearers" (see p. 59), and in Aphrodisias a large stele immortalizes the donations of Jews and Godfearers to a Jewish communal institution (see p. 67).*[34]

Patristic sources also reflect, with considerable chagrin, the attraction of Judaism for Christians. Thus, for example, the mid-fourth-century Council of Laodicea shows the church hierarchy attempting to keep Christians from adopting Jewish practices:[35]

> Christians should not Judaize and refrain from work on the Sabbath, but they should work on that day. As Christians, they should honor the day of the Lord [Sunday], [and], as much as possible, refrain from work. If they are found out to be Judaizers, let them be anathematized from Christ.
> (Council of Laodicea, Canon 29)[36]

This is strong indication that some Christians found Judaism quite attractive. Elsewhere in this document, Christians are admonished not

---

*See Angelos Chaniotis, "Godfearers in the City of Love," *BAR*, May/June 2010; Louis H. Feldman, "The Omnipresence of the God-Fearers," *BAR*, September/October 1986.

to purchase *matzah* from Jews at Passover.

The most extensive extant polemic against Christian esteem for Jews and Judaism appears in John Chrysostom's *Contra Judaeos* (*Against the Jews*), sensitively—if incorrectly—translated in the wake of the Second Vatican Council as *Discourses Against Judaizing Christians*.[37] Chrysostom spoke to his community in Antioch on the Orontes during the days before the Jewish fall holidays. He writes with considerable urgency:

> ... For if the enemies of the truth never have enough of blaspheming our Benefactor, we must be all the more tireless in praising the God of all. But what am I to do? Another very serious illness calls for any cure my words can bring, an illness which has become implanted in the body of the Church. We must first root out this ailment and then take thought for matters outside; we must first cure our own and then be concerned for others who are strangers.
>
> What is this disease? The festivals of the pitiful and miserable Jews are soon to march upon us one after the other and in quick succession: the feast of Trumpets, the feast of Tabernacles, the fasts. There are many in our ranks who say they think as we do. Yet some of these are going to watch the festivals and others will join the Jews in keeping their feasts and observing their fasts. I wish to drive this perverse custom from the Church right now. My homilies against the Anomoeans can be put off to another time, and the postponement would cause no harm. But now that the Jewish festivals are close by and at the very door, if I should fail to cure those who are sick with the Judaizing disease, I am afraid that, because of their ill-suited association and deep ignorance, some Christians may partake in the Jews' transgressions; once they have done so, I fear my homilies on these transgressions will be in vain. For if they hear no word from me today, they will then join the Jews in their fasts; once they have committed this sin it will be useless for me to apply the remedy ...
>
> (John Chrysostom, *Discourses Against Judaizing Christians* 1.1.4–5)

These homilies reflect considerable acquaintance with Judaism, with its attitudes toward scripture, toward the synagogue as a "holy place" and various rituals.[38] Chrysostom expresses considerable concern for the positive attitude of his community toward Judaism. Here are a few select passages chosen from the first discourse:

> Since there are some who think the synagogue is a holy place, I must say a few words to them. Why do you reverence that place? Must you not despise it, hold it an abomination, run away from it? They answer that the Law and the books of the prophets are kept there. What is this? Will any place where these books are be a holy place? By no means! This is the reason above all others why I hate the synagogue and abhor it. They have the prophets but do not believe them; they read the sacred writings but reject their witness—and this is a mark of men guilty of the greatest outrage ... (1.5.2)
>
> So the godliness of the Jews and the pagans is on a par. But the Jews practice deceit which is more dangerous. In their synagogue stands an invisible altar of deceit on which they sacrifice not sheep and calves but the souls of men. Finally, if the ceremonies of the Jews move you to admiration, what do you have in common with us? If the Jewish ceremonies are venerable and great, ours are lies. But if ours are true, as they *are* true, theirs are filled with deceit. I am not speaking of the Scriptures. Heaven forbid! It was the Scriptures which took me by the hand and led me to Christ. But I am talking about the ungodliness and present madness of the Jews. Certainly it is time for me to show that the demons dwell in the synagogue, not only in the place itself but in the souls of the Jews ... (1.6.4–6)
>
> What else do you wish me to tell you? Shall I tell you of their plundering, their covetousness, their abandonment of the poor, their thefts, their cheating in trade? The whole day long will not be enough to give you an account of these things. (1.7.1)

Little archaeological evidence exists for Jews in Antioch during late antiquity. A small piece of marble with the image of a menorah was discovered there, but is now lost (see p. 110).[39] A large synagogue was discovered in nearby Apamea and considerable evidence for Jewish life is extant throughout modern Turkey, Syria and Lebanon.[40] Chrysostom's homilies are in no way unique; texts similar to these, often fragmentary, are known from across the empire in Greek, Latin and Syriac.[41]

In the early seventh century, the relationship between imperial Christianity and the Jewish minority was transformed. In 614 C.E. the armies of Sassanian Persia crossed the Euphrates, conquering Antioch and Palestine. According to patristic accounts, as the Persian army marched south through Lebanon, it was joined by Jews as it burned churches. In Jerusalem, Christian chronicles suggest, Jews executed large numbers of Christian clergy.[42] A mass grave recently excavated just west of Jerusalem's Jaffa Gate has been associated with this massacre.*

The reconquest of Jerusalem in 629 C.E. was accompanied by a slaughter of Jews. It is not difficult to understand that many Jews greeted the Islamic conquest of Palestine in 636 C.E. with messianic zeal. It was far better to be a second-class "people of the book"—now on a par with Christians—than a persecuted "wretched" remnant. This transformation is well expressed in a lintel discovered in the Western Wall excavations, said to date to this period.[43] At the center of the lintel, Byzantine craftsmen had carved a cross within a roundel. The roundel was apparently filled with plaster and two menorahs were painted in red ocher, flanking the now largely invisible cross. Whether this transformation is the result of the kind of animus that we have suggested regarding the Laodicea column drum referred to earlier, in which a cross was carved over a menorah and both were likely visible, or is the result of Jews acquiring in a more benign way a room once owned by Christians, transforming it into a synagogue with menorahs on its lintel, we cannot know. What is clear, however, is that the effacement of a cross by Jews would have been unthinkable during the latter Byzantine empire. It occurred in the far more hospitable world of Islam, in which Jews were allowed to display menorahs publicly, but the public display of the cross—held by Muslims to be idolatrous[44]—was prohibited.

The story that I have told is not a happy one. It is surely a complex one. It is a story of two communities with shared origins who read many of the same holy books and who held much in common. It is a story of interaction and fascination, of conversion and at times even a degree of tolerance. It is also the history of supersession, violence, survival

*See Strata, "Ancient Persians Massacre Jerusalem Christians," *BAR*, November/December 2010; and Ronny Reich, "'God Knows Their Names': Mass Christian Grave Revealed in Jerusalem," *BAR*, March/April 1996.

DRAWING BY BRIAN LALOR, FROM EILAT MAZAR, *THE TEMPLE MOUNT EXCAVATIONS IN JERUSALEM, QEDEM 43*

BYZANTINE LINTEL REUSED IN A JERUSALEM SYNAGOGUE. Shortly after the Islamic conquest of Palestine in 636 C.E., this 4-foot-long stone lintel with a Byzantine cross carved within a roundel was reused in the doorway of a Jerusalem synagogue in the area of the Western Wall. With no apparent concern for erasing the lintel's Christian symbol, the synagogue's builders filled the roundel with plaster and painted red menorahs and other Jewish symbols on either side.

and vengeance. Literary and archaeological sources suggest that by the mid-fourth century or so the "parting of the ways" was truly an unequal relationship, in which a Jewish minority sought to maintain its balance within an empire that was malevolent toward "pagans," "heretics" and toward "Jews" as well. A pattern of anti-Judaism—rhetorical and often enacted—well known for its vehemence, was set in place. Alas, this pattern continued to reverberate well into the 20th century, when my grandparents—refugees from pogroms, saved by their earlier emigration from the horrors of the Second World War, met their Christian neighbors under the new umbrella of American tolerance. Alas, it is a pattern of disdain that members of all communities must continue to guard against even today.

13

From Sabbath to Sunday: Why, How and When?

LAWRENCE T. GERATY

JEWS HAVE OBSERVED THE SEVENTH-DAY SABBATH ACCORDING TO the biblical commandment (Exodus 20; Deuteronomy 5) for thousands of years. Jesus, being a Jew, did the same (see, for instance, Luke 4:16). The vast majority of his followers, however, calling themselves Christian, today observe the first day in lieu of the seventh day.[1] It is also common knowledge that Christianity grew out of Judaism. Why, how and when did this transition to a different day of worship occur?

Let me deal at the outset with what may be an underlying issue. I am a Seventh-day Adventist. Presumably editor Hershel Shanks asked me to write this chapter because I might reasonably be expected to have an interest in the subject, hopefully, an unbiased one! Although my first published paper dealt with this subject, I am heavily dependent here on the research of others, particularly on the doctoral research at the Vatican's

Pontifical Gregorian University of my (now deceased) friend, Samuele Bacchiocchi, also a Seventh-day Adventist scholar.* For what it is worth, his books have received the Vatican imprimatur.[2]

The New Testament and early church period

There is no evidence in the New Testament for any move on the part of Jesus' followers to replace the Jewish Sabbath. On the contrary, the Book of Acts describes the private gatherings of early Christians as not conflicting with the Temple or synagogue services, but rather as complementing them. These earliest Christians were known as Nazarenes (Acts 24:5), within the Jewish fold, similar to the Jewish parties of the Sadducees (Acts 5:17) and Pharisees (Acts 15:5, 26:5). There appears to be no desire to leave the parent religion. C.W. Dugmore, to whom we are indebted for an exhaustive study on the influence of the synagogue upon the Christian service, shows persuasively that the "synagogue did influence both the form of service and the times at which Christians met together for public prayer in the first four centuries of our era to a much greater extent than has sometimes been recognized."[3]

Some of the hostility of Jewish religious leaders toward Christians of course had theological motivations. In the words of Denise Judant:

> While the Judeo-Christians considered themselves to be the lawful heirs of the tradition of Israel, the Jewish religious leaders could not concede faith in the divinity of the Messiah, which to them appeared as a threat to monotheism or the suppression of the Mosaic observances, considered disobedience to the divine law, or the proclamation of the equality of all men before God, since this would have meant the abolition of the privileges of Israel.[4]

So, for instance, Jews followed Paul in his evangelistic itinerary, endeavoring to hinder and neutralize his work (see Acts 13:50, 14:5, 14:19, 17:5, 17:13, 18:6, 18:13, 20:3, 21:27, 23:12, 24:1–9, etc.). The accusation against and arrest of Paul on the part of the chief priests and elders accelerated the process of separation of Jews and Christians. This hostility, which was initially directed toward the Christians of Jewish birth and later

*See Samuele Bacchiocchi, "How It Came About: From Saturday to Sunday," *BAR*, September/ October 1978.

was extended to all Christians, induced the church fathers to assume an attitude of condemnation and separation from those traditions that were typically Jewish. Christians began to distinguish themselves from Jews in the eyes of the Romans and to affirm and safeguard at the same time their identity and rights.

The Jerusalem council (recounted in Acts 15) shows the concern of James and of the apostles to respect Jewish scruples regarding circumcision, food (including abstention from meat that had been offered to idols, and from anything strangled) and association with gentiles. This hardly allows us to imagine that a weightier matter like Sabbath observance would be abrogated. In such a climate it would be impossible to change the date of a millenarian institution like the Sabbath. Furthermore, Paul's reassurance to Jewish believers that he was loyal to their laws and customs (Acts 24:17–18) suffices to discredit any attempt to attribute to him the responsibility for the abrogation of the Sabbath and introduction of Sunday observance.

In Matthew, a gospel addressed to Jewish-Christians, Jesus speaks of the coming tribulation when his followers will flee to the mountains: "Pray that your flight may not be in winter or on the Sabbath" (Matthew 24:20).

In short, the primitive Christian community in Jerusalem was composed primarily of, and administered by, converted Jews who retained a deep attachment to Jewish religious customs such as Sabbath-keeping. It is difficult to imagine that a new day of worship was introduced by the Jerusalem church prior to the Roman destruction of the city in 70 C.E.

The martyrdom of James (c. 62 C.E.) reflects mounting Jewish hostility to Christians. And the flight of Christians to Transjordan (c. 68–70 C.E.) during the Jewish revolt against Rome (see Chapter IV, "The Christian Flight to Pella? The Archaeological Picture," by Pamela Watson) only resulted in further alienation of Christians from Jews.

After the Roman destruction of Jerusalem in 70 C.E., the rabbinical authorities reconstituted at Yavneh (Jamnia in Greek) (c. 80–90 C.E.). They appear to have introduced a "test" in the daily synagogue service to detect the presence of heretics consisting of a curse against heretics. It has long been suggested that this serves as evidence that there must have been Judeo-Christians still worshiping in the synagogues on Sabbath even after the fall of Jerusalem.[5] More recently, however, questions have been raised as to when this curse on heretics was added to the synagogue service, as well as to whether Christians were clearly intended as the object (see Chapter XI, "In Between: Jewish-Christians and the Curse of the Heretics," by Shaye J.D. Cohen).[6]

The Jerusalem church was administered successively by 15 bishops, all of Jewish extraction. We know for instance that at the time of Justin (150 C.E.), Jewish-Christians stressed Sabbath observance and no mention is made of their keeping Sunday. Had the latter been the case, Justin would surely have mentioned it in his anti-Jewish *Dialogue with Trypho*.[7]

In short, it would be difficult to find any argument that the Jerusalem church introduced so radical a liturgical innovation as Sunday observance before Hadrian's conquest of Jerusalem at the end of the Second Jewish Revolt in 135 C.E. After 135 C.E. Jerusalem was rebuilt as a pagan Roman colony—Aelia Capitolina—and Hadrian specifically forbade observance of the Sabbath. But by then the city had lost its political and religious prestige for both Jews and Christians.

The year 135, however, does mark a significant break in the relationships between Judaism and Christianity.[8] First, there was the total cessation of the sacrificial and sacerdotal system. But there was more: The proclamation of Bar-Kokhba, the leader of the Jewish revolt, as the Messiah effectively repudiated Jesus as the Messiah.[9] The persecution of the Judeo-Christians on the part of the rebellious Jews also contributed to the separation of Jews and Christians,[10] as did Hadrian's edict prohibiting the practice of Judaism and the entrance of Jews into Aelia Capitolina.[11]

All these factors must have created a Christian need to separate and differentiate themselves from the Jews. The abandoning of Sabbath and the adoption of Sunday by many Christians could have been the most evident sign of this process.[12]

As Bruce M. Metzger has expressed it:

> The difference between East and West in the observance of the Sabbath can be accounted for by a reasonable historical explanation. In the West, particularly after the Jewish rebellion under Hadrian, it became vitally important for those who were not Jews to avoid exposing themselves to suspicion; and the observance of the Sabbath was one of the most noticeable indications of Judaism. In the East, however, less opposition was shown to Jewish institutions.[13]

Scholars have suggested a number of factors to account for the transition from Sabbath to Sunday. I will list them first and then explore them in more detail.

- Anti-Judaism in the Roman Empire beginning as early as the first century C.E. could have motivated Christians to disassociate and differentiate themselves from Jews.

- During the spread of Christianity, particularly outside of Palestine, many early Christian converts may have come from Roman-era cults in which sun worship may have played a role.

- Other early Christians may have come from Jewish sects such as the Dead Sea Scroll sect that favored Sunday for certain cultic observances.

- Some early Christian writers were persuaded that the resurrection, having occurred on Sunday, offered a better Christian precedent for worship than creation (Genesis 1–2) and the Exodus redemption (Deuteronomy 5:13–15).

Anti-Judaism in the Roman Empire

As Samuele Bacchiocchi has observed:

> Two processes seem to have conditioned the relations between Jews and Christians in the first centuries. On the one hand ... Christians assimilated and adapted Jewish cultic traditions according to the exigencies of their New Faith. They still felt sufficiently united to Judaism to retain many of its characteristics. On the other hand, Christians considered themselves to be distinct and separated from the Old Faith, having accepted the message of Jesus Christ. This Christian awareness of distinction from Judaism became the primary cause of the hostility of Jews toward Christians and in time it contributed to the separation and differentiation of Christians from Jews. Unfortunately these two processes of assimilation and differentiation, continuity and discontinuity have not always been in balance or harmony. This has often given rise to conflicts, either in Christianity itself or in its relationship with Judaism.[14]

Concomitant factors in these processes may have contributed to the renunciation of the Sabbath and adoption of Sunday on the part of the majority of Christians, especially given the anti-Judaism in Rome.

The predominance of Christians of pagan extraction and their conflict with the Jews led to a break with Judaism in Rome even before it had occurred in the East. (See Chapter VIII, "Jews and Christians at Rome: An Early Parting of the Ways" by Margaret H. Williams.) In the year 49, Emperor Claudius, according to the Roman historian Suetonius (c. 70–122 C.E.), "expelled the Jews from Rome since they rioted constantly at the instigation of Chrestus."[15] Whether or not this is a reference to Christ, they were nevertheless expelled. Among the converted Jews who were expelled were Aquila and Priscilla (Acts 18:2), suggesting that the Roman police had not yet come to distinguish Christians from Jews. By 64 C.E., however, as F.F. Bruce has observed, Christians "were clearly differentiated at Rome," while it "took a little longer in Palestine (where practically all Christians were of Jewish birth)."[16]

The unpopularity of the Jews in Rome as well as the anti-Judaic measures taken by the emperors following the Jewish rebellions, such as the imposition of certain taxes only on Jews, could have influenced the attitude of the church of Rome toward the Sabbath (as well as toward the Jewish Passover)—anything to get out of paying taxes!

It was probably in Rome that Easter Sunday originated (at about the time of Pope Sixtus, c. 116–126 C.E.) in order for Christians to separate themselves from the date of the Jewish Passover.[17] Jews consistently observed Passover on Nisan 14, which coincided with Jesus' trial and crucifixion. That meant that whenever the Jews were celebrating Passover in subsequent years, Christians would be celebrating Passion week culminating in Easter. This was called the "Quartodeciman" practice. As Christians began differentiating themselves from Jewish practices, however, there arose the practice of always observing Easter on the nearest Sunday to Passover. In other words, there were Christians celebrating Easter at two different times, one according to Nisan 14, and the other always on a Sunday. Gradually the latter practice won out. As Emperor Constantine himself later stated:

> It appeared an unworthy thing that in the celebration of this most holy feast we should follow the practice of the Jews, who have impiously defiled their hands with enormous sin, and are,

therefore, deservedly afflicted with blindness of souls ... Let
us then have nothing in common with the detestable Jewish
crowd; for we have received from our Savior a different way.
(Quoted in Eusebius, *Life of Constantine* 3.18–19)[18]

Eusebius (c. 260–340 C.E.) describes the controversy that flared up
when Bishop Victor of Rome (189–199 C.E.) required observance of
Easter on Sunday in place of the older custom championed by Polycrates,
Bishop of Ephesus, of celebrating it in relation to the Jewish Passover on
Nisan 14 according to the Jewish calendar (the so-called Quartodeciman
[14th] observance).[19]

Finally, it is from Rome that we get the first detailed treatment of the
celebration of the Eucharist on Sunday (through Justin; see below) as well
as of the repudiation of the Sabbath, which was considered the mark of
the unfaithfulness of the Jews.[20] The weekly observance of Sunday may
well have been influenced by the Jewish custom in Rome of fasting on
the Sabbath.[21] To quote Bacchiocchi, "In the light of the close nexus
existing between the annual Paschal Sabbath fast and the weekly one, it is
reasonable to conclude that the latter originated in Rome as an extension
of the former, not only to express sorrow for Christ's death but also to
show contempt for the Jewish people and particularly for their Sabbath."[22]
In fact, this is one of the factors that contributed to the break between
the eastern church and the western church in 1054 C.E.[23]

In summary, we can again quote Bacchiocchi on the various factors
pointing to Rome as the place for the abandonment of the Sabbath and
the adoption of Sunday:

> The premature separation of the Christian community from
> the Jews, the pagan origin of the majority of its members, the
> unpopularity of the Jews in the capital city, the imperial fiscal
> anti-Judaic measures, Hadrian's repressive measures against
> Jewish worship such as the observance of Sabbath ... and the
> repudiation of the Jewish Quartodeciman Passover. Besides all
> these factors, present in their totality only in Rome, can be added
> the role of spiritual primacy exercised by the bishop of Rome, the
> only one capable of influencing the rest of Christianity to adopt
> such a new liturgical practice as that of the commemoration of
> the resurrection on Sunday, both as a weekly and a yearly feast.[24]

Canon 29 of the Council of Laodicea (c. 360 C.E.) explicitly condemns the veneration of the Sabbath as Judaizing and prescribes working on such a day in order to show a special respect for Sunday: "Christians must not Judaize by resting on the Sabbath, but must work on that day, honoring rather the Lord's Day by resting, if possible, as Christians. However if any shall be found Judaizing, let them be anathema from Christ."[25]

Such depreciations of the Sabbath and condemnation of "Judaizing" by such a day, along with the related appreciation of Sunday, reflect how the observance of Sunday was felt to be a clear sign of the separation and dissociation from Judaism. Even in the fourth century, such church fathers as Athanasius in Alexandria, Cyril in Jerusalem, Basil in Cappadocia and Chrysostom in Antioch all fought against the observance of the Sabbath on the part of some Christians.

Sun worship in the Roman Empire

While anti-Judaism prompted the rejection of the Sabbath, what determined the choice of Sunday?

One possibility is the planetary week, the days named for the seven planets.[26] If Sunday-keeping was introduced into Christianity in the early part of the second century, was the planetary week already in existence in the Greco-Roman world? Gaston H. Halsberghe presents persuasive texts and arguments indicating that Sun worship was "one of the oldest components of the Roman religion."[27] According to him, the Sun cult in ancient Rome experienced two phases: Until the end of the first century C.E., the Romans practiced what he calls an "autochthonous [i.e., native or indigenous] Sun-cult," but "starting in the second century [C.E.], Eastern Sun-worship began to influence Rome and the rest of the Empire."[28]

Dio Cassius (c. 150–235 C.E.)[29] says that the planetary week had come into use "not so very long ago," that the Romans regarded it as an ancestral custom, and that already back in 37 B.C.E., when Jerusalem was captured by Sosius and Herod the Great, the Sabbath "even then was called day of Saturn."[30] For such reasons, C.S. Mosna concludes that "the planetary week must have originated already in the first century B.C.,"[31] a fact confirmed by many finds from Pompeii, which was destroyed in the volcanic eruption of Mount Vesuvius in 79 C.E.[32]

According to Bacchiocchi, the preeminence of Sunday in the plane-tary-named days of the week is already implied by Justin Martyr:

Why in [Justin's] brief exposition of the Christian worship [*1 Apology* 67] did he mention three times "the day of the Sun"? Why did he present the creation of light on the first day as the first reason for the Christian Sunday gathering? Apparently because the day was venerated by the Romans. By associating Christian worship with both the day and the symbolism of the pagan Sun, Justin ... aimed at gaining from the Emperor a favorable appraisal of Christianity.[33]

Thus, Christians themselves were not immune to the popular veneration of the sun and astrological practices. Such is attested to by the frequent condemnation of these practices by the church fathers.[34] Reflexes of sun worship in the Christian liturgy can be seen in the theme of "Christ, the Sun,"[35] in the orientation toward the east,[36] and in the practice of observing Christ's birth (Christmas) on the day of the winter solstice, i.e., the birth of the sun.[37]

Bacchiocchi suggests that no deliberate attempt was made prior to Eusebius (c. 260–340 C.E.) to justify Sunday observance by means of the symbolism of the day of the Sun. Eusebius, however, on several occasions refers explicitly to the motifs of the light, of the sun and of the day of the Sun to explain Christian Sunday as the substitution for the Jewish Sabbath.[38] For instance:

The Logos has transferred by the New Alliance the celebration of the Sabbath to the rising of the light. In this day of light, first day and true day of the sun, when we gather after the interval of six days, we celebrate the holy and spiritual Sabbaths ... All things whatsoever that were prescribed for the Sabbath, we have transferred them to the Lord's Day, as being more authoritative and more highly regarded and first in rank, and more honorable than the Jewish Sabbath. In fact, it is on this day of the creation of the world that God said: "Let there be light and there was light." It is also on this day that the Sun of Justice has risen for our souls.
(Eusebius of Caesarea, *Commentary on Psalm 91*)[39]

As Bacchiocchi has suggested:

The existence of two distinct traditions, one Judaeo-Christian which associated the Deity with the Light and the Sun, and the other pagan which venerated the Sun, especially on Sun-day, could well have produced an amalgamation of ideas within the Christian community. The process could have predisposed those Christians who had previously venerated the Sun and who now needed to differentiate themselves from the Jewish Sabbath, to adopt the day of the Sun for their weekly worship.[40]

Sunday in Jewish sectarianism

The Jews associated with the Dead Sea Scrolls appear to have used a sectarian solar calendar,[41] but there is no hint that early Christians in Jerusalem abandoned the regular Jewish worship times.

Earle Hilgert has argued that "a psychological orientation toward Sunday derived from Qumran or related circles may well have been a contributing factor in the establishment of Sunday observance in the early church."[42] A similar Jewish sacerdotal calendar is reflected in the Book of Jubilees in which yearly feasts are held on specific days of the week.

If Sunday observance originated in Rome, however, rather than in Jerusalem, it would seem unlikely that it derived from a Jewish source or even from Paul. Indeed as Paul K. Jewett has noted, "[Paul] is the only New Testament writer who warns his converts against the observance of days [Colossians 2:16–17; Galatians 4:10; Romans 14:6]."[43]

The theology of Sunday worship

A number of theological motivations have been advanced to justify both the choice and the observance of Sunday for Christian worship. The major motives can best be grouped around three basic headings: resurrection, creation and the symbolism of the eighth day.

Resurrection

Jesus' resurrection occurred on the first day of the week. He was crucified on Friday and rose three days later, on Sunday, by Jewish counting. This became the dominant reason for Sunday observance. Augustine (354–430 C.E.) provides perhaps the most explicit enunciation of this: "The Lord's day was not declared to the Jews but to the Christians by the resurrection of the Lord and from that event its festivity had its origin."[44] But, as Bacchiocchi has observed, "This concise and explicit recognition of the resurrection as the cause of the origin of Sunday observance represents the culmination of long theological reflection."[45]

In the early second century, Ignatius of Antioch does not present the resurrection either as the first or the sole motivation for Sunday observance. The "divine prophets who lived according to Jesus Christ attained a new hope, no longer sabbatizing but living according to the Lord's life, on [or by] which also our life rose up through his death." Ignatius is contrasting ways of life rather than days.[46]

In both Barnabas and Justin Martyr, the resurrection is mentioned as the second of two reasons, important but not dominant, for Sunday observance.[47] This is especially noteworthy because both men lived at the very time when Sunday worship was rising, and yet both present the resurrection as a secondary or additional motivation for Sunday, apparently because this was not yet viewed as the fundamental reason.[48]

Creation

The commemoration of creation is a justification often adduced by the church fathers for observing Sunday. Justin Martyr presents this as the primary reason for the Christian Sunday gathering:

> Sunday, indeed, is the day on which we hold our common assembly because it is the first day on which God, transforming darkness and [prime] matter, created the world; and our Savior Jesus Christ arose from the dead on the same day.
>
> (Justin Martyr, *1 Apology* 67.5–7)

Justin was not alone in seeing a nexus between creation and resurrection. It is found even more explicitly in a sermon of Eusebius of Alexandria (c. 500 C.E.):

> The holy day of Sunday is the commemoration of the Lord. It is called Lord's because it is the Lord of all days ... It was on this day that the Lord established the foundation of the creation of the world and on the same day He gave to the world the first-fruits of the resurrection ... This day is therefore for us the source of all benefits; the beginning of the creation of the world, the beginning of the resurrection, the beginning of the week. Since this day contains three beginnings, it prefigures the principle of the Trinity.
>
> (Eusebius of Alexandria, *De Die Dominico*)[49]

The Eighth Day

Numerical symbolism was highly important for the early Christians, as the works of the church fathers make clear. This type of symbolism is alien to modern thought, but it provided early Christian preachers and theologians with practical and yet profound arguments that captivated much of the thinking of Christian antiquity. Barnabas of Alexandria famously stated:

> Further he says to them, "Your new moons and Sabbaths I cannot endure." [quoting Isaiah 1:13] You see what he means: It is not the present Sabbaths that are acceptable to me, but the one that I have made, on which having brought everything to rest, I will make the beginning of an eighth day, that is, the beginning of another world. This is why we also observe the eighth day with rejoicing, on which Jesus also rose from the dead, and having shown himself, ascended to heaven.
>
> (Epistle of Barnabas 15.8–9)[50]

Barnabas's cosmic-eschatological symbolism of the eighth day to justify Sunday observance is reiterated and elaborated by numerous church fathers, which bespeaks a widespread tradition that speculated on the duration of the world by means of the cosmic week.[51]

As Bacchiocchi observed, the rich symbology of the eighth day "became widely used primarily as a polemic argument to prove the fulfillment, the substitution, and the supersedure of Judaism and of its Sabbath as well as the superiority of Christianity and of its Sunday."[52]

Conclusion

The first explicit, but timid, reference to Christian Sunday is found in the Epistle of Barnabas (chapter 15), which mentions simply that Christians spent the eighth day rejoicing, inasmuch as it represented the prolongation of the eschatological Sabbath, to which is united the memory of the resurrection. Since Barnabas lived at the crucial time when Emperor Hadrian (117–138 C.E.) adopted rigorous and repressive measures against the Jews, outlawing their religious observances and particularly their Sabbath-keeping, both external pressures and internal needs encouraged many Christians at that time to break radically with the Jews. Externally, the existing conflict between the Jews and the empire made it necessary for

Christians to develop a new identity in order to avoid the repressive and punitive measures (fiscal, military, political and literary) aimed at the Jews.

Internally, the influence of the synagogue and of Judeo-Christians who insisted on the literal observance of certain Mosaic regulations prompted many Christians to sever their ties with Judaism. To develop this new identity, many Christians not only assumed a negative attitude toward the Jews as a people but also substituted characteristic Jewish religious observance such as Passover with Easter Sunday and the Sabbath with Sunday. This apparently served to make the Roman authorities aware that Christians, now liberated from Jewish religious ties, represented for the empire irreproachable subjects.

It is quite clear then that Sunday observance was introduced in a climate of controversy. Christians had a need to force a break with Judaism. That occurred first and to a greater degree in the church of Rome. In Rome most Christian converts were of pagan extraction; they experienced an earlier differentiation from Jews than converts in the East. The repressive measures adopted by the Romans against the Jews—particularly felt in the Roman capital—apparently encouraged the predominant gentile membership in the church of Rome to clarify to the Roman authorities their distinction from Judaism. The close nexus between Easter Sunday and weekly Sunday—the latter being viewed by many church fathers as an extension of the former[53]—suggests that both festivities originated contemporaneously in Rome because of the same anti-Judaic motivations.

Moreover, in the second century only the bishop of Rome enjoyed sufficient ecclesiastical authority to influence the greater part of Christendom to accept new customs or observances, even though some churches refused to comply with his instruction.

The specific choice of Sunday as the new Christian day of worship was suggested not by anti-Judaism but by other factors. Anti-Judaism caused a devaluation and repudiation of the Sabbath, thus creating the necessity to look for a new day of worship. The diffusion of the sun cults, which early in the second century caused the advance of the day of the Sun to the position of first day of the week, especially oriented Christian converts from paganism toward the day of the Sun.

The existence of a rich Judeo-Christian tradition associating the deity with the sun and light apparently predisposed Christians favorably toward the day and the symbolism of the sun. Christians also realized that the venerable day of the Sun provided a fitting symbolism that could efficaciously commemorate and explain to the pagan world two fundamental events in the history of salvation—creation and resurrection. Jerome himself said it: "It is on this day that the Light of the World has appeared and on this day that the Sun of Justice has risen."[54]

The origin of Sunday was the result of an interplay of Jewish, pagan and Christian factors. Judaism, as we have seen, contributed both negatively and positively to the rise of Sunday. The negative aspect is represented by the repressive measures adopted by the Romans against the rebelling Jews, as well as by the Jewish hostility toward Christians, both of which created the necessity of a radical Christian separation from Judaism. This need for differentiation was a determining factor in causing both the repudiation of the Sabbath and the exigency of a new day of worship.

The positive contribution of Judaism to the rise of Sunday may have been a psychological orientation toward Sunday derived from the sectarian Jubilees or Qumran calendar, but especially in the Jewish apocalyptic speculations on the cosmic week. The latter made it possible to defend the choice of Sunday in Jewish and Jewish-Christian circles since, as the eighth eschatological day representing the eternal new world, Sunday was superior to the seventh terrestrial millennium symbolized by the Sabbath.

Paganism suggested to those Christians who had previously known both the day and the cult of the sun the possibility of adopting the venerable day of the Sun as their new day of worship. This rich symbolism of the sun in the pagan world was conducive to worshiping the True Sun of Righteousness who on that day divided light from darkness.

Lastly, Christianity gave theological justification to Sunday observance by teaching that the day commemorated important events such as the inauguration of creation, the resurrection of Christ and the eschatological hope of the new world to come. It appears, therefore, that Jewish, pagan and Christian factors merged to give rise to an institution that satisfied the exigencies of many Jewish as well as pagan converts to the new religion.

In the end, Sunday worship does not rest on a foundation of biblical theology and/or apostolic authority, but on the later contributory factors suggested here. In the context of this book, it not only facilitated the parting of the ways, but is a cosmic summary of the process.[55]

14

Social Organization and Parting in East and West

ARYE EDREI AND DORON MENDELS

MANY CHURCH HISTORIANS AND JUDAIC SCHOLARS HAVE attempted to account for the gap that progressively widened between Judaism and Christianity in the early centuries of the common era.[1] Here we present our initial thoughts on a catalyst for the widening gap between the two religions—the rabbinic aspiration to develop a system of civil law and an autonomous community structure, in contrast to no such aspiration among contemporaneous Christians. This had a significant influence on the schism between the two religions, or, as it is commonly known, the parting of the ways.[2]

While the rabbinic tradition sought to develop an isolated community with its own legal system, Christianity tended to rely on the legal system of the government within which the church functioned. Interestingly, Judaism was the only religion in the ancient world that developed a comprehensive system of civil law that overtly addressed secular and communal matters as part of its religious system. Christianity, for its own reasons, did not develop a "civil" law during its first centuries, but rather relied on Roman law. For this reason, Christianity was able to integrate more easily into the various elements of the Roman public sectors, such as the market, the army, and the public administration and, to a certain degree, gradually assimilated into them. Not only did the rabbis not forgo their law and its significance, but they strengthened its importance as a component of religious observance.

Our argument—essentially a matter of political science—is that the gap that existed between the Jewish and Christian approaches to legal sovereignty significantly influenced the schism between them.

The Jewish position

Rabbinic Judaism sought to develop a "state within a state" or, more precisely, "a community within a state." Rabbinic Judaism emphasized its own legal culture, as distinct from the law of the host state. This rabbinic political stance, when contrasted to Christian political theology, explains the difference between the Christian aspiration to spread out and the Jewish aspiration for seclusion.

The manner in which the rabbis expanded the scope of certain rituals and religious laws reflects their eagerness to establish a separate community of believers. Augustine pointed this out already in the fifth century:

> This is really a wonder, that the Jewish tribe did not forfeit its law, neither under the rule of idolatrous monarchs nor under the hegemony of the Egyptians. In this way, they remained separate from other tribes and people. Every king or caesar who found them in his land was unable to effect a reality in which the Jews were not separated from the other people by means of observance of their laws.
>
> (Augustine, *Against Faustus*)[3]

It is not entirely clear whether Augustine was referring to Jewish religious and ritual law or, as it seems to us, also or primarily to the civil legal code. Indeed, there is no question that religious laws, such as *kashrut* (dietary laws) and the Sabbath, promoted the social separation and communal seclusion of the Jews. By these observances, "the Jews are separated from the family of nations."⁴ But far beyond this, one of the six orders of the Mishnah, the order of *Nezikin* (*Damages*), deals entirely with civil law—including laws of acquisition, damages, monetary and property issues, documents, jurisprudence and punishment. These topics arise frequently in other parts of the Mishnah as well as in other rabbinic sources. In both the Jerusalem and Babylonian Talmud, we find numerous instances in which Jewish courts issued rulings in civil litigation between Jews.⁵ The ideal that the rabbis were promoting was a separate legal system.

Moreover, the rabbis rejected a missionary approach; they had no aspiration to proselytize others. They fashioned the Torah as a *national* Torah without universalistic goals. They did, however, establish minimum requirements for mankind called the "seven Noahide laws," which included the prohibitions of murder, adultery, etc.⁶ The most intriguing in this regard is the "*denim*," which places an obligation upon every human society to establish a fair and egalitarian system of justice. In essence, the rabbis argued that every society needs a system of justice and that they therefore should create their own legal system, but they did not presume that the Jewish legal system should be adopted by other nations. In reality, the rabbis viewed civil law as an integral part of their own religious and national identity. Likewise, every nation should establish a fair judicial system, but they were not prepared to share their own system with the outside world. Their stubborn insistence that Jews are obligated to be subordinate to the Jewish legal system was not based on the notion that it was more just or more suitable, but because it was *theirs*, and this made them unique. The rabbis engaged in the study of law and jurisprudence not only as an instrument for maintaining their society, but also as part of divine law. Indeed, in addition to the Mishnah, a quarter of the Babylonian Talmud deals with societal order—what we call civil and criminal law. Not surprisingly, in rabbinic law it is forbidden for a Jew to litigate with another Jew in a non-Jewish court. And, conversely, there is no place for a non-Jew in the Jewish courts.

Ultimately, the rabbinic *halakhah* (law) that the rabbis sought to establish in the context of the dispersion and exile is based on a biblical model. It is described in Deuteronomy 17:8–11:

If there arise a matter too hard for you in judgment, between blood and blood [capital], between judgment and judgment [civil], and between affliction and affliction [skin afflictions], even matters of controversy within your gates; then shall you rise up and go up to the place which the Lord your God shall choose. And you shall come unto the priests the Levites, and unto the judge that shall be in those days; and you shall inquire; and they shall declare to you the sentence of judgment ...

The Babylonian Talmud cites a *Beraita* in the name of Rabbi Tarfon that expands upon this concept:

R. Tarfon used to say: In any place where you find heathen law courts, even though their law is the same as the Israelite law, you must not resort to them since it says: "These are the judgments which you shall set before them."

(BT *Gittin* 88b)[7]

A Jew who uses a non-Jewish court came to be considered as one who desecrates God's name:

"Before them," and not before gentiles: How do we know that Jewish litigants who have a controversy between them cannot appear before gentiles, even if they know that they judge [on this issue] in the same way as the Jewish law? Because the Torah says: "before them"—and not before non-Jews. For anyone who leaves Jewish judges and goes before non-Jews, first denies God, and afterwards denies the Torah, as it says [Deuteronomy 32:31]: "For not like our Rock is their rock—yet our enemies judge us."

(*Tanhuma, Parshat Mishpatim*, section 3)

The testimony of a gentile in a non-Jewish court is proper and valid, but it is invalid in a Jewish court. This follows not from a lack of trust, but from the desire for isolation and separation—the exclusion of non-Jews from Jewish courts.[8]

The Christian position

In his epistle to the Romans, Paul describes the contrasting Christian position:

Let every person be subject to the governing authorities. For there is no authority except by God's appointment, and the authorities that exist have been instituted by God. So the person who resists such authority resists the ordinance of God, and those who resist will incur judgment (for rulers cause no fear for good conduct but for bad). Do you desire not to fear authority? Do good and you will receive its commendation, for it is God's servant for your good. But if you do wrong, be in fear, for it does not bear the sword in vain. It is God's servant to administer retribution on the wrongdoer. Therefore it is necessary to be in subjection, not only because of the wrath of the authorities but also because of your conscience. For this reason you also pay taxes, for the authorities are God's servants devoted to governing. Pay everyone what is owed: taxes to whom taxes are due, revenue to whom revenue is due, respect to whom respect is due, honor to whom honor is due.

(Romans 13:1–7)[9]

Paul here elaborates on an idea that already appeared in the sayings of Jesus: "If so, grant unto Caesar what is Caesar's, and unto God what is God's" (Matthew 22:21). The only law that is valid for Christians is the law of the sovereign state; the church has no presumption of having a separate judicial system. Rather, it views the law of the sovereign as divinely ordained. At the same time, Christianity continued to promote and develop ethical concepts that might help in the crystallization of the community, but would not contribute in any way to the creation of a state or anything similar.[10] As argued by the church father Eusebius:

[T]he old covenant and the law given by Moses was only applicable to the Jewish race, and only to such of them as lived in their own land. It did not apply to other nations of the world nor to the Jews inhabiting foreign soil.

(Eusebius, *Proof of the Gospel* 1.5.1)[11]

And further:

Christ sojourned in this life, and the teaching of the new covenant was borne to all nations, and immediately the Romans themselves besieged Jerusalem, and destroyed it and the Temple there. At once the whole of the Mosaic law was abolished, with all that remained of the old covenant and its curse passed over to those who became lawbreakers, because they obeyed Moses' laws when its time had gone by, and still clung ardently to it, for at that very moment the perfect teaching of the new Law was introduced in its place.

(Eusebius, Proof of the Gospel 1.6.34–35)

Early on Christians said clearly and bluntly that they do not have and do not need a civil code of their own, whereas the Jews needed one.

In this way, Eusebius provides a theological anchor for Christianity vis-à-vis its lack of a legal system for its community. This nullification of the law also came hand-in-hand with the nullification of the idea of the divine election of the Jewish people. This enabled Christianity to undergo a process of integration into Roman society and to "conquer" it gradually.

The opposite was true of the Jewish people. The idea of divine selection and divine commandments engendered the aspiration for separation. The Christian approach outsourced to the empire everything related to law and aspects of communal organization. This theology and the communal organization that flowed from it contributed to the Roman Empire's adoption of Christianity at the time of Constantine the Great. Christianity relied on the universal state within which it existed. Since Christianity negated a legal sovereign approach in the first few centuries of its existence, it needed a political context for its existence. Even in the ancient world, a state could not exist on dogma alone. The Christians were therefore unable to create an autonomous society in the absence of a political context. The Roman Empire was an ideal political context for this purpose because it was a universalistic sovereign entity that could integrate a religion that had no legal framework of its own to conflict with the Roman legal system. The aspects of Christianity that bothered the Romans from time to time were matters of faith, not law. In the final analysis, the Roman Empire facilitated the spread of Christianity. The irony of history in the first few centuries of the common era was that even though Christians wanted to integrate into the Roman legal and political systems, the Romans perceived them as a threat, fearing a Christian conspiracy to dominate the empire. It is therefore easy to understand that in the first few centuries, Christians were the targets of Roman persecution much more than Jews.[12] In short, the Christian church was not designed to exercise sovereign political governance.

CONSTANTINE THE GREAT. By the time Emperor Constantine (right) converted to Christianity in the early fourth century, Christians, lacking an organized legal framework for governance, adapted to existing Roman legal codes, thereby facilitating the rapid spread of the faith.

By contrast, eastern Jews of the first centuries C.E. developed a legal system that was largely independent of the Roman system. This sense of social and legal autonomy continued to develop in the centuries after Jerusalem's destruction, as many Jews gravitated toward the more accommodating and laissez-faire rule of the Parthian empire. Western Jews, who were not part of this process, however, strongly adhered to biblical law and therefore were more directly influenced by Roman legal traditions.

TIMOTHY MCCARTHY/ART RESOURCE, NY

The relationship to the government and the geographic divide

The decline of the rabbinic centers in Palestine was accompanied by an increasing rabbinic presence in Parthia, centered primarily on Babylonia. At the same time, Christianity developed within the Roman Empire. In contrast to the Roman Empire, the Parthian empire was a much more comfortable fit for a community that aspired to legal autonomy. We refer not to the legal status of Jews in these empires,[13] but rather to their attitude toward their own legal system in relation to that of the empire.

This process had two conflicting implications. On the one hand, Christianity became more and more Roman in its political approach. On the other hand, its desire to assimilate into the legal and political structure of the Roman Empire led it at times to a direct confrontation with Roman rulers who feared a Christian conspiracy. When Constantine decreed that Christians would no longer be persecuted in 313 C.E., Christianity had already absorbed the concepts and political language of the empire.[14] As a result, there was no conflict between the law of the empire and the Christian religious system that had developed during the previous centuries. This fact facilitated the process initiated by Constantine.

In contrast, a significant portion of Rabbinic Judaism existed beyond the borders of the Roman Empire, and established itself in the Parthian empire. The relocation to a feudal or somewhat feudal empire that granted autonomy to its vassals greatly facilitated the Jewish aspiration to develop a segregated community and a separate legal system for adjudicating civil law. Thus the Jewish community exercised a considerable degree of independence and separation in the Parthian empire and aspired to sovereign autonomy, while the Christian community sought mainly theological autonomy. A community cannot conduct its day-to-day functions based on dogma, and those elements of law were outsourced by Christians to the host Roman Empire.[15]

In a recent book on the beginnings of political organization, the American political scientist Francis Fukuyama claims that legal systems constitute the beginning of states.[16] The laws that slowly came into being, such as English common law, or as one-time events, such as the American Constitution, led to the creation of the various state institutions of those countries. In that light, Fukuyama claims that the reliance of Christians on the Roman legal system led inevitably to Christianity's integration into the Roman Empire, for without a law, it could not develop an independent sovereign framework.

Judaism, we claim, developed independent laws that led to its crystallization as a semi-sovereign independent community within the host state. As such, the move to the Parthian empire by rabbinic Jews was not by chance. One of the prominent characteristics of the Parthian government was its total lack of centralization. It was essentially a feudal government that granted a high degree of independence to its subjects.

Babylonia, where Jewish centers came to be located in the East, went through numerous political and cultural changes during the centuries in which it served as the primary center of Jewish life. The Sassanid empire of Persia, which defeated the Parthians, began in the early third century.

As observed by Isaiah Gafni, "The Parthian Kingdom was different from its Achaemenid predecessor and the subsequent Sassanid Empire in ... that in effect it never constituted a unified empire with a strong central government, but rather a loose confederation of countries."[17] In contrast to the Parthians, the Sassanids established a centralized government, and even a centralized religion. Nevertheless, as other scholars have also claimed, the roots of the strength of Babylonian Jewry had already been established and developed during the 300 years of Parthian rule. It was during that period that the Babylonian Jewish community became the seminal component of the Jewish world, the first to compete with and provide an alternative to the centrality of the Jewish community in the land of Israel.

Rabbi Judah ha-Nasi, who in about 200 C.E. organized and edited the Mishnah and transformed it into a closed canon, understood that the Babylonian center of Judaism was gaining in strength; he wished to impart to it the Torah of the land of Israel. There were certainly many factors that created the special bond between the great rabbinic sage known as Rav and the Parthian king. Rav recognized that the Parthian regime enabled the Jewish community to develop unfettered and did not view it as a nuisance. Rav's arrival in Babylonia was a significant turning point in the history of Babylonian Jewry. Returning to Babylonia from the land of Israel, Rav brought with him the Mishnah of Judah ha-Nasi, which became the cornerstone for Babylonian Jewish creativity in the following centuries, including the Babylonian Talmud.

When Rav returned to Babylonia, he was surely cognizant of the Parthian reality and the situation of the Jews in Babylonia at that time, as well as the situation of the community under Roman rule in the land of Israel. His decision to return to Babylonia was no doubt influenced by a number of factors, but it is logical to assume that one of them was his recognition of the favorable circumstances of the Jewish community under Parthian rule as opposed to the communities under Roman rule, including the community in the land of Israel. He almost certainly saw the Babylonian community at that time as the most fertile ground for the development of Jewish life and learning. Ironically, it was soon after Rav's return that a political revolution brought about the fall of the Parthians and the rise of the Sassanid regime. In place of a feudal authority with no aspiration for centralization, a government that sought both political and religious centralization came to power. Rav's response to this revolution, recorded in the Babylonian Talmud, demonstrates his recognition of the benefits that enabled Judaism to flourish under the Parthian regime, and his fears regarding the political revolution underway.[18] It is important to note, however, that even the most troublesome periods of the Sassanid dynasty cannot be compared to the difficulties faced by Jews under the Roman decrees of the first half of the second century. Moreover, the tension with the Sassanid regime and its priests subsided rather quickly, and Sassanid rulers soon became tolerant and moderate toward the Jewish community.

The famous statement of the Babylonian *amora* Shmuel, a contemporary of Rav, that "the law of the land is the law" is probably also a reaction to the rise of the Sassanids and their demand for centralization. We can deduce from the fact that this axiom was not needed previously that the Jews were able to live in the Parthian empire as an autonomous community. In addition, an analysis of the cases in which Shmuel used this rule demonstrates that while it is clear that he sought ways to satisfy the ruling powers, his main emphasis was on maintaining autonomy vis-à-vis what was for him the most central and important issue—jurisdiction over any dispute between members of the Jewish community.[19]

There is no doubt that the aspiration of the rabbis to shape a separate Jewish community secluded from its surroundings required an environment such as the one provided by the Parthians. It would have been much more difficult for a legal separatist approach to develop under a centralized government such as Rome. This point is strengthened in light of the fact that the rabbinic desire for separation was not limited to areas of ritual and religion, but applied as well to areas that are usually an integral part of a centralized legal system, as if they wanted a "state within a state." Paradoxically, feudal regimes provide naturally fertile ground for the development of autonomous, partially sovereign societies from all perspectives. Fukuyama finds a similar process in relation to European feudalism:

> From the standpoint of political development, the critical aspect of European feudalism was not the economic relationship between lord and vassal but the decentralization of power it implied. In the words of the historian Joseph Strayer, "Western

European feudalism is essentially political—it is a form of government ... in which political authority is monopolized by a small group of military leaders, but is rather evenly distributed among members of the group." This definition, also associated with Max Weber, is the one I will use throughout this volume. The core of the institution was the grant of fiefdom, benefice, or appanage, a delineated territory over which the vassal exerted some degree of political control. Despite the theoretical revocability of feudal contracts, European vassals over time turned their fiefdoms into patrimony, that is, property that they could hand down to their descendants. They acquired political rights over these territories to raise armies, tax residents, and administer justice free from interference of the nominal lord.[20]

The Jewish masses wandered eastward for many reasons—economic, political and cultural. The Jewish leadership went eastward, however, not only in the wake of the masses, but also because of a calculated perspective on the possibility of advancing their idea of an autonomous community in the Parthian east rather than the Roman west.[21] The regime and the atmosphere in the Parthian empire provided fertile ground for the development of the rabbinic vision of the sovereign autonomous Jewish community. Thus, divisions in language (Hebrew and Aramaic vs. Greek and Latin), geography (East vs. West), and perceptions of communal sovereignty (political and legal vs. theological) contributed to the parting of the ways between Judaism and Christianity.*

*See also Doron Mendels, "Why Paul Went West" *BAR*, January/February 2011.

15

Did They Ever Part?

JAMES H. CHARLESWORTH

FOR APPROXIMATELY 1,400 YEARS, JEWISH AND CHRISTIAN scholars assumed that Christianity was something new in history. They held that while the matrix of Christianity was to be sought in the Greek and Roman world, something unprecedented clearly occurred in Jesus' life. Jesus simply did not fit within Judaism as known from traditional Jewish sources.

For Jews, Christianity was perceived to be a Greek phenomenon. After all, the texts were in Greek; scripture (Torah) was in Hebrew (and Aramaic). Hebrew scriptures, along with the Mishnah, Tosefta and Talmudim, emphasized *halakhot* (rules and regulations for faithful obedience to Torah). Jesus' followers rejected these Jewish customs and rules. Jesus and his followers were customarily considered outcasts. Jesus seems to have been one who broke with the Torah and rejected the traditional truths.

For Christians, focus was more on the canon, especially the New Testament's "good news," and less on the context out of which Christianity arose. Christian philosophers, theologians and apologists emphasized that God had acted in an unparalleled way in the early first century and that Jesus should be hailed as divine, even God. Theological and dogmatic reflections on revelation, not historical study, defined the academy—and it was controlled by the ecclesiastics. Judaism was disparaged and caricatured.

In light of archaeological discoveries that have informed us of the diversity and richness of early Judaism, and in light of the historical and philological research awakened by the study of the Dead Sea Scrolls, we may now observe a more scientific methodology for assessing the emergence of Christianity. Today, Jewish and Christian experts on Second Temple Judaism[1] recognize the Palestinian Jesus Movement as one aspect of early Judaism and acknowledge that what would become Christianity was for decades a sect within Judaism. Scholarly assumptions of the past and what had been perceived to constitute early Judaism appear misinformed and in need of new paradigms and explanations.

Problems with previous assumptions

First error. For centuries, savants have claimed incorrectly that the "parting of the ways" occurred in Jesus' lifetime.[2] Jews were united and Jesus' group caused a rift. After Jesus' death, the ways parted and two religions formed.

This age-old solution is now misrepresentative of what we know about pre-70 C.E. Judaism. Now we know about extreme divisions within Second Temple Judaism (c. 300 B.C.E. to 70 C.E.). The greatest hatred found in ancient Jewish and Christian writings is within not only so-called Christian anti-Christian (that is, unacceptable Christology) and anti-Jewish rhetoric, but in the Dead Sea Scrolls. In the documents composed at Qumran (MMT, 1QS, 1QHa, 1QM, the *Pesharim*), the priests in Jerusalem and those related to them are "the Sons of Darkness" who were predestined to walk in the ways of darkness. They lead the nation astray. Eventually, they will be cast into Sheol or hell and punished until they are annihilated (1QS 4). The Wicked Priest hunted down and persecuted the Righteous Teacher (*Pesharim*) and may have chained him and beat him, even breaking his bones (1QHa).

Samaritans murdered Galileans who were on the annual pilgrimage to worship the same God as the Samaritans, but in Jerusalem's Temple. Hillel and Shammai debated and decided to disagree on major *halakhot*; many scholars ponder that these two Palestinian geniuses were not pre-70 Pharisees but originally represented different, though closely related, groups. Jesus' group became a martyred group, from John the Baptizer in the 20s to James in 62 C.E. (and Simeon in the time of Hadrian); but Jesus' group was not hated by some Jews any more than these selfsame men despised other sects, notably the Samaritans. After 66 C.E., chaos that had appeared intermittently exploded throughout ancient Palestine, bringing an end to the holy city and the Temple. A scholar should not seek the parting of the ways within a chaos in which rival Jews were killing each other.

Second error. Some influential thinkers erroneously contend that the claim Jesus had been raised from the dead created a schism within Judaism. The parting of the ways began in 30 C.E. Those who believed in Jesus' resurrection constituted a new religion; many in it were gentiles.

This is a distortion of our data. Belief in the resurrection of Jesus did not constitute a new religion, and resurrection belief was not something unprecedented within Judaism. The belief in the resurrection of one who had lived, died and was raised by God to an eternal existence was known in Palestinian Judaism by the second century B.C.E. (e.g., the Books of Enoch). It was advocated by not only one Jewish group but was known to Essenes (On Resurrection, 4Q521), to the precursors of the Pharisees (Psalms of Solomon) and to the Pharisees (note the evidence in the New Testament and the *Amidah* or Eighteen Benedictions).[3] Paul, who claimed to have experienced a living Jesus after Jesus' resurrection, argued that he (Paul) was a faithful Jew: "I myself am an Israelite, a descendant of Abraham, a member of the tribe of Benjamin" (Romans 11:1). Mary Magdalene, Peter and James, and the first generation of Jews who affirmed that Jesus was the long-awaited Messiah and believed in his resurrection claimed to remain Jews faithful to Torah and *halakhah*. Belief in a Jew as the Messiah was tolerated within Judaism (cf. Bar-Kokhba); belief in resurrection was not a Christian intrusion within early Judaism.

Third error. Too many Christian apologists contend that Jesus was not a Jew; he came from the "Galilee of the gentiles." Teachers today unfortunately continue to claim that Galilee is the home of the gentiles and thus Jesus should be seen as a gentile.[4] They continue misperceiving history, casting it according to their own whims, even claiming that Jesus began a new religion. He did not observe the Sabbath (Shabbat). He sought to replace the Temple.

No. This solution mirrors old polemics. The phrase "Galilee of the gentiles," which is found in the Bible,[5] does not describe the culture of Jesus as non-Jewish. Archaeological research in Lower Galilee proves a link with Judea; most of the Jews living in Magdala, Nazareth and other cities most likely migrated north from Judea when the Hasmonean (i.e., Judean) army conquered Galilee under John Hyrcanus, Aristobulus I and Alexander Jannaeus.[6] The stone recovered from the center of the pre-70 synagogue in Magdala (Migdal) placards a strong symbolic link with the Temple in Jerusalem.* Lower Galilee was a land of Jews; they used stone vessels made in Jerusalem (John 2), and small oil lamps that were almost always made in Jerusalem (perhaps to symbolize the spiritual meaning of light).[7]

Jesus was admired by many Jews in Galilee, even though he cursed the three main centers in which he focused his itinerant ministry—Chorazin, Bethsaida and Capernaum (Matthew 11:20–24; Luke 10:13–16). According to traditions, thousands heard him speak, admired him and held some belief in him. We should explore the variety of beliefs held by those who believed in Jesus before 30 C.E. (perhaps we should ponder the continuing dimensions of a pre-cross Christology, maybe in the sources Q and Semeia†). Jesus was not a fool who taught absurd ideas, like loving your enemies (as held by some Jewish thinkers in the past); he was a genius who knew that love should have no boundaries (as the brilliant David Flusser perceived).[8]

Jesus honored and observed Shabbat as specified in the Torah (Exodus 20 and Deuteronomy 5). He healed the sick on Shabbat, because he knew that saving a life supersedes the laws of Shabbat. (In Mishnah *Shabbat* 7:2 healing is not included in the 39 generative categories of acts of labor prohibited on Shabbat. The Mishnah gives no precise legislation against healing on Shabbat, but healing is allowed sometimes according to *Shabbat* 14:3–4.) But according to some post-Torah and pre-70 traditions in early Judaism, Jesus did not obey the Shabbat commandment. E.P. Sanders rightly points out that Jesus himself observed Shabbat, and the New Testament is confused on this point, since later followers

*See Joey Corbett, "New Synagogue Excavations in Israel and Beyond," *BAR*, July/August 2011.
†"Q" (for German, *Quelle*) denotes the lost source of Jesus' sayings allegedly used by Matthew and Luke; *Semeia* means "signs" in Greek and denotes a "signs" source hypothetically used by the author of the Gospel of John.

COURTESY ISRAEL ANTIQUITIES AUTHORITY

MAGDALA SYNAGOGUE STONE. This 3-foot-long engraved stone with an early depiction of a seven-branched menorah and elaborate floral and heart designs was discovered in the first-century C.E. synagogue of Magdala on the shores of the Sea of Galilee. While the stone's function remains uncertain (some believe it served as a table on which Torah scrolls were rolled out and read), its iconography clearly links Galilean Jews with Jewish rituals and symbols known from Judea and the Jerusalem Temple.

retrojected their own ideas back into Jesus' life; moreover, within most Jewish communities, and most cities, Jews differed on how (if at all) to obey Shabbat.[9]

Some scholars have been convinced that Jesus never broke one commandment or rule in the Torah (the Pentateuch). For example, let us reflect on the sage advice of James D.G. Dunn in his *The Partings of the Ways*:

> It was not the law or law as a principle which Jesus called in
> question. *It was the law understood in a factional or sectarian
> way*—interpreted in narrowing terms so that those who could

not accept, or who would not conform, or who challenged that interpretation, were *ipso facto* categorized as "sinners," even though they were Jews themselves and willing or indeed eager to live within the covenant as they understood it.[10]

Let me add to this insight. When Jesus said that, on Shabbat, he was working as his father continued working (John 5:16–18), he was representing debates within Judaism and a valid interpretation of the Hebrew text of Genesis 2:2 (which was "corrected" by the translators of the Septuagint). The Hebrew text states that God finished his work on Shabbat, implying that he worked at the beginning of Shabbat. The Greek text (the Septuagint) states that God finished his work on the sixth day. Jesus sided with Jews who interpreted Genesis according to the Hebrew text; and Jesus claimed since God continued to work on Shabbat, he could also heal on Shabbat (note that Jesus believed that saving life overruled Shabbat rulings) and he otherwise "rested" and prayed on Shabbat, frequenting the synagogues (cf. Luke 4:16).

"Parting" options in need of refinement

Jesus' time. Some scholars argue that the parting of the ways may be adumbrated in Jesus' life and teachings; if so, it would be only in an embryonic form. Jesus could be aggressive and confrontational; he argued with many leading Jews in Galilee and especially in the Temple. He broke Shabbat, according to the Essenes, the Sadducees and some Pharisees. If he claimed to be God (Yahweh), then he was guilty of blaspheming, according to Torah and *halakhah*.[11]

The Jews of Jesus' time also bear responsibility for the parting of the ways. Many of them fiercely rejected Jesus, and some were behind his condemnation (perhaps a few may be behind his crucifixion—but the editing of early sources, especially by Matthew, blinds too many readers). A study of Matthew indicates that the community behind it, as Luke T. Johnson states, "knew that its Messiah had been rejected by the Jewish leadership and the populace of Jerusalem (Matthew 27:25), and that he continued to be rejected by those who worshiped in the synagogue down the street."[12]

Hostile debates within Judaism, however, do not constitute a parting of the ways; after all, Jews loved to agree to debate and disagree—and there was no set *halakhah* in Jesus' time. In summary, we should not ignore the foreshadowing of some parting of the ways during Jesus' earthly ministry, but the true parting of the ways should be observed when two separate religions recognize how different the other really has become. Jesus did not intend to establish a new religion. He was faithful to Torah and sought to bring his nation back to the piety of Isaiah and Jeremiah.[13] He loved the Temple;[14] and he customarily taught and worshiped there (developed later in this chapter).[15]

The first century C.E. If one ignores the full data from many countries, one might come to the conclusion that a parting of the ways occurred already in the first century C.E. One could point to Jesus' crucifixion, but the full evidence in the Gospels (despite the later editing) does not lead to the conclusion that Caiaphas, Annas or any member of the Sanhedrin is to blame for his crucifixion or condemnation.

One could point to the stoning of Stephen by Diasporic Jews, but his brilliance was defined by a hostile polemic against the Temple establishment; and his extremes advanced beyond those of Jesus, who loved the Temple but had some problems with certain aspects of the cult.

One could point to the martyrdom of James, Jesus' brother, and to the Sadducean high priest behind this murder;[16] but the Jewish establishment did not agree with this action and dismissed the Sadducean high priest after his unlawful action. Most likely, the Temple priests admired the piety, dedication and hope of James who (unlike Paul) did not advocate a break with Jewish *halakhot*.

One could posit that Paul caused the rift. He did reject the *kashrut* laws, affirming that one did not have to observe the Jewish dietary restrictions. Paul did abolish the demands of circumcision (Galatians 5:11–6:10), which did cause a parting of the ways, not only with the Jerusalem priests, but with all Sadducees and most Pharisees (according to the Mishnah and the Tosefta).

It is easy and popular to place all the blame on a schism with Paul. Regarding the *kashrut* laws, tradition indicates that Peter also rejected the dietary restrictions (Acts 10), and the arguments used in Acts were not new to early Jews. Moreover, many Jews, as is clear from texts and excavations, ate pig and other forbidden animals and did not always "wash the hands" in a halakhic fashion before meals.[17]

Circumcision does not seem to have been practiced by all Jews in the ancient world. Queen Helena of Adiabene's son, Izates, was not circumcised when he converted (only later), but many Jews apparently accepted him as a converted Jew (Josephus, *Antiquities* 20.41). Philo notes that some Jews in Alexandria were not circumcised (while some Egyptians were) and did not advocate this ritual;[18] evidently some Jews in the Diaspora and also in Palestine did not observe circumcision.[19] The practice of epispasm (the removal of the marks of circumcision) should warn us that some Jews who were circumcised removed the marks of circumcision so they would not be ostracized in the public baths or in athletic contests.[20] Today, scholars note more continuity between Paul and Jesus than did earlier scholars; the shift in perspective is due to an improved perception of the creative and complex thoughts in early Judaism.

Shabbat. Few social organizations are as important as the calendar, as we have learned studying the different calendars regnant within Second Temple Judaism, following Shemaryahu Talmon's sociological studies.*[21] From at least the time of David until today, Jews have followed a seven-day calendar. Worship and rest is on the final or seventh day. No cosmic movement supports this calculation,[22] so Jews can use a lunar or semi-solar calendar (there is no possible purely solar calendar on earth).[23] The rhythm of the week, and the name of the days in Hebrew (Day One, etc.) are based on creation beliefs.

When some followers of Jesus, sometime after 70 C.E., began to observe "the first day" as "the Sabbath,"[24] it indicated a parting of the ways for them and their group; but, as C.W. Dugmore shows, the synagogue for centuries influenced Christian services and the day for observing Shabbat.[25] The earliest evidence of resting and worshiping on "the first day," because that was the day God raised his Son from the dead, is in Revelation 1:10. Eventually, "Sunday" was observed almost everywhere as the Sabbath (but not today by Seventh-day Adventists); Canon 29 of the Council in Laodicea (about 360 C.E.) forbade worship and resting on Shabbat and labeled all who did so anathema. (See Chapter XIII, "From Sabbath to Sunday: Why, How and When?" by Lawrence T. Geraty.)

How could this be possible when the "Old Testament" made "the seventh day" Shabbat and Christians canonized all the books in the Old Testament as scripture? Of course, even today there are Christians who observe the commandment to rest on Shabbat (Exodus 20:8–11).

*See Strata, Milestones, "Shemaryahu Talmon (1920–2010)," *BAR*, March/April 2011.

Worshiping on the first day and not on the seventh day constitutes a parting of the ways. Before 100 B.C.E., the Qumranites parted (*prš*) from the priests in Jerusalem.[26] One reason was the observance of a solar-lunar calendar and a polemic against the lunar calendar that was a new development within the Jerusalem priestly circles. Recall Some Works of the Torah (MMT): "We have separated [(*š*)*pršnw*] from the mass of the [people and from all their impurity] ..." (Section C 7).

From 100 to 325 C.E. The foreshadowing of anti-Judaism can be seen in the Gospel of John, in which "the Jews" are portrayed as Jesus' opponents. Unfortunately, too many miss the point that sometimes the Greek *ioudaioi* means some "Judean" leaders.[27]

The term denoting being cast out of synagogues (*aposunagogos*) appears only in John 9:22, 12:42 and 16:2. In the Fourth Gospel, there are many statements in tension regarding Jesus' relations with God, thus signifying that the truth is to be found as such contrarieties are juxtaposed. If the earthly Jesus made the claims found in John, then it is understandable that Jews would have cast out any one who believed such confessions as these:

I and the Father are one.

(John 10:30)

He who has seen me has seen the Father.

(John 14:9)

One should not overlook the subordinationist statements also attributed to Jesus, among them these:

Jesus said to them: "Truly, truly, I say to you, the Son can do nothing of his own accord, but only what he sees the Father doing; for whatever he does, that the Son does likewise."

(John 5:19)

The Father is greater than I.

(John 14:28)

The first vestiges of anti-Judaism seem to be in Matthew, since this author added to the Passion narrative, the earliest written record behind the Gospels, the cry of "all the people" (obviously Jews according to

Matthew): "His blood be on us and our descendants" (Matthew 27:25). This horrible addition reverberates through the centuries, undermining the purity of Christian scripture. The escalation of anti-Judaism increases as one moves from the canonical New Testament to Barnabas, Justin Martyr[28] and Melito of Sardis (died c. 190 C.E.).[29]

A special case is presented by the compositions in the so-called Apocrypha and Pseudepigrapha of the New Testament. These documents should not be ignored. They were the scriptures of many early Christians. Only a select example may now be brought into focus. Note the anti-Judaism found, for example, in the Gospel of the Ebionites, referenced by Epiphanius; in this gospel, Jesus is reputed to have said: "I have come to abolish the sacrifices" (Epiphanius, *Panarion* 30.3–13). Also, according to the Gospel of the Ebionites, the Jews in Tiberias have Hebrew copies of the Gospel of John and Acts. Perhaps the texts could signify a continuing relationship among Jews and Christians, but the report is intended to emphasize the need for Jews to convert to Christianity.[30]

And in the Infancy Gospel of Thomas, Jesus calls a Jewish boy "you, insolent, godless ignoramus" (3:1).[31]

Far more disconcerting is the supersessionism in the noncanonical Preaching of Peter. The author, intent on stressing monotheism, states that Jews "do not know" God and that a "new covenant" was established for Christians:

> He [God] made a new one [covenant] with us: for the ways of the Greeks and Jews are old, but we are Christians who worship him in a new way as a third generation.
>
> (Clement of Alexandria, *Stromata* 2.15.68;
> *Eclogae Propheticae* 58)

> And according to the Acts of Pilate: "The Jews said to Pilate: 'We wish him to be crucified'" (4:4).[32]

As we move from the canonical New Testament to the extra-canonical New Testament, one dimension becomes obvious: The authors' increasing anti-Judaism.

Anti-Christ. The rhetoric of polemics in antiquity, explored insightfully by Luke T. Johnson,[33] is the perspective in which and through which to comprehend the origins of the parting of the ways. Is any ancient polemic as virulent as that found in the canonical Epistles of John? This polemic is addressed primarily to fellow Christians who have an unacceptable Christology: "By this you know the Spirit of God. Every spirit which confesses that Jesus Christ has come in the flesh is of God. And every spirit which does not confess Jesus is not of God. This is the spirit of the antichrist ..." (1 John 4:2–3).

Gentiles. Jesus' group began as a Jewish movement and all the first disciples and the Twelve were Jews. Apparently, Jesus called gentiles "sinners," as did most Palestinian Jews (Luke 6:34) and even "house dogs" (Mark 7:27).

Only Mark 13:10 implies that Jesus shared the universalism found in the Testaments of the Twelve Patriarchs and, surprisingly, in a section of the Thanksgiving Hymns.[34] This verse in Mark is clearly a Marcan addition (or perhaps from a Petrine source); it clashes with the abundant evidence that Jesus restricted his ministry to "the lost tribes of Israel."[35] Jesus seemed to include only Jews and was surprised when gentiles, like the centurion and the Syro-Phoenician woman,[36] obtained unexpected wisdom and belief. But Jesus did not invite them to follow him.

It is difficult, therefore, to attribute to the historical Jesus the eschatological influx of the gentiles. Despite attempts from Schleiermacker, Renan and Schweitzer to the present, universalism cannot be attributed clearly to the historical Jesus. If Jesus did not espouse this view,[37] his followers certainly attributed it to him. While the first generation was reticent to edit his views on the gentiles, the view is evident in the editing of some traditions (Matthew 18:11–12; Luke 13:28–29; cf. Mark 12:9).

Yet, the issue is complex. I am attracted to N.T. Wright's insight regarding the widespread belief in pre-70 traditions that all the tribes of Israel will return to Zion—and that this would include gentiles.[38] The importance of gentiles is evident in sacred traditions, as we know from the stories about Ruth, the Queen of Sheba and Aseneth. But, I do not find such emphases in the sayings that can be confidently attributed to Jesus.

Before 70 C.E., and increasingly over the next 100 years, non-Jews began to populate Christianity until it was almost exclusively a gentile religion. It is singularly important, therefore, to observe the paradigmatic distinction between polemics *within* Judaism *by Jews* and polemics from *outside* Judaism *by gentiles.* Within Judaism, and especially within Second Temple Judaism, most Jews were impressively tolerant of concepts that deviated from so-called Pharisaism.[39]

Parting of the Ways: more attractive options

What, then, constitutes a "parting of the ways"? Where is it evident and when? Two paradigmatically distinct answers appear.[40]

First viable answer. Historical origins and theologically shared traditions make any parting of the ways problematic and misrepresentative, hence the publication of *The Ways That Never Parted.*[41] Yet from a sociological perspective, the parting of the ways occurred sometime long ago and is demonstrably clear virtually everywhere on earth.[42] Jews and Christians today are not identical. Furthermore, defining a "Jew" or "Christian" today is either complex or demands ignoring some phenomena (for example, Israeli secularists despise Hasadim).

During the early centuries of Christianity, Jews were vilified by leading Christians in writings and in practice. In some translations of the Gospel of John, "the Jews" are presented as those who oppose and crucify Jesus. During the Middle Ages (not to mention the Shoah or Holocaust), many "Christians" claimed a Jew was a Christ-killer, even God-murderer (*Gottesmörder*).

Those who advocate that Jews and Christians are distinct would support Jacob Neusner's claim that while Jews and Christians share the so-called Hebrew scriptures, their interpretations are so different that one should acknowledge two different sources: the Torah (in Hebrew) and the Old Testament (in modern languages).[43] Thus, it is evident that during the first three centuries of Christianity a parting of the ways occurred; that is why not one Jew was seated or present at the first council, the Council at Nicaea in 325 C.E., when the emperor Constantine may have been in the chair.[44]

Second viable answer. Archaeological research and a focus on local issues lead to a perception that one cannot posit a parting of the ways. Schlomo Moussaieff, an Israeli antiquities collector,* has early glass that depicts a

*See Hershel Shanks, "Magnificent Obsession: The Private World of an Antiquities Collector," *BAR*, May/June 1996.

cross and the menorah. What does that mean? As Annette Yoshiko Reed and Adam H. Becker point out:

> Contrary to the "Parting" model, our sources suggest that developments in both traditions continued to be shaped by contacts between Jews and Christians, as well as by their shared cultural contexts. Even after the second century, the boundaries between "Jewish" and "Christian" identities often remained less than clear, consistent with the ambiguities in the definition of both "Jew" and "Christian."[45]

One of the many differences between *The Apocrypha and Pseudepigrapha of the Old Testament* (Oxford: Clarendon Press, 1913) and *The Old Testament Pseudepigrapha* (Garden City, NY: Doubleday, 1983, 1985) is that many documents were included in the latter collection that showed the fluid boundaries among Jewish works and Christian documents. Clearly, Christians transmitted Jewish works, sometimes without alteration, and sometimes with interpolations or additions (note how, for example, 4 Ezra became the Fourth Book of Ezra by about 250 C.E.). Since 1983, Jewish scholars have been pointing out that rabbinic compositions often mirror contacts with Christians. As I pointed out long ago, Jerome had to have learned Hebrew from a Jew or he could not have translated the Hebrew scriptures (the Old Testament).

In a deep sense, no parting of the ways can occur universally and conceptually. Almost all documents in the Bible were composed by Jews. Thus, if the books in the Bible were composed by Jews, how can Christianity part from its heritage? Likewise, if Christianity is defined by the belief that God raised up his son from the dead, then each of the elements are Jewish. The concept of God is Jewish. The man crucified was a Jew who was deeply dedicated to Torah and worshiped and taught in the Temple. The concept of resurrection came into Western culture by Jews and their writings, notably the Books of Enoch, the Testaments of the Twelve Patriarchs, Josephus's tomes and the Eighteen Benedictions that is chanted in synagogues today throughout the world.

If the heart of Christian confessions, and the Christian Bible, is Jewish, how can Christians and Christianity ever definitively separate from the mother, early Judaism? One can deny one's parentage, but that does not change DNA.

Moreover, we are changing paradigms in light of archaeological discoveries. The Dead Sea Scrolls are gifts to us because of the First Jewish Revolt (during which Qumran was destroyed) and their chance discovery by Bedouin. Likewise, the Old Testament Pseudepigrapha, ancient Jewish sacred texts that reveal the creativity and diversity of early Judaism, were preserved almost always only by Christians. How can we claim a parting of the ways when there was, in many centers, deep continuity?

If we seek to overcome the parochialism that has defined too much Christian thought, we will observe that in some countries there is no parting of the ways. For example, the priests and lay people in the Ethiopian Orthodox Täwahïdo Church—"the most Jewish of all Christian churches"[46]—honor and admire their Jewish heritage and Jews. Ephraim Isaac can report that when he is in Ethiopia, Christians admire that he is a Falasha, a Jew. He reports that priests visited his father: "They looked upon him as a member of the beloved Children of Israel, and used to sing his praises."[47]

Likewise, India must not be ignored; it became part of the Hellenistic world due to Alexander the Great's conquests in 326 B.C.E. What do we know assuredly about Jews in India in antiquity? India is mentioned in Esther (1:1, 8:9) and the elephants used in warfare by the Maccabees may have come from India (1 Maccabees 6:37).[48] The Parthian invasion of 40 B.C.E. may have brought India linen and gems to ancient Palestine. The fine linen and precious jewels worn by the high priest on Yom Kippur, described in detail by Josephus (*Antiquities* 3; *War* 5), conceivably came from India. To what extent is there reliable history in the stories about Thomas, one of the Twelve, reaching India?[49] Commerce between Egypt and India is evident in antiquity, and most likely by the first century C.E.[50]

If Christianity reached India via Edessa (the city of the Apostle Thomas, according to early traditions), then most likely the relations among Jews and Christians were cordial as they were in Syria. This valid assumption deepens as one more adequately perceives that as a very Jewish type of Christianity moved from Palestine and the west to Edessa[51] and other eastern cities, it migrated along the Silk and Spice Road[52] from synagogue to synagogue as if they were caravanserai.[53] The contact between Jerusalem and the East is obvious,[54] since in the 40s C.E. the royalty in Adiabene converted to Judaism,[55] the high priest Ananel (37–36 B.C.E.) under Herod the Great was from Babylonia, Hillel originated in Babylon, and Jewish pilgrims flowed to Jerusalem from the East to fulfill the laws of pilgrimage.[56]

The Edessan church thrived because of the support of the Jews;[57] note J.B. Segal's comment: "When the Christians of Edessa, like their co-religionists elsewhere in the Roman Empire, were persecuted by the Imperial authorities at the beginning of the fourth century, they had the open sympathy of the Jews."[58] Too many scholars ignore such primary evidence about India since it seems shaped by self-serving legends.

We need to be careful not to focus only on 70 or 136 C.E. (the latter being the revised date for the defeat of Bar-Kokhba[59]) in ancient Palestine.[60] Is it possible that Jewish-Christian relations in Judea could be an exception? Or is a global perspective so expansive as to cause a loss of focus?

The question must not redefine the data. That is, if we ask, "When did the parting of the ways occur?" we assume it has occurred. If we ask "Why did the parting of the ways occur?" we may be leaving the primary, and contradictory, sources we are pledged to interpret.

Perhaps the best way to observe the full issue is to argue that a parting of the ways has occurred and then use the same skills and knowledge to argue that no parting of the ways has nor can transpire. Do such reflections lead to a perception, as Gabrielle Boccaccini contends, that Christianity is one of the Judaisms of our times?[61]

While Neusner's point is fundamental and obvious, he tends to assume all Christians read "the Old Testament" in a similar fashion. Many Christians do not read the Old Testament Christologically, that is, seeking to find prophecies about Jesus in the prophets. Neusner was focusing on the United States and Europe, but there are a vast variety of biblical interpretations within the U.S. and Europe, and many more within all the forms of global Christianity (e.g., the Ethiopian Church, the Russian Church, the Greek Orthodox Church, the Armenians, the Nestorians, the Roman Catholic Church, the early Elkesaites [who were a mixture of Judaism, Christianity and "paganism"], the Latter-Day Saints, and the vast differences within so-called Protestantism). In interpreting prophecy and its fulfillment in Jesus, a fundamentalist would differ from a conservative, and each of them would be aghast at how some Protestant biblical scholars and theologians interpret prophecy.

Thus, since there is a vast amount of data to comprehend in order to explore how and in what ways,[62] if at all, a scholar should subscribe to "a parting of the ways," it is unwise to declare a once-and-for-all "parting of the ways." There certainly is discontinuity and parting of the ways in many places at certain times, but not at all times and, fortunately, not today in some areas (notably, in the United States and Germany, but not in Poland and Russia). Differences abound today within Judaism—within Israel alone aspersion is often cast by Ashkenazi Jews on Sephardic Jews (and the Haredim and Hasidim pose major problems for most Israelis)—and within Christianity (for example, the "parting of the ways" among the Southern Baptists). And today, sometimes one is impressed more by differences within both Judaism and Christianity than between Jews and Christians.[63]

Summary. Paul exacerbated the rift between Jews living in the Diaspora and those in the Holy Land. For believers-in-Jesus, he abolished the need for circumcision,[64] the dietary restrictions, and other distinct features of Jewish lifestyle that were clearly ridiculed by gentiles. He did not replace Shabbat with worship on the first day of the week,[65] and he continued to visit, even worship, in synagogues. He claimed to be a zealous and faithful Jew and redefined the descendants of Abraham as those who were faithful to God's covenant. Thus, heredity may have continued for Paul as an advantage; but far more important for Paul was believing in Jesus as the Christ and recognizing that belonging within the house of Israel meant having the obedience of Abraham.

The study of Jesus' commandment of love should not be isolated within a growing hatred of Jews by Christians from 30 to 325 C.E. In the process, no one would suggest that Christians were being obedient to Jesus' perspective: "A new commandment I give unto you, that you love one another as I have loved you" (John 13:34). If Jesus' followers during the four centuries after his death had heeded this commandment, it would be difficult to posit a parting of the ways.

Reflections on insights from the previous chapters

Having expressed my personal reflections on the topic of a parting of the ways, let me now, at the conclusion of the present collection of essays, share reflections on my colleagues' insights. Let me begin by lauding Hershel Shanks for convening this symposium (even if we never convened) and for the impressive reflections by all who contributed to the present volume. I was pleased by the inclusion of archaeology and the focus, intermittently, on different areas of the ancient world (but not all of it; India and Ethiopia were marginalized, and the focus was too often on only one locale).

Commonly shared points

A symposium is best when differing viewpoints are shared and heard sympathetically. The differences in the preceding pages are thus warranted. Agreeing to disagree is healthy, and divergent views are necessary since the issues are complex and do not allow for easy explanations. Yet there were some major areas of agreement; let me list them:

• It is extremely timely to discuss the issue of a parting of the ways, as new data and methodologies demand better, more representative terms and sophisticated paradigms.[66]

• The Jewish Jesus is not the cause for a parting of the ways.

• Jesus and his earliest followers did not consider Torah to be of secondary importance.[67]

• While most contributors argue that it is misleading to posit a parting of the ways before 66 C.E. (see especially Joan Taylor, Chapter V, "Parting in Palestine"), Geza Vermes concludes that Paul is "the primary source of the parting of the ways" (see p. 23).

• Dietary laws (*kashrut*) and observance of Shabbat established social separation and a communal seclusion of Jews (see especially Chapter XIV, "Social Organization and Parting in East and West," by Arye Edrei and Doron Mendels).

• The parting of the ways was clear, in many areas, by the fourth century C.E. Yet Jerome informs us of some people who wished to be both Jews and Christians (*sed dum volunt et Judaei esse et Christiani*).[68] How are we to be sensitive to the emic view and not impose on it our own etic perspective?* Only dogmatism can lead to the charge that these Ebionites or Nazoraeans are neither Jews nor Christians (*nec Judaei sunt, nec Christiani*). The Latin words reflect leaders in the western "church" attempting to define itself by eliminating perceived threats.

---

*Cultural anthropologists use "emic" to refer to the interpretations, beliefs and customs of those within a group or culture. "Etic" denotes an outsider's view of what is being studied (often in light of the examiner's own interests).

Insights and problems that need further discussion

• Arye Edrei and Doron Mendels (both Israelis) suggest the catalyst for the parting of the ways: "the rabbinic aspiration to develop a system of civil law and an autonomous community structure, in contrast to no such aspiration among contemporaneous Christians" (see p. 269).

• How can we obtain some insight into the arrival of "Christians" to Rome when Jewish history is a blank from 31 to 41 C.E. and yet hostility defined the relations among "Christians" and Jews in Rome before 50 C.E. (see Chapter VIII, "Jews and Christians at Rome," by Margaret H. Williams)?[69]

• Is it wise to claim that, although Jews and Christians continued a dialogue, and rabbinic texts reflect Christian thinking, this relationship in no way suggests "the parting of the ways"? (See Chapter XI, "In Between: Jewish-Christians and the Curse of the Heretics," by Shaye J.D. Cohen.)

• Finally, Eric Meyers's chapter (Chapter VII, "Living Side by Side in Galilee") presents one of the most insightful and nuanced perspectives. He concludes that the parting of the ways should not be posited until the Crusades. He rightly notes the importance of Christian success in the Holy Land long after 135/6 C.E.; after all, Origen and Eusebius flourished in Caesarea Maritima. He warns that it is a "great mistake" to think that in antiquity (especially in Palestine) Jews and Christians were enemies. They shared a common culture. Meyers concludes, "I believe we must view the parting of the ways pretty much as a family affair" (see p. 150). Indeed, there is much to be learned from architecture and archaeology; Jews and Christians shared a culture and similar structures (many early synagogues copied the architecture of churches). At Capernaum, the sixth-century synagogue is near the Byzantine church built over Peter's house.

Contributors who assume a parting by the fourth century[70]

Arye Edrei and Doron Mendels (from Rome to Babylonia), Robert Kraft and AnneMarie Luijendijk (in Egypt), Margaret Williams (Rome before 50 C.E.), Lawrence Geraty (in Palestine by 135/6 C.E.), Joan Taylor (in

Judea/Palestine before 135/6 C.E.), Shaye J.D. Cohen (by the early second century) and Geza Vermes (with Paul and before 50 C.E.).

Contributors who hesitate to posit a parting of the ways

Steven Fine (in the West), Annette Yoshiko Reed and Lily Vuong (in Roman Syria), Matt Jackson-McCabe (the Ebionites and Nazoraeans, primarily in eastern provinces of the Roman Empire), James D.G. Dunn (debates between Jews and Christians are not dissimilar to the factionalism within Second Temple Judaism) and Bruce Chilton (each context shows variations).

Some final thoughts

Complex issues, especially the parting of the ways, should not be simplified. I have tried to represent the problems by avoiding black-and-white answers. As made clear in this volume, Justin Martyr did not use the term "Christian," and rabbis did not use the term "Judaism." Helpful is John Meier's caveat regarding the murkiness from the beginning:

> Jesus persists in veiling himself in indirect references and metaphors ... It is almost as though Jesus were intent on making a riddle of himself ... Whoever or whatever Jesus was, he was a complex figure, not easily subsumed under one theological rubric or sociological model.[71]

Claims that by the fourth century C.E. "orthodox" Christianity and Rabbinic Judaism had clearly parted ways need contextualizing and modification. One may claim that conclusion by focusing on Rome (where the pope issued proclamations) and Tiberias (where Rabbi Judah the Prince edited the Palestinian Talmud), but such a claim focuses on only two portions of the West. Christian missionaries in the East, especially in Adiabene and Edessa, were supported by friendly Jews.[72]

I am personally convinced that any focused discussion needs to be aware that both "orthodox" Christianity[73] and Rabbinic Judaism evolved and changed due to complex issues, including competing ideologies, competitive stories, and the loss of Jerusalem and the Temple. Both departed from the creative (and perhaps too chaotic) world of Second Temple Judaism that ended in 70 C.E.

Moreover, have we answered our central question by including only "orthodox" Christianity and Rabbinic Judaism? What percentage of Christians and Jews have we included for contemplation? Many types of Judaism existed after 70 C.E.; for example, those who produced 3 Enoch, the Zohar, as well as the Hekhalot literature.[74] Many types of Christianity also existed; for example, the Gnostics, the Ebionites, the Manicheans, the members in the Ethiopian Orthodox, etc., would warn us that we have focused only on the few whom we know about because their writings (or their ramifications on writings) are now extant.

Notes

I. The Jewish Jesus Movement

[1] For an expansion of some of the ideas in this chapter, see chapter 2 of my book *Christian Beginnings: From Nazareth to Nicaea (AD 30–325)* (London: Penguin, 2012; New Haven, CT: Penguin, 2013).

[2] See Martin Goodman, *Mission and Conversion: Proselytizing in the Religious History of the Roman Empire* (Oxford: Clarendon, 1994), pp. 60–90; Brian C. McGing, "Population and Proselytism. How Many Jews Were There in the Ancient World?" in *Jews in the Hellenistic and Roman Cities*, ed. John R. Barlett (London: Routledge, 2002), pp. 88–106.

[3] See Vermes, *Christian Beginnings* (see endnote 1), chapter 1.

[4] On the Pharisees, see Emil Schürer, *The History of the Jewish People in the Age of Jesus Christ (175 B.C.–A.D. 135)*, 3 vols., rev. ed., eds. Geza Vermes, Fergus Millar and Martin Goodman (Edinburgh: T & T Clark, 1973–1987), vol. 2, pp. 381–414.

[5] *Antiquities* 13.171–173.

[6] Schürer, *History of the Jewish People* (see endnote 4), vol. 2, pp. 598–606; Martin Hengel, *The Zealots* (Edinburgh: T & T Clark, 1989).

[7] For the population of Palestine, see Magen Broshi, *Bread, Wine, Walls and Scrolls* (London: Sheffield Academic Press, 2002), pp. 91–92. As far as the Diaspora is concerned, according to Philo, the Jews of Egypt amounted to one million (Flaccus, 43). The 13th-century Syriac chronicler Bar Hebraeus asserts that the census of the emperor Claudius (41–54 C.E.) recorded 6,944,000 Jews in the Roman world (see S.W. Baron, "Population," *EJ*, vol. 13, col. 871), a figure probably confused by Bar Hebraeus with that of the census of the inhabitants of the whole empire put by Tacitus in *Annals* 11.25 as 5,984,072. All these numbers must be taken with a pinch of salt. For total skepticism regarding ancient Jewish demographic data, see McGing, "Population and Proselytism" (see endnote 2).

[8] Philo, *Quod omnis probus* 75; *Antiquities* 18.21.

[9] *Antiquities* 17.42 (during the reign of Herod), 18.15.

[10] *Letter of Aristeas* 95; *Apion* 2.108.

[11] See the list of Pentecost pilgrims in Acts 2:9–11.

[12] See JT *Sanhedrin* 10.5.

[13] For the Onias story, see *War* 1.33, 7.423–432; *Antiquities* 12.237, 387, 13.63–73, 20.236. See also Schürer, *History of the Jewish People* (see endnote 4), vol. 3, pp. 47–48, 145–147; Robert Hayward, "The Jewish Temple of Leontopolis: A Reconsideration," *JJS* 33 (1982), pp. 429–443; Abraham Wasserstein, "Notes on the Temple

of Onias at Leontopolis," *Illinois Classical Studies* (1993), pp. 119–129; Geza Vermes, "The Leadership of the Qumran Community: Sons of Zadok–Priests–Congregation," in *Geschichte— Tradition—Reflexion Festschrift für Martin Hengel*, ed. Peter Schäfer (Tübingen: Mohr Siebeck, 1996), pp. 381–384.

[14] See Geza Vermes and Martin D. Goodman, *The Essenes According to the Classical Sources* (Sheffield: JSOT Press, 1989).

[15] See Geza Vermes, *The Story of the Scrolls* (London: Penguin, 2010), pp. 191–202.

[16] For a brief outline of "The Age of Jesus in Its Wider Context," see Geza Vermes, *Who's Who in the Age of Jesus* (London/New York: Penguin, 2006), pp. 13–28.

[17] See Geza Vermes, *The Nativity* (London: Penguin, 2006). For a more traditionalist presentation, see Raymond E. Brown, *The Birth of the Messiah* (New York: Doubleday, 1993).

[18] See Joan E. Taylor, *The Immerser: John the Baptist Within Second Temple Judaism* (Grand Rapids, MI: Eerdmans, 2006).

[19] 1QS 8:12–16.

[20] *Antiquities* 18.119.

[21] *Antiquities* 18.63. See Geza Vermes, *Jesus in the Jewish World* (London: SCM, 2010), pp. 40–44.

[22] See BT *Shabbat* 108b.

[23] See Vermes, *Christian Beginnings* (see endnote 1), chapter 1; "Jewish Miracle Workers in the Late Second Temple Period," in *Jewish Annotated New Testament*, eds. Amy-Jill Levine and Marc Z. Brettler (New York: Oxford University Press, 2011), p. 536.

[24] See Geza Vermes, *The Authentic Gospel of Jesus* (London: Penguin, 2004), pp. 427–430. Concerning guidelines for disentangling the authentic from the inauthentic sayings of Jesus, see Vermes, *Authentic Gospel*, pp. 376–397, and *Jesus in the Jewish World* (see endnote 21), pp. 224–235.

[25] See A.Z. Idelsohn, *Jewish Liturgy and Its Development* (New York: Schocken, 1972), p. 84.

[26] CD 1:3–11; 20:13–15.

[27] *Seder Olam Rabbah* 30.

[28] Ferdinand Hahn, *The Titles of Jesus in Christology* (Cambridge: Lutterworth, 1969), p. 307.

[29] Ecclesiasticus [Ben Sirach] 23:1; see also 4:10, 23:4, 51:10 [Hebrew]; Tobit 13:4; 4Q200 6, 9–10; Wisdom 14:3, etc.

[30] Jubilees 19:29; see also 1:25, 28; Test. of Juda 17:2; 24:2; etc.

[31] 4Q372 1, 16; 1QH 17:35; 4Q502 39, 3; 4Q511 27, 1, etc.

[32] Eighteen Benedictions 5–6 [Palestinian version]; the Kaddish; Mishnah *Berakhot* 5:1, etc.

[33] Joachim Jeremias, *The Prayers of Jesus* (London: SCM, 1977), pp. 57–65.

[34] See Geza Vermes, *Jesus and the World of Judaism* (London: SCM, 1983), pp. 41–42; and especially James Barr, "Abba Isn't Daddy!" *JTS* 39 (1988), pp. 28–47.

[35] Ben Sirach 4:10; Wisdom 2:17–18; Jubilees 1:24–25, etc.

[36] See Geza Vermes, *Jesus the Jew* (London: SCM, 2001), pp. 168–73, 180–183.

[37] See Geza Vermes, *The Passion* (London: Penguin, 2005), pp. 81–93.

[38] Ernst Käsemann, *Essays on New Testament Themes* (London: SCM, 1964), p. 101.

[39] Mishnah *Yoma* 8:6.

[40] *Mekhilta of Rabbi Ishmael* on Exodus 31:14.

[41] See Geza Vermes, *The Changing Faces of Jesus* (London: Penguin, 2001), pp. 218–219.

[42] Philo, *Special Laws* 1.1.

[43] *Hypothetica* 7.6; BT *Shabbat* 31a.

[44] As for the lasting, i.e., institutional, character of the Lord's Supper, it is not mentioned in either Mark or Matthew and is only hinted at in Luke probably under Pauline influence in the added command: "Do this in remembrance of me" (Luke 22:19; 1 Corinthians 11:24–25).

[45] The total unexpectedness by his disciples of Jesus' downfall speaks powerfully against the genuineness of the repeated predictions of the passion and the cross as well as against the foretelling by Jesus of his glorious return. See Vermes, *Authentic Gospel* (see endnote 24), pp.

385–389; *Jesus in the Jewish World* (see endnote 21), pp. 233–235.

[46] Josephus mentions slabs inscribed in Greek and Latin displayed at regular intervals along the Temple boundaries prohibiting foreigners under death penalty to cross the line (*War* 5.194; *Antiquities* 15.417). Two such inscriptions, one complete and one fragmentary, were discovered in Jerusalem in 1871 and 1935. See eds. Hannah M. Cotton et al., *Corpus Inscriptionum Iudaeae/ Palestinae*, vol. 1, *Jerusalem, Part 1* (Berlin: De Gruyter, 2010), pp. 42–45.

[47] London: Penguin, 2005. Brief outlines may be found in Vermes, *Jesus and the World of Judaism* (see endnote 34), pp. viii–ix, and *Changing Faces of Jesus* (see endnote 41), pp. 258–262.

[48] *Antiquities* 18.65.

[49] *Antiquities* 18.117–119.

[50] *War* 6.300–310.

II. From the Crucifixion to the End of the First Century

[1] See, for example, S. Sandmel, *The First Christian Century in Judaism and Christianity* (New York: Oxford University, 1969), chapter 2, "Palestinian Judaisms"; *Judaisms and Their Messiahs at the Turn of the Christian Era*, eds. J. Neusner et al. (Cambridge: Cambridge University Press, 1987); A.F. Segal, *The Other Judaisms of Late Antiquity* (Atlanta: Scholars Press, 1987); J. Murphy, *The Religious World of Jesus: An Introduction to Second Temple Palestinian Judaism* (Hoboken, NJ: Ktav, 1991), p. 39.

[2] Ignatius, *Magnesia* 10.1–3; *Romans* 3:3; *Philippians* 6:1; *Martyrdom of Polycarp* 10.1. See further K.W. Niebuhr, "'Judentum' und 'Christentum' bei Paulus und Ignatius von Antiochien," *Zeitschrift für die Neutestamentliche Wissenschaft* 85 (1994), pp. 218–233, esp. 224–233.

[3] Acts 5:17, 15:5, 26:5; Josephus, *War* 2.119–166; *Antiquities* 18.11–15.

[4] Acts 9:2; see also 19:9,23, 22:4, 24:14, 22; cf. 18:25–26; 2 Peter 2:2; possibly reflected in 1 Corinthians 12:31.

[5] See J.D.G. Dunn, *Theology of Paul the Apostle* (Grand Rapids, MI: Eerdmans, 1998), p. 643, nn. 82–84.

[6] See further G.G. Porton, "Halakah," in *Anchor Bible Dictionary*, ed. David N. Freedman (New York: Doubleday, 1992), vol. 3, pp. 26–27; S. Safrai, "Halakha," in *The Literature of the Sages*, ed. S. Safrai, Compendia Rerum Iudaicarum ad Novum Testamentum II.3.1 (Assen: van Gorcum, 1987), pp. 121–209.

[7] Note particularly the absolute use ("the way") in 1QS 9.17–18, 21, 10.21; CD 1.13, 2.6.

[8] 1QS 4.22, 8.10,18,21, 9.5.

[9] The fact that the post-biblical Jewish writings, including those by Philo and Josephus, were retained by Christians rather than the rabbis, and that several Jewish writings, like the Testaments of the Twelve Patriarchs, became the basis of Christian writings should not be forgotten. See J.H. Charlesworth, "Christian and Jewish Self-Definition in Light of the Christian Additions to the Apocryphal Writings," in *Jewish and Christian Self-Definition*, vol. 2, *Aspects of Judaism in the Graeco-Roman Period*, ed. E.P. Sanders (London: SCM, 1981), pp. 27–55; M.A. Knibb, "Christian Adoption and Transmission of Jewish-Pseudepigrapha: The Case of 1 Enoch," *JSJ* 32 (2001), pp. 396–415.

[10] J. Lieu, "'The Parting of the Ways': Theological Construct or Historical Reality?" *Journal for the Study of the New Testament* 56 (1994), pp. 101–119, reprinted in *Neither Jew nor Greek? Constructing Early Christianity* (London: T & T Clark, 2003), pp. 11–29; she prefers the imagery of "a criss-crossing of muddy tracks" (at p. 119 or p. 29).

[11] See particularly E.K. Broadhead, *Jewish Ways of Following Jesus*, WUNT 266 (Tübingen: Mohr Siebeck, 2010).

[12] The main thesis of A.H. Becker and A.Y. Reed, eds., *The Ways That Never Parted*, TSAJ 95 (Tübingen: Mohr Siebeck, 2003) is obvious from the title, but unfortunately the editors see their task as dispelling "the notion of a single and simple 'Parting of the Ways' in the first or second century CE" (ibid., p. 22); but "single and simple" is too much of a straw man.

[13] My use of the plural ("Partings") in *The Partings of the Ways Between Christianity and Judaism* (London: SCM, 1991) was not always appreciated; but note also the "Preface to the Second Edition" (2006).

[14] In what follows I naturally draw on my *Beginning from Jerusalem* (Grand Rapids, MI: Eerdmans, 2009).

[15] S. Heschel, *Abraham Geiger and the Jewish Jesus* (Chicago: University of Chicago Press, 1998), p. 75. On the anti-Jewishness of 19th-century New Testament scholarship, see particularly pp. 66–75, 106–107, 117–118, 123, 153–157, 190–193, 212–213, 227. See also H. Moxnes, "Jesus the Jew: Dilemmas of Interpretation," in *Fair Play: Diversity and Conflicts in Early Christianity*, eds. I. Dunderberg et al., H. Räisänen FS (Leiden: Brill, 2002), pp. 83–103 (here 83–89, 93–94).

[16] A. von Harnack, *The Expansion of Christianity in the First Three Centuries* (London: Williams & Norgate, 1904): "By their rejection of Jesus the Jewish people disowned their calling and dealt the death-blow to their own existence" (pp. 81–82); quoted by Broadhead, *Jewish Ways* (see endnote 11), p. 354.

[17] "Those who seek smooth things" (the Pharisees) were "hanged alive on the tree" (Deuteronomy 21:22–23); Josephus displays a similar shock (*Antiquities* 13.380–381).

[18] L.T. Johnson, "The New Testament's Anti-Jewish Slander and the Conventions of Ancient Polemic," *JBL* 108 (1989), pp. 419–441.

[19] See, for example, E. Schürer, *The History of the Jewish People in the Age of Jesus Christ*, rev. and ed. G. Vermes and F. Millar, 4 vols. (Edinburgh: T & T Clark, 1973–1987), vol. 1, pp. 543–544.

[20] Detail in ibid., vol. 1, §18.

[21] Psalm 110:1 evidently played a crucial role in earliest reflection on what had happened to Jesus. See particularly D.M. Hay, *Glory at the Right Hand: Psalm 110 in Early Christianity*, SBL Monograph Series 18 (Nashville: Abingdon, 1973); and M. Hengel, "'Sit at My Right Hand!' The Enthronement of Christ at the Right Hand of God and Psalm 110.1," in *Studies in Early Christology* (Edinburgh: T & T Clark, 1995), pp. 119–225.

[22] *Pace* L.W. Hurtado, *How on Earth Did Jesus Become a God?* (Grand Rapids, MI: Eerdmans, 2005), pp. 34–36.

[23] Particularly as regards the law—reflected especially in Galatians and Philippians 3.

[24] Genesis 5:24 (Enoch); 2 Kings 2:11 (Elijah); the righteous martyrs (Wisdom of Solomon 5:5,15–16); 4 Ezra 14:9 (Ezra); 2 Baruch 13:3 (Baruch). G. Jossa, *Jews or Christians? The Followers of Jesus in Search of Their Own Identity*, WUNT 202 (Tübingen: Mohr Siebeck, 2006), p. 68: "The assertion of the heavenly exaltation of Jesus (and of Jesus crucified) in fact puts the group of his disciples in a completely different situation from that of the other Jewish groups of the time." But contrast J. Carleton Paget, "Jewish Christianity," in *The Cambridge History of Judaism*, vol. 3, *The Early Roman Period*, eds. W. Horbury et al. (Cambridge: Cambridge University Press, 1999), pp. 731–775: "At that early stage there was no sense on their part that a commitment to Jesus implied anything negative about their continuing commitment to their inherited faith" (p. 742).

[25] It is unclear that passages like 1 Corinthians 8:6 and Philippians 2:10–11 would have been heard by traditionalist Jews, at least initially, as a threat to the *Shema*; see J.D.G. Dunn, *Did the First Christians Worship Jesus?* (London: SPCK, 2010), pp. 101–112.

[26] M. Hengel, *Judaism and Hellenism*, trans. J. Bowden (London: SCM, 1974), and *The "Hellenization" of Judaea in the First Century After Christ* (London: SCM, 1989).

[27] Acts 6:1 uses the term ("Hellenist") only for one group of Jesus' followers, but it is clear from Acts 6:8–10 that the believing Hellenists belonged to a much larger group comprising Jews from Cyrenia, Alexandria, Cilicia and Asia.

[28] In Acts 9:2 Saul's persecuting zeal is directed against those "who belonged to the Way," that is, probably Hellenist believers-in-Jesus in particular.

[29] It is not clear that Stephen or the Hellenists had engaged in a radical critique of the law apart from its focus on the Temple, though such an inference is regularly drawn; see J.D.G. Dunn,

Beginning from Jerusalem (see endnote 14), p. 261, n. 81.

[30] Jesus was remembered as speaking negatively about the Temple (at least warning against its destruction [Mark 13:2]; his reported speech is presented by Matthew and Mark as false testimony (Mark 14:57–59 and parallels), but John attributes much the same words to Jesus himself (John 2:19).

[31] Leviticus 26:1,30; Isaiah 2:18, 10:11; etc.; Daniel 5:4,23; Judith 8:18; Wisdom of Solomon 14:8; Philo, *On the Life of Moses* 1.303, 2.165,168; Sibylline Oracles 3.605–606,722, 4.28a. In the Septuagint (LXX) *cheiropoiētos* almost always stands for the Hebrew *'elil*; on which, see H.D. Preuss, *"'elil,"* in *Theological Dictionary of the Old Testament*, eds. G. Johannes Botterweck and H. Ringgren, trans. J.T. Willis (Grand Rapids, MI: Eerdmans, 1977), vol. 1, pp. 285–287.

[32] But Luke is generally much more positive in his presentation of the role of the Temple, and so in his own attitude to the Temple; consequently, we should probably refer this very negative attitude to Luke's source.

[33] The completion of a Nazirite vow included a sin offering (Numbers 6:9–12).

[34] See further J.D.G. Dunn, "When Did the Understanding of Jesus' Death as an Atoning Sacrifice First Emerge?" in *Israel's God and Rebecca's Children: Christology and Community in Early Judaism and Christianity: Essays in Honor of Larry W. Hurtado and Alan F. Segal*, eds. D.B. Capes et al. (Waco, TX: Baylor University Press, 2007), pp. 169–181.

[35] The initial influence on the converted Paul came from the Hellenists whom he had been persecuting (in Damascus?); his first contact with more traditionalist members of the sect did not take place for another three years (Galatians 1:18).

[36] The Jewish Christian sect known as the Ebionites treasured a gospel (of Matthew?) in which Jesus claims, "I have come to abolish the sacrifices; if you do not cease from sacrificing, the wrath [of God] will not cease from weighing upon you" (as cited by J.K. Elliott, *The Apocryphal New Testament* (Oxford: Clarendon, 1994), p. 15.

[37] See particularly CD 3.12–4.12; 4QFlor[ilegium] 1.1–7; and further B. Gärtner, *The Temple and the Community in Qumran and the New Testament*, Society for New Testament Studies Monograph Series 1 (Cambridge: Cambridge University Press, 1965), chapters 2 and 3; G. Klinzing, *Die Umdeutung des Kultus in der Qumrangemeinde und im Neuen Testament*, Part 2 (Göttingen: Vandenhoeck & Ruprecht, 1971).

[38] The fact that Luke describes those scattered from Jerusalem as preaching to "the Hellenists" in Antioch (Acts 11:20) has caused some confusion (the New International Version and New Jerusalem Bible, for example, translate/ read "Greeks," and the Revised English Bible "gentiles"), but Luke's point is presumably to indicate that the link lay in the fact that both groups spoke/functioned in Greek; or perhaps we should speak more generally of their shared Hellenistic culture.

[39] According to Josephus, in Antioch in the period prior to the Jewish revolt, many Greeks were attracted to the Jewish synagogues' religious ceremonies and integrated socially with the Jews (*War* 7.3). And, notably, in the violence that marked relations between Jews and non-Jews in Syria in 66 C.E., Antioch was one of only three cities that spared their Jewish inhabitants (*War* 2.5).

[40] Juvenal seems to have a typical Godfearer in mind when he satirizes the God-fearing father, "who reveres the Sabbath, worships nothing but the clouds" and abstains from eating swine's flesh, and the son who takes the logical next step of accepting circumcision (*Satires* 14.96–106).

[41] See, for example, P. Trebilco, *Jewish Communities in Asia Minor*, SNTSMS 69 (Cambridge: Cambridge University Press, 1991), chapter 7; J.M. Lieu, "The Race of the God-fearers," *JTS* 46 (1995), pp. 483–501; I. Levinskaya, *The Book of Acts in Its Diaspora Setting* (Grand Rapids, MI: Eerdmans, 1996), chapters 4–7; B. Wander, *Gottesfürchtige und Sympathisanten: Studien zum heidnischen Umfeld von Diasporasynagogen*, WUNT 104 (Tübingen: Mohr Siebeck, 1998).

[42] See L.H. Schiffman, *Who Was a Jew? Rabbinic and Halakhic Perspectives on the Jewish-Christian Schism* (Hoboken, NJ: Ktav, 1985).

[43] Psalms 22:27–28, 86:9; Isaiah 2:2–4 = Micah 4:1–3; Isaiah 45:20–23, 56:6–8, 66:19–20,23; Jeremiah 3:17; Zephaniah 3:9–10; Zechariah 2:11–12, 8:20–23, 14:16–19; Tobit 13:11, 14:6–7; 1 Enoch 10:21, 90:30–36; Sibylline Oracle 3.715–719. See further J. Jeremias, *Jesus' Promise to the Nations* (London: SCM, 1958), pp. 56–62; and T.L. Donaldson, "Proselytes or 'Righteous Gentiles'? The Status of Gentiles in Eschatological Pilgrimage Patterns of Thought," *Journal for the Study of the Pseudepigrapha* 4 (1990), pp. 3–27.

[44] See J.D.G. Dunn, "Paul: Apostate or Apostle of Israel?" *Zeitschrift für die Neutestamentliche Wissenschaft* 89 (1998), pp. 256–271.

[45] There is broad agreement that Galatians 1:15–16 draws on Jeremiah 1:5 and Isaiah 49:1–6.

[46] Genesis 12:3, 18:18.

[47] For a full discussion, see Dunn, *Beginning from Jerusalem* (see endnote 14), §27.2.

[48] Deuteronomy 10:16; Jeremiah 4:4, 9:25–26; Ezekiel 44:9.

[49] Romans 2:26, 3:30; Galatians 2:7; Colossians 3:11.

[50] See J.D.G. Dunn, *The Epistles to the Colossians and to Philemon*, The New International Greek Testament Commentary (Grand Rapids, MI: Eerdmans, 1996).

[51] See particularly W. Meeks, *The First Urban Christians: The Social World of the Apostle Paul* (New Haven, CT: Yale University Press, 1983), pp. 97, 168; J.M.G. Barclay, "'Do We Undermine the Law?' A Study of Romans 14.1–15.6," in *Paul and the Mosaic Law*, ed. J.D.G. Dunn, WUNT 89 (Tübingen: Mohr Siebeck, 1996), pp. 287–308, here 303–308).

[52] See particularly R. Bauckham, "James and the Jerusalem Church," in *The Book of Acts in Its Palestinian Setting*, ed. R. Bauckham (Grand Rapids, MI: Eerdmans, 1995), pp. 458–462; J. Wehnert, *Die Reinheit des "christlichen Gottesvolkes" aus Juden und Heiden*, Forschungen zur Religion und Literatur des Alten und Neuen Testaments 173 (Göttingen: Vandenhoeck & Ruprecht, 1997), pp. 209–238; W. Kraus, *Zwischen Jerusalem und Antiochia: Die "Hellenisten," Paulus und die Aufnahme der Heiden in*

das endzeitliche Gottesvolk, Stuttgarter Biblestudien 179 (Stuttgart: Katholisches Bibelwerk, 1999), pp. 148–155.

[53] In his protest to Peter (Galatians 2:14–16), Paul may well have been influenced by Jesus' famed readiness to eat with "sinners" (Mark 2:16–17; Matthew 11:19; Luke 15:2); and his own denial that no food was "unclean" (Romans 14:14) seems to reflect Mark's account of Jesus' teaching on sources of impurity (Mark 7:14–23).

[54] See, for example, E. Haenchen, *The Acts of the Apostles*, trans. B. Noble and G. Shinn (Blackwell, 1971), pp. 471–472.

[55] See H. Karpp, "Christennamen," in *Reallexicon für Antike und Christentum*, vol. 2 (Leipzig: K.W. Hiersemann), pp. 114–138 (here 113); H.B. Mattingly, "The Origin of the Name Christiani," *JTS* 9 (1958), pp. 26–37 (here 28, n. 3); see also W. Bauer, *A Greek-English Lexicon of the New Testament and Other Early Christian Literature*, 3rd ed., revised by F.W. Danker (Chicago: University of Chicago Press, 2000), p. 1089.

[56] B. Reicke observes that the verb used (*chrēmatisai*) has the sense of "called officially" and translates Acts 11:26, "for the first time in Antioch the disciples were publicly known as Christians." See *Theological Dictionary of the New Testament*, ed. G. Kittel (Grand Rapids, MI: Eerdmans, 1974), vol. 9, pp. 481–482.

[57] "The Greek-speaking synagogues in Rome used the Greek suffix *-esioi* in their names. The suffix *-ianus* constitutes a political comment ... It is not used of the followers of a god. It classifies people as partisans of a political or military leader, and is mildly contemptuous." Quoted from E.A. Judge, "Judaism and the Rise of Christianity: A Roman Perspective," *TynB* 45 (1994), pp. 355–368 (here 363). See further Dunn, *Beginning from Jerusalem* (see endnote 14), pp. 303–306 and nn. 266, 271.

[58] Ambivalence between *Chrestus* and *Christus*, *Chrestianoi* and *Christianoi* was a feature of this period; see, for example, R.E. Van Voorst, *Jesus Outside the New Testament* (Grand Rapids, MI: Eerdmans, 2000), pp. 43–44.

[59] According to Acts 18:2, Aquila and Priscilla, Jews who were already disciples of Jesus Messiah, had been among those expelled from Rome.

⁶⁰ For example, U. Schnelle, *The History and Theology of the New Testament Writings*, trans. M.E. Boring (London: SCM, 1998): The expulsions of 49 "accomplished the final separation between the Christian community and the synagogue" (p. 112); S. Spence, *The Parting of the Ways: The Roman Church as a Case Study* (Leuven: Peeters, 2004), p. 117.

⁶¹ P. Lampe, *From Paul to Valentinus: Christians at Rome in the First Two Centuries*, trans. M. Steinhauser, ed. M. Johnson (Minneapolis: Fortress Press, 2003), pp. 167–170.

⁶² I follow the influential argument of W. Wiefel, "The Jewish Community in Ancient Rome and the Origins of Roman Christianity," *Judaica* 26 (1970), pp. 65–88, reprinted in *The Romans Debate*, ed. K.P. Donfried (Peabody, MA: Hendrickson, 1991), pp. 85–101.

⁶³ See Acts 2:10; see, for example, Lampe, *From Paul to Valentinus* (see endnote 61), pp. 7–10; R. Hvalvik, "Jewish Believers and Jewish Influence in the Roman Church until the Early Second Century," in *Jewish Believers in Jesus: The Early Centuries*, eds. O. Skarsaune and R. Hvalvik (Peabody, MA: Hendrickson, 2007), pp. 179–216 (here 187–189).

⁶⁴ Often cited is the note of Ambrosiaster (fourth century) that the Romans "embraced faith in Christ, though according to Jewish rite, without seeing any sign of miracles and without any of the apostles" (*Patrologia Latina* 17 col. 46). Note also Tertullian's observation that the "school" of Christianity insinuated its claims "under cover of a very famous religion [Judaism] and one certainly permitted by law" (*Apology* 21.1).

⁶⁵ See further J.D.G. Dunn, "The Legal Status of the Earliest Christian Churches," in *The Making of Christianity: Conflicts, Contacts and Constructions, Essays in Honor of Bengt Holmberg*, eds. M. Zetterholm and S. Byrskog (Winona Lake, IN: Eisenbrauns, 2012), pp. 75–93.

⁶⁶ There is an ongoing debate as to whether Philippians was written from Ephesus or Rome, though I find the case for Rome slightly more compelling (see Dunn, *Beginning from Jerusalem* [see endnote 14], pp. 1009–1014).

⁶⁷ Argued for strongly by Spence in particular (*Parting of the Ways* [see endnote 60], pp. 119–137, 170; though see also pp. 235–237); see also Jossa, *Jews or Christians?* (see endnote 24), pp. 133–135.

⁶⁸ E.M. Smallwood (*The Jews Under Roman Rule from Pompey to Diocletian* [Leiden: Brill, 1981], pp. 218–219) discusses whether there was any Jewish involvement in the denunciation of the "Christians."

⁶⁹ Referred to by Jossa, *Jews or Christians?* (see endnote 24), p. 134, n. 27, who also notes that the accusation that Tacitus levels against the Christians, of "hatred of the human race" (*Annals* 15.44.4), is the same accusation that he levels against the Jews (*Histories* 5.5.1).

⁷⁰ However, we should note the Jewish uprising in Cyrene in 115–117 C.E. (Schürer, *History of the Jewish People* [see endnote 19], vol. 1, pp. 529–534).

⁷¹ But we cannot assume that this happened before the third century; see P.S. Alexander, "'The Parting of the Ways' from the Perspective of Rabbinic Judaism," in *Jews and Christians: The Parting of the Ways A.D. 70 to 135*, ed. J.D.G. Dunn, WUNT 66 (Tübingen: Mohr Siebeck, 1992), pp. 1–25.

⁷² The tradition comes down to us from two sources (Eusebius, *Ecclesiastical History* 3.5.3; Epiphanius, *Panarion* 29.7.7–8). See further C. Koester, "The Origin and Significance of the Flight to Pella Tradition," *CBQ* 51 (1989), pp. 90–106; and Dunn, *Beginning from Jerusalem* (see endnote 14), §36.3.

⁷³ See J.D.G. Dunn, *Unity and Diversity in the New Testament*, 3rd ed. (London: SCM, 2006); also D.F. Wright, "Ebionites," and D.A. Hagner, "Jewish Christianity," in *Dictionary of the Later New Testament and Its Developments*, eds. R.P. Martin and P.H. Davids (Downers Grove, IL: InterVarsity Press, 1997), pp. 313–317, 583–587.

⁷⁴ See further Broadhead, *Jewish Ways of Following Jesus* (see endnote 11).

⁷⁵ Schürer, *History of the Jewish People* (see endnote 19), vol. 2, pp. 271–272.

⁷⁶ Text in *GLAJJ*, vol. 2, p. 128. See further M. Goodman, "Nerva, the *fiscus Judaicus* and

Jewish Identity," *JRS* 79 (1989), pp. 40–44; and further M. Heemstra, *The Fiscus Judaicus and the Parting of the Ways*, WUNT 277 (Tübingen: Mohr Siebeck, 2010).

77 For full discussion, see Heemstra, Fiscus Judaicus (see endnote 76), chapter 2.

78 "From the year 96 onward it was possible for Roman authorities to recognize Christians, because they were exclusive monotheists, who did not pay the Jewish tax" (ibid., p. 196).

79 Notably J.T. Sanders, *The Jews in Luke-Acts* (Philadelphia: Fortress Press, 1987). Sanders quotes regularly from E. Haenchen, "The Book of Acts as Source Material for the History of Early Christianity," in *Studies in Luke-Acts*, eds. L.E. Keck and J.L. Martyn (Philadelphia: Fortress Press, 1966), pp. 258–278, particularly Haenchen's judgment that "Luke has written the Jews off" (p. 278).

80 See further Dunn, "The Question of Anti-semitism in the New Testament Writings," in *Jews and Christians* (see endnote 71), pp. 177–211 (here 187–195), and *Beginning from Jerusalem* (see endnote 14), pp. 1006–1009.

81 See particularly G.N. Stanton, *A Gospel for a New People: Studies in Matthew* (Edinburgh: T & T Clark, 1992), Part 2: "The Parting of the Ways."

82 The assembly of believers-in-Jesus is referred to by James as a "synagogue" (James 2:2). Matthew also speaks of "their scribes" (7:29), but in 8:19 and 23:34 scribes are portrayed in a positive light, and 13:52 is usually taken as a self-reference to Matthew himself as a scribe.

83 See, for example, J.D.G. Dunn, "Pharisees, Sinners and Jesus," in *Jesus, Paul and the Law* (London: SPCK, 1990), pp. 61–86 (here 73–77); also *Jesus Remembered* (Grand Rapids, MI: Eerdmans, 2003), pp. 528– 532.

84 See further, Dunn, "The Question of Anti-semitism" (see endnote 80), pp. 203–210.

85 D.C. Allison, *The New Moses: A Matthean Typology* (Edinburgh: T & T Clark, 1993).

86 See particularly W.D. Davies, *The Setting of the Sermon on the Mount* (Cambridge University Press, 1964), pp. 256–315.

87 John 5:10,15,16,18, 7:1,13, 8:48,52,57(?), 9:18,22, 10:31,33, 11:8. In 5:15, 7:13, 9:18,22, 11:8 an individual or individuals who are themselves Jews are distinguished from "the Jews."

88 John 6:41,52, 7:11–12,15,31,35, 8:22,31, 10:19,24, 11:19,31,33,36,42,45,54, 12:9,11.

89 John 6:52, 7:11–12,31,35,40–44, 10:19, 12:11,17–19, 12:34.

90 C.H. Dodd (*The Interpretation of the Fourth Gospel* [Cambridge: Cambridge University Press, 1960], pp. 352–353) pointed out that what he called "the Book of Signs" (chapters 3–12) is constructed with a view to bringing out the divisive effect of Christ, the escalating process of separation (*krisis*–3:19, 5:22,24,27,29,30, 7:24, 8:16, 12:31) and division (*schisma*–7:43, 9:16, 10:19) that was the inevitable effect of the light shining (3:19–21).

91 The most recent discussion, with bibliography, is by W.E.S. North, "'The Jews' in John's Gospel: Observations and Inferences," in *Judaism, Jewish Identities and the Gospel Tradition: Essays in Honour of Maurice Casey*, ed. J.G. Crossley (London: Equinox, 2010), pp. 206–226. She concludes: John's usage "stems from his desire to promote his own group as an alternative and authentic form of Judaism" (p. 221).

92 The revision of the 12th benediction to make it a malediction on apostates is attributed to Samuel the Small in about 85 C.E. (BT *Berakhot* 28b). The thesis that the *Birkat ha-Minim* lay behind John 9:22 was given influential statement by J.L. Martyn, *History and Theology in the Fourth Gospel* (Nashville: Abingdon, 1968; revised 1979). Davies argued the less clear case that the *Birkat ha-Minim* similarly lay behind Matthew's hostility to the Pharisees/rabbis (*Setting* [see endnote 86], pp. 275–282).

93 Discussion subsequent to Martyn's thesis has shown it to be likely that the *Birkat ha-Minim* did not emerge until later, and that any explicit reference to Christians is unlikely to have been part of its original formulation. See now D. Boyarin, *Border Lines: The Partition of Judaeo-Christianity* (Philadelphia: University of Pennsylvania Press, 2004), pp. 67–73 and further bibliography there, including particularly P.W. van der Horst, "The *Birkat ha-Minim* in Recent Research," in *Hellenism-Judaism-Christianity:*

Essays on Their Interaction (Kampen: Pharos, 1994), pp. 99–111.

[94] See particularly W. Horbury, "The Benediction of the *Minim* and Early Jewish-Christian Controversy," *JTS* 33 (1982), pp. 19–61, also *Jews and Christians in Contact and Controversy* (Edinburgh: T & T Clark, 1998), chapter 2 and pp. 240–242.

[95] The classic collection of data is R.T. Herford, *Christianity in Talmud and Midrash* (London: Williams & Norgate, 1903).

[96] Boyarin, *Border Lines* (see endnote 93), Part 2.

[97] B. Lindars, *The Theology of the Letter to the Hebrews* (Cambridge: Cambridge University Press, 1991), pp. 4–15. "To the Hebrews" was not part of the original title, but it appears already in p[46], that is, about 200 C.E.

[98] See already in Barnabas and Melito of Sardis. Horbury observes that "a Christian sense of accepted separation from the Jewish community seems first clearly detectable in writings from about the end of the first century onward, notably the Epistle of Barnabas" (*Jews and Christians* [see endnote 94], pp. 11–13).

[99] See, for example, H. von Campenhausen, *The Formation of the Christian Bible*, trans. J.A. Baker (London: A & C Black, 1972), pp. 232–233.

[100] See J.D.G. Dunn, "Two Covenants or One? The Interdependence of Jewish and Christian Identity," in *Geschichte-Tradition-Reflexion: Festschrift für Martin Hengel. III. Frühes Christentum*, ed. H. Lichtenberger (Tübingen: Mohr Siebeck, 1996), pp. 97–122; reprinted in the second ed. of *Partings of the Ways* (see endnote 13), pp. 339–365 (§2).

III. The Godfearers: From the Gospels to Aphrodisias

[1] See John M.G. Barclay, *Jews in the Mediterranean Diaspora: From Alexander to Trajan (323 BCE–117 CE)*, Hellenistic Culture and Society 33 (Berkeley: University of California Press, 1996).

[2] Bradley Blue, "Acts and the House Church," in *The Book of Acts in its Graeco-Roman Setting*,

eds. David W.J. Gill and Conrad Gempf (Grand Rapids, MI: Eerdmans, 1994), pp. 119–222, at pp. 178–183.

[3] See Louis B. Feldman, *Jew and Gentile in the Ancient World: Attitudes and Interactions from Alexander to Justinian* (Princeton, NJ: Princeton University Press, 1993), p. 152.

[4] See Joyce Reynolds and Robert Tannenbaum, *Jews and God-Fearers at Aphrodisias: Greek Inscriptions with Commentary: Texts from the Excavations at Aphrodisias Conducted by Kenan T. Erim* (Cambridge: Cambridge Philological Society, 1987).

[5] *Juvenal and Persius with an English Translation*, Loeb, trans. G.G. Ramsay (London: W. Heinemann, 1979), with the translation slightly revised.

[6] See Mishnah *Demai* 2:2–3 and the discussion in Richard S. Sarason, *Demai*, The Talmud of the Land of Israel 3 (Chicago: University of Chicago Press, 1993), pp. 75–84.

[7] So A.T. Kraabel, "The Disappearance of the 'God-Fearers,'" *Numen* 28.2 (1981), pp. 113–126, at p. 114.

[8] Kraabel, "Disappearance of the 'God-Fearers'" (see endnote 7); Louis H. Feldman, "Jewish 'Sympathizers' in Classical Literature and Inscriptions," *Transactions and Proceedings of the American Philological Association* 81 (1950), pp. 200–208; and Ralph Marcus, "The Sebomenoi in Josephus," *Jewish Social Studies* 14.3 (1952), pp. 247–250.

[9] See Paul F. Stuehrenberg, "The 'God-Fearers' in Martin Luther's Translation of Acts," *The Sixteenth Century Journal* 40.3 (1989), pp. 407–415.

[10] This suggestion, from Charlotte Roueché, is accepted in Joyce Reynolds and Robert Tannenbaum, *Jews and God-Fearers at Aphrodisias* (see endnote 4), p. 51 (cf. n. 204).

[11] A probable awareness of the *Birkat ha-Minim* causes him to reinterpret Galatians 3:10 in *Dialogue* 95–96. As Judith M. Lieu ("Accusations of Jewish Persecution in Early Christian Sources with Particular Reference to Justin Martyr and the *Martyrdom of Polycarp*," in *Tolerance and Intolerance in Early Judaism and Christianity*,

eds. Graham N. Stanton and Guy G. Stroumsa [Cambridge: Cambridge University Press, 1998], pp. 279–295, at p. 291) says: "On the one hand, the scriptural 'cursed be everyone who hangs on a tree' anticipates how the Jews would treat both Christ and Christians, yet, on the other, it also sets into sharp relief the Christian response of steadfastness and forgiveness ..."

[12] Rodney Werline, "The Transformation of Pauline Arguments in Justin Martyr's *Dialogue with Trypho*," *HTR* 92.1 (1999), pp. 79–93, at p. 90.

[13] Philippe Bobichon, *Justin Martyr: Dialogue avec Tryphon, édition critique*, Paradosis 47.1,2 (Fribourg: Academic Press, 2003). I have interacted further with his views in "Justin and Israelite Prophecy," *Justin Martyr and His Worlds*, eds. Sara Parvis and Paul Foster (Minneapolis: Fortress Press, 2007), pp. 77–87.

[14] Irina A. Levinskaya, "The Inscription from Aphrodisias and the Problem of God-Fearers," *TynB* 41.2 (1990), pp. 312–318; see also Martin Goodman's review in *JRS* 78 (1988), pp. 261–262; Margaret H. Williams, "The Jews and Godfearers Inscription from Aphrodisias: A Case of Patriarchal Interference in Early 3rd Century Caria?" *Historia: Zeitschrift für Alte Geschichte* 41.3 (1992), pp. 297–310; and Paul Trevilco, "The Jews in Asia Minor, 66–c. 235 CE," in *The Cambridge History of Judaism*, vol. 4: *Late Roman-Rabbinic Period*, ed. Steven T. Katz (Cambridge: Cambridge University Press, 2006), pp. 80–81.

[15] "New Inscriptions from Aphrodisias (1995–2001)," *American Journal of Archaeology* 108.3 (2004), pp. 377–416; "The Jews of Aphrodisias: New Evidence and Old Problems," *Scripta Classica Israelica* 21 (2002), pp. 209–242.

[16] A. Andrew Das, *Solving the Romans Debate* (Minneapolis: Fortress Press, 2007), p. 81. See also Martin Hengel, "The Interpenetration of Judaism and Hellenism in the Pre-Maccabean Period," in *The Cambridge History of Judaism*, vol. 2: *Hellenistic Age*, eds. W.D. Davies and Louis Finkelstein (Cambridge: Cambridge University Press, 2003), pp. 167–228.

[17] Reynolds and Tannenbaum, *Jews and God-Fearers at Aphrodisias* (see endnote 4), p. 23.

[18] Ibid., p. 45.

[19] Ibid.

[20] Ibid., pp. 54–56.

[21] See *Discourses Against Judaizing Christians*, trans. Paul W. Harkins (Washington, DC: Catholic University of America, 1979). For a characterization, see Lee I. Levine, *The Ancient Synagogue: The First Thousand Years* (New Haven, CT: Yale University Press, 2005), pp. 294–302; and Robert L. Wilken, *John Chrysostom and the Jews: Rhetoric and Reality in the Late 4th Century* (Berkeley: University of California Press, 1983).

[22] See Wilken, *John Chrysostom and the Jews* (see endnote 21).

[23] See Feldman, *Jew and Gentile in the Ancient World* (see endnote 3), pp. 369–370.

[24] For a discussion, see Shaye J.D. Cohen, *The Beginnings of Jewishness: Boundaries, Varieties, Uncertainties* (Berkeley: University of California Press, 1999), pp. 175–197.

[25] See F.J. Elizabeth Boddens Hosang, *Establishing Boundaries: Christian-Jewish Relations in Early Council Texts and the Writings of Church Fathers* (Leiden: Brill, 2010), pp. 91–107.

[26] Steven Fine, "The Menorah and the Cross: Historiographical Reflections on a Recent Discovery from Laodicea on the Lycus," *New Perspectives on Jewish-Christian Relations in Honor of David Berger*, eds. Elisheva Carlebach and Jacob J. Schacter, Brill Reference Library of Judaism (Leiden: Brill, 2012), pp. 31–50, at p. 47.

[27] See Judith Lieu, *Neither Jew Nor Greek? Constructing Early Christianity* (London: T & T Clark, 2005), pp. 38–40.

IV. The Christian Flight to Pella? The Archaeological Picture

[1] The debate has recently been summarized by Jonathan Bourgel, "'The Jewish Christians' Move from Jerusalem as a Pragmatic Choice," in *Studies in Rabbinic Judaism and Early*

Christianity, ed. Dan Jaffé (Leiden: Brill, 2010), pp. 107–138, especially references pp. 107–108; see also Vicky Balabanski, *Eschatology in the Making: Mark, Matthew, and the Didache* (Cambridge: Cambridge University Press, 1997), pp. 101–102.

² See, for example, *Jews and Christians: The Parting of the Ways, A.D. 70 to 135*, ed. James D.G. Dunn (Tübingen: Mohr Siebeck, 1992); *The Ways That Never Parted: Jews and Christians in Late Antiquity and the Early Middle Ages*, eds. A.H. Becker and A.Y. Reed (Minneapolis: Fortress Press, 2007).

³ Further discussed in B. Van Elderen, "Early Christianity in Transjordan," *TynB* 45.1 (1994), pp. 97–117.

⁴ This approach is advocated in D.R. Edwards and C.T. McCollough, *Archaeology and the Galilee: Texts and Contexts in the Graeco-Roman and Byzantine Periods* (Atlanta: Scholars Press, 1997), see especially James F. Strange, "First Century Galilee from Archaeology and from the Texts," pp. 39–48.

⁵ Judith Lieu, "'The Parting of the Ways': Theological Construct or Historical Reality?" in *Neither Jew nor Greek? Constructing Early Christianity* (London: T & T Clark, 2002), pp. 11–29. Lieu distinguishes theological concerns with the universal and the abstract from historical realities, encouraging "a more nuanced analysis of the local and the specific" (p. 18) and consideration of "the social realia that must have occupied most people most of the time" (p. 52).

⁶ Trans. Kirsopp Lake (London: Heinemann, 1926).

⁷ Epiphanius, *Against Heresies* 29.7, 30.2; and *De Mensuris et Ponderibus*, 15.9 (ed. J.P. Migne, Paris 1857–1899).

⁸ R.H. Smith, *Pella of the Decapolis I: The 1967 Season of the Wooster Expedition to Pella* (Wooster, OH: College of Wooster, 1973), pp. 42–43.

⁹ See endnote 1. Notably against the historicity of the tradition was S.G.F. Brandon, *The Fall of Jerusalem and the Christian Church: A Study of the Effects of the Jewish Overthrow of A.D. 70 on Christianity* (London: SPCK, 1978 [first published 1951]), pp. 168–173, followed by

Gerd Lüdemann, "The Successors of Pre-70 Jerusalem Christianity: A Critical Evaluation of the Pella-Tradition," in *Jewish and Christian Self-Definition*, vol. 1, ed. E.P. Sanders (Philadelphia: Fortress Press, 1980), pp. 161–173. See also G. Lüdemann and M.E. Boring, *Opposition to Paul in Jewish Christianity* (Minneapolis: Fortress Press, 1989); Lüdemann, *Heretics: The Other Side of Early Christianity* (Westminster: John Knox Press, 1996); and J. Verheyden, "The Flight of the Christians to Pella," *Ephemerides Theologicae Lovanienses* 66 (1990), pp. 368–384. This view has been considerably debated, for example, by Sidney Sowers, "The Circumstances and Recollection of the Pella Flight," *Theologische Zeitschrift* 26 (1970), pp. 305–320; R.A. Pritz, *Nazarene Jewish Christianity: From the End of the New Testament Period Until Its Disappearance in the Fourth Century* (Leiden: Brill, 1988); C. Koester, "The Origin and Significance of the Flight to Pella Tradition," *CBQ* 51 (1989), pp. 90–106; Balabanski, *Eschatology in the Making* (see endnote 1); and Bourgel, "'The Jewish Christians' Move from Jerusalem" (see endnote 1).

¹⁰ For the principal results of archaeological excavations at Pella, see Smith, *Pella of the Decapolis I* (see endnote 8); A.W. McNicoll, R.H. Smith and J.B. Hennessy, *Pella in Jordan 1* (Canberra: Australian National Gallery, 1982); R.H. Smith and L.P. Day, *Pella of the Decapolis II: Final Report on the College of Wooster Excavations in Area IX, the Civic Complex, 1979–1985* (Wooster, OH: College of Wooster Art Museum, 1989); A.W. McNicoll, P.C. Edwards, J. Hanbury-Tenison, J.B. Hennessy, T.F. Potts, R.H. Smith, A.G. Walmsley and P.M. Watson, *Pella in Jordan 2* (Sydney: Meditarch, 1992). Preliminary reports are found in the *Annual of the Department of Antiquities of Jordan* from 1980 onward.

¹¹ For the collection of ancient texts mentioning Pella, see Smith, *Pella of the Decapolis I* (see endnote 8), pp. 23–82.

¹² Josephus, *Antiquities* 13.4; Smith, *Pella of the Decapolis I* (see endnote 8), pp. 37–39.

¹³ P. Watson and J. Tidmarsh, "Pella/Tall al-Husn Excavations 1993: The University of Sydney–15th Season," *Annual of the Department of Antiquities of Jordan* 40 (1996), pp. 305–308. The earliest Roman public buildings such as the odeon and

the bathhouse in the wadi are dated to the late first century C.E.

[14] *Antiquities* 14.4. These discoveries allow a revision of Robert Smith's earlier view that Pella "lay in ruins" when Pompey passed by some 20 years later (see "Pella," in the *Anchor Bible Dictionary*, ed. David N. Freedman [New York: Doubleday, 1992], vol. 5, p. 220).

[15] Pliny, *Natural History* 5.16.74.

[16] *War* 2.1–2.

[17] Smith and Day, *Pella of the Decapolis II* (see endnote 10).

[18] G. Schumacher, *Pella* (London: Palestine Exploration Fund, 1895). For a comprehensive account of early explorations of the site, see Smith, *Pella of the Decapolis I* (see endnote 8), pp. 2–14.

[19] Schumacher, *Pella* (see endnote 18), pp. 39–42.

[20] Ibid., pp. 36–38.

[21] J. Richmond, "Khirbet Fahil," *Palestine Exploration Fund Quarterly Statement* (1934), pp. 20–22.

[22] R.W. Funk and H.N. Richardson, "The 1958 Sounding at Pella," *Biblical Archaeologist* 21.4 (1958), pp. 81–96.

[23] Smith, *Pella of the Decapolis I* (see endnote 8), pp. 143–149, "A Sarcophagus from Pella: New Light on Earliest Christianity," *Archaeology* 26 (1973), pp. 250–256.

[24] The Pella Hinterland Survey was directed by the author and Dr. Margaret O'Hea with the sponsorship of the British Institute at Amman for Archaeology and History and the University of Adelaide.

[25] Briefly reported in P.M. Watson, Research Reports, *Levant* 30 (1998), p. 219. Further studies of the tunnels and caves found in the Pella Hinterland Survey are found in P.M. Watson, "Roman Water Installations in the Vicinity of Pella," *Studies in the History and Archaeology of Jordan VII* (Amman: Department of Antiquities of Jordan, 2001), pp. 485–491, and "The Cave of Refuge at Pella," in *Australians Uncovering Ancient Jordan: Fifty Years of Middle Eastern Archaeology*, ed. A.G. Walmsley (Sydney: University of Sydney, 2001), pp. 113–120. For a

general account of the survey, see P.M. Watson and M. O'Hea, "The Pella Hinterland Survey 1994: Preliminary Report," *Levant* 28, pp. 63–76.

[26] Richmond, "Khirbet Fahil" (see endnote 21), p. 20.

[27] For a discussion of the geology, see P.G. Macumber, "The Geological Setting of Palaeolithic Sites at Tabaqat Fahl, Jordan," *Paléorient* 18.2 (1992), pp. 31–44.

[28] Richmond, "Khirbet Fahil" (see endnote 21), p. 21, fig. 1, "anchorite tunnels," from top to bottom, respectively. Compare Watson, "Roman Water Installations" (see endnote 25), fig. 8, p. 488.

[29] Watson, "Roman Water Installations" (see endnote 25).

[30] For a fully illustrated account, see Watson, "The Cave of Refuge at Pella" (see endnote 25).

V. Parting in Palestine

[1] See Hanan Eshel, "The Bar Kochba Revolt, 132–135 CE," in *The Cambridge History of Judaism*, vol. 4, *The Late Roman-Rabbinic Period*, ed. Steven T. Katz (Cambridge: Cambridge University Press, 2006), pp. 105–127.

[2] See Fergus Millar, *The Roman Near East, 31 BC–AD 337* (Cambridge, MA: Harvard University Press, 1993), pp. 374–386.

[3] For a common assumption, see Seth Schwartz, "Political, Social and Economic Life in the Land of Israel 66 to c. 235," in Katz, *Cambridge History of Judaism* [see endnote 1], pp. 23–52, who suggests that *Roman* law was in effect in Judea from 70 C.E.

[4] *Apion* 1.32, 90, 160, 228, 310; 2.21, 25.

[5] *Apion* 1.171.

[6] For courts in the land of Israel, see *The Jewish People in the First Century: Historical Geography, Political History, Social, Cultural and Religious Life*, eds. Shemuel Safrai and Mordecai Stern, Compendia Rerum Iudaicarum ad Novum Testamentum (Assen: Van Gorcum, 1974), vol. 1, pp. 377–419, and the examination of private law, pp. 504–533.

[7] For example, Dio Cassius, *Roman History* 69.12.1–69.14.3; Eusebius, *Ecclesiastical History* 4.6; Justin Martyr, *1 Apology* 31.6; Lamentations Rabbah 2:2.

[8] See Hannah M. Cotton, W.E.H. Cockle and Fergus G.B. Millar, "The Papyrology of the Roman Near East: A Survey," *JRS* 85 (1995), pp. 214–235, at p. 228. I am grateful to Fergus Millar for this reference.

[9] Yigael Yadin, *Bar-Kokhba: The Rediscovery of the Legendary Hero of the Second Jewish Revolt Against Rome* (London: Weidenfeld and Nicolson, 1971); Eshel, "Bar Kochba Revolt" (see endnote 1), pp. 117–127; Millar, *Roman Near East* (see endnote 2), pp. 370–375.

[10] See *Hadashot Arkeologiyot*, online edition: http://www.hadashot-esi.org.il/report_detail_eng.asp?id=179&mag_id=110

[11] See Stuart S. Miller, "Stepped Pools, Stone Vessels and Other Identity Markers of 'Complex Common Judaism,'" *JSJ* 41 (2010), pp. 214–243, at pp. 225–242; David Amit and Yonatan Adler, "The Observance of Ritual Purity after 70 CE: A Reevaluation of the Evidence in Light of Recent Archaeological Discoveries," in *'Follow the Wise': Studies in Jewish History and Culture in Honor of Lee I. Levine*, eds. Zeev Weiss, Oded Irshai, Jodi Magness and Seth Schwartz (Winona Lake, IN: Eisenbrauns, 2010), pp. 121–143.

[12] Yonatan Adler, "Ritual Baths Adjacent to Tombs: An Analysis of the Archaeological Evidence in Light of the Halakhic Sources," *JSJ* 40 (2009), pp. 55–73.

[13] Amit and Adler, "Observance of Ritual Purity" (see endnote 11), pp. 123–124, citing in particular the study by Yaakov Sussman, *Babylonian Sugiyot to the Orders Zera'im and Tohorot*, Ph.D. dissertation (Hebrew University of Jerusalem, 1969), pp. 310–313 (in Hebrew).

[14] Joan E. Taylor, "A Second Temple in Egypt: The Evidence for the Zadokite Temple of Onias," *JSJ* 29 (1998), pp. 1–25.

[15] Photius, *Bibliotheca* 33; Dio Cassius, *Roman History* 66:15.

[16] Especially *War* 6.1–8; 353–355; 7.1–5; 216, cf. *Life* 76; Benjamin Isaac, "Judaea after 70," in *The Near East Under Roman Rule: Selected Papers* (Leiden: Brill, 1998), pp. 112–121, originally published in *JJS* 35 (1984), pp. 44–50.

[17] Benny Arubas and Haim Goldfus, "The Kilnworks of the Tenth Legion Fretensis," in *The Roman and Byzantine Near East: Some Recent Archaeological Research*, *JRA* Supplement 14 (Ann Arbor, MI: *JRA*, 1995), pp. 95–107.

[18] Mordecai Gichon and Benjamin H. Isaac, "A Flavian Inscription from Jerusalem," *Israel Exploration Journal* 24 (1974), pp. 117–123.

[19] See for example, Mordecai Aviam and Danny Syon, "Jewish Ossilegium in Galilee," in *What Athens Has to Do with Jerusalem: Essays on Classical, Jewish and Christian Art and Archaeology in Honor of Gideon Forster*, ed. Leonard V. Rutgers (Leuven: Peeters, 2002), pp. 151–187, at 171–172, 195; and see *Supplementum Epigraphicum Graecum* 44 (1994), p. 1349; see also 46, 2014, 2015 in L.Y. Rahmani, *A Catalogue of Jewish Ossuaries in the State of Israel* (Jerusalem: Israel Antiquities Authority, 1994), pp. 319, 322.

[20] For example, the tomb in which the Abba inscription was found in Givat ha-Mivtar, just north of Jerusalem, had coins dating from both the first and second revolts (this also suggests the dating of the inscription itself is therefore open to review). Likewise, the ossuary of "Mother Mariam" had coins dating at least to 80–81 C.E. For the Abba inscription, see *Corpus Inscriptionum Iudaeae/Palaestinae*, vol. 1: *Jerusalem*, eds. Hannah M. Cotton et al. (Berlin: de Gruyter, 2010), p. 100, no. 55; for the "Mother Mariam" ossuary, see ibid., p. 509, no. 488.

[21] Sifre on Deuteronomy 43; *Corpus I* (see endnote 20), p. 17.

[22] Aviam and Syon, "Jewish Ossilegium" (see endnote 19), p. 184.

[23] See also *War* 3.30–34.

[24] Danny Syon, "Galilean Mints in the Early Roman Period: Politics, Economy and Ethnicity," in *Judaea and Rome in Coins, 65 BCE–135 CE*, eds. David M. Jaconson and Nikos Kokkinos (London: SPINK, 2012).

[25] See Mishnah *Rosh Hashanah* 4:1–3; BT *Sanhedrin* 32b.

[26] Mishnah *Ketubbot* 1:5.

27 Philip Alexander, "What Happened to the Jewish Priesthood After 70?" in *A Wandering Galilean: Essays in Honour of Sean Freyne*, ed. Zuleika Rodgers with M. Daly-Denton and A. Fitzpatrick-McKinley, JSJ Supplements 132 (Leiden: Brill, 2009), pp. 3-34, at 29-30.

28 Martin Goodman, *State and Society in Roman Galilee, AD 132-212* (Totowa, NJ: Rowman & Allanheld, 1983), pp. 51, 104, 107, 177, 181.

29 BT *Menahot* 65a; BT *Baba Bathra* 115b; Mishnah *Yadayim* 4:5; Tosefta *Parah* 3:8.

30 See Shaye Cohen, "The Significance of Yavneh: Pharisees, Rabbis and the End of Jewish Sectarianism," *Hebrew Union College Annual* 55 (1984), pp. 27-53.

31 See the critique in Daniel Boyarin, *Border Lines: The Partition of Judaeo-Christianity* (Philadelphia: University of Pennsylvania Press, 2004), pp. 151-201.

32 Benjamin Isaac and Isaac Roll, "Judea in the Early Years of Hadrian's Reign," in *Near East Under Roman Rule* (see endnote 16), pp. 182-197, originally published in *Latomus* 28 (1979), pp. 54-66.

33 There may well also have been a ban on circumcision; for discussion, see Eshel, "Bar Kochba Revolt" (see endnote 1), pp. 107-108.

34 See *The History of the Jewish People in the Age of Jesus Christ*, revised edition, ed. Emil Schürer with Geza Vermes, Fergus Millar and Matthew Black (Edinburgh: T & T Clark, 1973), vol. 1, p. 544.

35 See Leo Mildenberg, *The Coinage of the Bar Kokhba War*, ed. Patricia Erhart Mottahedeh, Typos: Monographien zur antiken Numismatik 6 (Aarau: Sauerländer, 1984); and see Eshel, "Bar Kochba Revolt" (see endnote 1), pp. 113-116.

36 *Roman History* 69.14.2.

37 Amos Kloner and Boaz Zissu, "Hiding Complexes in Judaea: An Archaeological and Geographical Update on the Area of the Bar Kochba Revolt," in *The Bar Kokhba Revolt Reconsidered*, ed. Peter Schäfer (Tübingen: Mohr Siebeck, 2003), pp. 181-216, at pp. 181-182.

38 Tertullian, *Against the Jews* 13; Justin Martyr, *Dialogue with Trypho* 16; *1 Apology* 77; Eusebius, *Ecclesiastical History* 4.6; Midrash Lamentations Rabbah 2:2. For discussion, see Benjamin Isaac, "Cassius Dio on the Revolt of Bar Kokhba," in *Near East Under Roman Rule* (see endnote 16), pp. 211-219. For the period following, see Joan Taylor, *Christians and the Holy Places: The Myth of Jewish-Christian Origins* (Oxford: Oxford University Press, 1993), pp. 48-85; and Michael Avi Yonah, *The Jews of Palestine: A Political History from the Bar Kochba Revolt to the Arab Conquest* (Oxford: Blackwell, 1976), pp. 50-51, see map (p. 17) for the exclusion zone.

39 Taylor, *Christians and the Holy Places* (see endnote 38), pp. 19-20. For a good overview and definition, see James Carleton Paget, *Jews, Christians and Jewish-Christians in Antiquity*, WUNT 251 (Tübingen: Mohr Siebeck, 2010), pp. 289-324, which follows a praxis-based approach.

40 As argued initially by John Knox, *Marcion and the New Testament: An Essay in the Early History of the Canon*, rev. ed. (Chicago: University of Chicago Press, 1980); John T. Townsend, "The Date of Luke-Acts," in *Luke-Acts: New Perspectives from the Society of Biblical Literature Seminar*, ed. Charles H. Talbert (New York: Crossroad, 1984), pp. 47-62; Richard I. Pervo, *Dating Acts: Between the Evangelists and the Apologists* (Santa Rosa: Polebridge, 2006); Joseph Tyson, *Marcion and Luke-Acts: A Defining Struggle* (Columbia: University of South Carolina Press, 2006); Shelly Matthews, *Perfect Martyr: The Stoning of Stephen and the Construction of Christian Identity* (Oxford: Oxford University Press, 2010), pp. 5-6.

41 See Robert L. Brawley, *Luke-Acts and the Jews: Conflict, Apology, and Conciliation*, SBL Monograph Series 33 (Atlanta: Scholars Press, 1987); Jacob Jervill, "The Divided People of God," in *Luke and the People of God* (Minneapolis: Augsburg, 1972), pp. 41-74.

42 Acts 24:5. See Joan E. Taylor, "The *Nazoraeans* as a 'Sect' in 'Sectarian' Judaism? A Reconsideration of the Current View via the Narrative of Acts and the Meaning of *Hairesis*," in *Sects and Sectarianism in Jewish History*, ed. Sacha Stern (Leiden: Brill, 2011), pp. 87-118.

43 Alan Segal, "Acts 15 as Jewish and Christian History," *Forum* 4 (2001), pp. 63-87, especially 75.

[44] John A. Zeisler, "Luke and the Pharisees," *NTS* 25 (1979), pp. 146–157; Amy-Jill Levine, "Luke's Pharisees," in *In Quest of the Historical Pharisees*, eds. Jacob Neusner and Bruce Chilton (Waco, TX: Baylor University Press, 2007), pp. 113–130.

[45] For a critique of the hypothesis that Jewish-Christians are evidenced by archaeology at later Christian holy places as early as the second century, see Taylor, *Christians and the Holy Places* (see endnote 38).

[46] Eusebius, *Ecclesiastical History* 4.5.1–4; 6.4. The names of the leaders (overseers/bishops) are given as James, Simeon, Justus, Zacchaeus, Tobias, Benjamin, John, Matthias, Philip, Seneca, Justus, Levi, Ephres, Joseph and Judas. Since James was killed in 62 C.E., the many names here may well indicate short lives, as Eusebius suggests.

[47] *Ecclesiastical History* 3.5.3, cf. Epiphanius, *Panarion* 29.7.7–8; *On Weights and Measures* 15; Taylor, *Christians and the Holy Places* (see endnote 38), pp. 43–44.

[48] *On Weights and Measures* 14; cf. Bordeaux Pilgrim, *Itinerary* 592; see also Taylor, *Christians and the Holy Places* (see endnote 38), pp. 208–213.

[49] See *Ecclesiastical History* 4.8.1, 4.22; William Telfer, "Was Hegesippus a Jew?" *HTR* 53 (1960), pp. 143–153; and J. Stanley Jones, "Hegesippus as a Source for the History of Jewish-Christianity," in *Le Judéo-christianisme dans tous ses états: actes du colloque de Jérusalem, 6–10 juillet 1998*, ed. Simon-Claude Mimouni (Paris: Cerf, 2001), pp. 201–212.

[50] For a detailed examination of this passage and its correct translation, see Joan Taylor, *The Essenes, the Scrolls, and the Dead Sea* (Oxford: Oxford University Press, 2012), pp. 173–175.

[51] Curiously, in using the expression "the tribe of the Christ" there is a reflection of the language of the Testimonium Flavianum, as cited by Eusebius (*Ecclesiastical History* 1.11): "the tribe of the Christians" (Josephus, *Antiquities* 18.64) is found elsewhere in Eusebius in summarizing Pliny's letter to Trajan and its response (*Ecclesiastical History* 3.33.2–3) when it does not appear in the source material.

[52] *1 Apology* 31.5–6; Eusebius, *Ecclesiastical History* 4.8.4.

[53] *Eusebii Chronicorum Libri duo*, 2 vols., ed. Alfred Schoene (Berlin: Weidmann, 1866–1875), pp. 166–167.

[54] See discussion in Eshel, "Bar Kochba Revolt" (see endnote 1), pp. 114–115.

[55] *Ecclesiastical History* 4.5.1–4; *Demonstration of the Gospel* 3.5.

[56] *Ecclesiastical History* 7.19.

[57] Joan E. Taylor, "Golgotha: A Reconsideration of the Evidence for the Sites of Jesus' Crucifixion and Burial," *NTS* 44 (1998), pp, 180–203.

[58] As suggested in Taylor, *Christians and the Holy Places* (see endnote 38), p. 43.

[59] See Justin Martyr, *Dialogue with Trypho* 47, cf. 46.1–2.

[60] See Eusebius, *Life of Constantine* 3.26–27; Jerome, *Epistles* 58.3; Socrates, *Ecclesiastical History* 1.17; Sozomon, *Ecclesiastical History* 2.1; Rufinus, *Ecclesiastical History* 9.60.

[61] Taylor, *Christians and the Holy Places* (see endnote 38), pp. 113–142, and Shimon Gibson and Joan E. Taylor, *Beneath the Church of the Holy Sepulchre, Jerusalem: The Archaeology and Early History of Traditional Golgotha* (London: Palestine Exploration Fund, 1994), pp. 65–71.

[62] See Hershel Shanks, *Jerusalem's Temple Mount* (New York: Continuum, 2007), p. 43; Joseph Patrich, "The Early Church of the Holy Sepulchre in the Light of Excavations and Restoration," in *Ancient Churches Revealed*, ed. Yoram Tsafrir (Jerusalem: Israel Exploration Society, 1993), pp. 103–104; Gibson and Taylor, *Beneath the Church of the Holy Sepulchre* (see endnote 61), pp. 65–71.

[63] Eusebius, *Ecclesiastical History* 4.9; Justin Martyr, *1 Apology* 68.6–10.

[64] For a thorough examination, see Paul Keresztes, "Hadrian's Rescript to Minucius Fundanus," *Phoenix* 21 (1967), pp. 120–129.

[65] BT *Berakhot* 28b–29a, cf. JT *Berakhot* 4:3, Jerome, *Epistles* 112.13. This is the 12th of the Eighteen Benedictions, said within synagogue prayer.

[66] *Commentary on Isaiah* 1.5.18–19; 13 on 49.7; 14 on 52.4–6; *Commentary on Amos* 1.1.11–12. Epiphanius assumed it referred only to Nazoraeans, i.e., Jewish-Christians, in *Panarion* 29.9.

[67] See BT *Taanit* 27b; BT *Avodah Zarah* 6a and 7b; amended BT *Gittin* 57a.

[68] BT *Avodah Zarah* 17a; BT *Sanhedrin* 43a; BT *Berakhot* 17b; BT *Sotah* 47a; BT *Sanhedrin* 103a, 107a et al. See the discussion in Philip Mayo, "The Role of the *Birkat HaMinim* in Early Jewish-Christian Relations: A Reexamination of the Evidence," *Bulletin for Biblical Research* 12 (2006), pp. 325–344, at 332–338.

[69] For a survey of scholarship from the 1980s to 1994, see Pieter van der Horst, "The *Birkat ha-Minim* in Recent Research," *The Expository Times* 105 (September 1994), pp. 363–368. For a recent argument for a late addition, see Ruth Langer, *Cursing the Christians?: A History of the Birkat ha-Minim* (Oxford: Oxford University Press, 2012).

[70] This Cairo Genizah text in Hebrew was published by Solomon Schechter, "Genizah Specimens," *Jewish Quarterly Review* 10 (1898), pp. 654–659, at 657.

[71] Yaakov Y. Teppler, *Birkat HaMinim: Jews and Christians in Conflict in the Ancient World*, trans. Susan Weingarten (Tübingen: Mohr Siebeck, 2007).

[72] Mayo, "The Role of the *Birkat HaMinim*" (see endnote 68), pp. 338–341.

[73] Langer, *Cursing the Christians?* (see endnote 69), pp. 29–30, from Reuven Kimelman, "Birkat ha-Minim and the Lack of Evidence for an Anti-Christian Jewish Prayer in Late Antiquity," in *Jewish and Christian Self-Definition: Aspects of Judaism in the Graeco-Roman Period*, eds. E.P. Sanders with A.I. Baumgarten and Alan Mendelsohn (Philadelphia: Fortress Press, 1980–1981), vol. 2, pp. 226–244, at 235–236.

[74] Origen knew of curses against Christ, as Justin indicates (*Homilies on Psalms* 37.2.8; *Homilies on Jeremiah* 10.8.1; 19.12.3), but not a cursing of Christians.

[75] The attribution to Gamaliel II derives from much later material.

[76] Origen, *Against Celsus* 4.36.

[77] For evidence of this, see Taylor, *Christians and the Holy Places* (see endnote 38), pp. 48–56, now with archaeological and further analysis such as that of Mordecai Aviam, "Distribution Maps of Archaeological Data from the Galilee," in *Religion, Ethnicity and Identity in Ancient Galilee: A Region in Transition*, eds. Jürgen Zangenberg, Harold W. Attridge and Dale B. Martin (Leiden: Brill, 2007), pp. 115–132, which shows that central Galilee was mainly inhabited by Jews between the second and fourth centuries, but this study also tends to underscore the small extent of this area, which is ultimately only about 40 square kilometers.

[78] I am not sure that this translates into ethnic hybridity as argued by Michael Peppard, "Personal Names and Ethnic Hybridity in Late Ancient Galilee: The Data from Beth Shearim," in *Religion, Ethnicity and Identity* (see endnote 77), pp. 99–114.

[79] For a review of the literature on this large topic, see Anders Runesson, Donald D. Binder and Birger Olsson, *The Ancient Synagogue from Its Origins to 200 CE: A Source Book* (Leiden: Brill, 2008); and see also Jodi Magness, "Heaven on Earth: Helios and the Zodiac Cycle in Ancient Palestinian Synagogues," *Dumbarton Oaks Papers* 59 (2005), pp. 1–52, and "When Were the Galilean-Type Synagogues Built?" *Cathedra* 101 (2001), pp. 39–70 (in Hebrew; English summary, pp. 204–205).

[80] Uzi Leibner, "Excavations at Khirbet Wadi Hamam (Lower Galilee): The Synagogue and the Settlement," *JRA* 23 (2010), pp. 220–238.

[81] Epiphanius, *Panarion* 29.1.1–9.4; Jerome, *Commentary on Isaiah* 8.14.19–22; 9.1–4; 29.17–21; 31.6–9.

[82] Epiphanius, *Panarion* 29.7.7; cf. 30.2.8–9, 18.1. See map in Taylor, *Christians and the Holy Places* (see endnote 38), p. 37 with discussion pp. 36–41, and the summary provided by Edwin K. Broadhead, *Jewish Ways of Following Jesus* (Tübingen: Mohr Siebeck, 2010), pp. 346–349.

[83] Eusebius, *Onomasticon* 172.1–3, see *Palestine in the Fourth Century: The Onomasticon by Eusebius of Caesarea*, introduced and edited by Joan E. Taylor, translated by Greville

Freeman-Grenville and indexed by Rupert Chapman III (Jerusalem: Carta, 2003), p. 95.

[84] Gottlieb Schumacher, *The Jaulan* (London: Richard Bentley, 1888), pp. 116, 183, figs. 23, 27, 74–76.

[85] W.F. Albright, "Bronze Age Mounds of Northern Palestine and the Hauran: The Spring Trip of the School in Jerusalem," *BASOR* 19 (1925), pp. 5–19, at 14.

[86] Claudine Dauphin, "Farj en Gaulanitide: refuge judéo-chrétien," *Prôche-Orient Chrétien* 34 (1984), pp. 233–245; "Jewish and Christian Communities: A Study of Evidence from Archaeological Surveys," *Palestine Exploration Quarterly* 114 (1982), pp. 129–142; and Claudine Dauphin and Shimon Gibson, "Ancient Settlements in their Landscapes: The Results of Ten Years of Survey on the Golan Heights (1978–1988)," *Bulletin of the Anglo-Israel Archaeological Society* 12 (1992–1993), pp. 7–31.

[87] See Gibson and Taylor, *Beneath the Church of the Holy Sepulchre* (see endnote 61), pp. 80–83.

[88] Avraham Negev, "The Chronology of the Seven-Branched Candelabrum," *Eretz-Israel* 8 (1963), pp. 193–210 (in Hebrew); Daniel Sperber, "The History of the Menorah," *JJS* 16 (1965), pp. 135–159.

[89] Taylor, *Christians and the Holy Places* (see endnote 38); and summary in Broadhead, *Jewish Ways* (see endnote 82), pp. 301–351.

[90] *Panarion* 30.11–12. Taylor, *Christians and the Holy Places* (see endnote 38), pp. 226–227, 288–290.

[91] See http://peregrinations.kenyon.edu/vol2_3/notices.html

[92] Taylor, *Christians and the Holy Places* (see endnote 38).

[93] For further discussion, see ibid., pp. 56–64.

[94] Ibid., p. 57.

[95] The prayer hall was dated by excavator Yotam Tepper to c. 230 C.E., abandoned c. 305 C.E., dating that is also plausible, given the attested evidence of Christians in Palestine at this time (see Yotam Tepper and Leah Di Segni, *A Christian Prayer Hall of the Third Century CE at Kefar 'Othnay (Legio): Excavations at the*

Megiddo Prison 2005 (Jerusalem: Israel Antiquities Authority, 2006); and see the summary and commentary by Edward Adams, "The Ancient Church at Megiddo: The Discovery and an Assessment of Its Significance," *The Expository Times* 120 (2008), pp. 62–69.

[96] The sanctuary on Gerizim and the city of Shechem had apparently been destroyed by John Hyrcanus in 128 B.C.E., so Josephus, *Antiquities* 13.255–256; this sanctuary was replaced by a temple to Zeus by Hadrian, see Menachem Mor, "The Samaritans and the Bar-Kokhbah Revolt," in *The Samaritans*, ed. Alan Crown (Tübingen: Mohr Siebeck, 1989), pp. 19–31.

VI. Christianity in Antioch: Partings in Roman Syria

[1] For reasons explained below, we here focus on northern Syria (i.e., roughly corresponding to modern Lebanon, Syria and southeast Turkey).

[2] For the former, see Galatians 1:17; 2 Corinthians 11:32–33; Acts 9:2, 22:5, 26:12; for the latter, see Galatians 2:11–14; Acts 15.

[3] For a summary of opinions, see Magnus Zetterholm, *The Formation of Christianity in Antioch: A Social-Scientific Approach to the Separation Between Judaism and Christianity* (New York: Routledge, 2003), pp. 129ff.

[4] Ignatius, *Magnesians* 10.1–3; *Philadelphians* 3.3.3; 6.1.3; *Trallians* 10.4.4. On the meaning of these and other *-ismos* nouns in Greek, see Steve Mason, "Jews, Judeans, Judaizing, Judaism: Problems of Categorization in Ancient History," *JSJ* 38 (2007), pp. 457–512, esp. pp. 470–471. "Whereas the author of 2 Maccabees had championed *Ioudaismos* as response to the threat of *Hellênismos*," Mason there suggests, "Ignatius coins *Christianismos* as remedy for a threatening *Ioudaismos*."

[5] For late antiquity, see Daniel Boyarin, "Semantic Differences, or, 'Judaism'/'Christianity,'" in *The Ways That Never Parted: Jews and Christians in Late Antiquity and the Early Middle Ages*, eds. Adam H. Becker and Annette Yoshiko Reed, TSAJ 95 (Tübingen: Mohr Siebeck, 2003), pp.

65–86. On the relationship between late antique and modern developments, see Adam H. Becker, "Martyrdom, Religious Difference, and 'Fear' as a Category of Piety in the Sasanian Empire," *Journal of Late Antiquity* 2.2 (2009), pp. 300–306 at 302–303 and references there.

6 On the Syrian interest in Peter and works written in his name, see Eusebius, *Ecclesiastical History* 6.12.3–6; Markus Bockmuehl, "Syrian Memories of Peter: Ignatius, Justin and Serapion," in *The Image of Judaeo-Christians in Ancient Jewish and Christian Literature*, eds. Peter J. Tomson and Doris Lambers-Petry, WUNT 158 (Tübingen: Mohr Siebeck, 2003), pp. 124–142.

7 The most useful discussion of problems of defining this term remains J. Carleton Paget, "Jewish Christianity," in *The Cambridge History of Judaism*, vol. 3: *The Early Roman Period*, eds. William Horbury, W.D. Davies and John Sturdy (Cambridge: Cambridge University Press, 1999), pp. 733–742.

8 On the slow process by which the Christian anti-Jewish rhetoric came to shape social reality in the Roman Empire, see Paula Fredriksen, "What 'Parting of the Ways'? Jews, Gentiles, and the Ancient Mediterranean City," in *Ways That Never Parted* (see endnote 5), pp. 35–64; Fredriksen, "Roman Christianity and the Post-Roman West: The Social Correlates of the *Contra Iudaeos* Tradition," in *Jews, Christians, and the Roman Empire: The Poetics of Power in Late Antiquity*, eds. Natalie B. Dohrmann and Annette Yoshiko Reed (Philadelphia: University of Pennsylvania Press, in press).

9 On the challenges of defining "Syria" as well as the shifting scope of provinces bearing that name and variations thereof, see Kevin Butcher, *Roman Syria and the Near East* (Los Angeles: Getty Publications with the British Museum Press, 2003), pp. 10–15, 79–121. On regional features and long-term settlement patterns, see also Getzel M. Cohen, *Hellenistic Settlements in Syria, the Red Sea Basin, and North Africa* (Berkeley: University of California Press, 2006), pp. 21–26. Notably, ancient sources use the term "Syria" in different ways as well, ranging from a broad regional sense to a specific administrative sense (e.g., Strabo 16.2.1–2; Luke 2:2).

10 Han J.W. Drijvers, "Syrian Christianity and Judaism," in *The Jews Among Pagans and Christians in the Roman Empire*, eds. Judith Lieu, John North and Tessa Rajak (London: Routledge, 1992), pp. 124–146 at 125.

11 For a map of "the cities of northern Syria," see Butcher, *Roman Syria* (see endote 9), p. 107, fig. 31. We here omit Palmyra and Dura Europos from our survey due to our focus on literary evidence, which is sadly lacking from these desert trade-cities.

12 For the history of the city, see J.B. Segal, *Edessa: The Blessed City* (Piscataway, NJ: Gorgias, 2005).

13 As John Barclay notes, for instance, Josephus can state that "the Jewish *genos* ... is especially numerous in Syria because of its *proximity*" (*War* 7.43), even though the Jewish homeland was for much of its history technically *part of* "Syria," "Coele-Syria," etc., in a political or administrative sense; see *Jews in the Mediterranean Diaspora: From Alexander to Trajan (323 B.C.E.–117 C.E.)* (Edinburgh: T & T Clark, 1996), pp. 242–243. The shifting circles of imperial governance, in other words, did not override longstanding biblical and Jewish notions of the land of Israel.

14 Drijvers, "Syrian Christianity and Judaism" (see endnote 10), pp. 125–127.

15 On Jews in Antioch in the Hellenistic period, see Barclay, *Jews in the Mediterranean Diaspora* (see endnote 13), pp. 244–249.

16 Ibid., p. 242.

17 Unless otherwise noted, translations from Josephus here and below have been revised from those of Henry St. John Thackeray et al., in the Loeb Classical Library (Cambridge, MA: Harvard University Press, 1926–1965), vols. 242, 281, 326, 365, 410, 433, 456, 489 and 490.

18 Jacob Neusner, "The Conversion of Adiabene to Judaism," *JBL* 83.1 (1964), pp. 60–66.

19 Lee I. Levine, *The Ancient Synagogue* (New Haven, CT: Yale University Press, 2000), pp. 124–126, at p. 124. For a summary of the evidence for different Syrian cities, see Leonard Rutgers, *Hidden Heritage of Diaspora Judaism* (Leuven: Peeters, 1998), p. 130.

20 As evidence for a connection, Tessa Rajak points to epigraphical evidence that "a gerousiarch of the Antiochene Jewish community named Aidesios [was able] to obtain a desirable burial in the Galilee, close to rabbinic tombs"; see Rajak, "The Maccabaean Martyrs in Jewish Memory: Jerusalem and Antioch," in *Envisioning Judaism: Essays in Honor of Peter Schäfer on the Occasion of His Seventieth Birthday*, eds. Ra'anan Boustan et al. (Tübingen: Mohr Siebeck, in press), pp. 63–80 at p. 71. See further Rajak, "The Rabbinic Dead and the Diaspora Dead at Beth She'arim," repr. in Rajak, *The Jewish Dialogue with Greece and Rome: Studies in Cultural and Social Interaction*, Arbeiten zur Geschichte des antiken Judentums und des Urchhristentums 48 (Leiden: Brill, 2001), pp. 479–502, at 491; M. Schwabe and B. Lifschitz, eds., *Beth She'arim*, vol. 2: *The Greek Inscriptions* (Jerusalem: Massada, 1974), no. 141.

21 So Rajak, "Maccabaean Martyrs" (see endnote 20), p. 70; see further Arthur Droge, *Homer or Moses?* (Tübingen: Mohr Siebeck, 1989), pp. 70–72.

22 So Isaiah M. Gafni, "Syria, Biblical and Second Temple Period," in *EJ*, vol. 19, p. 388, pointing the expansion of some *halakhot* about the land of Israel to include Syria in the Mishnah (e.g., Mishnah *Hallah* 4:11) and discussions about the halakhic status of Syria in relation to the land of Israel in the Tosefta (e.g., Tosefta *Terumoth* 2:9–13; Tosefta *Abodah Zara* 2:8; cf. Tosefta *Peah* 4:6).

23 It was also the stopover city between Palestine and Asia Minor, as well as an important commercial and administrative center in the Roman Empire; Wayne A. Meeks and Robert L. Wilken, *Jews and Christians in Antioch in the First Four Centuries of the Common Era*, SBL Sources for Biblical Study Series 13 (Missoula, MT: Scholars Press, 1978), p. 1.

24 Barclay, *Jews in the Mediterranean Diaspora* (see endnote 13), pp. 250–255, 322. On the possibility that some Jewish captives from the revolt were taken to Antioch, see John Chrysostom, *Against the Judaizers* 6.2–33.

25 That this hostility also stretched to Syrian non-Jews sympathetic to Jews and Judaism is suggested by Josephus, *War* 2.461–463.

26 Rajak, "Maccabean Martyrs" (see endnote 20).

27 That it is critical *not* to assume that all references to Torah observance imply Jewish ethnicity, particularly given our ample evidence for ancient interest in Jewish practices among non-Jews, is nicely explained in Charlotte Fonrobert, "Jewish Christians, Judaizers, and Christian Anti-Judaism," in *Late Ancient Christianity*, ed. Virginia Burrus, People's History of Christianity 2 (Minneapolis: Fortress Press, 2005), pp. 234–254.

28 To be sure, Paul's own references to Damascus are terse (Galatians 1:17; 2 Corinthians 11:32–33). Luke-Acts reports that Saul was on his way from Jerusalem to "synagogues at Damascus," when he received his vision of the risen Christ and commission to become "apostle to the Gentiles" (Acts 9:2, 22:5, 26:12). The blindness caused by the vision is said to have been healed by a Jewish disciple from Damascus, Ananius (Acts 9:10–18), "a devout man according to the law, well spoken of by all the Jews who lived there" (22:12).

29 According to Luke-Acts, this harmony was broken after Paul's baptism, when he is said to have proclaimed Jesus as Messiah in the city's synagogues in a manner that raised the ire of other Damascene Jews (Acts 9:20) causing him to flee the city (9:23–26). The incident is intriguing, especially in light of Josephus's reference to the plentitude of Damascene women who were proselytes to Judaism (*War* 2.559–561). Yet the historicity of Luke-Acts' account remains uncertain, not least due to 2 Corinthians 11:32–33, where Paul himself alludes to his flight from the city due to persecution from the Roman governor. Unfortunately, there is no further mention of the city in the New Testament.

30 Meeks and Wilken, *Jews and Christians in Antioch* (see endnote 23), pp. 14–16.

31 Although the precise origins of the name remains debated, Luke-Acts' account may encode a memory of its early use—at least in Syrian locales—perhaps even to denote a sect or group *within* Judaism; see Anders Runesson, "Inventing Christian Identity: Paul, Ignatius, and Theodosius I," in *Exploring Early Christian Identity*, ed. Bengt Holmberg, WUNT 226 (Tübingen: Mohr Siebeck, 2008), pp. 59–92.

32 See further, e.g., Robert R. Hann, "Judaism and Jewish Christianity in Antioch: Charisma and Conflict in the First Century," *Journal of Religious History* 14 (1987), pp. 341–60; Martin Hengel, *Between Jesus and Paul: Studies in the Earliest History of Christianity* (Eugene, OR: Wipf & Stock, 2003), pp. 11–20.

33 According to Acts 14:19, for instance, Jews from Antioch were among those who tried to stone Paul—presumably due to their familiarity with his teachings from their home-city.

34 See above for the evidence from Josephus. Furthermore, as in the case of the success of Paul and other apostles in spreading their message to gentiles who frequented synagogues elsewhere (e.g., Acts 13, 17:17), it seems likely that "pagans" with some knowledge of Jewish Scriptures, and respect for Jewish monotheism and piety, might have been especially receptive to the Christian message.

35 I.e., having only met—Paul claims—with Peter and James (Galatians 1:18–19), and not returning to Jerusalem for 14 years (Galatians 2:1).

36 See further Mason, "Jews, Judeans, Judaizing, Judaism" (see endnote 4), esp. p. 469; Shaye J.D. Cohen, *The Beginnings of Jewishness: Boundaries, Varieties, Uncertainties* (Berkeley: University of California Press, 2001).

37 For the range of ancient Jewish perspectives on the question of whether and how a non-Jew could be impure, see Christine Hayes, *Gentile Impurities and Jewish Identities: Intermarriage and Conversion from the Bible to the Talmud* (Oxford: Oxford University Press, 2002).

38 See now Charlotte Hempel, "Who Is Making Dinner at Qumran?" *JTS* 63.1 (2012), pp. 49–65. For speculations that the problem of eating in Galatians and Acts was related to the Eucharist, see Heinrich Schlier, *Der Brief an die Galater*, 12th ed., Kritisch-exegetischer Kommentar 9 (Göttingen: Vandenhoeck & Ruprecht, 1962), pp. 83–84; Justin Taylor, "The Jerusalem Decrees (Acts 15:20, 29 and 21:25) and the Incident at Antioch (Galatians 2:11–14)," *NTS* 47 (2001), p. 379.

39 Translation here follows Shaye J.D. Cohen, "Respect for Judaism" [1987], repr. in Cohen, *The Significance at Yavneh and Other Essays in Jewish*

Hellenism, TSAJ 136 (Tübingen: Mohr Siebeck, 2011), pp. 194–195. As Cohen there notes, *The Jewish War* does not distinguish between "adherence" and "conversion" to Judaism.

40 The importance of common meals to maintaining Jewish solidarity and community in the Diaspora in the first century is suggested by the letters and decrees concerning Jewish rights and privileges quoted by Josephus in *Antiquities* 14.185–264, where—as Seth Schwartz notes—"the most commonly mentioned ritual activities are neither prayer nor sacrifice but common meals and fund-raising"; *Imperialism and Jewish Society, 200 B.C.E. to 640 C.E.* (Princeton, NJ: Princeton University Press, 2002), pp. 221–222.

41 As Richard Bauckham notes, Luke-Acts reduces the possibilities to two options: "that of Peter, with which Barnabas and Paul agree, and that of the group who require the circumcision of Gentile converts. There is no indication of a middle way that might envisage two separate Christian communities"; "James, Peter, and the Gentiles," in *The Missions of James, Peter, and Paul: Tension in Early Christianity*, eds. Bruce Chilton and Craig Evans (Leiden: Brill, 2005), pp. 91–142, at 117.

42 For the pentateuchal conception of the "moral impurity" resultant from sins of idolatry, sexual impropriety and bloodshed as it differs from the dynamics of the "ritual impurity" temporarily caused by contact with corpses, menstruation, seminal emissions, etc.—as well as various Second Temple developments—see Jonathan Klawans, *Impurity and Sin in Ancient Judaism* (Oxford: Oxford University Press, 2000), pp. 26–60.

43 On Syria, see endnote 15 above. On purity and eating, see Hayes, *Gentile Impurities and Jewish Identities* (see endnote 37); Charlotte E. Fonrobert, *Menstrual Purity: Rabbinic and Christian Reconstructions of Biblical Gender* (Stanford, CA: Stanford University Press, 2000); Jordan Rosenblum, *Food and Identity in Early Rabbinic Judaism* (Cambridge: Cambridge University Press, 2010). We are not suggesting any influence or connection here, but rather pointing to a parallel development.

[44] So, e.g., David C. Sim, *The Gospel of Matthew and Christian Judaism: The History and Social Setting of the Matthean Community*, Studies of the New Testament and Its World (Edinburgh: T & T Clark, 1998), pp. 31–40, 53–62. Notably, since ancient times, Matthew has been deemed the gospel closest to Judaism (e.g., Papias *apud* Eusebius, *Ecclesiastical History* 3.39; Irenaeus, *Against Heresies* 3.1.1; Eusebius, *Ecclesiastical History* 3.24.5–6; 5.10.3; 6.25.4; John Chrysostom, *Homilies on Matthew* 1.7; Jerome, *On Illustrious Men* 3); modern scholars who make the same point typically point to its engagement with halakhic debates concerning divorce and marriage (Matthew 5:27–32, 19:3–9), ritual purity (15:1–9) and Sabbath observance (12:1–14) as well as its style of exegetical argumentation from the Hebrew Bible (see, e.g., 9:13, 12:3–7, 19:4–5,7–8). Contrast L. Gaston, "The Messiah of Israel as Teacher of Gentiles," *Interpretation* 29 (1975), pp. 24–40; Douglas Hare, "How Jewish Is the Gospel of Matthew?" *CBQ* 63 (2000), pp. 264–277.

[45] See, for example, Zetterholm, *Formation of Christianity in Antioch* (see endnote 3), p. 211; David C. Sim, "Matthew and Ignatius of Antioch," in *Matthew and His Christian Contemporaries*, eds. David C. Sim and Boris Repschinski, Library of New Testament Studies 333 (New York: T & T Clark, 2008), pp. 140–141; J.P. Meier, "Matthew and Ignatius: A Response to William R. Schoedel," in *Social History of the Matthean Community: Cross-Disciplinary Approaches*, ed. David L. Balch (Minneapolis: Fortress Press, 1991), pp. 178–186.

[46] Arguments for a Galilean provenance include J. Andrew Overman, *Matthew's Gospel and Formative Judaism: The Social World of the Matthean Community* (Minneapolis: Fortress Press, 1990), pp. 158–159; Anthony J. Saldarini, "The Gospel of Matthew and Jewish-Christian Conflict in Galilee," in *Studies on Galilee in Late Antiquity*, ed. Lee I. Levine (New York: Jewish Theological Seminary, 1992), pp. 23–28; Aaron M. Gale, *Redefining Ancient Borders: The Jewish Scribal Framework of Matthew's Gospel* (London: T & T Clark, 2004), pp. 41–63. For the possibility of a combination of the two—i.e., pre-70 Galilean/Palestinian and post-70 Antiochene/Syrian origins—see Wim Weren, "The History and Social Setting of the Matthean Community,"

in *Matthew and the Didache: Two Documents from the Same Jewish-Christian Milieu?* ed. Hubertus van de Sandt (Minneapolis: Fortress Press, 2005), pp. 51–62.

[47] Elsewhere in the New Testament, we find references to various Pharisees who were also followers of Jesus—most famously Paul (Acts 23:6), of course, but also Nicodemus (John 3:1–21) and those Jerusalemites who speak up to defend circumcision and Torah observance for gentile "adherents" or "converts" in Acts 15:5. On Christian Pharisaism, see further Anders Runesson, "Rethinking Early Jewish-Christian Relations: Matthean Community History as Pharisaic Intragroup Conflict," *JBL* 127.1 (2008), pp. 95–132, at 120–132.

[48] Weren, "History and Social Setting" (see endnote 46), p. 58.

[49] The contrast between John Chrysostom's *Homilies on Matthew* and the Pseudo-Clementine *Homilies* is perhaps most striking in this regard; see further Annette Y. Reed, "When Did Rabbis Become Pharisees?" in *Envisioning Judaism* (see endnote 20), pp. 859–896.

[50] Zetterholm, *Formation of Christianity in Antioch* (see endnote 3), p. 204. So, too, Meeks and Wilken, *Jews and Christians in Antioch* (see endnote 23), p. 20. For docetists and others condemned by Ignatius, see Jerry L. Sumney, "Those Who 'Ignorantly Deny Him': The Opponents of Ignatius of Antioch," *JECS* 1.4 (1993), pp. 347–349.

[51] Shaye J.D. Cohen, "Judaism Without Circumcision and 'Judaism' Without 'Circumcision' in Ignatius," *HTR* 95.4 (2002), p. 397.

[52] Translations of Ignatius are based on William R. Schoedel, *Ignatius of Antioch: A Commentary* (Philadelphia: Fortress Press, 1985), albeit revised with reference to the Greek, especially for key terms here under discussion.

[53] Paul Foster, "The Epistles of Ignatius of Antioch," in *The Writings of the Apostolic Fathers*, ed. Paul Foster (Edinburgh: T & T Clark, 2007), p. 91. See also Meeks and Wilken, *Jews and Christians in Antioch* (see endnote 23), p. 20; cf. C.K. Barrett, "Jews and Judaizers in the Epistles of Ignatius," in *Jews, Greeks, and Christians: Religious Cultures in Late Antiquity: Essays in*

Honor of William David Davies, eds. Robert Hamerton-Kelly and Robin Scroggs (Leiden: Brill, 1976), pp. 220–244; Jakob Speigl, "Ignatius in Philadelphia: Ereignisse und Anliegen in den Ignatiusbriefen," *VC* 41 (1987), pp. 360–376, at 370; Schoedel, *Ignatius of Antioch* (see endnote 52), p. 20; Charles Munier, "Où en est la question d'Ignace d'Antioche?" *Aufstieg und Niedergang der Romischen Welt* 2.27.1 (1993), pp. 404–407. In Syria, moreover, circumcision was hardly limited just to Jews—as the case of the Roman emperor Elagabalus makes clear.

⁵⁴ Cf. R.M. Grant, *The Apostolic Fathers: Ignatius of Antioch* (Camden, NJ: Thomas Nelson and Sons, 1966), vol. 4, p. 103; Zetterholm, *Formation of Christianity in Antioch* (see endnote 3), pp. 204–211.

⁵⁵ Notably, at the time, the concept and collection of the "New Testament" had not yet taken shape, and there was not yet a sense of *Christian* scripture. The scriptures of Christians, rather, were the Jewish scriptures, while distinctively Christian teachings were associated with oral preaching and proclamation by Ignatius, Papias and others. In the early second century, the term and concept of "gospel" maintained its original sense as spoken and preached proclamation, rather than a written text or record. See further Annette Yoshiko Reed, "*Euangellion*: Orality, Textuality, and the Christian Truth in Irenaeus' *Adversus Haereses*," *VC* 56 (2002), pp. 11–46.

⁵⁶ Mason, "Jews, Judeans, Judaizing, Judaism" (see endnote 4), pp. 471–475; Cohen, "Judaism Without Circumcision" (see endnote 51), p. 398.

⁵⁷ Judith M. Lieu, *Image and Reality: The Jews in the World of the Christians in the Second Century* (Edinburgh: T & T Clark, 1996), p. 29; italics mine.

⁵⁸ For a recent example of this tendency, see Thomas A. Robinson, *Ignatius of Antioch and the Parting of the Ways: Early Jewish–Christian Relations* (Peabody, MA: Hendrickson, 2010). Contrast Zetterholm's *Formation of Christianity in Antioch* (see endnote 3), which adopts the same stopping point but cautions against extrapolating from the social dynamics in one specific time and place to "Christianity" and "Judaism" writ large.

⁵⁹ The classic study remains Adolf von Harnack, *Marcion: The Gospel of the Alien God*, trans. John E. Steely and Lyle D. Bierma (Durham: Labyrinth, 1990). For a recent reassessment, see Sebastian Moll, *The Archheretic Marcion*, WUNT 250 (Tübingen: Mohr Siebeck, 2010). Also Robert M. Grant, *Heresy and Criticism* (Louisville: Westminster/John Knox Press, 1993), pp. 33–48; Judith Lieu, "The Battle for Paul in the Second Century," *Irish Theological Quarterly* 75.1 (2010), pp. 3–14.

⁶⁰ Frances Young, *Biblical Exegesis and the Formation of Christian Culture* (Cambridge: Cambridge University Press, 2007), esp. pp. 63–70, 290–291; Grant, *Heresy and Criticism* (see endnote 59), pp. 89–113.

⁶¹ Although Marcion never took up residency in Syria, Marcionism became so influential there that the *Chronicles of Edessa* record "in the year 449 [of the Seleucid era, i.e., 137/138 C.E.] Marcion left the Catholic Church"; Han J.W. Drijvers, "Marcionism in Syria: Principles, Problems, Polemics," *Second Century* 6 (1987–1988), p. 153.

⁶² Drijvers, "Marcionism in Syria" (see endnote 61), pp. 153–172; Drijvers, "Syrian Christianity and Judaism" (see endnote 10), pp. 131–133; Sidney Griffith, "Christianity in Edessa and the Syriac-Speaking World: Mani, Bar Daysan and Ephraem; The Struggle for Allegiance on the Aramean Frontier," *Journal of the Canadian Society for Syriac Studies* 2 (2002), pp. 5–20.

⁶³ On Theophilus and Bardaisan, see Eusebius, *Ecclesiastical History* 4.24, 30. In addition, Hippolytus notes that the Marcionite Prepon, an Assyrian, wrote against Bardaisan (*Refutation of All Heresies* 7.31). Ephrem's *Hymni contra Haereses* and *Prose Refutations* counter Marcion, Bardaisan and Mani.

⁶⁴ Drijvers, "Syrian Christianity and Judaism" (see endnote 10), pp. 140–141; Grant, *Heresy and Criticism* (see endnote 59), pp. 89–91.

⁶⁵ The degree to which this interest in biblical exegesis reflects direct contacts with Jews and/or the activities of Jewish converts remains debated; not all scholars share Drijver's skepticism in this regard. On Theophilus, see Robert M. Grant, "The Bible of Theophilus of Antioch," *JBL* 66.2 (1947), pp. 173–196; Grant, "Scripture, Rhetoric

and Theology in Theophilus," *VC* 13.1 (1959), pp. 33–45; cf. William R. Schoedel, "Theophilus of Antioch: Jewish Christian?" *Illinois Classical Studies* 18 (1993), pp. 279–297. With respect to the Peshitta, Sebastian Brock concludes that "[t]he translators all worked basically from the Hebrew text ... In some books the translators seem to have consulted or made use of other translations: thus at various places in the Pentateuch (Genesis, Deuteronomy), there are some remarkable links between the Peshitta and the Jewish Aramaic Targums and for some of the Prophets and Wisdom books the translators probably consulted the Septuagint on occasion ..."; *The Bible in the Syriac Tradition* (Piscataway, NJ: Gorgias, 2006), p. 23. See also Michael Weitzman, "From Judaism to Christianity: The Syriac Version of the Hebrew Bible," in *Jews Among Pagans and Christians* (see endnote 10), pp. 147–173.

⁶⁶ F. Stanley Jones, *Pseudoclementina Elchasaiticaque inter Judaeochristiana: Collected Studies*, Orientalia Lovaniensia Analecta 203 (Leuven: Peeters, 2012), p. 205.

⁶⁷ Ibid., p. 206.

⁶⁸ See further Denise Kimber Buell, *Why This New Race: Ethnic Reasoning in Early Christianity* (New York: Columbia University Press, 2005).

⁶⁹ See further Nicole Kelley, *Knowledge and Religious Authority in the Pseudo-Clementines*, WUNT-2 213 (Tübingen: Mohr Siebeck, 2006).

⁷⁰ See, for example, Laura Nasrallah, "Mapping the World: Justin, Tatian, Lucian, and the Second Sophistic," *HTR* 98.3 (2005), pp. 283–314, and further citations there. For the later trajectories of the Hellenized anti-Hellenism of early Syrian Christianity, see Sebastian Brock, "From Antagonism to Assimilation: Syrian Attitudes Towards Greek Learning," repr. in Brock, *Syriac Perspectives on Late Antiquity* (London: Variorum, 1984), V.19.

⁷¹ See further Tacitus, *Annals* 11.10; 12.11,13,14; Dio Cassius, *Roman History* 68.18,21; Segal, *Edessa* (see endnote 12), pp. 110–192; Fergus Millar, *The Roman Near East, 31 B.C.–A.D. 337* (Cambridge, MA: Harvard University Press, 1993), pp. 472–481, 553–562; Steven K. Ross, *Roman Edessa: Politics and Culture on the Eastern Fringes of the Roman Empire, 114–242 C.E.* (London: Routledge, 2001).

⁷² On the latter, see the problematic but suggestive account in *Scriptores Historia Augusta*, Heliogabalus 13.4–5.

⁷³ Drijvers stresses the "pagan" origins of Christianity in Edessa, in part to counter older approaches that romanticized this Mesopotamian city as preserving an archaic Aramaic Christianity; "Jews and Christians at Edessa," *JJS* 36 (1985), pp. 88–102. Contrast Robert Murray, *Symbols of Church and Kingdom: A Study in Early Syriac Christianity*, rev. ed. (London: T & T Clark, 2006), pp. 3–17; R.B. ter Haar Romeny, "Hypotheses on the Development of Judaism and Christianity in Syria in the Period after 70 C.E.," in *Matthew and the Didache* (see endnote 46), pp. 13–33. Most recently, F. Stanley Jones (*Pseudoclementina* [see endnote 66], pp. 434, 473) dates the *Book of Elchasai* to 116–117 C.E. and suggests that it represents "a founding document of early Syrian Christianity" and "chronologically the earliest identifiable witness to Christianity" in Mesopotamia—culturally proximate to Bardaisan of Edessa (154–222 C.E.), and closely linked in a chain of influence both with the Pseudo-Clementines (i.e., Basic Writing, c. 220 C.E.) and with Mani (c. 216–274 C.E.).

⁷⁴ Murray, *Symbols of Church and Kingdom* (see endnote 73), pp. 7–9.

⁷⁵ William Adler, "The Kingdom of Edessa and the Creation of a Christian Aristocracy," forthcoming in *Jews, Christians, and the Roman Empire* (see endnote 8).

⁷⁶ On Edessa and the development of Syriac, see John F. Healey, "The Edessan Milieu and the Birth of Syriac," *Hugoye* 10.2 (2007), pp. 115–127; and for an introduction to Syriac literature, see Sebastian P. Brock, *An Introduction to Syriac Studies*, rev. ed. (Piscataway, NJ: Gorgias, 2006). On the formative fourth century and the foundational works of Ephrem (306–373 C.E.) and Aphrahat (c. 270–c. 345 C.E.), see Murray, *Symbols of Church and Kingdom* (see endnote 73).

⁷⁷ On the importance of this work for the study of Jewish/Christian relations and "Jewish-Christianity" in Syria, see esp. Charlotte Fonrobert,

"The *Didascalia Apostolorum*: A Mishnah for the Disciples of Jesus," *JECS* 9 (2001), pp. 483–509, there building on Marcel Simon, *Verus Israel: A Study in the Relations Between Christians and Jews in the Roman Empire (AD 135–425)*, trans. H. McKeating (London: Littman Library of Jewish Civilization, 1986), esp. pp. 88–90, 94, 310–318, 324–325; Georg Strecker, "Appendix 1: On the Problem of Jewish Christianity," in Walter Bauer, *Orthodoxy and Heresy in Earliest Christianity*, trans. and ed. Robert A. Kraft and Gerhard Kroedel with a team from the Philadelphia Seminar on Christian Origins (Philadelphia: Fortress Press, 1971), pp. 244–257.

[78] As a possible parallel for the practices not paralleled in Torah law and rabbinic *halakhot*, Fonrobert ("*Didascalia Apostolorum*" [see endnote 77], pp. 491–502) points to Tosefta *Sotah* 15.11 (as paralleled and expanded in BT *Baba Batra* 60b), which counters Jews who refrained from meat and wine after the destruction of the Temple. On asceticism in Syrian Christianity, see Sebastian Brock, "Early Syrian Asceticism," *Numen* 20 (1973), pp. 1–19.

[79] Fonrobert ("*Didascalia Apostolorum*" [see endnote 77], pp. 499–501) posits that those critiqued for such practices include those of Jewish lineage but are not limited to them; cf. Strecker, "On the Problem" (see endnote 77), p. 354.

[80] See Joseph Mueller, "The Ancient Church Order Literature: Genre or Tradition?" *JECS* 15 (2007), pp. 337–380 on the *Didache*, *Apostolic Tradition* and *Didascalia Apostolorum* as "a self-consciously apostolic tradition that presents such rules as flowing from halakhic and aggadic interpretation of the OT" (p. 379).

[81] Annette Yoshiko Reed, "Parting Ways over Blood and Water? Beyond 'Judaism' and 'Christianity' in the Roman Near East," in *La croisée des chemins revisitée*, eds. Simon Claude Mimouni and Bernard Pouderon, Collection de la Revue des Études Juives (Paris: Cerf, 2012), pp. 227–259.

[82] Hillel Newman, "The Normativity of Rabbinic Judaism," in *Jewish Identities in Antiquity: Studies in Memory of Menachem Stern*, eds. Lee I. Levine and Daniel R. Schwartz, TSAJ 130 (Tübingen: Mohr Siebeck, 2009), p. 169.

[83] William Horbury, "The New Testament and Rabbinic Study: An Historical Sketch," in *The New Testament and Rabbinic Literature*, eds. Reimund Bieringer et al. (Leiden: Brill, 2010), pp. 3–6, quote at 6.

[84] Fonrobert, "*Didascalia Apostolorum*" (see endnote 77), pp. 501–508. She further suggests that the *Didascalia Apostolorum*'s critiques are mostly plausibly understood as having been "triggered by the author(s)' knowledge of the consolidation of the mishnaic traditions into a canonical text" (p. 496). For a different reading of the conflicts here described, see Charlotte Metheun, "Widows, Bishops, and the Struggle for Authority in the *Didascalia Apostolorum*," *Journal of Ecclesiastical History* 46 (1995), p. 204.

[85] I.e., the *Didascalia Apostolorum* provides indirect evidence for the Torah-observant Christians whom its authors address, but it also reveals the authors' own engagement with Jews and Judaism.

[86] For an introduction to the corpus, see Jones, *Pseudoclementina* (see endnote 66), pp. 7–49.

[87] Another Syrian Christian example of this phenomenon may be found in the *Protevangelium of James*; see Lily Vuong, "Purity, Piety, and the Purpose(s) of the Protevangelium of James," in *"Non-Canonical" Religious Texts in Early Judaism and Early Christianity*, eds. James H. Charlesworth and Lee M. McDonald, Jewish and Christian Texts 14 (New York: T & T Clark, 2012), pp. 205–221; Vuong, "'Let Us Bring Her Up to the Temple of the Lord': Exploring the Boundaries of Jewish and Christian Relations Though the Presentation of Mary in the *Protevangelium of James*," in *Infancy Gospels: Stories and Identities*, eds. Claire Clivaz et al. (Tübingen: Mohr Siebeck, 2011), pp. 418–432.

[88] This aim shapes multiple strata and sources of this literature; see F. Stanley Jones, "An Ancient Christian Rejoinder to Luke's Acts of the Apostles" [1999], repr. in Jones, *Pseudoclementina* (see endnote 66), pp. 207–229; Annette Yoshiko Reed, "'Jewish Christianity' as Counter-History? The Apostolic Past in Eusebius' *Ecclesiastical History* and the Pseudo-Clementine *Homilies*," in *Antiquity in Antiquity: Jewish and Christian Pasts in the Greco-Roman World*, eds.

Gregg Gardner and Kevin Osterloh, TSAJ 123 (Tübingen: Mohr Siebeck, 2008), pp. 173–216.

89 Pseudo-Clementine *Homilies* 7.4,8; 11.28–30; 13:4,9,19; *Recognitions* 2.71–72; 6.9–11; 7.29,34; 8.68. Peter models this ideal, particularly in the *Homilies*, by insisting that true Christians do not eat with those who are impure; see further Reed, "Parting Ways over Blood and Water?" (see endnote 81).

90 See further Annette Yoshiko Reed, "Jewish Christianity After the Parting of the Ways: Approaches to Historiography and Self-Definition in the Pseudo-Clementine Literature," in *Ways That Never Parted* (see endnote 5), pp. 188–231.

91 See also Pseudo-Clementine *Homilies* 3.19; the notion there that Moses and Jesus are manifestations of the same True Prophet is distinctive to the *Homilies*.

92 Most famously: Joyce Reynolds and Robert Tannebaum, *Jews and God-Fearers at Aphrodisias: Greek Inscriptions with Commentary* (Cambridge: Cambridge University Press, 1987), pp. 48–66.

93 This assertion is especially significant inasmuch as the authors of the Pseudo-Clementine *Homilies* view the written Scriptures as corrupted by interpolations. See *Homilies* 2.38–52, 3.4–6, 3.9–11, 3.17–21, 3.37–51, 16.9–14, 18.12–13, 18.18–22; Georg Strecker, *Das Judenchristentum in den Pseudoklementinen* (Berlin: Akademie, 1958), pp. 166–186; Karl Shuve, "The Doctrine of the False Pericopes and Other Late Antique Approaches to the Problem of Scripture's Unity," in *Nouvelles intrigues pseudo-clémentines*, eds. Frédéric Amsler et al. (Prahins: Zèbre, 2008), pp. 437–445.

94 Amram Tropper, "Tractate *Avot* and Early Christian Succession Lists," in *Ways That Never Parted* (see endnote 5), pp. 159–188.

95 See, for example, *Sifre Deuteronomy* 351; JT *Megillah* 4.1; JT *Pe'ah* 2.6; *Pesikta Rabbati* 14b; BT *Shabbat* 13a; Martin S. Jaffee, *Torah in the Mouth: Writing and Oral Tradition in Palestinian Judaism, 200 B.C.E.–400 C.E.* (New York: Oxford University Press, 2001).

96 Albert Baumgarten, "Literary Evidence for Jewish Christianity in the Galilee," in *The Galilee*

in *Late Antiquity*, ed. Lee I. Levine (New York: Jewish Theological Seminary of America, 1992), p. 43.

97 See my more detailed discussions in "'Jewish-Christianity' as Counter-History?" (see endnote 88) and "When Did Rabbis Become Pharisees?" (see endnote 49).

98 I.e., just as Moses' teachings are kept by the Pharisees who sit on his seat (*kathedra*; *Homilies* 11.29), so Jesus' teachings are faithfully kept by Peter, who passes his knowledge and authority onto the bishops who sit on his seat (*kathedra*; *Homilies* 3.70). See further Reed, "'Jewish Christianity' as Counter-History?" (see endnote 88).

99 As F. Stanley Jones (*Pseudoclementina* [see endnote 66], pp. 22–24) notes, some of the hypothetical sources of the Pseudo-Clementines—such as the *Kerygmata Petrou*—are largely modern scholarly fictions. See Jones's extensive survey of the source-critical research in "The Pseudo-Clementines: A History of Research, Part I" [1984], repr. in Jones, *Pseudoclementina* (ibid., pp. 50–80), as well as my discussion in "Jewish Christianity After the Parting of the Ways" (see endnote 90).

100 See now Jones, *Pseudoclementina* (see endnote 66), pp. 114–206.

101 On the Pseudo-Clementines' anti-Marcionite concerns, see F. Stanley Jones, "Marcionism in the Pseudo-Clementines" [2007] and "Jewish Christians as Heresiologists and as Heresy" [2009] repr. in Jones, *Pseudoclementina* (see endnote 66), pp. 152–171, 516–533.

102 James Carleton Paget, *Jews, Christians, and Jewish Christians in Antiquity* (Tübingen: Mohr Siebeck, 2010), pp. 427–492.

103 On the function of these materials in the *Homilies*, see Annette Yoshiko Reed, "From Judaism and Hellenism to Christianity and Paganism: Cultural Identities and Religious Polemics in the Pseudo-Clementine *Homilies*," in *Nouvelles intrigues pseudo-clémentines* (see endnote 93), pp. 351–361.

104 See further Reed, "From Judaism and Hellenism" (see endnote 103); Reed, "Heresiology and the (Jewish-)Christian Novel: Narrativized Polemics in the Pseudo-Clementines *Homilies*," in *Heresy and Identity in Late Antiquity*, eds.

Eduard Iricinschi and Holger Zelletin, TSAJ 119 (Tübingen: Mohr Siebeck, 2008), pp. 273–298; Dominique Côté, "Le problème de l'identité religieuse dans la Syrie du IVe siècle: Le cas des Pseudo-Clémentines et de l'*Adversus Judaeos* de saint Jean Chrysostome," in *La croisée des chemins revisitée* (see endnote 81), pp. 339–370.

[105] See further Côté, "Le problème de l'identité religieuse" (see endnote 104).

[106] For references and discussion, see Mason, "Jews, Judeans, Judaizing, Judaism" (see endnote 4), pp. 471–480.

[107] See further Robert L. Wilken, *John Chrysostom and the Jews: Rhetoric and Reality in the Late Fourth Century* (Berkeley: University of California Press, 1983), pp. 66–94; Christine Shepardson, "Controlling Contested Places: John Chrysostom's *Adversus Iudaeos Homilies* and the Spatial Politics of Religious Controversy," *JECS* 15.4 (2007), pp. 483–516, esp. 498–501.

[108] John G. Gager, "Jews, Christians, and the Dangerous Ones in Between," in *Interpretation in Religion*, eds. Shlomo Biderman and Ben-Ami Scharfstein (Leiden: Brill, 1992), pp. 249–257.

[109] For a lucid summary of late fourth-century factors, see Shepardson, "Controlling Contested Places" (see endnote 107), pp. 488–495.

[110] Griffith, "Christianity in Edessa and the Syriac-Speaking World" (see endnote 62).

[111] See further Adam H. Becker, *Fear of God and the Beginning of Wisdom: The School of Nisibis and the Development of Scholastic Culture in Late Antique Mesopotamia* (Philadelphia: University of Pennsylvania Press, 2006). On so-called "Nestorianism" see also Sebastian Brock, "The 'Nestorian' Church: A Lamentable Misnomer," *Bulletin of the John Rylands Library of Manchester* 78 (1996), pp. 23–36.

[112] See Sebastian Brock, "Jewish Traditions in Syriac Sources," *JJS* 30 (1979), pp. 212–232, on the incorporation of Jewish traditions into Syriac literature, including the Peshitta's dependence on the proto-Masoretic Hebrew text, targumic traditions attested in and beyond the Peshitta, and apocrypha and pseudepigrapha of Jewish origins. For the challenges of comparison with Babylonian Jews, however, see Adam H. Becker, "The Comparative Study of 'Scholasticism' in

Late Antique Mesopotamia: Rabbis and East Syrians," *AJS Review* 34 (2010), pp. 91–113; Becker, "Polishing the Mirror: Some Thoughts on Syriac Sources and Early Judaism," in *Envisioning Judaism* (see endnote 20), pp. 897–916.

[113] See further references and discussion in Annette Yoshiko Reed, "Beyond the Land of Nod: Syriac Images of Asia and the Historiography of 'the West'," *History of Religions* 49.1 (2009), pp. 48–87.

[114] Adam H. Becker, "Beyond the Spatial and Temporal *Limes*: Questioning the 'Parting of the Ways' Outside the Roman Empire," in *Ways That Never Parted* (see endnote 5), pp. 343–362.

VII. Living Side by Side in Galilee

[1] This sort of language and point of reference and consideration of the question was the subject of a consultation between Princeton and Oxford universities entitled "Ways That Never Parted." A summary of those meetings may be found in Annette Yoshiko Reed's essay "Parting of the Ways," in *The Eerdmans Dictionary of Early Judaism*, eds. John J. Collins and Daniel C. Harlow (Grand Rapids, MI: Eerdmans, 2010), pp. 1029–1031. A more detailed presentation of views on this subject may be found in the volume *The Ways That Never Parted: Jews and Christians in Late Antiquity and the Early Middle Ages*, eds. Adam H. Becker and Annette Yoshiko Reed (Minneapolis: Fortress Press, 2007), especially in the "Introduction" by the editors, pp. 1–34.

[2] Becker and Reed, *Ways That Never Parted* (see endnote 1), pp. 1–2.

[3] Seth Schwartz, *Imperialism and Jewish Society, 200 B.C.E. to 640 C.E.* (Princeton, NJ: Princeton University Press, 2001), p. 103.

[4] This issue is dealt with extensively by Eric M. Meyers and Mark A. Chancey in their volume *Alexander to Constantine: Archaeology of the Land of the Bible* (New Haven, CT: Yale University Press, 2012), especially chapter 7. In addition, see Joan Taylor, *Christians and*

the Holy Places: The Myth of Jewish Christian Origins (Oxford: Oxford University Press, 1993); and Yotam Tepper and Leah Di Segni, *A Christian Prayer Hall of the Third Century CE at Kefar 'Othnay (Legio): Excavations at the Megiddo Prison 2005* (Jerusalem: Israel Antiquities Authority, 2006).

[5] The belief that the Jesus movement fled to Pella in Transjordan is based on Eusebius (*Ecclesiastical History* 3.5.3) and Epiphanius (*Panarion* 29.7.7–8, 30.2.7–9), both fourth-century writers. There is no archaeological evidence in Pella to support this at such an early date, though a menorah with a stork was found in a Byzantine church context. For a summary of the Franciscan point of view, see Ignazio Mancini. *Archaeological Discoveries Relative to the Judaeo-Christians: Historical Survey* (Jerusalem: Franciscan Printing Press, 1970).

[6] Oded Irshai, "From Oblivion to Fame: The History of the Palestinian Church, 135–303 CE," in *Christians and Christianity in the Holy Land: From the Origins to the Latin Kingdoms*, eds. Ora Limor and Guy G. Stroumsa (Turnout, Belgium: Brepols, 2006), pp. 91–139.

[7] For a fuller discussion of this question, see Jonathan Reed, *Archaeology and the Galilean Jesus: A Re-Examination of the Evidence* (Harrisburg, PA: Trinity Press, 2002), pp. 100–108.

[8] Tepper and Di Segni, *Christian Prayer Hall* (see endnote 4).

[9] Taylor, *Christians and the Holy Places* (see endnote 4), pp. 273–284.

[10] Ibid., pp. 384–385, and also by James F. Strange, in his review of the publication of Emmauele Testa, *Cafarnao IV: graffiti della casa de S. Pietro* (Jerusalem: Franciscan Printing Press, 1972), "Capernuam and Herodium Publications," *BASOR* 226 (1977), pp. 65–73, and in part 2, *BASOR* 233 (1979), pp. 63–69.

[11] James F. Strange and Hershel Shanks, "Where Jesus Stayed in Capernaum," in *Where Christianity Was Born*, ed. Hershel Shanks (Washington, DC: Biblical Archaeological Society, 2006), p. 78.

[12] This question is the short title of a Forum featured in the volume *Jewish Identities in Antiquity: Studies in Memory of Menahem Stern*, eds. Lee I. Levine and Daniel R. Schwartz (Tübingen: Mohr Siebeck, 2009), pp. 267–268.

[13] Uzi Leibner, *Settlement and History in Hellenistic, Roman, and Byzantine Galilee: An Archaeological Survey of the Eastern Galilee*, TSAJ 127 (Tübingen: Mohr Siebeck, 2009), and his summary in the *Stern Festschrift* (see endnote 12), "Settlement Patterns in the Eastern Galilee: Implications Regarding the Transformation of Rabbinic Culture in Late Antiquity," pp. 269–295, and his response to Magness in the same volume, "The Settlement Crisis in Eastern Galilee During the Late Roman and Early Byzantine Periods: Response to Jodi Magness," pp. 314–319. Magness's critique of Leibner and of the author's work at Meiron and Sepphoris may be found in her article, "Did Galilee Experience a Settlement Crisis in the Mid-Fourth Century?" in *Jewish Identities in Antiquity* (see endnote 12), pp. 296–313.

[14] See Eric M. Meyers and Carol L. Meyers, "Response to Jodi Magness's Review of the Final Publication of Nabratein," *BASOR* 359 (2010), pp. 67–76.

[15] In his preface to the articles by Leibner and Magness, in Levine, "Forum" (see endnote 12), p. 267.

[16] Eric M. Meyers, "The Problem of Scarcity of Synagogues from 70 to ca. 250 C.E.: The Case of Synagogue I at Nabratein (2nd–3rd Century C.E.)," in *"Follow the Wise": Studies in Jewish History and Culture in Honor of Lee. I. Levine*, eds. Zeev Weiss, Oded Irshai, Jodi Magness and Seth Schwartz (Winona Lake, IN: Eisenbrauns, 2010), pp. 435–448.

[17] Meyers and Chancey, *Alexander to Constantine* (see endnote 4), pp. 208–224.

[18] A major case in point is the site of Sepphoris in Lower Galilee where among many significant structures that may be dated to the middle Roman period, which is coterminous with the tannaitic period, we may date the Dionysos Mansion on the western summit. Talgam and Weiss, who base their conclusions on the data compiled by the Joint Sepphoris Project led by Eric Meyers, Ehud Netzer and Carol Meyers, date the founding of the structure to the later second or early third century or c. 200 C.E., *The Mosaics of the House of Dionysos at Sepphoris,*

Qedem 44 (Jerusalem: The Institute of Archaeology, The Hebrew University, 2004), p. 29. This
is supported by both ceramics and numismatic
evidence. Chancey and I deal with this issue
extensively in our book *From Alexander to
Constantine* (see endnote 4).

[19] Contra Schwartz, *Imperialism and Jewish
Society* (see endnote 3; see also endnote 21
below).

[20] Joseph Patrich, "Early Christian Churches in
the Holy Land," in *Christians and Christianity
in the Holy Land* (see endnote 6), pp. 355–399.

[21] Seth Schwartz has grossly overstated the case
in his book *Imperialism and Jewish Society* (see
endnote 3), pp. 14–15 and *passim*. His thesis is
that the Jews were left shattered by the two wars
with Rome and that most had only a vestigial
identity with their tradition. The rabbinic
literature reflects only the views of an elite, and
the archaeology demonstrates that only after
the rise of imperial Christianity did the Jewish
community begin to reassert its identify and
build synagogues, etc.

[22] Doron Bar, "The Christianisation of Rural
Palestine in Late Antiquity," *Journal of Ecclesiastical History* 54 (2003), pp. 401–421.

[23] Ibid., p. 402.

[24] Yoram Tsafrir, "Some Notes on the Settlement
and Demography of Palestine in the Byzantine
Period: the Archaeological Evidence," in
*Retrieving the Past: Essays on Archeological
Research and Methodology in Honor of G.W.
van Beek*, ed. Joe D. Seger (Winona Lake, IN:
Eisenbrauns, 1996), pp. 269–283.

[25] John Gager, "Aspects of Palestinian Paganism
in Late Antiquity," in *Sharing the Sacred:
Religious Contacts and Conflicts in the Holy
Land*, eds. Aryeh Kofsky and Guy Stroumas
(Jerusalem: Yad Izhak Ben Zvi, 1998), pp. 2–18.

[26] Bar, "Christianisation of Rural Palestine" (see
endnote 22), p. 405.

[27] Mordechai Aviam, *Jews, Pagans and Christians
in the Galilee* (Rochester, NY: University of
Rochester Press, 2004), pp. 181–205.

[28] Ibid., pp. 181–201.

[29] Ibid., pp. 202–203.

[30] Ibid.

[31] See above endnotes 10 and 11.

[32] Aviam, *Jews, Pagans and Christians in the
Galilee* (see endnote 27), p. 203.

[33] Ibid., p. 204

[34] Ibid.

[35] Leibner, *Settlement and History in Hellenistic,
Roman, and Byzantine Galilee* (see endnote 13),
p. 371.

[36] Bar, "Christianisation of Rural Palestine" (see
endnote 22), p. 406.

[37] Ibid., p. 408.

[38] Hagith Sivan, *Palestine in Late Antiquity*
(Oxford: Oxford University Press, 2008), pp.
326–328.

[39] Zeev Weiss, "Sepphoris," in *The New Encyclopedia of Archaeological Excavations in the Holy
Land*, 5 vols., ed. Ephraim Stern (Jerusalem:
IES and Carta, 1993; vol. 5, 2008), vol. 5, pp.
2032–2034.

[40] Bar, "Christianisation of Rural Palestine" (see
endnote 22), p. 409.

[41] On the dating of synagogues, in addition
to my article "The Problem of the Scarcity of
Synagogues" (see endnote 16), see also most
recently Eric M. Meyers and Carol L. Meyers,
"Response to Jodi Magness's Review" (see
endnote 14), pp. 67–76. It should be stressed that
no one doubts that the majority of synagogue
buildings in Israel may be dated to the Byzantine
period. The question of what existed before and
why there are not more physical remains is at
issue. This explanation of the spread of Christianity in the rural areas, however, may well be a
factor that has allowed for the anomaly of why
so many more remains are preserved in the late
period.

[42] Amnon Linder, *The Jews in Roman Imperial
Legislation* (Detroit: Wayne State University
Press/Jerusalem: Israel Academy of Sciences
and Humanities, 1987).

[43] Bar, "Christianisation of Rural Palestine" (see
endnote 22), p. 416 and n. 73. See also Zvi Ma'oz,
"Golan: Synagogues," in *New Encyclopedia* (see
endnote 39), vol. 2, pp. 539–545.

44 Bar, "Christianisation of Rural Palestine" (see endnote 22), pp. 417–418.

45 Ibid., p. 418.

46 Ibid., p. 419.

47 Schwartz, *Imperialism and Jewish Society* (see endnote 3), pp. 179, 181. (And see endnote 19.)

48 Fergus Millar, "Transformation of Judaism under Graeco-Roman Rule: Responses to Seth Schwartz's 'Imperialism and Jewish Society'" *JJS* 57 (2006), pp. 139–158.

49 Quoted and translated by Adiel Schremer in his article, "The Christianization of the Roman Empire and Rabbinic Literature," in *Jewish Identities in Antiquity* (see endnote 12), p. 353.

50 Ibid. Hayim Lapin has recently suggested that the period from 500–800 C.E. was one that saw the rabbinic community of Palestine transform from an urban, voluntary religious confraternity into a widespread, hegemonic one that spread far beyond Palestine. Such a view supports the idea that Christianity had not made the kind of inroads into Jewish life that many have assumed in the Byzantine period. See his essay, "Aspects of the Rabbinic Movement in Palestine, 500–800 C.E.," in *Shaping the Middle East: Jews, Christians, Muslims in an Age of Transition, 400–800 C.E.*, eds. K.G. Holum and H. Lapin (Bethesda, MD: University Press of Maryland, 2011), pp. 181–196.

51 Reuven Kimmelman, "Identifying Jews and Christians in Roman Syria-Palestine," in *Galilee Through the Centuries: Confluence of Cultures*, ed. Eric M. Meyers (Winona Lake, IN: Eisenbrauns, 1999), pp. 307–308.

52 Ibid, p. 307. See for example, Origen, *Homily on Jeremiah* 12.13; *Commentary on Matthew*, sermon 79 or Chrysostom, *Homilies Against the Jews* 3.4.

53 In regard to tableware and purity, see Andrea Berlin, *Gamla I: The Pottery of the Second Temple Period* (Jerusalem: Israel Antiquities Authority, 2006), pp. 133–156; and Adan-Bayewitz, *Common Pottery in Roman Galilee: A Study of Local Trade* (Ramat-Gan: Bar-Ilan University Press, 1993).

54 Robert C. Gregg and Dan Urman, *Jews, Christians, and Pagans in the Golan Heights* (Atlanta: Scholars Press, 1996), pp. 294–298, maps 4, 5 and 6.

55 The best presentation of the material heritage of Palestinian Christianity is the catalogue *Cradle of Christianity*, eds. Yael Israeli and David Mevorah (Jerusalem: The Israel Museum, 2000).

56 Reed, "Parting of the Ways" (see endnote 1), p. 1031.

VIII. Jews and Christians at Rome: An Early Parting of the Ways

1 Trans. J.C. Yardley (Oxford: Oxford World Classics, 2008), pp. 359–360.

2 For the account of the entire year, see Tacitus, *Annals* 15.33–47. For the date of the actual outbreak (that is, July 19), see Tacitus, *Annals* 15.41. This, so it was believed, was the anniversary of the Gallic sack of Rome in 390 B.C.E.

3 Jesus' death is dated variously from 27 to 33 C.E. See L.W. Hurtado, *Lord Jesus Christ: Devotion to Jesus in Earliest Christianity* (Grand Rapids, MI: Eerdmans, 2003), p. 59. For Pilate's official title, *praefectus*, see C.M. Lehmann and K.G. Holum, *The Greek and Latin Inscriptions of Caesarea Maritima* (Boston: ASOR, 2000), no. 43. Tacitus's designation of him as procurator in *Annals* 15.44, our opening passage, is an anachronism.

4 For the literary references to Judaism as a "superstition," see M.H. Williams, "The Disciplining of the Jews of Ancient Rome—Pure Gesture Politics?" in *Studies in Latin Literature and Roman History*, vol. 15, ed. C. Deroux, Collection Latomus 323 (Bruxelles: Éditions Latomus, 2010), pp. 79–102, especially p. 80, n. 5. For the use of the word "superstition" in relation to the Christians, see, for instance, Suetonius, *Life of Nero* 16.2, and Pliny, *Letters* 10.96.8.

5 Valerius Maximus, *Memorable Deeds and Sayings* 1.3.3 in the abridged versions of Iulius Paris and Ianuarius Nepotianus (fourth/fifth century C.E.). For these passages and their translations, see *GLAJJ*, vol. 1, nos. 147a and 147b. For discussion of the episode itself, see Williams,

"Disciplining of the Jews" (see endnote 4), pp. 94–97.

6 According to the version of Iulius Paris (Stern no. 147b), the Jews were ordered to "return to their homes"—a phrase strongly suggesting that their domicile was elsewhere.

7 Implied clearly by Cicero's remarks at *In Defense of Flaccus* 66. For discussion, see E.M. Smallwood, *The Jews Under Roman Rule from Pompey to Diocletian* (Leiden: Brill, 1976), p. 131.

8 Cicero, ibid.

9 As shown at the obsequies of Julius Caesar in 44 B.C.E. See Suetonius, *Life of the Deified Julius* 84.5.

10 M.H. Williams, "Latin Authors on Jews and Judaism," in *The Dictionary of Early Judaism*, eds. J.J. Collins and D. Harlow (Grand Rapids, MI: Eerdmans, 2010), pp. 870–875, especially p. 871.

11 E.S. Gruen (*Diaspora: Jews Amidst Greeks and Romans* [Cambridge, MA: Harvard University Press, 2002], pp. 15 and 260, n. 1) puts its size at around 20,000 but several scholars have argued that it might have been twice or even three times larger than that.

12 Philo, *Embassy to Gaius* 155.

13 Williams, "Disciplining of the Jews" (see endnote 4), pp. 87–89.

14 Macrobius, *Saturnalia* 2.4.11: "It is better to be Herod's pig than Herod's son." In the original Greek, the joke is much funnier. See discussion at Stern (endnote 6), vol. 2, no. 543.

15 Tacitus, *Annals* 2.85.5.

16 Josephus, *Antiquities* 18.84.

17 Philo, *Embassy to Gaius* 160.

18 E.M. Smallwood, *Philonis Alexandrini Legatio ad Gaium* (Leiden: Brill, 1961), p. 244.

19 For two recent discussions, see Williams, "Disciplining of the Jews" (see endnote 4), pp. 98–100, who takes issue with Gruen, *Diaspora* (see endnote 11), pp. 29–36.

20 Philo, *Embassy to Gaius* 155–158. According to Philo (ibid., 156), their prayer houses (*proseuchai*) also functioned as depositories for

the Temple tax before the transferral of those monies to Jerusalem.

21 For a full account of this and the important role played in it by Herod Agrippa I, see Josephus, *Antiquities* 19.212–275.

22 L.I. Levine, *Jerusalem: Portrait of the City in the Second Temple Period (538 B.C.E.–70 C.E.)* (Philadelphia: JPS, 2002), p. 252.

23 For discussion, see D.W. Hurley, *Suetonius: Divus Claudius* (Cambridge: Cambridge University Press, 2001), pp. 177–178. For the long-running debate about Claudius's anti-Jewish measures, see discussion and full bibliography at S. Cappelletti, *The Jewish Community of Rome: From the Second Century B.C. to the Third Century C.E.* (Leiden: Brill, 2006).

24 M. Heemstra, *The Fiscus Judaicus and the Parting of the Ways* (Tübingen: Mohr Siebeck, 2010), p. 91.

25 Hurley, *Suetonius* (see endnote 23), p. 177.

26 Acts 14:19 (Lystra), 17:5 (Thessalonica), 17:13 (Beroea).

27 For the epigraphic and literary evidence for these people, see I. Levinskaya, *The Book of Acts in Its Diaspora Setting*, The Book of Acts in Its First Century Setting 5 (Grand Rapids, MI: Eerdmans, 1996), chapters 4 and 7.

28 See, for instance, Horace, *Satires* 1.9.60–78 (Aristius Fuscus, allegedly a sympathiser); Josephus, *Antiquities* 18.82 (Fulvia, a proselyte); Philo, *Embassy to Gaius* 245 (Publius Petronius, sympathetic to Judaism).

29 For its generally accepted Pauline authorship, see J.D.G. Dunn, "The Spread of Christianity from Jerusalem to Rome: 30–70 C.E.," in *Christianity and Rabbinic Judaism: A Parallel History of Their Origins and Early Development*, 2nd ed., ed. H. Shanks (Washington, DC: Biblical Archaeology Society, 2011), p. 95; for our purposes, however, the identity of the author is not important.

30 We need not assume with Heemstra (*Fiscus Judaicus* [see endnote 24], p. 91) that Nero had given formal permission for their return on his accession in 54 C.E. As noted in the text above, once an expulsion had occurred, the authorities tended to lose interest in the fate of the expelled.

31 Romans 14:1–15:13; quotes from 14:20 and 15:2 (trans. New English Bible).

32 Tacitus, *Annals* 15.44.

33 For the common accusations made against Christians, especially by second- and early third-century C.E. writers, see M. Beard, J. North and S. Price, *Religions of Rome*, vol. 1 (Cambridge: Cambridge University Press, 1998), pp. 225–226.

34 On the role of the mob in inciting the authorities to persecute the Christians, see R.L. Williams, "Persecution," in *Encyclopedia of Early Christianity*, 2nd ed., ed. E. Ferguson (New York: Garland Publishing, 1999), pp. 896–897.

35 On the "eschatological (end time) fervor" in early church circles, see Dunn, "Spread of Christianity" (see endnote 29), p. 105.

36 Tacitus, *Annals* 15.44.5. Whether their confession was to incendiarism or to being Christians is disputed. From the discussion later in the chapter, it will become clear that I favor the former.

37 So claims the writer of 1 Clement 5–6, a letter composed in the 90s C.E. and thus our earliest source for the persecution of 64 C.E.

38 Tacitus, *Annals* 15.44.5.

39 Josephus, *Life* 16.

40 Josephus, *Antiquities* 20.195. For Poppaea's Jewish sympathies, see M.H. Williams, "*Theosebes gar en*—The Jewish Tendencies of Poppaea Sabina," *JTS* 39 (1988), pp. 97–111; T. Gruell and L. Benke, "A Hebrew/Aramaic Graffito and Poppaea's Alleged Jewish Sympathy," *JJS* 62 (2011), pp. 37–55, esp. 52–55.

41 There is no hard evidence to back the claim of W.H.C. Frend (*Martyrdom and Persecution in the Early Church* [Oxford: Blackwell, 1965], pp. 164–165) and others that it was the malice and machinations of the Jews that led to the sadistic punishment of the Christians.

42 Clearing out the pockets of resistance, however, lasted until 73/74 C.E., when the last rebel stronghold, Masada, was finally taken. See Josephus, *War* 7.163–408.

43 On the relative obscurity of the Flavians' origins, see Suetonius, *Life of the Deified Vespasian* 1.

44 On the deliberately dynastic character of the triumph, see Josephus, *War* 7.121; for Josephus's detailed eyewitness account, see *War* 7.121–157.

45 See F. Millar, "Last Year in Jerusalem: Monuments of the Jewish War in Rome," in *Flavius Josephus and Flavian Rome*, eds. J. Edmondson, S. Mason and J. Rives (Oxford: Oxford University Press, 2005), pp. 101–128, esp. 102.

46 For some examples, see I.A. Carradice and T.V. Buttrey, *The Roman Imperial Coinage II, Part I: From AD 69–96, Vespasian to Domitian*, 2nd ed. (London: Spink, 2007), pp. 71–72 (nos. 159–169) and p. 75 (nos. 233–236) with plates 21, 22 and 25.

47 Millar, "Last Year in Jerusalem" (see endnote 45).

48 Josephus, *War* 7.161.

49 Ibid., 7.148–149.

50 For the visit there by the Jewish sage Rabbi Eliezer ben Jose, see the passages cited by Smallwood, *Jews Under Roman Rule* (see endnote 7), p. 329, n. 161. For the visit of the Christian emperor Constantius, see Ammianus Marcellinus, *The Chronicles of Events* 16.10.

51 For the universal application of the tax, see Josephus, *War* 7.218. For its ethnic character (*imposita genti tributa*), Suetonius, *Life of Domitian* 12.2.

52 For epigraphic attestation of the *Fiscus Judaicus* at Rome, see M.H. Williams, *The Jews Among the Greeks and Romans: A Diasporan Sourcebook* (Baltimore: Johns Hopkins University Press, 1998), IV.65: epitaph of a "procurator for the capitation tax on the Jews."

53 For a brief discussion, see Smallwood, *Jews Under Roman Rule* (see endnote 7), pp. 124–125.

54 For discussion and documentation, see V.A. Tcherikover and A. Fuks, *Corpus Papyrorum Judaicarum*, vol. 2 (Cambridge, MA: Harvard University Press, 1960), pp. 108–136.

55 Williams, "Latin Authors" (see endnote 10), p. 873.

56 They had known this since the time of Pompey's capture of the Temple in 63 B.C.E. at the very least. For the evidence from the

Augustan historian Livy, see *GLAJJ*, vol. 1, no. 133.

[57] Dio Cassius, *Roman History* 66.7.2. For the burning down of the Temple, first in the civil wars of 69 C.E. and then again shortly after Vespasian's death in 79 C.E., see Plutarch, *Publicola* 15. For its second rebuilding in the Flavian period, this time by the emperor Domitian, see Suetonius, *Life of Domitian* 5. To soften the blow for his Jewish readers, Josephus (*War* 7.218) conceals the fact that their money was going towards the rebuilding of a pagan temple, preferring instead the more neutral term "capitol."

[58] For Martial's flattery of the Flavians and his crude anti-Jewish humor, see the passages listed in *GLAJJ*, vol. 1, nos. 238–246. For a more detailed analysis of these poems, see D.S. Barrett, "Martial, Jews and Circumcision," *Liverpool Classical Monthly* 9.3 (1984), pp. 42–46.

[59] Originally it was called the Flavian Amphitheatre, the nickname Colosseum only being acquired at a much later date. Construction had started under Vespasian but completion and dedication took place only under Titus. See Suetonius, *Life of the Deified Vespasian* 9 and *Life of the Deified Titus* 7.3.

[60] In the inscription on the arch, he is referred to as "the deified Titus," indicating that he is now dead. See the *Corpus Inscriptionum Latinarum* 6.945.

[61] A. Claridge, *Rome: An Oxford Archaeological Guide* (Oxford: Oxford University Press, 1998), p. 278.

[62] For an illustration of this relief, the only triumphal procession ever depicted on a Roman triumphal arch, see M.H. Williams, "Jews and Jewish Communities in the Roman Empire," in *Experiencing Rome: Culture, Identity and Power in the Roman Empire*, ed. J. Huskinson (London: Routledge, 2000), p. 331, fig. 11.8.

[63] For this less well known image, see M. Beard, *The Roman Triumph* (Cambridge, MA: Belknap Press, 2007), p. 44, fig. 8.

[64] For examples of Titus's *Judea Capta* coinage, see Carradice and Buttrey, *Roman Imperial Coinage* (see endnote 46), p. 208 (nos. 145–153) with plates 93 and 94. The coin taken until fairly

recently to show that Domitian issued *Judea Capta* coins in 85 C.E. has been declared by Carradice and Buttrey (ibid., p. 399) to be a fake.

[65] For the date, see M.H. Williams, "Domitian, the Jews and the 'Judaizers'—A Simple Matter of *cupiditas* and *maiestas*?" *Historia* 39 (1990), pp. 196–211, especially p. 204; and Heemstra, Fiscus Judaicus (see endnote 24), p. 27, arguing on slightly different grounds.

[66] Suetonius, *Life of Domitian* 12.1–2. One reason for this discrimination against the Jews may have been their refusal to acknowledge Domitian's godhead, a practice upon which he had recently begun to insist (ibid., 13.2). Another reason may have been a determination to maximize the revenues for the cult of Jupiter Capitolinus, a deity Domitian particularly favored. Besides rebuilding his temple, which once again had been burned down (ibid., 5), he also in 86 C.E. instituted an international festival in that god's honor, the Capitoline Games (ibid., 4.4). Both projects will have required large amounts of money.

[67] What had driven the informers on was the handsome profits that could be made from bringing about successful prosecutions. The penalty for evasion of the Jewish tax was the confiscation of property. In accordance with Roman law (Tacitus, *Annals* 4.20.3), 25 percent of the value of that property went to the successful informer, with the rest going to the state.

[68] For the analysis offered here, see Williams, "Domitian, the Jews and the 'Judaizers'" (see endnote 65), pp. 198–202; and Heemstra, Fiscus Judaicus (see endnote 24), pp. 24–66. The views of Goodman that (1) only Jews were affected by Domitian's maladministration, and (2) Nerva's reforms consisted in the temporary abolition of the Jewish tax (from 96–98 C.E.) strike me as implausible and so are not followed here. For those views, see M. Goodman, "Nerva, the *Fiscus Judaicus* and Jewish Identity," *JRS* 79 (1989), pp. 40–44, "The *Fiscus Iudaicus* and Gentile Attitudes to Judaism in Flavian Rome," in *Flavius Josephus and Flavian Rome*, eds. J. Edmondson, S. Mason and J. Rives (Oxford: Oxford University Press, 2005), pp. 167–177, and *Rome and Jerusalem: The Clash of Ancient Civilizations* (London: Penguin, 2008), pp.

469–470 and p. 614, n. 25. For cogent criticisms of Goodman's thesis, see Heemstra, Fiscus Judaicus (see endnote 24), pp. 73–74.

[69] Also caught up in the witch hunt and included in this category may have been pagans who had adopted various Jewish customs without fully comprehending their meaning. On these people, see Seneca, De Superstitione (Concerning Superstition), as cited by Augustine, The City of God 6.11. Josephus at Against Apion 2.282 also speaks of the popularity of Jewish customs with non-Jews throughout the Roman world.

[70] Such as Philo's high-flying nephew, Tiberius Julius Alexander. For his apostasy, see Josephus, Antiquities 20.100.

[71] For a neat tabulation of all the likely categories, see Heemstra, Fiscus Judaicus (see endnote 24), p. 33.

[72] Williams, "Domitian, the Jews and the 'Judaizers'" (see endnote 65), pp. 200–201.

[73] Dio Cassius, Roman History 68.1.2.

[74] Ibid.

[75] H. Mattingly and E.A. Sydenham, The Roman Imperial Coinage II (London: Spink, 1926), p. 227 (nos. 58–59) for Nerva's first issue of this coin type and p. 228 (no. 82) for the second in 97 C.E.

[76] Josephus, War 7.218.

[77] Dio Cassius, Roman History 66.7.2, with Heemstra, Fiscus Judaicus (see endnote 24), p. 80.

[78] Heemstra, Fiscus Judaicus (see endnote 24), pp. 21–23. The synagogue had performed a similar function in respect of the Temple tax prior to the destruction. See, for instance, Philo, Embassy to Gaius 156–157.

[79] The use in some late-first-century C.E. Christian texts from Rome of the title synagogue for the Christian assembly (e.g., Shepherd of Hermas, Mandata [Instructions] 11.9) suggests that in such cases the membership may well have been largely or wholly Jewish.

[80] The famous anti-Christian oration of Marcus Cornelius Fronto, tutor to the future emperor Marcus Aurelius is lost. See S. Benko, Pagan Rome and the Early Christians (London: B.T. Batsford, 1985), p. 54. Fronto was also well informed about the Jews and particularly their end-of-sabbath rituals. See M.H. Williams, "Being a Jew in Rome: Sabbath Fasting as an Expression of Romano-Jewish Identity," in Negotiating Diaspora: Jewish Strategies in the Roman Empire, ed. J.M.G. Barclay (London/New York: T & T Clark, 2004), pp. 8–18, esp. 14–15.

[81] Tacitus, Annals 15.44.

[82] Revealed especially in his notorious ethnographic excursus on the Jews at Histories 5.4–5, but see also Annals 2.85.5.

[83] These were adherents of a pernicious superstition (exitiabilis superstitio) and so deserving of exemplary punishment. See Annals 15.44.

[84] For discussion of all of Suetonius's Jewish references, see Williams, "Latin Authors" (see endnote 10), pp. 873–874.

[85] Suetonius, Life of Nero 16.2.

[86] For useful discussion of this point, see GLAJJ, vol. 2, p. 39.

[87] At Letters 10.96.8, he describes them as a "superstitio prava et immodica" ("a degenerate sort of cult carried to extravagant lengths") (trans. B. Radice, Penguin 1963, reprinted 1969, p. 294).

[88] For powerful arguments on this point, see Heemstra, Fiscus Judaicus (see endnote 24), pp. 202–203. The crime for which the Christians had been executed by Nero was probably incendiarism.

[89] Pliny, Letters 10.96.5. It is entirely possible that the last test, cursing Christ, had been suggested to Pliny by some of the Jews in his province. Who but they at that time would have known of this vital distinction between Jews and Christians? I am indebted to Dr. Sara Parvis for pointing this out to me. The Jewish cursing of Christ in Jewish synagogues and the part it played in dividing Jews from Christians is discussed briefly under "Christian Sources" later in this chapter.

[90] Pliny, Letters 10.97.2

[91] Acts 18:12–16.

[92] Suetonius, Life of Nero 16.2.

[93] The first recorded instances of this term come in the writings of Ignatius of Antioch: Letter to

the *Magnesians* 10.3 and *Letter to the Philadelphians* 6.1. In both of these passages, *Christianismos* is contrasted with *Ioudaismos*. Ignatius
himself lived at the time of Trajan (98–117 C.E.).

94 S.G. Wilson, "Marcion and the Jews," in *Anti-
Judaism in Early Christianity*, vol. 2, *Separation
and Polemic*, ed. S.G. Wilson (Waterloo, ON:
Wilfrid Laurier Press, 1986), pp. 45–58, esp. 45.

95 For useful, brief discussions of the careers and
principal beliefs of these two men, see Hurtado,
Lord Jesus Christ (see endnote 3), pp. 523–532
(Valentinus and Valentinianism), pp. 549–558
(Marcion).

96 For instance, Luke's gospel, the only one of the
four to be judged appropriate for inclusion in
the canon, was stripped of its opening nativity
narrative! Likewise, from those Pauline epistles
that had met with Marcion's approval "all
statements referring to the Old Testament as
Scripture" were deleted. Ibid., p. 553.

97 Wilson, "Marcion and the Jews" (see endnote
94), p. 52.

98 S.G. Wilson, *Related Strangers: Jews and
Christians 70–170 C.E.* (Minneapolis: Fortress
Press, 1995), p. 218. The suggestion, first made by
R.M. Grant (*Gnosticism and Early Christianity*
[New York: Columbia University Press, 1959],
pp. 121–128), has found general acceptance.

99 Dio Cassius, *Roman History* 69.14.3. Dio's
claims about the scale of the revolt, once
dismissed as exaggerated, have now been conclusively proved on the basis of newly published
inscriptions. See, for instance, W. Eck, "The Bar
Kokhba Revolt: The Roman Point of View," *JRS*
89 (1999), pp. 76–89, and "New Perspectives on
Hadrian and the Bar Kokhba Revolt" at http://
www.currentepigraphy.org/2008/02/19/werner-
eck-new-perspectives-on-hadrian-and-the-bar
-kokhba-revolt/ (abstract of a paper delivered
in Cambridge on February 16, 2008, expanding
on the arguments presented in the earlier *JRS*
paper).

100 See, for instance, Justin Martyr, 1 *Apology* 31.6.

101 Hurtado, *Lord Jesus Christ* (see endnote 3), p.
555, quoting A. Balás.

102 For the existence of Marcionite congregations
as late as the fifth century C.E., see Wilson,
"Marcion and the Jews" (see endnote 94), p. 45.

103 J. Lieu, *Image and Reality: The Jews in the
World of the Christians in the Second Century*
(London: T & T Clark, 1996), p. 103.

104 The Bar-Kokhba Revolt has only recently
ended. See *Dialogue with Trypho* 1.3.

105 Eusebius, *Ecclesiastical History* 4.18.6.

106 Lieu, *Image and Reality* (see endnote 103), p.
139; and Hurtado, *Lord Jesus Christ* (see endnote
3), p. 607.

107 For the history and scope of the *Birkat
ha-Minim*, the 12th section of the *Amidah*, see
the detailed study of W. Horbury, "The Benediction of the *Minim* and Early Jewish-Christian
Controversy," in *Jews and Christians in Contact
and Controversy*, ed. W. Horbury (Edinburgh: T
& T Clark, 1998), pp. 67–110.

108 *Dialogue with Trypho* 16.4, cf. 96.2: "In your
synagogues you curse all those who through him
are called Christians."

109 "*Birkat ha-Minim*," in *The Oxford Dictionary
of the Jewish Religion*, eds. R.J. Zwi Werblowsky
and Geoffrey Wigoder (Oxford: Oxford
University Press, 1997), p. 131.

110 Hurtado, *Lord Jesus Christ* (see endnote 3),
pp. 607–608.

111 For a useful overview of both the Jewish
and the Christian catacombs, see L.V. Rutgers,
*Subterranean Rome: In Search of the Roots of
Christianity in the Catacombs of the Eternal City*
(Leuven: Peeters, 2000). Rutgers's comments (p.
149) on their relative dating, however, should
be ignored. They are invalidated by his own
subsequent research, for which see endnote 113
below.

112 For a clear map of the principal Jewish and
Christian catacombs, see J. Stevenson, *The
Catacombs: Rediscovered Monuments of Early
Christianity* (London: Thames and Hudson,
1978), p. 8; for more detail but less clarity, see
the map in *Encyclopedia of Early Christianity*
(see endnote 34), p. 222 (under "Catacombs").

113 L.V. Rutgers, A.F.M. de Jong and K. van der
Borg, "Radiocarbon Dates from the Jewish

Catacombs of Rome," *Radiocarbon* 44 (2002), pp. 541–547, and L.V. Rutgers, "Radiocarbon Dating: Jewish Inspiration of Christian Catacombs," *Nature* 436 (2005), p. 339.

[114] L.V. Rutgers (*The Jews in Late Ancient Rome: Evidence of Cultural Interaction in the Roman Diaspora* [Leiden: Brill, 1995], pp. xvii–xviii and 96–98) suggests a date in the late second century C.E.

[115] Hippolytus, *Refutation of All Heresies* 9.12.14, where it is shown to have been initiated by Zephyrinus, bishop of Rome, c. 198–217 C.E.

[116] L.V. Rutgers, *The Hidden Heritage of Diaspora Judaism* (Leuven: Peeters, 1998), pp. 69–70: "Whether one inspects funerary inscriptions, wall-paintings, sarcophagi, gold glass fragments, or pottery remains, all of these materials belong chronologically, without exception to the late antique period," by which he means "the third and fourth centuries C.E."

[117] The sole exception are the *kokhim*, a type of grave common in Palestine, found in the Vigna Randanini catacomb. On these, see Rutgers, *Jews in Late Ancient Rome* (see endnote 114), pp. 61–64. For illustrations, see H.J. Leon, *The Jews of Ancient Rome*, rev. ed. (Peabody, MA: Hendrickson, 1995), plate VIII, figs. 10 and 11.

[118] For illustrations, see Leon, *Jews of Ancient Rome* (see endnote 117), plates VI and VII, figs. 8 and 9.

[119] Neither Jews nor Christians practiced cremation, the former mostly because burial was an "ancestral practice," the latter because of their fervent belief in bodily resurrection. Pagan Romans, by contrast, tended to cremate. For mainstream (i.e., pagan) practice at Rome, see "Dead, disposal of," in the *Oxford Classical Dictionary*, 3rd ed., eds. S. Hornblower and A. Spawforth (Oxford: Oxford University Press, 2003).

[120] Examples at Leon, *Jews of Ancient Rome* (see endnote 117), plates X and XI, figs. 15 and 16: *arcosolia* in the Vigna Randanini catacomb for single burials; plate XXIV, figs. 41 and 42: *arcosolia* for double burials in the Villa Torlonia catacomb, referred to in Leon by its old name, Via Nomentana.

[121] On these, see A. Konikoff, *Sarcophagi from the Jewish Catacombs of Ancient Rome: A Catalogue Raisonée*, rev. ed. (Stuttgart: Franz Steiner Verlag, 1990).

[122] For these, see *JIWE*, vol. 2. About 75 percent of these texts are written in Greek; the remainder, apart from one Aramaic text, are in Latin.

[123] For the occurrence of *hosios* at Rome, see Rutgers, *Jews in Late Ancient Rome* (see endnote 114), pp. 192–193. From his table, which sets out all the Greek epithets found in pagan, Jewish and early Christian epitaphs at Rome, we see that *hosios* not only is the most frequently occurring Judeo-Greek epithet, but it does not feature in pagan or Christian epitaphs at all.

[124] See *JIWE*, vol. 2, p. 536 (Index IIIf).

[125] Curiously omitted from the *JIWE* index of epithets (IIIf). It occurs in three epitaphs: *JIWE*, vol. 2, no. 68 (Monteverde catacomb) and nos. 270 and 374, both from the Vigna Randanini.

[126] *JIWE*, vol. 2, no. 307 (Vigna Randanini).

[127] *JIWE*, vol. 2, no. 544 (perhaps from Trastevere?). On this title, see Leon, *Jews of Ancient Rome* (see endnote 117), p. 193, who notes that the term *Talmid Hakam* was "applied to scholars of the law who were held in special honour"; and "Talmid Hakam," in *The Oxford Dictionary of the Jewish Religion* (see endnote 109), p. 668.

[128] On the various office holders of Rome, see M.H. Williams, "The Structure of Roman Jewry Re-considered—Were the Synagogues of Rome Entirely Homogeneous?" *Zeitschrift für Papyrologie und Epigraphik* 104 (1994), pp. 129–141.

[129] *JIWE*, vol. 2, no. 577 (the present location and original provenance of her sarcophagus at Rome are unknown).

[130] *JIWE*, vol. 2, no. 171 (Monteverde). The other epithets applied to this man are devout (*hosios*), just, a lover of his children and a lover of his brothers—so altogether a model Jew!

[131] For a full discussion of this common blessing, almost exclusively Jewish in its usage, see J.S. Park, *Conceptions of Afterlife in Jewish Inscriptions: With Special Reference to Pauline Literature* (Tübingen: Mohr Siebeck, 2000), pp. 98–112. See also the sensible comments by P. van der Horst on death as sleep in his *Ancient Jewish Epitaphs*

(Kampen, Netherlands: Kok Pharos, 1991), pp. 115–117.

132 Park, *Conceptions of Afterlife in Jewish Inscriptions* (see endnote 131), pp. 21–26; and Van der Horst, *Ancient Jewish Epitaphs* (see endnote 131), p. 42.

133 M. Schwabe and B. Lifshitz, *Beth She'arim II: The Greek Inscriptions* (New Brunswick, NJ: Rutgers University Press, on behalf of the Israel Exploration Society and the Institute of Archaeology, Hebrew University, 1974), pp. 223–224; and Park, *Conceptions of Afterlife in Jewish Inscriptions* (see endnote 131).

134 The only certain examples are *JIWE*, vol. 2, nos. 39, 173, 521 (father and son with that name) and 596.

135 M.H. Williams, "Image and Text in the Jewish Epitaphs of Late Ancient Rome," *JSJ* 42.3 (2011), pp. 328–350.

136 On this, see Konikoff, *Sarcophagi from the Jewish Catacombs* (see endnote 121), no. 22 (pp. 53–56 and plate 16, IV-22), who accepts it as Jewish. Other scholars who cannot conceive of Jews breaking the second commandment view it as an intrusive object, possibly taken from some nearby pagan or Christian burial site.

137 These problematic frescoes originated in an independent hypogeum (underground burial chamber) that later became incorporated into the Jewish catacomb. Whether that hypogeum was constructed originally for Jews and the frescoes therefore commissioned by Jews cannot be determined. All we can say for certain is that the Jews who subsequently used these rooms for burial purposes (shown by the presence of *kokhim*) did not object to their presence and have them removed. For discussion, see Rutgers, *Jews in Late Ancient Rome* (see endnote 114), pp. 44 and 54–55.

138 Konikoff, *Sarcophagi from the Jewish Catacombs* (see endnote 121), no. 14 (pp. 38–41 and plate 11, III-14). For illustrations of this famous artifact, see, for instance, Leon, *Jews of Ancient Rome* (see endnote 117), plate XXVI, fig. 44; and J.M.C. Toynbee, *Death and Burial in the Roman World* (London: Thames and Hudson, 1971), plate 74.

139 For a comprehensive list of the various symbols found in the Jewish catacombs of Rome, see Williams, "Image and Text in the Jewish Epitaphs" (see endnote 135), pp. 346–349 (Appendix 1). The absence of the incense shovel indicates that the iconography relates to the synagogue rather than to the Temple.

140 See Leon, *Jews of Ancient Rome* (see endnote 117), plate XV, fig. 24, for a clear example of menorah marking an anonymous grave.

141 On the possible explanations for this (e.g., religious scruple, artistic licence, sheer sloppiness), see S. Fine, *Art and Judaism in the Greco-Roman World: Toward a New Jewish Archaeology*, rev. ed. (Cambridge: Cambridge University Press, 2010), p. 155.

142 For some examples, see Williams, "Image and Text in the Jewish Epitaphs" (see endnote 135), Appendix 1 under "uncertain object."

143 See P.C. Finney, *The Invisible God: The Earliest Christians on Art* (Oxford: Oxford University Press, 1994), pp. 256–262, figs. 6.87, 6.88, 6.90 and 6.93; and R. Hachlili, *Ancient Jewish Art and Archaeology in the Diaspora* (Leiden: Brill, 1998), color plates VI-10 and VI-15.

144 *JIWE*, vol. 2, plate XIV (illustration of no. 331).

145 L.I. Levine ("The History and Significance of the Menorah in Antiquity," in *From Dura to Sepphoris: Studies in Jewish Art and Society in Late Antiquity*, eds. L. Levine and Z. Weiss, JRA Supplement Series 40 [Portsmouth, RI: JRA, 2000], pp. 131–153) has a useful summary of the most popular recent interpretations at pp. 147–148.

146 For the former, an interpretation omitted from Levine's list, see M.H. Williams, "The Menorah in a Sepulchral Context—A Protective (Apotropaic) Symbol?" in *The Image and Its Prohibition in Jewish Antiquity*, ed. S. Pearce, JJS Supplements (Leiden: Brill, 2013).

147 Williams, "Image and Text in the Jewish Epitaphs" (see endnote 135), pp. 349–350 (Appendix 2).

148 Philo, *Embassy to Gaius* 156–157 (time of Augustus).

149 M.H. Williams, "The Shaping of the Identity of the Jewish Community in Rome in Antiquity,"

in *Christians as a Religious Minority in a Multi-cultural City: Modes of Interaction and Identity Formation in Early Imperial Rome*, eds. J. Zangenberg and M. Labahn (London: T & T Clark, 2004), pp. 33–46.

[150] Whereas only a handful of Jewish examples are found at Rome, Solin lists more than 100 from the Christian catacombs there. See H. Solin, *Die Griechische Personennamen in Rom: Ein Namenbuch*, 2nd ed., vol. 3 (Berlin: de Gruyter, 2003), pp. 1282–1284.

[151] Of the handful of examples listed at *JIWE*, vol. 2, pp. 540–541 (Index VI: Dates), one is not from Rome (no. 564) and two (nos. 401 and 530) are considered by some scholars to be Christian rather than Jewish. The latter (*JIWE*, vol. 2, no. 530) was not actually found in a Jewish catacomb but on the Via Flaminia.

[152] Witness the tiny amount of space given to the Jewish fresco material in Finney's study of early Christian art (*Invisible God* [see endnote 143]), in which they rate only a brief appendix (pp. 247–263).

[153] For Jonah as a symbol of resurrection, see the words attributed to Jesus at Matthew 12:39–40. For the popularity of his story in early Christian catacomb art, see R.M. Jensen, *Understanding Early Christian Art* (London: Routledge, 2000), pp. 69 and 172–174.

[154] Jensen (ibid., pp. 167–171) notes that one of the earliest examples comes from the catacomb of Callistus (early third century C.E.).

[155] See "Persecution," in *Encyclopedia of Early Christianity* (see endnote 34).

[156] For this understanding of these tales, see Jensen, *Understanding Early Christian Art* (see endnote 153), pp. 79–84 and 174–175. Also extremely popular was the story of the binding of Isaac by Abraham, in which the former was saved from sacrifice through the latter's faith in God. See Jensen (pp. 143–145) who notes, however, that other interpretations of this tale are possible.

[157] See the table of Greek epithets at Rutgers, *Jews in Late Ancient Rome* (see endnote 114), pp. 192–193. There are no occurrences in Jewish epitaphs.

[158] *The Ways That Never Parted: Jews and Christians in Late Antiquity and the Early Middle Ages*, eds. A.H. Becker and A.Y. Reed (Tübingen: Mohr Siebeck, 2003).

[159] Only the name Anastasios, for which see *JIWE*, vol. 2, references in endnote 134 above, and the adoption (three instances only) of the popular Christian epithet *agapetos* (beloved). On this, see Rutgers's table in *Jews in Late Ancient Rome* (see endnote 114), pp. 192–193.

[160] I would like to thank my colleague, Dr. Sara Parvis, for several stimulating discussions prior to the writing of this chapter.

IX. Christianity's Rise After Judaism's Demise in Early Egypt

[1] On the origins of Christianity in Egypt in general, see Adolph Harnack, *Mission and Expansion of Christianity in the First Three Centuries*, trans. James Moffatt (London: Williams & Norgate, 1908); and Walter Bauer, *Orthodoxy and Heresy in Earliest Christianity*, trans. and eds. Robert Kraft and Gerhard Kroedel (Philadelphia: Fortress Press, 1971). In some ways, treating Alexandria and "Egypt" together can be misleading, since representatives of the former often proudly distinguished themselves from the "Egyptians." But with our present state of knowledge, and for the topic at hand, this otherwise important nuance does not seem to be sufficiently significant to merit close attention. Similarly, for present purposes we are not attempting to draw fine definitional lines between "Judaism" and/or "Christianity" as identifiable communities in the Egyptian world, and individual "Jews" and/or "Christians" who lived there. That is, the presence of isolated individual Jews or Christians would not in itself establish the presence of Judaism or Christianity as social entities. And, indeed, it cannot be taken for granted that every identifiable Jew (or Christian) would be in essential agreement with every other—it is clear that there were different types (groups) within these general categories, upon which we tend to impose our artificially unifying terms.

[2] On the rebellion(s) in 115–117 C.E., see especially Joseph Mélèze-Modrzejewski, *The Jews of Egypt: From Rameses II to Emperor Hadrian*, trans. Robert Cornman (Philadelphia: JPS, 1995), and Mélèze-Modrzejewski's subsequent 1987 and 1989 articles in French cited by Bagnall (see endnote 4), p. 353.

[3] See Colette Sirat, *Les papyrus en caractères hébraïques trouvés en Egypte* (avec la contribution de M. Beit-Arié, M. Dukan, F. Klein-Franke, H. Harrauer. Calligraphie et illustration par A. Yardeni) (Paris: CNRS, 1985). On a marriage contract from Antinoopolis published in 1986, Sirat says: "It was a magnificent papyrus rotulus (a roll written across the narrow dimension) in Hebrew characters, some 80 cm [32 in] long and 30 cm [12 in] wide. For a papyrus, the 27 lines of text were well preserved. It turned out to be a Jewish marriage contract written in the year 417 C.E. in Antinoopolis, Egypt. The first four and a half lines are in Greek; the rest is Aramaic" (in Colette Sirat et al., *La Ketouba de Cologne: Un contrat de mariage juif à Antinoopolis*, Papyrologica Coloniensia 12 [Opladen: Westdeutscher Verlag, 1986]). See also Eldon Jay Epp, "The Jews and the Jewish Community in Oxyrhynchus: Socio-Religious Context for the New Testament Papyri," in *New Testament Manuscripts: Their Texts and Their World*, eds. Thomas J. Kraus and Tobias Nicklas, Texts and Editions for New Testament Study 2 (Leiden: Brill, 2006), pp. 13–52; and A. Kasher, "The Jewish Community of Oxyrhynchus in the Roman Period." *JJS* 32 (1981), pp. 151–157.

[4] Roger S. Bagnall, *Egypt in Late Antiquity* (Princeton, NJ: Princeton University Press, 1993, with subsequent corrected reprints), pp. 275–276, 278.

[5] See David T. Runia, *Philo in Early Christian Literature: A Survey*, Compendia Rerum Iudaicarum ad Novum Testamentum 3.3 (Minneapolis: Fortress Press, 1993).

[6] Eusebius, *Ecclesiastical History* 2.17.

[7] See Jean Riaud, "Les Thérapeutes d'Alexandrie dans la tradition et dans la recherche critique jusqu'aux découvertes de Qumran," *Aufstieg und Niedergang der Romischen Welt* 2.20.2 (1987), pp. 1189–1295; and Sabrina Inowlocki, "Eusebius of Caesarea's *Interpretatio Christiana* of Philo's *De*

vita contemplativa," *HTR* 97 (2004), pp. 305–328. See further, Joan E. Taylor, *Jewish Women Philosophers of First Century Alexandria: Philo's 'Therapeutae' Reconsidered* (Oxford: Oxford University Press, 2006).

[8] There is no supporting evidence that Philo and Peter ever met.

[9] On the Epistle of Barnabas, see R. Kraft, *Barnabas and the Didache*, vol. 3, *The Apostolic Fathers: A New Translation and Commentary*, ed. Robert M. Grant (New York: Nelson & Sons, 1965).

[10] Barnabas preached in Rome and Alexandria according to the Clementine *Recognitions* 1.7–11 and the Clementine *Homilies* 1.9–14.

[11] So Eusebius, *Ecclesiastical History* 2.16.

[12] So Tertullian, *On Modesty [De Pudicitia]* 20 (as well as other later writers).

[13] See, for instance, Jörg Frey, "Zur Vielgestaltigkeit judenchristlicher Evangelienüberlieferungen," in *Jesus in apokryphen Evangelienüberlieferungen*, eds. J. Frey and J. Schröter (Tübingen: Mohr Siebeck, 2010), pp. 115–118 (116: "eine Herkunft aus dem alexandrinischen Judenchristentum").

[14] Bauer, *Orthodoxy and Heresy in Earliest Christianity* (see endnote 1).

[15] See Annewies van den Hoek, *Clement of Alexandria and His Use of Philo in the Stromateis: An Early Christian Reshaping of a Jewish Model*, VC Supplements 3 (Leiden: Brill, 1988).

[16] See Nicholas deLange, *Origen and the Jews: Studies in Jewish-Christian Relations in Third Century Palestine* (Cambridge: Cambridge University Press, 1977), p. 67: "We know hardly anything of Judaism in Alexandria at this time, and any information Origen could offer would be most welcome. He knew the city well, having been born and brought up there, and having lived there for the greater part of his life. In the works produced before he left Alexandria there are some interesting remarks about Jews and Judaism. What is to be made of these?" in view of the fact that after 117 C.E., "Jewish community life appears to have come to an end and the power of the Jews in Alexandria was destroyed." Origen continued

to consult with Jewish informants in Caesarea and along the way he obtained copies of various Jewish Greek translations of Scriptures (Aquila, Symmachus, Theodotion et al.). See the theory developed by D. Barthélemy on this subject (in R. Kraft, "Reassessing the Impact of Barthélemy's *Devanciers*, 40 years later," *Bulletin of the International Society for Septuagint Studies* 37 [2005], n. 21). On Origen's activities in Caesarea, see also Anthony Grafton and Megan Williams, *Christianity and the Transformation of the Book: Origen, Eusebius, and the Library of Caesarea* (Cambridge, MA: Harvard University Press, 2006).

[17] On "Jewish" traditions in "Gnostic" materials, see Birger A. Pearson, *Gnosticism, Judaism, and Egyptian Christianity*, Studies in Antiquity and Christianity (Minneapolis: Fortress Press, 1990, reissued with new preface 2006).

[18] According to the nearly contemporaneous fifth-century church historian Socrates (*Ecclesiastical History* 7.13), the following took place: Many Jews attended performances in the theater on the Sabbath. Since these gatherings were prone to disorderly behavior, Orestes, the prefect, attempted to regulate them. The Christians sent an observer, a certain Hierax, whom the Jews suspected of instigating trouble. Orestes had Hierax tortured in the theater. This infuriated Cyril, who summoned the leaders of the Jews and threatened them with expulsion. In reaction to Cyril's intimidation, however, the Jews attacked Christians at night, luring them out of their homes by means of a false fire alarm.

[19] Christopher J. Haas, *Alexandria in Late Antiquity: Topography and Social Conflict* (Baltimore: Johns Hopkins University Press, 1997), p. 299; for the context in general, see especially his chapter 4, "The Jewish Community," pp. 91–127. As Haas remarks, "Cyril's opposition to the Jewish community grew out of his exegesis of scripture" (p. 308, see also pp. 300–301).

[20] *Festal Letter One* 5.45; see also Haas, *Alexandria in Late Antiquity* (see endnote 19), p. 300.

[21] Socrates, *Ecclesiastical History* 7.13. See also Haas, *Alexandria in Late Antiquity*, pp. 299–304.

[22] Ibid., p. 304.

[23] The earliest surviving account is found in Josephus, *War* 7.10, which also tells of the flight of Palestinian Jewish rebels to Alexandria and Thebes in the wake of the destruction of the Jerusalem Temple in 70 C.E. See further Allen Kerkeslager, "The Jews in Egypt and Cyrenaica, 66–c. 235," in *The Cambridge History of Judaism*, vol. 4, *The Late Roman-Rabbinic Period*, ed. Steven T. Katz (Cambridge: Cambridge University Press, 2006), pp. 53–67.

[24] For a collection of these documents, see Victor A. Tcherikover and Alexander Fuks, *Corpus Papyrorum Judaicarum (CPJ)*, 3 vols. (Cambridge, MA: Harvard University Press, 1957–1964). Tcherikover used onomastics as an important criterion for identifying Jews in documentary texts (*CPJ* 1, xvii), see also endnote 29 below. On identifying Christians in papyrus documents, see AnneMarie Luijendijk, *Greetings in the Lord: Early Christians and the Oxyrhynchus Papyri*, Harvard Theological Studies 60 (Cambridge, MA: Harvard University Press, 2008), pp. 25–55.

[25] See Joseph van Haelst, *Catalogue des papyrus littéraires juifs et chrétiens* (Paris: Sorbonne 1976); and R. Kraft, "Connecting the Dots: Early Jewish and Early Christian Greek Evidence in Context" (http://ccat.sas.upenn.edu/rak//temp/Connect-Dots.html), and the materials referenced there.

[26] See Kurt Treu, "The Significance of Greek for Jews in the Roman Empire," *Kairos* 15 (1973), pp. 123–144, trans. William Adler and (http://ccat.sas.upenn.edu/rak//publics/notrak/Treu.htm), (the excursus "On the Question of Greek Bible Manuscripts of Jewish Origin" is especially relevant here). Note also the surviving fragments of a third-century codex of some of Philo's writings [= van Haelst #695–696], described in detail by James R. Royse, "The Oxyrhynchus Papyrus of Philo," *Bulletin of the American Society of Papyrologists* 17 (1980), pp. 155–165, which also preserved some discarded Christian gospel fragments used as cover stiffener—who created such a cover is unclear (Jewish, Christian or unaffiliated bookmaker).

[27] P.Oxy 9.1205 dated 14 April 291 C.E. records a manumission *inter amicos*: The Jewish community (συναγωγή) of Oxyrhynchus manumitted a Jewish slave woman named Paramone together with two or three of her

children for the large amount of 14 silver talents. One important implication of this document is that by the end of the third century a Jewish community in Egypt had the financial means to afford such a transaction.

28 See Sirat, *papyrus en caractères hébraïques* (see endnote 3); also A.E. Cowley, "Notes on Hebrew Papyrus Fragments from Oxyrhynchus," *Journal of Egyptian Archaeology* 2 (1915), pp. 209–213 (plates xxvii-xxix) = *Corpus Papyrorum Judaicarum* 1. 101–102; and Mark Harding, "§11. A Hebrew Congregational Prayer from Egypt," *New Documents Illustrating Early Christianity* 8 (1984–1985), pp. 145–147.

29 Roger S. Bagnall, "Conversion and Onomastics: A Reply," *Zeitschrift für Papyrologie und Epigraphik* 69 (1987), pp. 243–250, "Religious Conversion and Onomastic Change in Early Byzantine Egypt," *Bulletin of the American Society of Papyrologists* 19 (1982), pp. 105–124; Ewa Wipszycka, "La valeur de l'onomastique pour l'histoire de la christianisation de l'Égypte: À propos d'une étude de R. S. Bagnall," *Zeitschrift für Papyrologie und Epigraphik* 62 (1986), pp. 173–181. More generally, see now Tal Ilan, *Lexicon of Jewish Names in Late Antiquity*, 4 vols. (Tübingen: Mohr Siebeck, 2002–2011).

30 P. Oxy. 44.3203. See G. Horsley, *New Documents Illustrating Early Christianity*, vol. 1 (North Ryde, NSW: Macquarie University, 1976), #82; and Epp, "Jews and Jewish Community in Oxyrhynchus" (see endnote 3), pp. 43–46. The nuns are described as "apotactic," which probably refers to their renunciation of certain undesirable practices; it could also be a group name ("the renouncers").

31 Roberts's theory is repeated in his *Manuscript, Society and Belief in Early Christian Egypt* (Oxford: Oxford University Press [for the British Academy], 1979), p. 24, n. 5. A useful discussion of this particular fragment, P. Oxy. 17.2070, may be found in Eldon J. Epp's "The Oxyrhynchus New Testament Papyri: 'Not Without Honor Except in Their Hometown'?" *JBL* 123 (2004), pp. 40–42; see also Luijendijk's *Greetings in the Lord* (see endnote 24), p. 150, n. 98. For a convenient if dated survey of such dialogue materials, see A. Lukyn Williams, *Adversos Judaeos: A Bird's-Eye View of Christian Apologiae until the Renaissance* (Cambridge: Cambridge University Press,

1935). Note that the lamentably lost "Dialogue of Jason and Papiscus" might be relevant to this discussion, with Papiscus identified as an Alexandrian Greek Jew in one source.

32 On the Christian palimpsests, see Michael Sokoloff and Joseph Yahalom, "Christian Palimpsests from the Cairo Geniza," *Revue d'Histoire des Textes* 8 (1978), pp. 107–132, following on older studies such as Charles Taylor, *Hebrew-Greek Cairo Genizah Palimpsests from the Taylor-Schechter Collection Including a Fragment of the Twenty-Second Psalm According to Origen's Hexapla* (Cambridge: Cambridge University Press, 1900); and Agnes S. Lewis and Margaret D. Gibson, *Palestinian Syriac Texts from Palimpsest Fragments in the Taylor-Schechter Collection* (London: C.J. Clay, 1900). On the Cairo Geniza materials in general, see Stefan C. Reif, *A Jewish Archive from Old Cairo: The History of Cambridge University's Genizah Collection* (Richmond, Surrey: Curzon, 2000), and also *The Cambridge Genizah Collections: Their Contents and Significance,* ed. S. Reif, Cambridge University Library Genizah series 1 (Cambridge: Cambridge University Press, 2002). On differences in treatment of remains of sacred texts, see also AnneMarie Luijendijk, "Sacred Scriptures as Trash: Biblical Papyri from Oxyrhynchus" *VC* 64 (2010), pp. 217–254.

33 It is widely reported that the Coptic authorities sold the Old Cairo (Fustat) Church dedicated to the Archangel Michael to Jews in 882 C.E., although a few modern sources claim an earlier date. The first major period of Jewish documents in the Geniza dates from the tenth through the 13th centuries. The reused Christian materials date from the fifth to the ninth centuries.

34 On repurposing manuscripts, see Mauro Perani (Perugia Exhibit): "It was commercial factors that determined the movement of parchment books for reuse which were sold by second hand dealers over distances of hundreds of kilometers, thereby often leaving in a binder's store in one region, parts of books bought for reuse in another" (http://documentiebraici. unipg.it/galleriaENG.php).

X. Ebionites and Nazoraeans: Christians or Jews?

[1] For a helpful sociological analysis of sect movements, see Rodney Stark and William Sims Bainbridge, *The Future of Religion: Secularization, Revival, and Cult Formation* (Berkeley: University of California Press, 1985), pp. 19–26, 99–167.

[2] For a treatment of "cults" in the more neutral, sociological sense of new religions, see ibid., pp. 24–36, 171–303.

[3] For a helpful entrée into this issue, see the collection of essays in *The Ways That Never Parted: Jews and Christians in Late Antiquity and the Early Middle Ages*, eds. Adam H. Becker and Annette Yoshiko Reed (Minneapolis: Fortress Press, 2007).

[4] On the matter of archaeological evidence, see the general analytical survey in James F. Strange, "Archaeological Evidence for Jewish Believers?" in *Jewish Believers in Jesus: The Early Centuries*, eds. Oskar Skarsaune and Reidar Hvalvik (Peabody, MA: Hendrickson, 2007), pp. 710–741. On the question of literary remains, see below.

[5] See especially *Against Heresies* 1.26.2, but also 3.11.7, 3.21, 4.33.4 and 5.1.3. For a convenient collection of these and other passages from Irenaeus, see *Patristic Evidence for Jewish-Christian Sects*, eds. A.F.J. Klijn and G.J. Reinink, Supplements to Novum Testamentum 36 (Leiden: Brill, 1973), pp. 105–107.

[6] *Against Heresies* 1.26, *iudaico charactere vitae*; for text and translation here and in the remainder of this paragraph, see Klijn and Reinink, *Patristic Evidence* (see endnote 5), pp. 104–105. On Ebionite Christology, see further below; and on Cerinthus, see Matti Myllykoski, "Cerinthus," in *A Companion to Second-Century "Heretics,"* eds. A. Marjanen and P. Luomanen, VC Supplements 76 (Leiden: Brill, 2005), pp. 213–246; also Gunnar af Hällström and Oskar Skarsaune, "Cerinthus, Elxai, and Other Alleged Jewish Christian Teachers or Groups," in *Jewish Believers in Jesus* (see endnote 4), pp. 488–502, esp. 488–495.

[7] It is frequently assumed that Irenaeus depends on a prior written source rather than personal knowledge. Sakari Häkkinen suggests he had a re-worked version of Justin's *Syntagma*; see his "Ebionites," in *A Companion to Second-Century "Heretics"* (see endnote 6), pp. 247–278, here 250–251.

[8] For recent evaluations of the patristic sources, see James Carleton Paget, "The Ebionites in Recent Research," in *Jews, Christians and Jewish Christians in Antiquity*, WUNT 251 (Tübingen: Mohr Siebeck, 2010), pp. 325–379, esp. 327–343; Edwin K. Broadhead, *Jewish Ways of Following Jesus*, WUNT 266 (Tübingen: Mohr Siebeck, 2010), pp. 188–212; Oskar Skarsaune, "The Ebionites," in *Jewish Believers in Jesus* (see endnote 4), pp. 419–462, esp. 423–424; Häkkinen, "Ebionites" (see endnote 7), pp. 248–258; Klijn and Reinink, *Patristic Evidence* (see endnote 5), pp. 19–43.

[9] Irenaeus, *Against Heresies* 1.26.1–3.

[10] Origen's references to the Ebionites are found in Klijn and Reinink, *Patristic Evidence* (see endnote 5), pp. 125–135. The apparently exceptional reference to "Ebion" is found only in the Latin rendering of what would have been Origen's Greek in *Commentary on Romans* 3.11 (p. 133), and so may have been introduced by the translator as Häkkinen suggests ("Ebionites" [see endnote 7], p. 254, n. 20).

[11] See the passages from Eusebius collected in Klijn and Reinink, *Patristic Evidence* (see endnote 5), pp. 136–151.

[12] It is striking that Tertullian, around the turn of the third century, already speaks only of Ebion as a teacher rather than of Ebionites as a group; see the passages collected in Klijn and Reinink, *Patristic Evidence* (see endnote 5), pp. 107–111. Hippolytus mentions Ebion in *Refutation of All Heresies* 7.35.1 but otherwise speaks collectively of Ebionites (*Refutation of All Heresies* Prologue 7.8, 7.34.1, 10.22.1); cf. Klijn and Reinink, *Patristic Evidence* (see endnote 5), pp. 111–123.

[13] This point is generally recognized in the recent scholarly literature; see, for example, Paget, "The Ebionites in Recent Research" (see endnote 8), pp. 344–349, and further Skarsaune, "Ebionites" (see endnote 8), pp. 419–421. On the actual derivation of the name "Ebionites," see below.

[14] Epiphanius, *Panarion* 30.1.1–3, citing no less than seven different heretical groups in this connection. All translations of the *Panarion* come from Frank Williams, *The Panarion of Epiphanius of Salamis: Book I (Sects 1–46)*, Nag Hammadi and Manichaean Studies 35 (Leiden: Brill, 1987). Greek citations are taken from Karl Holl, *Epiphanius. Erster Band: Ancoratus und Panarion Haer. 1–33* (Leipzig: Hinrchs, 1915).

[15] The information about the group's origins is found in *Panarion* 30.2.7–9; cf. 30.1.1: "He was of the Nazoraeans's school, but preached and taught differently from them." Ebion's subsequent activity in Asia and Rome is reported in 30.18.1.

[16] See Eusebius, *Ecclesiastical History* 3.5; cf. Häkkinen, "Ebionites" (see endnote 7), p. 274. Indeed, Eusebius knows nothing at all about a heretical sect called "Nazoraeans."

[17] Certainly such a story would have been consistent with the group's reported veneration of Jerusalem (Irenaeus, *Against Heresies* 1.26.2). Note also, however, the analogous legend developed around Jericho in the source underlying the Pseudo-Clementine *Recognitions* 1.27–71; see esp. *Recognitions* 1.71.2–6, and on the source more generally F. Stanley Jones, *An Ancient Jewish Christian Source on the History of Christianity: Pseudo-Clementine Recognitions 1.27–71*, SBL Texts and Translations Series 37 (Atlanta: Scholars Press, 1995). This latter legend would be all the more significant if the Pseudo-Clementine literature, as Epiphanius would have it, is to be assigned to the Ebionites. That, however, is a big if. See below.

[18] See Eusebius's report of a village called Choba "in which live those Hebrews who believed in Christ, called Ebionites" (*Onomasticon*, p. 172, 1–3 [=Klijn and Reinink, *Patristic Evidence* (see endnote 5)], pp. 150–151); further Häkkinen, "Ebionites" (see endnote 7), pp. 272–275; Klijn and Reinink, *Patristic Evidence* (see endnote 5), p. 29.

[19] Irenaeus, *Against Heresies* 1.26.1–2; cf. Pseudo-Tertullian, *Against All Heresies* 3, which following Irenaeus, styles Ebion as a "successor" of Cerinthus. Apparently so interchangeable are these heresies in the mind of Epiphanius, in fact, that a long-traded story about an incident involving the apostle John and Cerinthus in a bathhouse becomes in his account a story about John and Ebion; compare Epiphanius, *Panarion* 30.24.1–7 with Irenaeus, *Against Heresies* 3.4 and Eusebius, *Ecclesiastical History* 4.14.6. Conversely, this juxtaposition also seems to have led to an increasing attribution of Ebionite-like traits to Cerinthus in the developing heresiological tradition; see Myllykoski, "Cerinthus" (see endnote 6); and Hällström and Skarsaune, "Cerinthus, Elxai, and Other Alleged Jewish Christian Teachers or Groups" (see endnote 6), pp. 488–495.

[20] Epiphanius, *Panarion* 30.1.1–3; cf. the very ambiguous connection drawn between the Nazoraeans and the Cerinthians in 29.1.1.

[21] See further on the Nazoraeans below.

[22] We glimpse Epiphanius's general method when we find him openly speculating that the cause of such "conflicting accounts of Christ" between Ebion on one hand and his later followers on the other "may be ... because Elxai–the false prophet ... was connected with them" (*Panarion* 30.3.1–2). Note that this speculation is subsequently treated as fact in 30.17.5–8. As it happens, this Elxai is probably as much a legendary invention as Ebion himself; see Hällström and Skarsaune, "Cerinthus, Elxai, and Other Alleged Jewish Christian Teachers or Groups" (see endnote 6), pp. 496–501; and further Gerard Luttikuizen, "Elchasaites and Their Book," in *A Companion to Second-Century Heretics* (see endnote 6), pp. 335–364.

[23] On marriage, see *Panarion* 30.2. Regarding the Jewish scriptures, compare Epiphanius's report (e.g., *Panarion* 30.18.4–9) regarding the Ebionite rejection of prophets after Moses and cursing of David with earlier indications of an Ebionite Christology that included a Davidic genealogy of Jesus; see Tertullian, *On the Flesh of Christ* 14, and further Skarsaune, "Ebionites" (see endnote 8), pp. 431–434.

[24] For more skeptical positions, see Klijn and Reinink, *Patristic Evidence* (see endnote 5), pp. 28–38, 43; Skarsaune, "Ebionites" (see endnote 8), pp. 423–424; more trusting of Epiphanius in this respect are, for example, Petri Luomanen, "Ebionites and Nazarenes," in *Jewish Christianity Reconsidered*, ed. M. Jackson-McCabe

(Philadelphia: Fortress Press, 2007), pp. 85–102; and Simon Claude Mimouni, *Les Chrétiens d'Origine Juive dans l'Antiquité* (Paris: Albin Michel, 2004), pp. 161–194.

[25] Despite this, a number of scholars display a remarkable confidence in the basic outlines of Epiphanius's account, identifying the Ebionites as a group that separated with the Nazoraeans; so, for example, Mimouni, *Les Chrétiens d'Origine Juive* (see endnote 24), pp. 176–178; cf. A. Pritz, *Nazarene Jewish Christianity* (Jerusalem: Hebrew University Magnes Press, 2010), pp. 37–39. The most recent and elaborate reconstruction of Ebionite history is found in the recent works of Petri Luomanen in *Recovering Jewish-Christian Sects and Gospels*, VC Supplements 110 (Leiden: Brill, 2012), pp. 44–49; and "Ebionites and Nazarenes" (see endnote 24), pp. 81–118, esp. 99–102. See, however, the sobering comments in Paget, "Ebionites in Recent Research" (see endnote 8), pp. 361–374.

[26] See Origen, *Commentariorum series in evangelium Matthaei* 79; Pseudo-Tertullian, *Against All Heresies* 3; and Epiphanius, *Panarion* 30.26.2 and 30.33.4–30.34.5; further Skarsaune, "Ebionites" (see endnote 8), pp. 438–439; Broadhead, *Jewish Ways* (see endnote 8), pp. 211–212.

[27] For example, Irenaeus, *Against Heresies* 1.26.2; Origen, *Homilies on Jeremiah* 19.12; *Against Celsus* 5.66; Epiphanius, *Panarion* 30.16.8–9 and 30.25.1–14. Tertullian, conversely, sees Paul arguing against both the practice (*Prescription Against Heretics* 32.2–5) and the Christology (*Prescription Against Heretics* 32.11; cf. *On the Veiling of Virgins* 6.1) of "Ebion."

[28] Note that while heresiologists call, for example, those who follow Cerinth "Cerinthians" or Marcion "Marcionites" or Valentinus "Valentinians," etc., they do not generally follow this convention for their own group: They do not typically call themselves, say, "Paulists," but "Christians," i.e., simply those who follow Christ—which claim, if not which name, each of these other groups no doubt would also have made for themselves. The invention of a founder of the Ebionites called "Ebion" is an inversion of this rhetorical strategy.

[29] *Panarion* 30.1.5.

[30] *Panarion* 30.1.4. Cf. Jerome's strategy for dealing with the Nazoraeans: "since they want to be both Jews and Christians, they are neither Jews nor Christians" (*Epistles* 112.13). Interestingly, Jerome's rhetoric is different regarding Ebion, whom he calls *semi-Christianus et semi-Judaeus* but in any case all *haeresiarches*! See *Commentary on Galatians* 3.13–14 (Klijn and Reinink, *Patristic Evidence* [see endnote 5], pp. 204–205).

[31] Epiphanius, *Panarion* 30.1.3; cf. Origen, *Against Celsus* 5.61, which portrays them "boasting to be Christians" [*Christianoi einai auchountes*] (text from Klijn and Reinink, *Patristic Evidence* [see endnote 5], p. 134); cf. Eusebius's explanation of the group's rise with reference to the same "evil *daimon*" that inspired "sorcerers" like Simon Magus to adopt the name "Christian" in order "to destroy the teaching of the Church" (*Ecclesiastical History* 3.26.4–3.27.1). All citations of Eusebius's *Ecclesiastical History* are taken from the Loeb edition (trans. K. Lake) unless otherwise noted.

[32] Eusebius, *Ecclesiastical History* 3.27.1.

[33] Cf. Origen, *On First Principles* 4.3.8; *Homilies on Genesis* 3.5; *Commentary on Matthew* 16.12; cf. Epiphanius, *Panarion* 30.17.1–3. Note that this etymology occurs in the early sources that don't refer to a founder called Ebion; but see endnote 35 below on Epiphanius.

[34] Cf. Acts 4:32–37.

[35] Richard Bauckham, "The Origin of the Ebionites," in *The Image of the Judaeo-Christians in Ancient Jewish and Christian Literature*, eds. Peter J. Tomson and Doris Lambers-Petry, WUNT 158 (Tübingen: Mohr Siebeck, 2003), pp. 162–181, here 177–178; Skarsaune, "Ebionites" (see endnote 8), p. 452. Epiphanius suggests that "the poor, wretched [Ebion] got the name from his father and mother by prophecy."

[36] Skarsaune, "Ebionites" (see endnote 8), p. 425; further Paget, "Ebionites in Recent Research" (see endnote 8), pp. 344–349. Bauckham ("Origin of the Ebionites" [see endnote 35], pp. 177–180) points out the particular connection between this idea and eschatological inheritance of the covenantal land.

[37] See 4QpPs[alms]a 2.9–12 (on Psalm 37:11): "And the poor shall inherit the land ... Its interpretation concerns the congregation of the poor who will tolerate the period of distress and will be rescued from the snares of Belial. Afterwards, all who shall inherit the land will enjoy and grow fat with everything..."; cf. 3:10 (on Psalm 37:21–22): ... "Its interpretation concerns the congregation of the poor [for them is] the inheritance of the whole world"; translations from Florentino García Martinez, *The Dead Sea Scrolls Translated* (Leiden: Brill, 1994). See further Bauckham, "Origin of the Ebionites" (see endnote 35), p. 179.

[38] For a recent analysis of this long-standing issue, see Paget, "Ebionites in Recent Research" (see endnote 8), pp. 345–346.

[39] For example, Matthew 5:3; James 2:5; but also Luke 4:16–19.

[40] Note, for example, Epiphanius's comment on the Nazoraeans: "these sectarians ... did not ... keep the name 'Jews' ... but [took] 'Nazoraeans' ... However they are simply complete Jews" (*Panarion* 29.7.1, translation slightly modified); and again at the close of his discussion in 29.9.1: "my brief discussion [of the Nazoraeans] will be enough. People like these are refutable at once and easy to cure—or rather, they are nothing but Jews [*kai Ioudaioi mallon kai ouden heteron*]."

[41] Pseudo-Tertullian, *Against All Heresies* 2; text and translation in Klijn and Reinink, *Patristic Evidence* (see endnote 5), pp. 124–125; cf. Jerome, *Commentary on Daniel* prologue (Klijn and Reinink, *Patristic Evidence* [see endnote 5], pp. 218–219), which clarifies "Ebionite" as referring to "another kind of Jew" (*Ebionitam, qui altero genere Iudaeus est*).

[42] Origen, *Against Celsus* 2.1 (Klijn and Reinink, *Patristic Evidence* [see endnote 5], pp. 134–135), *Ebiônaioi chrêmatizousin hoi apo Ioudaiôn ton Iêsoun hôs christon paradexamenoi*; cf. in the same passage "those from the Jews who believe in Jesus" [*hoi apo Ioudaiôn eis ton Iêsoun pisteountes*], with which compare also *Commentary on Matthew* 16.12.

[43] Eusebius, *Onomasticon* p. 138, 24–25 (=Klijn and Reinink, *Patristic Evidence* [see endnote 5], pp. 150–151), *Hebraiôn hoi eis Christon pisteusantes, Ebiônaioi kaloumenoi*.

[44] Epiphanius, *Panarion* 30.1.5: "And while professing to be a Jew, he is the opposite of Jews—though he does agree with them in part [*Ioudaion de heauton homologôn Ioudaiois antikeitai, kaitoi sumphônôn autois en merei*]." Cf. Eusebius, *Demonstration of the Gospel* 7.1 (Klijn and Reinink, *Patristic Evidence* [see endnote 5], pp. 138–139), [Ebionites were] a heresy of some so-called Jews [*hairesis ... kaloumenôn tinôn Ioudaiôn*] who claim to believe in Christ." Note that Epiphanius pursues the opposite strategy with the Nazoraeans, arguing that they are "Jews and nothing else"; see above endnote 41 and further below.

[45] Origen, *On First Principles* 4.3.8, alluding to Romans 9:8.

[46] Epiphanius, *Panarion* 30.16.8–9, relating how Paul was said to be a son of Greek parents who became circumcised only after falling in love with the daughter of the high priest—and who subsequently became hostile to the law as a result of unrequited love; cf. the extensive refutation of the charge in *Panarion* 30.25.1–14. The story is not known from the Pseudo-Clementine literature or any other extant source; but compare Origen's unfortunately vague reference to the fact that "up to the present day the Ebionites strike [Paul] the Apostle of Jesus Christ with shameful words incited by the unlawful word of the high priest" (*Homilies on Jeremiah* 19.12, alluding to Acts 23:3 [Klijn and Reinink, *Patristic Evidence* (see endnote 5), pp. 126–129]).

[47] Thus, for example, the extensive account by Hans Joachim Schoeps, *Theologie und Geschichte des Judenchristentums* (Tübingen: Mohr Siebeck, 1949); and in a condensed English version, *Jewish Christianity: Factional Disputes in the Early Church* (Philadelphia: Fortress Press, 1969).

[48] Irenaeus, *Against Heresies* 1.26.2; Hippolytus, *Refutation of All Heresies* 7.8 and 7.34.1–2; Tertullian, *Prescription Against Heretics* 32.3–5; Pseudo-Tertullian, *Against All Heresies* 3; Origen, *Against Celsus* 2.1; *Commentary on Matthew* 11.12; Eusebius, *Ecclesiastical History* 3.27.3; cf. Epiphanius, *Panarion* 30.2.2.

[49] Circumcision: Irenaeus, *Against Heresies* 1.26.2; Origen, *Homilies on Genesis* 3.5; Tertullian, *Prescription Against Heretics* 32.3–5; Epiphanius,

Panarion 30.2.2 and more extensively 30.26.1–30.28.9 and 30.33.1–30.34.5; dietary restrictions: Origen, *Commentary on Matthew* 11.12; Sabbath and festivals: Origen, *Commentariorum series in evangelium Matthaei* 79; Eusebius, *Ecclesiastical History* 3.27.5; Epiphanius, *Panarion* 30.2.2; 30.34.5; reverence for Jerusalem: Irenaeus, *Against Heresies* 1.26.2.

[50] The situation is substantially different if we include elements of practice Epiphanius found in his supposed Ebionite texts: immersion for purposes of purification (*Panarion* 30.2.4–5; 30.15.3; 30.16.1), particularly in connection with sex (30.2.4)—an item he explicitly links to the *Periodoi Petrou* (*Panarion* 30.15.3); vegetarianism, which is also apparently associated with the *Periodoi Petrou* (*Panarion* 30.15.4; cf. 30.19.1–5 and 30.22.1–11); a rejection, in principle, of sacrifices, which he derives from their gospel and links further to the Ascents of James (*Panarion* 16.4–5, 7); and various (and, Epiphanius points out, conflicting) views on marriage and sexuality, referring to treatises addressed to "elders and virgins" on one hand (*Panarion* 30.2.6) and the *Periodoi Petrou* on the other (*Panarion* 30.15.2); cf. also the healing ritual apparently derived from the Book of Elchasai (*Panarion* 30.17.4). The source of his notice about restrictions placed by the group on contact with gentiles (*Panarion* 30.2.3) is not immediately clear but, as Williams points out, finds interesting analogies in the literature of the Dead Sea sect (*The Panarion of Epiphanius* [see endnote 14], p. 120, n. 5). Most of these items, notably, have clear points of contact with the extant Pseudo-Clementine literature; see the helpful notes throughout Williams's translation of *Panarion* 30 (ibid.), and further Klijn and Reinink, *Patristic Evidence* (see endnote 5), pp. 30–38.

[51] Eusebius, *Ecclesiastical History* 3.27.5.

[52] Irenaeus, *Against Heresies* 5.1.3; cf. Epiphanius, *Panarion* 30.16.1, who also refers in this connection to their use of unleavened bread, but seems to suggest an annual rather than weekly rite.

[53] Origen, *Against Celsus* 5.61, 65 (Klijn and Reinink, *Patristic Evidence* [see endnote 5], pp. 134–135); so also Eusebius, *Ecclesiastical History* 3.27, apparently having learned this from Origen.

[54] Origen, *Commentary on Matthew* 16.12, in this case apparently referring to their Christology in particular as the explanation of their name; cf. *Homiliae in Lucan* 17 (Klijn and Reinink, *Patristic Evidence* [see endnote 5], pp. 126–127), "The Hebionites ... [say] that [Jesus] was born of man and woman in the same way as we also are born"; further the text from *In Epistulam ad Titum* in Klijn and Reinink, *Patristic Evidence* (see endnote 5), pp. 132–133. Compare Eusebius, *Ecclesiastical History* 3.27.1

[55] Some have argued that Origen here reflects a distinction between Ebionites and Nazoraeans, mistakenly classifying the latter as a second type of Ebionite; so, for example, Pritz, *Nazarene Jewish Christianity* (see endnote 25), p. 21. Häkkinen ("Ebionites" [see endnote 7], p. 254) makes the more general (and more plausible) assumption that Origen simply "seems to have called all Jewish Christians Ebionites" at this point; cf. in this respect the provocative suggestion by Skarsaune, "Ebionites" (see endnote 8), pp. 419–423, that Origen (and Eusebius) were essentially correct to do so insofar as the whole idea of a distinct Ebionite sect was a heresiological invention to begin with, prompted by a more diffuse presence of a variety of Jewish Jesus people. This suggestion merits more detailed consideration than it can be given here; see though the appraisal in Paget, "Ebionites in Recent Research" (see endnote 8), pp. 348–349.

[56] Hippolytus, *Refutation of All Heresies* 7.34.2; Irenaeus, *Against Heresies* 3.21.1, 9; 4.33.4; Tertullian, *On the Veiling of Virgins* 6.1; *On the Flesh of Christ* 14; cf. Epiphanius, *Panarion* 30.2.2; 30.3.1; further 30.20.1–11 and *passim*.

[57] See especially Irenaeus, *Against Heresies* 3.21. Compare in this respect his comment regarding their "diligent" (so Klijn and Reinink) interpretation of the prophetic writings in 1.26.2 (*quae autem sunt prophetica, curiosius exponere nituntur*). Cf. Epiphanius, *Panarion* 30.20.1–11, though he, apparently drawing from supposedly Ebionite literature (cf. 30.15.2), notes derisively that "the misguided Ebionites are very unfortunate to have abandoned the testimonies of the prophets" (30.20.8). So associated with this

interpretation of Isaiah were the Ebionites that Symmachus may have come to be characterized as an Ebionite by the orthodox fathers simply on the basis of a translation of Isaiah along these lines; see Skarsaune, "Ebionites" (see endnote 8), pp. 448–449.

[58] This apparently is the point of Irenaeus's comparison of the Ebionites with Cerinthus; compare *Against Heresies* 1.26.2 and 1.26.1, and perhaps also the unfortunately ambiguous remarks in Hippolytus, *Refutation of All Heresies* 7.35.1–2; further Epiphanius, *Panarion* 30.29.1–11. Regarding the textual problem surrounding this key issue in *Against Heresies* 1.26.2, see the convincing treatment by Skarsaune, "Ebionites" (see endnote 8), p. 428; contrast Klijn and Reinink, *Patristic Evidence* (see endnote 5), pp. 19–20. I borrow the phrase "distinctly more than human" from Bruce Lincoln, *Holy Terrors: Thinking About Religion After September 11* (Chicago: University of Chicago Press, 2003), p. 55.

[59] For a critical survey of the current discussion, see Paget, "Ebionites in Recent Research" (see endnote 8), pp. 349–357.

[60] Hippolytus, *Refutation of All Heresies* 7.34.1–2, and further Skarsaune, "Ebionites" (see endnote 8), pp. 434–435; though note the cautionary remarks in Klijn and Reinink, *Patristic Evidence* (see endnote 5), pp. 22–23. Hippolytus characterizes the Ebionites further as believing that "they themselves, having done the same [i.e., observe the Torah], are able to become Christs"; but whether this represents their actual belief or Hippolytus's own mocking conclusion is not clear. Compare in this connection the Ebionite appeal to the imitation of Christ, on which see above. It is also conceivable that this belief about Jesus reflects some particular interpretation of the Torah attributed to Jesus himself—i.e., that no one else had previously observed the law because no one else knew its proper interpretation.

[61] Tertullian, *On the Flesh of Christ* 14; further Skarsaune, "Ebionites" (see endnote 8), pp. 431–434; cf. Irenaeus, *Against Heresies* 3.21.9, where Irenaeus's attempt to refute the Ebionite rejection of the virgin birth includes the rather remarkable argument that Matthew's Davidic genealogy of Joseph, because it runs through Jechoniah, is actually conveying a line of descent that is "disinherited" and "cursed," citing several passages from Jeremiah to prove his point. Irenaeus says that the Holy Spirit conveyed these statements about Jechoniah precisely to anticipate "the doctrines of the evil teachers" like the Ebionites.

[62] I use the term "possession" here with the same generic sense it has when used, for example, in the study of Israelite prophecy—not with Michael Goulder's more specific (and less than persuasive) thesis that the Ebionites distinguished the human Jesus from the spiritual being, "Christ," that possessed him; see Goulder, "A Poor Man's Christology," *NTS* 45 (1999), pp. 332–348; and further *St. Paul versus St. Peter: A Tale of Two Missions* (Louisville: Westminster/John Knox Press, 1994).

[63] See in this connection Tertullian's comment that, if Jesus were entirely human, "he would be nothing more than Solomon and Jonah, as in Ebion's opinion one had to believe" (*On the Flesh of Christ* 18 [Klijn and Reinink, *Patristic Evidence* (see endnote 5), pp. 110–111]). The juxtaposition of prophet and king here, however, seems to come from Irenaeus, *Against Heresies* 4.33.4, and may reflect nothing more than Irenaeus's attempt to refute the Ebionites out of their own gospel; cf. Matthew 12:41–42.

[64] The picture expands dramatically—and also becomes much more complex—if we accept as Ebionite the range of views found in the various texts Epiphanius considers Ebionite; see especially *Panarion* 30.3.1–6 and 30.16.2–5; further Klijn and Reinink, *Patristic Evidence* (see endnote 5), pp. 33–34; and more generally Luomanen, "Ebionites and Nazarenes" (see endnote 24), pp. 86–102.

[65] Epiphanius, *Panarion* 29.5.4 and 29.7.5.

[66] *Panarion* 29.7.7; on their use of Hebrew, see 29.7.4 and 29.9.4.

[67] The relevant passages are among those conveniently collected from Jerome's works in Klijn and Reinink, *Patristic Evidence* (see endnote 5), pp. 199–229. All citations of Jerome come from this collection unless otherwise noted.

[68] *Epistles* 112.13: "What shall I say of the Ebionites who claim to be Christians? Until now a heresy

is to be found in all parts of the East where Jews have their synagogues; it is called 'of the Minaeans' and cursed by the Pharisees up to now. Usually they are named Nazoraeans."

[69] Jerome, *Commentary on Isaiah* 8.11–15; cf. *Commentary on Ezekiel* 16.16: "the Nazoraeans who try to connect the observance of the Law with evangelical grace." While a number of modern interpreters emphasize that Jerome was less than entirely negative about the group, his classification of them as heresy is clear from both this latter passage (*Nazaraei ... et omnes haeretici*) and *Epistles* 112.13.

[70] Jerome, *On Illustrious Men* 3.

[71] Jerome, *Epistles* 112.13.

[72] Klijn and Reinink, *Patristic Evidence* (see endnote 5), pp. 44–46; most fully Pritz, *Nazarene Jewish Christianity* (see endnote 25), pp. 29–47, who assumes the existence of some source at least behind *Panarion* 29.7; so too Broadhead, *Jewish Ways* (see endnote 8), pp. 177–178, evidently repeating Pritz's analysis at this point.

[73] For example, Pritz, *Nazarene Jewish Christianity* (see endnote 25), pp. 49–53; cf. Klijn and Reinink, *Patristic Evidence* (see endnote 5), pp. 46–50. Most troubling here is Jerome's apparent willingness to freely invent both an apocryphal book of Jeremiah supposedly read by the Nazoraeans and "a Hebrew person of the Nazoraean sect" who had given it to him (*Commentary on Matthew* 27.9–10); see Pritz, ibid., pp. 56–57. Compare in this respect the claims Jerome makes regarding the Nazoraeans's gospel, on which see especially Luomanen, *Recovering Jewish-Christian Sects and Gospels* (see endnote 25), pp. 89–103.

[74] More than a century ago, Alfred Schmidtke (*Neue Fragmente und Untersuchungen zu den judenchristlichen Evangelien: Ein Beitrag zur Literatur und Geschichte der Judenchristen*, Texte und Untersuchungen zur Geschichte der altchristlichen Literatur 37.2 [Leipzig: Hinrichs, 1911]) argued that both Epiphanius and Jerome drew primarily on Apollinaris of Laodicaea for their knowledge of the group; cf. more recently Wolfram Kinzig, "The Nazoraeans," in *Jewish Believers in Jesus* (see endnote 4), pp. 464–465 and 474; and with caveats where the exegetical work on Isaiah is concerned, Pritz, *Nazarene*

Jewish Christianity (see endnote 25), pp. 50–51, 56–57, 60–61, 66–67.

[75] *Panarion* 29.7.3, 6, citing specifically Cerinthus and Merinthus; compare also his treatment of "Ebion" (if not his followers) in, for example, *Panarion* 30.2.2; 30.3.1; 30.20.1, etc., on which see above.

[76] *Panarion* 29.7.2–3.

[77] Jerome, *Epistles* 112.13. When speaking of Ebionites elsewhere he assumes, in a manner more typical of the heresiological tradition, that they believe in a "merely human" Jesus; for example, *Commentary on Galatians* 1.1, 11–12; cf. *Commentary on Ephesians* 4.10; *On Illustrious Men* 9.

[78] *Panarion* 29.7.5 and 29.8.1.

[79] It is thus unclear what we are to make of Jerome's passing characterization elsewhere of the "erring Nazoraeans" as "serving the sacrifices which have been abolished" (*Commentary on Jeremiah* 3.14–16). Does he mean to say they actually continue to perform sacrifices (so apparently Kinzig, "Nazoraeans" [see endnote 74], p. 472)? Or does he simply assume that a principled (if now purely theoretical) affection for the sacrificial cult is part and parcel of their continued observance of the Torah?

[80] Jerome, *Commentary on Isaiah* 9.1. Cf. in this respect the distinction drawn by Justin (*Dialogue with Trypho* 47) between Jewish Jesus groups who require Torah observance of everyone and those who require it only of Jews. See further on the "Nazoraean" interpretation of Isaiah below.

[81] Epiphanius, *Panarion* 29.1.3; 29.6.2–8; cf. Jerome, *De Situ et Nominibus Locorum Hebraeorum* 143; further H.H. Schaeder, "Nazarênos, Nazôraios," in *Theological Dictionary of the New Testament*, 10 vols., ed. G. Kittel (Grand Rapids, MI: Eerdmans, 1967), vol. 4, pp. 874–879.

[82] Jerome, *Commentary on Amos* 1.11–12, *sub nomine Nazarenorum blasphemant populum christianum*; also *Commentary on Isaiah* 5.18–19; 52.4–6; 49.7; so too already Tertullian, *Against Marcion* 4.8.

[83] Epiphanius, *Panarion* 29.9.1–3.

[84] Jerome, *Epistles* 112.13. His equation here of the Nazoraeans with "the Minaeans" (cf. *minim*), particularly when coupled with the statement that they are found specifically wherever synagogues are found, makes it plain that the *Birkat ha-Minim* stands behind this claim.

[85] See Joseph Verheyden, "Epiphanius on the Ebionites," in *The Image of the Judaeo-Christians in Ancient Jewish and Christian Literature* (see endnote 35), p. 184: "the Nazoraeans of *Panarion* 29 may well be to a large degree the product of Epiphanius' imagination." An interpretation along these lines has been argued forcefully by Petri Luomanen in a series of recent publications: See Luomanen, "Nazarenes," in *Companion to Second-Century "Heretics"* (see endnote 6), pp. 279–314; "Ebionites and Nazarenes" (see endnote 24), pp. 102–117; and most recently, *Recovering Jewish-Christians Sects and Gospels* (see endnote 25).

[86] Luomanen, "Nazarenes" (see endnote 85), p. 309.

[87] Jerome, *Epistles* 112.13.

[88] Compare in this respect Epiphanius's strategy regarding Ebion: "But since he is practically midway between all the sects, he is nothing" (*Panarion* 30.1.4).

[89] He discusses the name "Jessaeans" at length in *Panarion* 29.1.3–29.5.4; see further Pritz, *Nazarene Jewish Christianity* (see endnote 25), pp. 39–42.

[90] Compare *Panarion* 29.6.7 and 29.7.1. The notice about the group's secession from the apostolic community in *Panarion* 29.5.4 is in any case based on Eusebius's account of Philo's Therapeutae, whom Epiphanius (like Eusebius) takes to be early followers of Jesus; cf. *Ecclesiastical History* 2.16–17, which however makes no mention of "Nazoraeans."

[91] *Panarion* 29.7.1: *ta panta de eisin Ioudaioi kai ouden heteron*. Interestingly, he takes the opposite strategy with "Ebion," to whom he denies this name; see above.

[92] Epiphanius makes this case with little appreciation for the irony that most of the items on it characterize his own group as well. Note in this connection his final concession: "They are different from Jews, and different from Christians, only in the following. They disagree with Jews because they have come to faith in Christ; but since they are still fettered by the Law ... they are not in accord with Christians."

[93] Fragments of the supposed "Gospel of the Nazoraeans" provide little help in this respect. For a recent and convenient reconstruction of the text and translation, see Bart D. Ehrman and Zlatko Plese, *The Apocryphal Gospels: Texts and Translations* (Oxford: Oxford University Press, 2011), pp. 201–211. Note in any case Luomanen's view that there was in fact no distinct "Gospel of the Nazoraeans," only a collection of anti-Pharisaic passages from Matthew that add little to what we already learn from the Isaiah interpretation; see *Recovering Jewish-Christian Sects and Gospels* (see endnote 25), pp. 83–119; and "Ebionites and Nazarenes" (see endnote 24), pp. 108–109.

[94] The earliest possible date is established by its reference to Rabbi Meir, who was active in the mid-second century; Pritz (*Nazarene Jewish Christianity* [see endnote 25], p. 68) suggests a date "in the mid-third century, and at least after 200, when the Mishnah was compiled"; so too Luomanen, *Recovering Jewish-Christian Sects and Gospels* (see endnote 25), p. 75. Whether Jerome had access to the original Hebrew or Aramaic of this work, or only to already-translated fragments of it, is a matter of dispute; see above endnote 74.

[95] The five fragments generally accepted as belonging to this work are found in Jerome, *Commentary on Isaiah* 8:11–15; 8.19–22; 9.1; 29.17–21; 31:6–9; all references to these passages in what follows are taken from Klijn and Reinink, *Patristic Evidence* (see endnote 5), pp. 220–225 unless otherwise noted. For discussion, see Schmidtke, *Neue Fragmente und Untersuchungen* (see endnote 74), pp. 108–123; A.F.J. Klijn, "Jerome's Quotations from a Nazoraean Interpretation of Isaiah," *Recherches de Science Religieuse* 60 (1972), pp. 241–255; Pritz, *Nazarene Jewish Christianity* (see endnote 25), pp. 57–70; Kinzig, "Nazoraeans" (see endnote 74), pp. 474–477; Luomanen, *Recovering Jewish-Christian Sects and Gospels* (see endnote 25), pp. 71–75. Broadhead (*Jewish Ways* [see endnote 8], pp. 166–171) entertains the possibility that at least some of the content from Jerome, *Commentary*

on Isaiah 11:1–3 might also have come from this work. The rationale for doing this is rather thin, however, and the passage is not included in what follows.

[96] Remarkably, "the Scribes and Pharisees" are explicitly named in four of the five extant fragments (*Commentary on Isaiah* 8.11–15; 8.19–22; 9.1; and 29.17–21) and are clearly in view in the fifth (on Isaiah 31:6–9).

[97] H.L. Strack and Günter Stemberger point out that the term *Mishnayot* likely underlies *deuteróseis* here (*Introduction to the Talmud and Midrash* [Minneapolis: Fortress Press, 1992], p. 65); see further on the implications of the use of this term here and elsewhere in the fragments Pritz, *Nazarene Jewish Christianity* (see endnote 25), pp. 66–68.

[98] For discussion of the puns underlying Jerome's (or his source's) Latin, see Schmidtke, *Neue Fragmente und Untersuchungen* (see endnote 74), pp. 113–114; Klijn, "Jerome's Quotations" (see endnote 95), p. 250; Pritz, *Nazarene Jewish Christianity* (see endnote 25), pp. 61–62; Kinzig, "Nazoraeans" (see endnote 74), p. 475, nn. 66–67.

[99] See the fragment on Isaiah 8:19–22; and cf. the comments on Isaiah 31:6–9 and Isaiah 9:1.

[100] Jerome, *Commentary on Isaiah* 8.11–15.

[101] On the interpretation of Zebulon and Naphtali as the land of Israel more generally, see Klijn, "Jerome's Quotations" (see endnote 95), p. 251, who rightly notes the contrasting use in Matthew 4:12–17.

[102] Jerome, *Commentary on Isaiah* 8.11–15.

[103] Ibid., 29.17–21.

[104] Ibid., 8.19–22.

XI. In Between: Jewish-Christians and the Curse of the Heretics

[1] The application of the phrase "the parting of the ways" to the separation of Christianity from Judaism became popular through the 1934 work of James Parkes, *The Conflict of the Church and the Synagogue* (New York: JPS, often reprinted), see the title of chapter 3.

[2] Thus in this essay I speak about the parting of the ways between Jews and Christians, not between "Judaism" and "Christianity," because for a historian "Judaism" and "Christianity" have no meaning except as convenient labels for the beliefs, practices, institutions, etc., of Jews and Christians, respectively. If instead one speaks about "Judaism" and "Christianity" as a collection of theological abstractions, one might conclude that they were, and perhaps still are, one and the same, an approach and a conclusion that I reject. This is (one of) my objection(s) to Daniel Boyarin, *Border Lines: The Partition of Judaeo-Christianity* (Philadelphia: University of Pennsylvania, 2004).

[3] Thus I take issue with the conclusion of the symposium convened by James D.G. Dunn, *Jews and Christians: The Parting of the Ways* (Tübingen: Mohr Siebeck, 1992; reprinted Grand Rapids, MI: Eerdmans, 1999). Dunn writes, "The Symposium remained divided regarding Christology, not on the fact that Christian claims regarding Jesus were the crucial factor in "the parting of the ways," but on how and when these christological claims made the breach inevitable" (p. 36). This is to assume what needs to be demonstrated: Were Christian claims regarding Jesus the crucial factor in the parting of the ways? Christian texts, beginning with the Gospel of John, would have us think so, but this fact hardly settles the matter.

[4] Thus I take issue with the viewpoint of the editors of the anthology *The Ways That Never Parted: Jews and Christians in Late Antiquity and the Early Middle Ages*, eds. Adam Becker and Annette Y. Reed (Minneapolis: Fortress Press, 2007), who seem to think that discussion between Jews and Christians in antiquity is evidence against a parting of the ways, and that the "old model" of the parting of the ways (e.g., the view of James Parkes) did not allow for ongoing contacts between Jews and Christians. Parkes was well aware of ongoing contacts between Jews and Christians, but these contacts did not for Parkes (or for me) call into question the reality of the parting of the ways. For ongoing interchange between Jews and Christians, see Parkes, *Conflict of the Church and the Synagogue*

(see endnote 1), pp. 113–119, and also his "Rome, Pagan and Christian," in *Judaism and Christianity*, vol. 2, *The Contact of Pharisaism with Other Cultures*, ed. H. Loewe (1937; repr. New York: Ktav, 1969), pp. 115–144. On one point, at least, Parkes is wrong; in *Conflict of the Church and the Synagogue* (p. 153) he writes that in Babylonia there was practically no theological discussion between Jew and Christian, a position that we now know to be wrong. For contacts between rabbis and Christians in late antiquity, see the bibliography assembled in Shaye J.D. Cohen, "Antipodal Texts," in the *Peter Schäfer Festschrift* (forthcoming). Peter Schäfer (*The Jewish Jesus* [Princeton, NJ: Princeton University Press, 2012], p. 84) writes, "We have all learned by now that the old model of the 'parting of the ways' of Judaism and Christianity needs to be abandoned in favor of a much more differentiated and sophisticated model, taking into consideration a long process of mutual demarcation *and* absorption." I do not know how long a process has to be in order to be considered "long," but, as I argue in this essay, I believe that the mutual demarcation had been achieved by the early decades of the second century C.E.

5 See Chapter III, "The Godfearers: From the Gospels to Aphrodisias," by Bruce Chilton in this volume.

6 Shaye J.D. Cohen, *The Beginnings of Jewishness* (Berkeley: University of California Press, 1999), p. 152, n. 41.

7 The best place to begin is *Jewish Believers in Jesus: The Early Centuries*, eds. Oskar Skarsaune and Reidar Hvalvik (Peabody, MA: Hendrickson, 2007).

8 See, for example, W.H.C. Frend, "Persecutions: Genesis and Legacy," in *The Cambridge History of Christianity*, vol. 1, *Origins to Constantine* (Cambridge: Cambridge University Press, 2006), pp. 503–523. See now Candida Moss, *Ancient Christian Martyrdom*, Yale Anchor Bible Reference Library (New Haven, CT: Yale University Press, 2012).

9 The earliest appearance of this motif is the *Martyrdom of Polycarp* 12:2, 13:1, 17:2, 18:1, in *The Apostolic Fathers: Greek Texts and English Translations*, ed. Michael Holmes, 3rd ed. (Grand Rapids, MI: Baker Academic, 2007). Polycarp

was martyred about 160 C.E., and the text of the martyrdom was written shortly after the event.

10 Eusebius, *Ecclesiastical History* 6.12.1 (during the reign of Septimus Severus). See also Jerome, *Commentary on Galatians* 6.12, in *St. Jerome's Commentaries on Galatians, Titus and Philemon*, trans. Thomas Scheck (Notre Dame, IN: University of Notre Dame, 2010), pp. 268–269 (slightly modified): "Gaius [Julius] Caesar, Octavian Augustus, and Tiberius, the successor of Augustus, had promulgated laws that permitted the Jews, who had been dispersed throughout the whole sphere of the Roman Empire, to live by their own rites and observe their ancestral ceremonies. Whoever had been circumcised, therefore, even if he believed in Christ, was reckoned as a Jew by the gentiles. But anyone without circumcision, who proclaimed by his foreskin that he was not a Jew, became liable to persecution from both Jews and gentiles. So those who were subverting the Galatians, wishing to avoid these persecutions, were persuading the disciples to circumcise themselves for protection."

11 Peter Schäfer, ed., *The Bar Kokhba War Reconsidered: New Perspectives on the Second Jewish Revolt Against Rome* (Tübingen: Mohr Siebeck, 2003).

12 Justin Martyr, *1 Apology* 31.6; Eusebius, *Annals* 2149; Orosius 7.13.4. These texts are conveniently available in Emil Schürer, *The History of the Jewish People in the Age of Jesus Christ*, rev. and ed. Geza Vermes et al. (Edinburgh: T & T Clark, 1973), vol. 1, p. 545, n. 141. The Bar-Kokhba documents from the Judean desert do not mention Christians (at least not explicitly).

13 Intellectuals of the second and third centuries C.E. also knew how to distinguish Judaism from Christianity. See the excerpts from Galen, Celsus and Porphyry in *GLAJJ*, vol. 2.

14 Marius Heemstra, *The Fiscus Judaicus and the Parting of the Ways* (Tübingen: Mohr Siebeck, 2010).

15 Suetonius, *Life of Domitian* 12.1–2 (= *GLAJJ*, vol. 2, no. 320).

16 The standard survey is Heinz Schreckenberg, *Die christlichen Adversus-Judaeos-Texte und*

ihr literarisches und historisches Umfeld, vol. 1 (Frankfurt: Peter Lang, 1982).

[17] For the dating and attribution of early Christian texts, I follow Siegmar Döpp and Wilhelm Geerlings, eds., *Dictionary of Early Christian Literature* (New York: Crossroad, 2000). The works of the Apostolic Fathers are cited from Holmes, *Apostolic Fathers* (see endnote 9).

[18] The term also appears in Magnesians 10:3 and Romans 3:3. See Shaye J.D. Cohen, "Judaism Without Circumcision and 'Judaism' Without 'Circumcision' in Ignatius," *HTR* 95 (2002), pp. 395–415, reprinted in my *The Significance of Yavneh and Other Essays in Jewish Hellenism* (Tübingen: Mohr Siebeck, 2010).

[19] See endnote 9.

[20] A convenient and accessible translation is *St. Justin Martyr Dialogue with Trypho*, trans. Thomas B. Falls, rev. Thomas Halton, ed. Michael Slusser (Washington, DC: Catholic University of America Press, 2003).

[21] Melito of Sardis, *On Pascha*, trans. Alistair Stewart-Sykes (Crestwood, NY: St. Vladimir's Seminary Press, 2007), stanzas 90–99. See the chapter on Melito in Jeremy Cohen, *Christ Killers: The Jews and the Passion from the Bible to the Big Screen* (New York: Oxford University Press, 2007). The Romans play no role in Christ's death according to Melito.

[22] Justin, *Dialogue with Trypho* 23.3; 80.1; 122–123 (proselytes); cf. Epistle of Barnabas 3.6. See *Iustini Martyris Dialogus cum Tryphone*, ed. Miroslav Marcovich (Berlin/New York: de Gruyter, 1997), pp. 64–65. On the larger question, see, for example, Judith Lieu, *Image and Reality: The Jews in the World of the Christians in the Second Century* (Edinburgh: T & T Clark, 1996); and Miriam S. Taylor, *Anti-Judaism and Early Christian Identity* (Leiden: Brill, 1995).

[23] See the numerous passages assembled by Adolf von Harnack, *Die Mission und Ausbreitung des Christentums in den ersten drei Jarhunderten*, 4th ed. (Leipzig: Hinrichs, 1924), pp. 262–267 and 281–289; see also Denise Kimber Buell, *Why This New Race? Ethnic Reasoning in Early Christianity* (New York: Columbia University Press, 2005).

[24] Bishops, presbyters and deacons are attested already in *1 Clement*, written c. 96 C.E.

[25] "As I stated above" alludes to 17.1; see also 138.

[26] Justin does not identify precisely who sent these messengers.

[27] Justin does not identify precisely who received these messages.

[28] See also 69.7 (Jesus is accused of having been a magician).

[29] There is remarkable confluence between the Jewish view of Jesus in this passage and the Jewish view of Jesus in BT *Sanhedrin* 43a, which also sees Jesus as an idolater and deceiver, and which also attributes his execution to Jewish authorities acting without any involvement of the Romans. See Peter Schäfer, *Jesus in the Talmud* (Princeton, NJ: Princeton University Press, 2007), pp. 63–74.

[30] Paul himself does not claim any commission from the high priest (1 Corinthians 15:9; Galatians 1:13; Philippians 3:6).

[31] William Horbury, "Jewish-Christian Relations in Barnabas and Justin Martyr," in *Jews and Christians* (see endnote 3), p. 342, reprinted in W. Horbury, *Jews and Christians in Contact and Controversy* (Edinburgh: T & T Clark, 1998), pp. 127–161. The anti-Christian messengers are also mentioned by Eusebius and Jerome.

[32] The Jews Curse Christ and/or Christians: *Dialogue with Trypho* 16.4,* 47.4, 93.4, 96.2,* 108.3, 133.6, 137.2* (the asterisked passages place the cursing in the synagogue).

[33] Aside from Horbury ("Jewish-Christian Relations" [see endnote 31]), none of the contributors to Dunn's symposium even mentions Justin's reported messengers.

[34] In 47.2–3, Justin mentions gentile Christians who observe the law, and Jewish-Christians who seek to impose the law on gentile Christians. In Justin's eyes both belong to the community of Christians.

[35] Herbert Danby, *The Mishnah* (Oxford: Oxford University Press, 1933; frequently reprinted).

[36] As Danby notes, a variant reading is "Sadducees."

37 Translation and meaning are not certain. See Cohen, *Beginnings of Jewishness* (see endnote 6), pp. 253–255.

38 Printed editions read "Sadducees" (perhaps as a result of conflation with 3:9), but the manuscripts read "heretics" (*minim).*

39 Translation uncertain. Perhaps: "an opportunity to mock us."

40 Printed editions read "Sadducee" but the manuscripts read "heretic" (*min).*

41 The number is approximate because the editions vary.

42 Jacob N. Epstein, *Mavo le Nusah ha Mishnah* (Jerusalem: Magnes Press, 1964), p. 967 (in Hebrew).

43 Or is Rabbi Yosi afraid of the heretics' reaction to the Mishnah's post-70 textual description of the Parah ritual, rather than their reaction to the pre-70 Temple ritual itself?

44 The grab-bag quality of the term is well emphasized by Daniel Sperber, "*min,*" *EJ,* vol. 14, pp. 263–264.

45 Standard printed editions add "from the Torah," that is "one who says that the resurrection of the dead has no basis in the Torah," but the words "from the Torah" are not found in the manuscripts.

46 My translation is based on that of Herbert Danby. For a recent discussion, see David M. Grossberg, "Orthopraxy in Tannaitic Literature," *JSJ* 41 (2010), pp. 517–561.

47 Is this the same as denying that the Torah is from heaven? Perhaps. I cannot discuss this point here.

48 Josephus, *Antiquities* 10.277–281 and 18.16–17; Matthew 22:23; see also *Fathers According to Rabbi Nathan,* version A, chapter 5.

49 Sadducees in the Mishnah: *Parah* 3:9, *Niddah* 4:2, *Yadayim* 4:6–8, *Eruvin* 6:2. The variant readings of some of our Mishnaic passages (nos. 1, 8, 9) suggest a connection between *minim* and *tzeduqim,* "Sadducees," but this connection is probably the result of the work of much later scribes and printers. In the age of printing, Jews knew that Christians knew that *minim* might well refer to Christians, so to avoid trouble with the censor they emended the potentially offensive word *min* to "Sadducee(s)." There is real anti-Sadducean polemic in the Mishnah (Mishnah *Yadayim* end), but not in our nine passages.

50 The Tosefta ad loc., which is a secondary expansion of the Mishnah, adds *minim.*

51 This is the main point of my article "The Significance of Yavneh," *Hebrew Union College Annual* 55 (1984), pp. 27–53, reprinted in *Significance of Yavneh and Other Essays* (see endnote 18). See now Adiel Schremer, "Thinking About Belonging in Early Rabbinic Literature," *JSJ* 43 (2012), pp. 249–275.

52 Just to be clear: The Tosefta has other non-Mishnaic references to *minim* (e.g., Tosefta *Megillah* 3:37), but because they cannot be shown to refer to Christians they are not treated here.

53 Or "the gospels," *ha gilyonim*; see below.

54 Wilhelm Bacher, "Le mot *minim* dans le Thalmud désigne-t-il quelquefois des chrétiens?" *Revue des études juives* 38 (1899), pp. 38–46, at 42, argues that *sifrei minim* are Torah scrolls written by *minim.* For discussion, see Daniel Sperber, "*Sifrei ha-minim,*" *EJ,* vol. 18, pp. 564–565.

55 Lieberman ed., pp. 58–59.

56 "Surely" means "not so surely." Adiel Schremer is not convinced that this passage is talking about Christian *minim*; see his *Brothers Estranged: Heresy, Christianity, and Jewish Identity in Late Antiquity* (Oxford: Oxford University Press, 2010), pp. 84–86.

57 The *evangelia* seem to be written in Hebrew, too. I have translated *sefer/sefarim* throughout as "scrolls," but perhaps in connection with Christians we should translate "books" or "codices."

58 This time I am sure.

59 *Mamzerim,* usually translated "bastards," are the offspring of strongly prohibited sexual unions who are not marriageable by Israelites of good pedigree. The word was also used as a term of abuse.

60 On the Tosefta's harsh laws about *minim,* see Schremer, *Brothers Estranged* (see endnote 56),

pp. 69–86. I agree with Schremer that there is no reason to assume that Christians are the target of the polemic. Another harsh anti-*minim* passage is Tosefta *Bava Metzia* 2:33, and there, too, we should not assume that Christians are meant (see Schremer, p. 61).

⁶¹ First story is Tosefta *Hulin* 2:22–23 (M.S. Zuckermandel ed., p. 503; Freiman ed., pp. 87–88); my translation is based on that of Jacob Neusner, *The Tosefta* (Peabody, MA: Hendrickson, 2002), p. 1380. The second story is Tosefta *Hulin* 2:24 (Zuckermandel ed., p. 503; Freiman ed., pp. 88–89; my translation is based on that of Joshua Schwartz and Peter J. Tomson, "When Rabbi Eliezer Was Arrested for Heresy," available at the website of the *Jewish Studies Internet Journal* (http://www.biu.ac.il/js/JSIJ/10–2012/SchwartzandTomson.pdf). The first story appears with variations in JT *Shabbat* 14 end (and *Avodah Zarah* 40d); BT *Avodah Zarah* 27b; the second story appears with variations in BT *Avodah Zarah* 17b; *Ecclesiastes Rabbah* 1:8. I cannot discuss those versions here.

⁶² That is, R. Yishmael did not permit R. Eleazar to be healed by Jacob. It is possible that the text means that R. Yishmael did not permit Jacob to heal R. Eleazar, but the following sentences turn on what R. Eleazar is permitted to do. Jacob himself is somewhere off-stage, and is not present in the dialogical space inhabited by R. Yishmael and R. Eleazar.

⁶³ The Vienna manuscript of the Tosefta has "they," which seems to be an error.

⁶⁴ Text and meaning uncertain. The syntax of this paragraph seems garbled. I am not persuaded by the interpretation of Schäfer, *Jesus in the Talmud* (see endnote 29), pp. 43–44.

⁶⁵ A weakness of the analysis of Schwartz and Thomson ("When Rabbi Eliezer Was Arrested" [see endnote 61]) is their confusion of narrative truth with historical truth.

⁶⁶ Origen, *Against Celsus* 1.32 (trans. H. Chadwick, p. 31; and n. 3); Schäfer, *Jesus in the Talmud* (see endnote 29), pp. 15–24.

⁶⁷ This explanation is advanced by the Yerushalmi. The commentators on BT *Avodah Zarah* 27b (and BT *Shabbat* 110a) explain it

differently. Schäfer (*Jesus in the Talmud* [see endnote 29], pp. 55–56) misconstrues the Bavli.

⁶⁸ All modern scholars understand the story this way. It is worth noting, however, that several important medieval Jewish commentators understand the opening line of the story not as "When R. Eliezer was arrested on a suspicion of *minut*," but as "When the *minim* arrested R. Eliezer." In this reading the governor is a leader of the *minim* and wants to know why R. Eliezer does not follow the *minim*.

⁶⁹ R. Eliezer is seeking a theological explanation for his ordeal, not a historical one: for the sin of consorting with a *min* he is punished by being arrested on a suspicion of *minut*. Schwartz and Thomson explain that some informer saw R. Eliezer in the marketplace with a *min* and reported the encounter to the Romans. This is beside the point.

⁷⁰ There are many recent scholarly studies of the *Birkat ha-Minim*. The fullest is Yaakov Teppler, *Birkat ha Minim* (Tübingen: Mohr Siebeck, 2007); the best is Ruth Langer, *Cursing the Christians? A History of the* Birkat HaMinim (Oxford: Oxford University Press, 2012). See also Uri Ehrlich, "*Birkat Ha-Minim*," *EJ*, vol. 3, pp. 711–712.

⁷¹ Perhaps to be vocalized *paroshim*.

⁷² Lieberman ed., pp. 17–18. The translation of this text that appears in Teppler (*Birkat ha Minim* [see endnote 70], p. 100) is wrong (perhaps the mistake belongs to the translator, not the author). The Vienna manuscript of the Tosefta at Tosefta *Taanit* 1:10 (Lieberman ed., p. 326) also refers to the *Birkat ha-Minim*, but the reference is absent from the Erfurt and London manuscripts and the printed editions. I do not discuss it here.

⁷³ JT *Berakhot* 4:3 7d (Zussman ed., col. 37); BT *Berakhot* 28b–29a.

⁷⁴ On these separatists, see David Flusser, "4QMMT and the Benediction against the Minim," in *Judaism of the Second Temple Period*, vol. 1, *Qumran and Apocalypticism*, trans. Azzan Yadin (Grand Rapids, MI: Eerdmans, 2007), chapter 9; Schremer, *Brothers Estranged* (see endnote 56), pp. 57–68.

[75] JT *Berakhot* 4:3 8a (Zussman ed., col. 37)// *Taanit* 2:2 65c (Zussman ed., col. 713).

[76] Some scholars have suggested that "sinners" (*posh`im*) is a variant reading of "separatists" (*perushim*).

[77] JT *Berakhot* 4:3 8a (Zussman ed., col. 37) // *Taanit* 2:2 65c (Zussman ed., col. 713).

[78] See Mishnah *Sanhedrin* quoted on p. 220.

[79] JT *Berakhot* 5:4 9c (Zussman ed., col. 47).

[80] BT *Berakhot* 28b-29a and *Megillah* 17b.

[81] I leave aside the question of whether heretics and separatists would recognize themselves as heretics and separatists; probably not.

[82] David Henshke suggests that the cursing of enemies is to ensure that God will listen to our prayers, not theirs; see Henshke, "From *Parashat ha Ibbur* to *birkat ha minim*," in *From Qumran to Cairo: Studies in the History of Prayer*, ed. Joseph Tabory (Jerusalem: Orhot, 1999), pp. 75–102 (in Hebrew).

[83] That the *Dialogue* was set in Ephesus is stated by Eusebius, *Ecclesiastical History* 4.18.6. Justin was born in Samaria.

[84] Regarding Epiphanius and Jerome, see William Horbury, "The Benediction of the *Minim* and Early Jewish-Christian Controversy," *JTS* 33 (1982), pp. 19–61, reprinted in Horbury, *Jews and Christians* (see endnote 31), pp. 67–110. In Antioch in the 380s, John Chrysostom does not know the *Birkat ha-Minim*, for if he knew it he surely would have mentioned it in his sermons against the Jews, translated under the title *Discourses Against Judaizing Christians*, trans. Paul W. Harkins (Washington DC: Catholic University of America, 1979). According to the *Martyrdom of Pionius*, which is set in Asia Minor in 250 C.E. and written (probably) not long after, and which contains much anti-Jewish material, the Jews try to seduce Christians away from Christianity by inviting them to their synagogues. "They will invite you to their synagogues"—no *Birkat ha-Minim* here (*Martyrdom of Pionios* 13). See Louis Robert, *Le martyre de Pionios prêtre de Smyrne*, eds. G.W. Bowersock and C.P. Jones (Washington, DC: Dumbarton Oaks, 1994), pp. 82–83. In contrast to the argument developed here, David

Rokeah argues that Justin is referring to the *Birkat ha-Minim*; see his Hebrew translation of the *Dialogue with Trypho* (Jerusalem: Magnes Press, 2005), n. 192 on *Dialogue* 16.4.

[85] John 9:22, 12:42 and 16:2.

[86] The classic statement of this theory is by J. Louis Martyn, *History and Theology in the Fourth Gospel*, 3rd ed. (Louisville: Westminster/ John Knox Press, 2003; 1st ed. 1968).

[87] For summaries of the critique, see John S. Kloppenborg, "Disaffiliation in Associations and the *Aposynagôgos* of John," *HTS Theological Studies* 67.1 (2011), art. 962 (http://www.hts.org. za/index.php/HTS/article/view/962/html) and Langer, *Cursing the Christians?* (see endnote 70), pp. 27–33.

[88] The exceptions are some Sibylline Oracles and a small corpus of synagogue prayers; for the latter, see Pieter van der Horst and Judith H. Newman, *Early Jewish Prayers in Greek* (Berlin: de Gruyter, 2008).

[89] Justin Martyr, *Dialogue with Trypho* 119.3–4, 123.9 and 135.3. These points were implicit a generation earlier in the *Epistle of Barnabas*.

[90] Larry Hurtado, *The Earliest Christian Artifacts: Manuscripts and Christian Origins* (Grand Rapids, MI: Eerdmans, 2006).

[91] See the story of Pope Callistus (Calixtus) in Hippolytus, *Refutatio omnium heresium* 9.12 (ed. Miroslav Marcovich [Berlin: de Gruyter, 1986], p. 351).

[92] The Jewish cemetery at Jaffa and the Jewish catacombs of Beth Shearim and Rome contain no demonstrably Christian burials. The Christian catacombs of Rome contain no demonstrably Jewish burials.

[93] See the chapter "Judaizing," in Cohen, *Beginnings of Jewishness* (see endnote 6).

[94] The standard discussion is Robert L. Wilken, *John Chrysostom and the Jews* (Berkeley: University of California Press, 1983). I would observe, too, that there is far more evidence (all of it Christian) for Christians in synagogues than for Jews in churches.

[95] The information that we do have derives from inscriptions; see Paul Trebilco, *Jewish*

Communities in Asia Minor (Cambridge: Cambridge University Press, 1991).

[96] Peter Schäfer, The Jewish Jesus: How Judaism and Christianity Shaped Each Other (Princeton, NJ: Princeton University Press, 2012), reacting to the work of Daniel Boyarin.

XII. The Complexities of Rejection and Attraction, Herein of Love and Hate

[1] The first story was told to me by my mother, Jane Fine, and the latter by Ray Hurvitz of Baltimore Hebrew University, 1999. See the Italian-American Dialect Dictionary, http://xeroth.wordpress.com/2009/04/14/italian/ (accessed January 2013).

I have discussed many of the sources presented in this chapter in "Non-Jews in the Synagogues of Palestine: Rabbinic and Archaeological Perspectives," in Jews, Christians and Polytheists in the Ancient Synagogue: Cultural Interaction During the Greco-Roman Period, ed. Steven Fine (London: Routledge, 1999), pp. 226–230, and in "The Menorah and the Cross: Historiographic Reflections on a Recent Discovery from Laodicea on the Lycus," in New Perspectives on Jewish-Christian Relations in Honor of David Berger, eds. Elisheva Carlebach and Jacob J. Schacter (Leiden: Brill, 2012), pp. 31–50, updated and revised in my Art, History and the Historiography of Judaism in Roman Antiquity (Leiden: Brill, forthcoming). In these essays the reader will find full references to the vast bibliography on the subjects discussed.

[2] The most recent volume on the relationship between Judaism and Christianity through the ages is New Perspectives on Jewish-Christian Relations (see endnote 1).

[3] James Parkes, The Conflict of the Church and Synagogue: A Study in the Origins of Anti-Semitism (London: Soncino Press, 1934), pp. 71–120.

[4] For example, Adam H. Becker and Annette Yoshiko Reed, eds., The Ways That Never Parted: Jews and Christians in Late Antiquity and the

Early Middle Ages (Minneapolis: Fortress Press, 2007).

[5] See, for example, Steven M. Cohen and Arnold M. Eisen, The Jew Within: Self, Family, and Community in America (Bloomington: Indiana University Press, 2000); Lila Corwin Berman, Speaking of the Jews: Rabbis, Intellectuals and the Creation of an American Public Identity (Berkeley and Los Angeles: University of California Press, 2009); Yoel Finkelman, Strictly Kosher Reading: Popular Literature and the Condition of Contemporary Orthodoxy (Boston: Academic Studies Press, 2011).

[6] For a most readable introduction to the Cairo Geniza, see Adina Hoffman and Peter Cole, Sacred Trash: The Lost and Found World of the Cairo Geniza (New York: Schocken Books, 2011).

[7] The best discussions of these sources are still Parkes, Conflict of the Church and Synagogue (see endnote 3); Marcel Simon, Verus Israel: A Study of the Relations Between Christians and Jews in the Roman Empire AD 135–425, trans. H. McKeating (London: Littman Library of Jewish Civilization, 1996). See now Leonard V. Rutgers, Making Myths: Jews in Early Christian Identity Formation (Leuven: Peeters, 2009), esp. 79–115, whose overall assessment is very similar to my own.

[8] See, for example, Peter Schäfer's Jesus in the Talmud (Princeton, NJ: Princeton University Press, 2009); Adiel Schremer, Brothers Estranged: Heresy, Christianity, and Jewish Identity in Late Antiquity (Oxford: Oxford University Press, 2010). On general historiographic trends, see Stuart S. Miller, "Roman Imperialism, Jewish Self-Definition, and Rabbinic Society: Belayche's Iudaea-Palaestina, Schwartz's Imperialism and Jewish Society, and Boyarin's Border Lines Reconsidered," Association for Jewish Studies Review 31.2 (2007), pp. 1–34.

[9] On the approach to the Dura synagogue presented here, see my Art and Judaism in the Greco-Roman World: Toward a New Jewish Archaeology, rev. ed. (Cambridge: Cambridge University Press, 2010), pp. 174–187; and "Jewish Identity at the Limus: The Jews of Dura Europos Between Rome and Persia," in Cultural Identity and the Peoples of the Ancient Mediterranean,

ed. Erich S. Gruen (Los Angeles: Getty Research Institute, 2011), pp. 289–306, updated in *Art, History and the Historiography* (see endnote 1).

[10] On the Dura church, see Carl H. Kraeling, *The Christian Building: The Excavations at Dura-Europos Conducted by Yale University and the French Academy of Inscriptions and Letters, Final report,* vol. 8, pt. 2 (New Haven, CT: Yale University Press, 1967).

[11] Jefim Schirmann, "Hebrew Liturgical Poetry and Christian Hymnology," *Jewish Quarterly Review* 44 (1953), pp. 152–155; A. Thomas Kraabel, "Melito the Bishop and the Synagogue at Sardis: Text and Context," in *Studies Presented to George M.A. Hanfmann,* eds. D.G. Mitten et al. (Mainz: Philipp von Zabern, 1971), pp. 77–85.

[12] Amnon Linder, *The Jews in Roman Imperial Legislation* (Detroit: Wayne State University Press; Jerusalem: Israel Academy of Sciences and Humanities, 1987).

[13] Cited in ibid., pp. 287–289.

[14] The most complete discussion and bibliography on Ilici appears in *JIWE,* vol. 1, pp. 241–247. On Stobi, see Dean L. Moe, "The Cross and the Menorah," *Archaeology* 30 (1977), pp. 148–157. On Gerasa, see John W. Crowfoot, "The Christian Churches," in *Gerasa: City of the Decapolis,* ed. Carl H. Kraeling (New Haven, CT: ASOR, 1938), pp. 234–241.

[15] Dan Barag, Yosef Porat and Ehud Netzer, "The Synagogue at 'En-Gedi," in *Ancient Synagogues Revealed,* ed. Lee I. Levine (Jerusalem: Israel Exploration Society, 1981), pp. 116–119. Michael Avi-Yonah (*The Jews Under Roman and Byzantine Rule: A Political History of Palestine from the Bar Kokhba War to the Arab Conquest* [Jerusalem: Magnes Press, 1984], p. 251) notes that "the evidence even included particles of sulfur." On Huseifa, see Michael Avi-Yonah and Na'im Makhouly, "A Sixth Century Synagogue at 'Isfiya," *Quarterly of the Department of Antiquities of Palestine* 3 (1933), pp. 118–131.

[16] Simcha Assaf, "An Early Lament on the Destruction of Communities in the Land of Israel," in *Texts and Studies in Jewish History* (Jerusalem: Rav Kook Institute, 1946), pp. 9–16 (in Hebrew); Mordechai A. Friedman, "Ono—New Insights from the Writings of the Cairo Genizah," in *Between Yarkon and Ayalon* (Ramat Gan: Bar Ilan University, 1983), p. 74; and Fine, "Non-Jews in the Synagogues of Palestine" (see endnote 1), pp. 234–235.

[17] See Steven Fine, *This Holy Place: On the Sanctity of the Synagogue in the Greco-Roman Period* (Notre Dame, IN: Notre Dame University Press, 1997), pp. 100–101; and *Art, History and the Historiography* (see endnote 1), chapter 7, "'Epigraphical' Study Houses in Late Antique Palestine: A Second Look."

[18] Robert L. Scranton, *Mediaeval Architecture in the Central Area of Corinth* (Princeton, NJ: American School of Classical Studies at Athens, 1957), p. 116.

[19] Steven Fine and Leonard V. Rutgers, "New Light on Judaism in Asia Minor During Late Antiquity: Two Recently Identified Inscribed Menorahs," *Jewish Studies Review* 3.1 (1996), pp. 1–23.

[20] Theodor Wiegand and Hans Schrader, *Priene: Ergebnisse der Ausgrabungen und Untersuchungen in den Jahren 1895–1898* (Berlin: G. Reimer, 1904), p. 481.

[21] Celal Şimşek, "A Menorah with a Cross Carved on a Column of Nymphaeum A at Laodicea Ad Lycum," *JRA* 91.1 (2006), pp. 343–346; and Fine, "Menorah and the Cross" (see endnote 1). On the history of the Jewish community at Laodicea, see Paul R. Trebilco, *Jewish Communities in Asia Minor* (Cambridge: Cambridge University Press, 1992), pp. 14, 17, 31, 101–103 and 198.

[22] In Linder, *The Jews in Roman Imperial Legislation* (see endnote 12), pp. 126–132, with slight alteration.

[23] Egon Wellesz, *A History of Byzantine Music and Hymnology* (Oxford: Clarendon Press, 1961), pp. 179–197; and Schirmann, "Hebrew Liturgical Poetry and Christian Hymnology" (see endnote 11), pp. 155–161.

[24] See Moshe D. Herr, "Hellenistic Influences in the Jewish City in Eretz Israel in the Fourth and Sixth Centuries C.E." *Cathedra* 8 (1978), pp. 90–94 (in Hebrew); and Hillel Newman, *The Ma'asim of the People of the Land of Israel* (Jerusalem: Yad Izhak Ben-Zvi Institute, 2011), pp. 1–12 (in Hebrew).

²⁵ See now Alexei M. Sivertsev, *Judaism and Imperial Ideology in Late Antiquity* (Cambridge: Cambridge University Press, 2011); and Fine, *Art, History and the Historiography* (see endnote 1), chapter 8, "Furnishing God's Study House: An Exercise in Rabbinic Imagination."

²⁶ *The Liturgical Poetry of Rabbi Yannai,* vol. 2, ed. Z.M. Rabinovitz (Jerusalem: Bialik Institute, 1985–1987), pp. 221–222 (in Hebrew).

²⁷ See now Ruth Langer, *Cursing the Christians?: A History of the Birkat HaMinim* (Oxford: Oxford University Press, 2011).

²⁸ See Schäfer, *Jesus in the Talmud* (see endnote 8); Fine, *Art and Judaism in the Greco-Roman World* (see endnote 9), pp. 117–118.

²⁹ See most recently *Toledot Yeshu ("The Life Story of Jesus") Revisited: A Princeton Conference,* eds. Peter Schäfer, Michael Meerson and Yaacov Deutsch (Tübingen: Mohr Siebeck, 2011).

³⁰ See, for example, Eberhard Sauer, *The Archaeology of Religious Hatred in the Roman and Early Medieval World* (London: Tempus, 2003); and John Pollini, "Christian Destruction and Mutilation of the Parthenon," *Athenische Mitteilungen* 122 (2007), pp. 207–228.

³¹ Andrew Jacobs, *Relics of the Jews: The Holy Land and Christian Empire in Late Antiquity* (Stanford, CA: Stanford University Press, 2004).

³² Louis Ginzberg, "Aquila," *The Jewish Encyclopedia* (New York: Funk and Wagnalls, 1902), vol. 2, pp. 36–38.

³³ See Fine, "Non-Jews in the Synagogues of Palestine" (see endnote 1) and the bibliography cited there.

³⁴ These sources are assembled by Louis H. Feldman, *Jews and Gentiles in the Ancient World* (Princeton, NJ: Princeton University Press, 1993), pp. 342–382.

³⁵ See F.J. Elizabeth Boddens Hosang, *Establishing Boundaries: Christian-Jewish Relations in Early Council Texts and the Writings of Church Fathers* (Leiden: Brill, 2010), pp. 91–107.

³⁶ Ibid., p. 93.

³⁷ John Chrysostom, *Discourses Against Judaizing Christians,* trans. P.W. Harkins (Washington, DC: Catholic University of America Press, 1979).

³⁸ See Fine, *This Holy Place* (see endnote 17), esp. pp. 137–157. In general, see Robert Wilken, *John Chrysostom and the Jews: Rhetoric and Reality in the Late Fourth Century* (Berkeley/Los Angeles: University of California Press, 1983), esp. 83–94.

³⁹ David Noy and Hanswulf Bloedhorn, *Inscriptiones Judaicae Orientis,* vol. 3, *Syria and Cyprus* (Tübingen: Mohr Siebeck, 2004), pp. 117–118, illustrated in Bernadette Brooton, "The Jews of Ancient Antioch," in *Antioch: The Lost Ancient City,* ed. Christine Kondoleon (Princeton, NJ: Princeton University Press, 2000), pp. 28, 34.

⁴⁰ See Leah Roth-Gerson, *The Jews of Syria as Reflected in the Greek Inscriptions* (Jerusalem: Zalman Shazar Center for Jewish History, 2001), *passim.*

⁴¹ The basic discussion of these sources is still Parkes, *Conflict of the Church and Synagogue* (see endnote 3).

⁴² Elliott Horowitz, *Reckless Rites: Purim and the Legacy of Jewish Violence* (Princeton, NJ: Princeton University Press, 2006), pp. 238–239 and 228–247; Gideon Avni, "The Persian Conquest of Jerusalem (614 C.E.)—An Archaeological Assessment," *BASOR* 357 (2010), pp. 35–48.

⁴³ See Eilat Mazar, *The Temple Mount Excavations in Jerusalem 1968–1978 Directed by Benjamin Mazar, Final Reports,* vol. 2, *The Byzantine and Early Islamic Periods,* Qedem 43 (Jerusalem: The Institute of Archaeology, The Hebrew University of Jerusalem, 2003), pp. 163–186.

⁴⁴ Seth Ward, *Construction and Repair of Churches and Synagogues in Islamic Law: A Treatise by Taqī al-Dīn ʿAlī b. ʿAbd al-Kāfī al-Subkī,* Ph.D. dissertation (New Haven, CT: Yale University, 1984).

XIII. From Sabbath to Sunday: Why, How and When?

¹ The Christians who today observe the seventh-day Sabbath, such as Seventh-Day Adventists, Seventh Day Baptists and some Church of God groups, do so as "restorers of

the original Sabbath," mostly since the Protestant Reformation.

² *An Examination of the Biblical and Patristic Texts of the First Four Centuries to Ascertain the Time and the Causes of the Origin of Sunday as the Lord's Day*, Ph.D. dissertation (Rome: Pontifical Gregorian University, 1975), hereinafter referred to as *Origin of Sunday*. See also *From Sabbath to Sunday: A Historical Investigation of the Rise of Sunday Observance in Early Christianity* (Rome: Pontifical Gregorian University, 1977), hereinafter referred to as *From Sabbath to Sunday*. A synopsis of that work by the author can be found as an appendix in his *Divine Rest for Human Restlessness* (self published, 1980). Extensive use of these sources has been made, sometimes without direct acknowledgment. A good summary of Bacchiocchi's views is found in his chapter, "The Rise of Sunday Observance in Early Christianity," in *The Sabbath in Scripture and History*, ed. Kenneth Strand (Washington, DC: Review & Herald, 1982), pp. 132–150. For an authoritative and recent analysis of the subject, see Herold Weiss's short but masterful "Introduction" to *A Day of Gladness: The Sabbath Among Jews and Christians in Antiquity* (Columbia, SC: University of South Carolina Press, 2003), pp. 1–9. Weiss rightly takes issue with Bacchiocchi's less than adequate, uncritical treatment of the New Testament sources, as well as his evangelical respondents, in *From Sabbath to Lord's Day: A Biblical, Historical and Theological Investigation*, ed. D.A. Carson (Grand Rapids, MI: Zondervan, 1982), esp. the concluding article by A.T. Lincoln, pp. 343–412.

³ C.W. Dugmore, "Lord's Day and Easter," in *Neotestamentica et Patristica*, Supplements to Novum Testamentum 6 (Leiden: Brill, 1962), p. 272.

⁴ Denise Judant, *Judaisme et christianisme, dossier patristique* (Paris: Éditions du Cèdre, 1969), p. 63.

⁵ Marcel Simon, *Verus Israel: étude sur les relations entre Chrétiens et Juifs dans l'Empire romain (135–425)* (Paris: E. De Boccard, 1964), p. 235; confirmed by James Parkes, *The Conflict of the Church and Synagogue: A Study of the Origins of Antisemitism* (London: Soncino Press, 1934), p. 78.

⁶ See comments in *Christianity and Rabbinic Judaism: A Parallel History of Their Origins*

and Development, 2nd ed., ed. Hershel Shanks (Washington, DC: Biblical Archaeology Society, 2011) by Geza Vermes (p. xxiii), Shaye J.D. Cohen (pp. 230–231), James H. Charlesworth (p. 340) and Isaiah M. Gafni (p. 399, n. 40).

⁷ Justin Martyr, *Dialogue with Trypho* 47 (in *Ante-Nicene Fathers*, vol. 1: *The Apostolic Fathers*, eds. Alexander Roberts and James Donaldson [Grand Rapids, MI: Eerdmans, 1950]), p. 218. Some have suggested that some of the heterodox Jewish-Christian sect members called the Ebionites may have observed Sunday; regardless they can hardly be placed before the second century C.E. See *From Sabbath to Sunday* (see endnote 2), pp. 153–156 for a good discussion.

⁸ Simon, *Verus Israel* (see endnote 5), chapter 4 ("Rome, Judaisme et Christianisme"), pp. 125f, recognizes the historical importance of this event.

⁹ James Parkes writes on this point (*Church and Synagogue* [see endnote 5], pp. 78, 93): "Until the Jews had not in large numbers decided for another Messiah, they [Christians] might continue to hope that they would accept Jesus. But when led by the famous Akiba the bulk of the population followed Barkokeba [Bar-Kokhba], then the position became hopeless."

¹⁰ Justin Martyr, *1 Apology* 31.6 (trans. Thomas B. Falls, *Writings of Saint Justin Martyr* [New York: Christian Heritage, 1948], p. 67) reports: "In the recent Jewish war, Barkokeba, the leader of the Jewish uprising, ordered that only the Christians should be subjected to dreadful torments, unless they renounced and blasphemed Jesus Christ."

¹¹ S. Kraus ("Hadrian" in *Jewish Encyclopedia* [New York: Funk and Wagnalls, 1907]) synthesizes the situation as follows: "The Jews now passed through a time of bitter persecution; Sabbaths, festivals, the study of the Torah and circumcision were interdicted and it seemed as if Hadrian desired to annihilate the Jewish people."

¹² Bacchiocchi (*Origin of Sunday* [see endnote 2], n. 103) suggests "That Easter-Sunday was introduced in Jerusalem by the Gentile-Christians after 135, is implied in Epiphanius' statement where he says that 'the controversy arose after the time of the exodus of the bishops of the circumcision' (*Patrologiae Graeca*, vol. 42, pp. 355–356)."

[13] Bruce M. Metzger, *Studies in Lectionary Text of the Greek New Testament* (Chicago: University of Chicago Press, 1944), vol. 2, sec. 3, p. 12.

[14] *Origin of Sunday* (see endnote 2), p. 17.

[15] Suetonius, *Life of Claudius* 25.4. See also Stephen Benko, "The Edict of Claudius of A.D. 49 and the Instigator Chrestus," *Theologische Zeitschrift* 25 (1969), pp. 406–418.

[16] F.F. Bruce, *The Spreading Flame* (Grand Rapids, MI: Eerdmans, 1958), p. 157.

[17] See Bacchiocchi, *Origin of Sunday* (see endnote 2), pp. 49–52, 61, 86 and references there.

[18] The letter of Constantine is found also in Socrates, *Ecclesiastical History* 1.9.

[19] Eusebius, *Ecclesiastical History* 5.23–24.

[20] Justin Martyr, *1 Apology* 67.3–7.

[21] On fasting in the early church, see Bacchiocchi, *Sunday Observance* (see endnote 2), pp. 137–139. A recent comprehensive study is by Radisa Antic, "The Controversy Over Fasting on Saturday Between Constantinople and Rome," *AUSS* 49.2 (2011), pp. 337–352.

[22] Bacchiocchi, *From Sabbath to Sunday* (see endnote 2), p. 194.

[23] R.L. Odom, "The Sabbath in A.D. 1054," *AUSS* 1 (1963), pp. 74–80.

[24] Bacchiocchi, *Origin of Sunday* (see endnote 2), pp. 88–89; compare *From Sabbath to Sunday* (see endnote 2), pp. 211–212.

[25] *Sacrorum Conciliorum Nova et Amplissima Collectio*, ed. Joannes Dominicus Mansi (Graz: Akademische Druck-u. Verlagsanstalt, 1960–1961), vol. 2, pp. 569–570.

[26] For a comprehensive treatment of this topic, see S. Douglas Waterhouse, "The Planetary Week in the Roman West," in *The Sabbath in Scripture and History* (see endnote 2), pp. 308–322, appendix A.

[27] Gaston H. Halsberghe, *The Cult of Sol Invictus* (Leiden: Brill, 1972), p. 26. This thesis was proposed earlier by Alfred von Domaszewski, *Abhandlungen zur Römischen Religion* (Leipzig: B.C. Tubner, 1909), p. 173.

[28] Bacchiocchi presents a sampling of evidence that demonstrates the first- and second-centuries' C.E. presence and influence of the Sun cult, including Augustus's import in 31 B.C.E. of two obelisks to Rome who had them dedicated to the sun—*Soli donum dedit*. See *From Sabbath to Sunday* (see endnote 2), pp. 239–241.

[29] Dio Cassius, *Roman History* 37.18.

[30] *Roman History* 49.22.

[31] C.S. Mosna, *Storia della domenica* (Rome: Libreria editrice dell'Università Gregoriana, 1969), p. 69. Attilio Degrassi agrees, based on archaeological evidence, that the planetary week was already in use during the Augustinian era (27 B.C.E.–14 C.E.). See "Un Nuovo frammento di calendario Romano e la settimana planetaria dei sette giorni," in *Atti del Terzo Congresso Internazionale de Epigrafia Greca e Latina* (Rome: L'Erma di Bretschneider, 1957), p. 104.

[32] Evidence summarized in Bacchiocchi, *From Sabbath to Sunday* (see endnote 2), pp. 245–246.

[33] Ibid., p. 251.

[34] Jack Lindsay (*Origin of Astrology* [London: Muller, 1972]) provides in his chapter 20 ("Pagan and Christians") a helpful survey of the influence of astrological beliefs on early Christianity.

[35] Bacchiocchi gives evidence for his claim that "The motif of the Sun was used not only by Christian artists to portray Christ but also by Christian teachers to proclaim Him to the pagan masses who were well acquainted with the rich Sun-symbology. Numerous Fathers abstracted and reinterpreted the pagan symbols and beliefs about the Sun and used them apologetically to teach the Christian message ... It would require only a short step to worship Christ-the-Sun, on the day specifically dedicated to the Sun." See *From Sabbath to Sunday* (see endnote 2), pp. 253–254 and notes.

[36] After an extensive analysis of patristic references dealing with the orientation toward the east, Francis A. Regan concludes: "A suitable, single example of the pagan influence may be had from an investigation of the Christian custom of turning toward the East, the land of the rising sun, while offering their prayers ... For in the transition from the observance of the Sabbath to the celebration of the Lord's day, the primitive Christians not only substituted the first day of the week for the seventh, but they

went even further and changed the traditional Jewish practice of facing toward Jerusalem during their daily period of prayer." See *Dies Dominica and Dies Solis: The Beginnings of the Lord's Day in Christian Antiquity* (Washington, DC: Catholic University of America Press, 1961), p. 196.

[37] Josef A. Jungmann states, "It has become progressively clear that the real reason for the choice of the 25th of December was the pagan feast of the '*dies natalis Solis Invicti*' which was celebrated in those days with great splendor." See *The Early Liturgy to the Time of Gregory the Great* (Notre Dame, IN: University of Notre Dame Press, 1962), p. 147. Likewise Mario Righetti, a renowned Catholic liturgist, writes, "The Church of Rome, to facilitate the acceptance of the faith by the pagan masses, found it convenient to institute the 25th of December as the feast of the temporal birth of Christ, to divert them from the pagan feast, celebrated on the same day in honor of the 'Invincible Sun' Mithras, the conqueror of darkness." See *Manuale di Storia Liturgica* (Milan: Ancora, 1955), vol. 2, p. 67.

[38] *From Sabbath to Sunday* (see endnote 2), p. 261.

[39] In *Patrologiae Cursus Completus*, Series Graeca, ed. J.P. Migne (Paris: Garnier Freres, 1857), vol. 23, pp. 1169–1172.

[40] *From Sabbath to Sunday* (see endnote 2), p. 264.

[41] Ibid., p. 139; see also Shemaryahu Talmon, *The Importance of the Qumran Calendar in Early Judaism* (North Richland Hills, TX: D & F Scott, 2002).

[42] Earle Hilgert, "The Jublilees Calendar and the Origin of Sunday Observance," *AUSS* 1 (1963), pp. 49, 50.

[43] Paul K. Jewett, *The Lord's Day: A Theological Guide to the Christian Day of Worship* (Grand Rapids, MI: Eerdmans, 1971), p. 56.

[44] Augustine, *Letter 55* 23.1 (*Corpus Scriptorum Ecclesiasticorum Latinorum*, vol. 34 [Vienna: Apud C. Geroldi filium, 1897], p. 194).

[45] *From Sabbath to Sunday* (see endnote 2), p. 271.

[46] Ibid.

[47] Ibid.

[48] Ibid., pp. 271–272.

[49] In *Patrologie Cursus Completes*, Series Graeca, ed. J.P. Migne (Paris: 1857), vol. 86, p. 416.

[50] Trans. Edgar J. Goodspeed, *The Apostolic Fathers* (New York: Independent Press, 1950), p. 41.

[51] *From Sabbath to Sunday* (see endnote 2), p. 283.

[52] Ibid., p. 285.

[53] See Lawrence T. Geraty, "The Pascha and the Origin of Sunday Observance," *AUSS* 3 (1965), pp. 85–96.

[54] Jerome, *In die dominica Paschae homilia*, *Corpus Christianorum, Series Latina* 78, p. 550.

[55] No less a Catholic authority than Thomas Aquinas states unambiguously: "In the New law the observance of the Lord's day took the place of the observance of the Sabbath not by virtue of the precept but by the institution of the Church and the custom of Christian people." See *Summa Theologica* (New York: Benzinger, 1947), vol. 2, Q122, art. 4, p. 1702.

XIV. Social Organization and Parting in East and West

[1] For a good discussion, see Anders Klostergaard Petersen, "At the End of the Road—Reflections on a Popular Scholarly Metaphor," in *The Formation of the Early Church*, ed. Jostein Ådna (Tübingen: Mohr Siebeck, 2005), pp. 45–72 (with some of the older literature).

[2] This chapter is a summary of a longer, scientific article by Arye Edrei and Doron Mendels, "Sovereignty and the Parting of the Ways: A Note on Law, Community and Theology," forthcoming in the *Journal for the Study of the Pseudepigrapha*.

[3] Jacques-Paul Migne, *Patrologia Latina*, vol. 42.8, p. 261.

[4] Some rabbinic laws in these two areas were designed specifically to create social separation. For example, the rabbis prohibited food cooked by gentiles, as well as using the bread, milk, oil

and cheese of gentiles—all for the purpose of creating distance and seclusion. See, for example, Mishnah *Avodah Zarah* 2:6 and the associated discussions in the Babylonian Talmud and the Jerusalem Talmud. This topic has been discussed at length in the scholarly literature, and this is not the place to expand upon it. Even the prohibition of drinking wine handled by gentiles, which is generally justified by the concern that the wine was used for idolatrous libations, might also logically be explained by the reasoning of "because of marriage" (i.e., in order to prevent marriages with gentiles), or in simple terms, to create social distance. Also in the context of Sabbath observance, the rabbis created innovative concepts and halakhic rules related to separation and seclusion. The most prominent example is the rabbinic enactment that forbids transporting items on the Sabbath between different private domains, between houses within a courtyard or between courtyards in an alley. The rabbis enacted the *eruv chatzerot*, which permits transport between the houses if the inhabitants agreed to become partners. This permit is not valid, however, when one of the residents is a gentile. The Talmud explains the invalidation of the permit in this case by the desire of the rabbis to encourage Jews not to live in the vicinity of non-Jews (see Mishnah and Talmud tractate *Eruvin*, chapter 6). Thus we find many rabbinic enactments and decrees that were designed to shape the community and isolate it from the gentile environment, a goal that was accomplished through acceptance of the commandments rather than through theological ideas.

⁵ See, for example, Hanina Ben-Menahem, *Judicial Deviation in Talmudic Law* (New York: Harwood Academic Publishers, 1991); היסטוריות בית דין בתלמוד הבבלי: צורות ספרותיות והשלכות מעשי גפני ישעיהו, in *Proceedings of the American Academy for Jewish Research* 49 (1982), pp. 23–40.

⁶ BT *Sanhedrin* 56a. See Bernard S. Jackson, "The Jewish View of Natural Law," *JJS* 52.1 (2001), pp. 136–145; and Suzanne Stone, "Sinaitic and Noahide Law: Legal Pluralism in Jewish Law," *Cardozo Law Review* 12.3–4 (1991), pp. 1157–1214.

⁷ Cf. parallel sources in the name of other *tannaim*.

⁸ The Jerusalem Talmud (1:4) states the following in this context: "A document that was produced in Beth-Shean and the witnesses were non-Jews. [...] Resh Lakish says that it is valid. [...] What is the reasoning of Resh Lakish? [...] Rabbi Yudan says, so as to not close the door before a person who tomorrow wants to borrow money and can't find [a lender]." Beth-Shean was a city in which most of the residents were gentiles, and according to the explanation of the Jerusalem Talmud, the position of Resh Lakish is that a document from Beth-Shean with non-Jewish witnesses should be valid because disqualification of the witnesses in a city like Beth-Shean would cause the cessation of loans. However, it is clear from the statement that this is an exception, and that the ideal would be if the community could sustain itself in accordance with the Jewish witnesses and courts of law.

Indeed, the Babylonian Talmud explains this law using Shmuel's dictum that "the law of the land is the law." The Tosafot (*Gittin* 9b, "Even though") explained that the testimony of a non-Jew is invalid because "he is not your brother in the fulfillment of the commandments." In other words, it is clear that in the discussion of this issue among the *Rishonim* (early medieval scholars), the issue is not one of credibility, but of being part of the community. The judicial system is separated for the exclusive use of "brothers." Rabbi Mordechai Ben-Hillel (Germany, 13th century) in *Gittin* (1:324) cites the opinion of Rabbeinu Yakir, who held that gentiles known to be telling the truth were not disqualified as witnesses. Ben-Hillel rejects this opinion, however, and states that the testimony of a non-Jew, while valid in the general system, is not valid in Jewish courts because they are not "brothers in the fulfillment of the commandments." Thus, the judicial system is exclusive and is designed to serve only the Jewish community. Maimonides wrote in the *Mishneh Torah, Hilkhot Edut* (*The Laws of Testimony*) 9:4 as follows: "Slaves are disqualified as witnesses from the Torah, for it says regarding witnesses: 'You shall do to them what they tried to do to their brother.' From this we learn that his brother is like him—just as his brother is Jewish (the son of the covenant), so too the witness must be Jewish. How much more so with regard to gentiles—if slaves who observe some commandments are invalid, should not gentiles even more so be invalid [because they observe no commandments]." Thus Maimonides as well understood that the disqualification derived from a desire for separation (that he is not your brother in the fulfillment of the commandments) and not from a lack of credibility.

[9] See also the Epistle to Titus 3:1: "Remind them to be subject to rulers and authorities, to be obedient, to be ready for every good work." So too in the First Epistle of Peter 2:13–17: "Be subject to every human institution for the Lord's sake, whether to a king as supreme or to governors as those he commissions to punish wrongdoers and praise those who do good. For God wants you to silence the ignorance of foolish people by doing good. Live as free people, not using your freedom as a pretext for evil, but as God's slaves. Honor all people, love the family of believers, fear God, honor the king."

[10] Regarding Christian and pagan notions of morality, Isaiah Berlin ("The Originality of Machiavelli," in *Against the Current: Essays in the History of Ideas* [London: Pimlico, 1997], p. 289) cites Machiavelli who differentiates "between two incompatible ideals of life, and therefore two moralities. One is the morality of the pagan world: Its values are courage, vigor, fortitude in adversity, public achievement, order, discipline, happiness, strength, justice, above all assertion of one's proper claims and the knowledge and power needed to secure their satisfaction ... Against this moral universe ... stands in the first and foremost place Christian morality. The ideals of Christianity are charity, mercy, sacrifice, love of God, forgiveness of enemies, contempt for the goods of this world, faith in the hereafter ... Machiavelli lays it down that out of men who believe in such ideals, and practice them, no satisfactory human community, in his Roman sense, can in principle be constructed."

[11] The *midrash* in *Sifre Deuteronomy* 43:17 (Finkelstein ed., p. 102), which states that the Jews have to observe the commandments outside of Israel in order not to forget them and preserve their knowledge of them for the time they would come back, may reflect an echo of the polemic on the validity of Jewish law outside the land of Israel.

[12] On the persecution of the Christians, see the still useful book of W.H.C. Frend, *Martyrdom and Persecution in the Early Church: A Study of a Conflict from the Maccabees to Donatus* (Oxford: Blackwell, 1965), and for the later empire, see Peter Brown, "Christianization and Religious Conflict," in *Cambridge Ancient History*, vol. 13, *The Late Empire: A.D. 337–425*, eds. Averil Cameron and Peter Garnsey (Cambridge: Cambridge University Press, 1998), pp. 632–664; and chapter 3 in Doron Mendels, *The Media Revolution of Early Christianity* (Grand Rapids, MI: Eerdmans, 1999), pp. 51–110.

[13] See Amnon Linder, "The Legal Status of the Jews in the Roman Empire," in *Cambridge History of Judaism*, vol. 4, *The Late Roman-Rabbinic Period*, ed. Steven Katz (Cambridge: Cambridge University Press, 2006), pp. 128–173; and "The Legal Status of Jews in the Byzantine Empire," in *Jews in Byzantium: Dialectics of Minority and Majority Cultures*, eds. Robert Bonfil et al. (Leiden: Brill, 2012), pp. 149–217.

[14] See Mendels, *Media Revolution* (see endnote 12).

[15] We wish to draw attention to an idea that is worthy of study in its own right. The absence of legal and political sovereignty in the Christian church, and its reliance on a sort of theological sovereignty (dogma) may explain the phenomenon of heresy in the early church, as opposed to Judaism that did not experience heresies.

[16] Francis Fukuyama, *The Origins of Political Order: From Prehuman Times to the French Revolution* (London: Profile Books, 2011).

[17] See Isaiah M. Gafni, *The Jews of Babylonia in the Talmudic Era* (Jerusalem: Magnes Press, 1990), p. 31.

[18] See Moshe Beer, "The Political Background and Activity of Rav in Babylonia," *Zion* 55 (1985), pp. 155–172, at pp. 158–159 (in Hebrew).

[19] See Shmuel Shilo, *Dina De-Malkhuta Dina: The Law of the State Is Law* (Jerusalem: Defus Akademi Jerushalayim, 1975), pp. 4–43.

[20] Fukuyama, *Origins of Political Order* (see endnote 16), p. 106.

[21] This may be yet another reason for the so-called split Diaspora, namely that the rabbis did not naturally move westward. See Doron Mendels and Arye Edrei, *Zweirlei Diaspora: Zur Spaltung der antiken juedischen Welt* (Goettingen: Vandenhoeck & Ruprechet, 2010).

XV. Did They Ever Part?

[1] In this book, Joan Taylor argues that "Second Temple Judaism" did not end in 70 C.E. (See Chapter V, "Parting in Palestine.") Clearly, 70 C.E. is the end of the Temple, the cult and the Sadducees. Obviously, Jews continued to be influential in Judea or Palestine after 70, as is evident in Josephus and in light of recent excavations in and around Jerusalem; and the apocalyptic fervor did not wane but exploded in 4 Ezra and 2 Baruch and led to the final revolt under Bar-Kokhba.

[2] The words "parting of the ways" have been used of Protestants departing from Roman Catholics and other religious phenomena. The one who made famous "parting of the ways" to explain the different development of Judaism and Christianity was James Parkes in *The Conflict of the Church and the Synagogue* (New York: JPS, 1934); see also Parkes, "Rome, Pagan and Christian," in *Judaism and Christianity*, ed. Herbert Loewe (New York: Ktav, 1937), pp. 115–144.

[3] For a discussion on the relevant early Jewish texts that contain resurrection beliefs, see James H. Charlesworth, *Resurrection* (New York/London: T & T Clark, 2006).

[4] I was surprised when some of my former students told me that Jesus was a gentile because he was from Galilee; this is what is being taught in their seminaries. How can this nonsense be tolerated?

[5] See Isaiah 9:1; 1 Maccabees 5:15; Matthew 4:15.

[6] See my review of Uzi Leibner's *Settlement and History in Hellenistic, Roman, and Byzantine Galilee* in *Journal for the Study of the Historical Jesus* 8 (2010), pp. 175–184.

[7] I am indebted to Motti Aviam for discussions on the origin of Herodian clay lamps in Lower Galilee.

[8] See especially David Flusser, *The Sage from Galilee: Rediscovering Jesus' Genius*, with R. Steven Notley (Grand Rapids, MI: Eerdmans, 2007).

[9] See E.P. Sanders, *The Historical Figure of Jesus* (London: Penguin Press, 1993), pp. 122–123.

[10] James D.G. Dunn, *The Parting of the Ways*, 2nd ed. (London: SCM Press, 2006), p. 149.

[11] Too many scholars misread the Gospel of John, assuming it proclaims that Jesus is God. Commentators on John rightly point out that in the Fourth Gospel Jesus is identical to God in will and mission. John never suggests that Jesus and God were of one substance; the subordinationist Christology in John should not be ignored nor should we try to explain away the conflicting so-called high Christology. Opposite thoughts help us perceive the true meaning within the tension.

[12] Luke T. Johnson, *The Writings of the New Testament* (Minneapolis: Fortress Press, 1999), p. 205.

[13] According to the Ebionites (see Epiphanius, Origen, Hippolytus) and Nazoraeans (see Epiphanius), and a tenth-century text published by Shlomo Pines, Jesus was the first to complete the Torah (cf. also the Pseudo-Clementines). Pines's text reports that the debates among Christians took precedence over the conflicts with the Jews. See Pines, "The Jewish Christians of the Early Centuries of Christianity According to a New Source," *Proceedings of the Israel Academy of Sciences and Humanities* 2.13 (1966), pp. 1–74. Reflections on such fragmentary texts should protect us from sweeping conclusions.

[14] See the insightful discussion by James D.G. Dunn in "Jesus and the Temple," in *Parting of the Ways* (see endnote 10), pp. 49–75.

[15] See *Jesus and the Temple*, ed. James H. Charlesworth (Grand Rapids, MI: Eerdmans, in press).

[16] Josephus implies (*Antiquities* 20.197–203; see also Eusebius, *Ecclesiastical History* 2.23.22), and the author of the Second Apocalypse of John reports, that James was stoned to death.

Hegesippus (*Ecclesiastical History* 2.23.3–18) and Eusebius (*Ecclesiastical History* 2.23.3) state that James was thrown from the top of the Temple (actually the "sanctuary"), stoned and then clubbed.

[17] See Mishnah *Yadayim* for rules about pouring water over the hands.

[18] *On the Migration of Abraham* 86–93; *Questions and Answers on Exodus* 2.2.

[19] See Moriz Friedlander, *Die religiösen Bewegungen innerhalb des Judentums im Zeitalter Jesu* (Berlin: Georg Reimer, 1905; reprinted in Amsterdam in 1974); and Peder Borgen, "Debates on Circumcision in Philo and Paul," in *Paul Preaches Circumcision and Pleases Men* (Trondheim: Tapir, 1983), pp. 15–32.

[20] See R.G. Hall, "Epispasm and the Dating of Ancient Jewish Writings," *Journal for the Study of the Pseudepigrapha* 1 (1988), pp. 71–86.

[21] Shemaryahu Talmon, *The World of Qumran from Within* (Jerusalem/Leiden: Magnes Press/Brill, 1989), see esp. 147–185.

[22] Consult Eviatar Zerubavel, *The Seven Day Circle: The History and Meaning of the Week* (Chicago: University of Chicago Press, 1985).

[23] Hebrew *shavu'a* is etymologically derived from *sheva*, "seven"; and thus we get *Shabbat*. See Jubilees, in which early Jews explained a cycle of seven-year periods.

[24] See Revelation 1:10, "I was in the Spirit on the Lord's day ..."

[25] See C.W. Dugmore, "Lord's Day and Easter," in *Neotestamentica et Patristica*, Supplements to Novum Testamentum 6 (Leiden: Brill, 1962), pp. 272–281. Dugmore rightly points out a point of continuing contact. The synagogue influenced the form of services and the times when Christians met in the first four centuries C.E. (p. 272).

[26] Gabriele Boccaccini is so convinced of a "parting of the ways" between two forms of Judaism that he can use that term in one of his books: *Beyond the Essene Hypothesis: The Parting of the Ways Between Qumran and Enochic Judaism* (Grand Rapids, MI: Eerdmans, 1998). Many leading scholars demur from speaking about a form of Judaism that could be called "Enochic Judaism."

[27] See James H. Charlesworth, "The Gospel of John: Exclusivism Caused by a Social Setting Different from That of Jesus (John 11:54 and 14:6)," in *Anti-Judaism and the Fourth Gospel: Papers of the Leuven Colloquium, 2000*, eds. R. Bieringer, D. Pollefeyt and F. Vandecasteele-Vanneuville (Assen: Royal Van Gorcum, 2001), pp. 479–513.

[28] William Horbury argues that, for the author of Barnabas and for Justin Martyr, the ways "have parted already," yet adding "the ways still run close together." See Horbury, "Jewish-Christian Relations in Barnabas and Justin Martyr," in *Jews and Christians: The Parting of the Ways, A.D. 70 to 135*, ed. James D.G. Dunn (Grand Rapids, MI: Eerdmans, 1999), p. 315.

[29] See James H. Charlesworth, "Christians and Jews in the First Six Centuries," in *Christianity and Rabbinic Judaism*, 2nd ed., ed. Hershel Shanks (Washington, DC: Biblical Archaeology Society, 2011), p. 356.

[30] See *The Apocryphal New Testament*, ed. James K. Elliott (Oxford: Clarendon Press, 1993), pp. 14–15.

[31] Ibid., p. 76.

[32] See Edgar Hennecke, *New Testament Apocrypha*, ed. Wilhelm Schneemelcher, English trans. and ed. R. McL. Wilson (London: Lutterworth Press, 1963), vol. 1, p. 455.

[33] Luke T. Johnson, "The New Testament's Anti-Jewish Slander and the Conventions of Ancient Polemic," *JBL* 108.3 (1989), pp. 419–441. Johnson rightly admits that the scurrilous polemic against Jews is "a source of shame (finally) to Christians," p. 419.

[34] See 1QHa 14.15: "And all peoples shall know your truth and all nations your glory."

[35] See, for example, Matthew 10:5–6, 15:24; John 4:22. See Dunn, *The Parting of the Ways* (see endnote 10), pp. 149–153.

[36] Matthew 8:5–13; Luke 7:1–10; and Mark 7:24–30.

[37] Anti-gentile attitudes abound in the Jewish apocryphal works and in the Qumran scrolls

(especially the *Pesharim*). See Martin Goodman, *The Ruling Class of Judaea* (Cambridge: Cambridge University Press, 1987), p. 108.

[38] N.T. Wright, *The New Testament and the People of God* (London: SPCK, 1993); *Jesus and the Victory of God* (London: SPCK, 1996), pp. 206–209; *The Challenge of Jesus* (Downers Grove, IL: InterVarsity Press, 1999), p. 47. Wright's eschatological and apocalyptic perspective has been caricatured. Here is his position: "Eschatology as the climax of Israel's history, involving events from which end-of-the world language is the only set of metaphors adequate to express the significance of what will happen, but resulting in a new and quite different phase *within* space-time history" *(Jesus and the Victory of* God, p. 208 [his italics]).

[39] Ephraim E. Urbach emphasized that point when we discussed the past. See his *The Sages* (Jerusalem: Magnes Press, 1979).

[40] See *Jews and Christians* (see endnote 28); see also Dunn, *The Parting of the Ways* (see endnote 10).

[41] *The Ways That Never Parted*, eds. Adam H. Becker and Annette Yoshiko Reed (Tübingen: Mohr Siebeck, 2003).

[42] Looking at Onias IV and the temple at Leontopolis and the Essene schism, Geza Vermes, in the present book, states: "So in more than one sense, the parting of the ways antedated the birth of Jesus" (see p. 3).

[43] Jacob Neusner has offered this opinion in numerous publications. Interpretation does sometimes give us different texts. *Tradutore traditore*; that is, (too often) a translator becomes a traitor. I am deeply moved by Neusner's profound and personal *Christian Faith and the Bible of Judaism* (Grand Rapids, MI: Eerdmans, 1987) and its dedication and comments on pp. xvii–xviii.

[44] See F.J.E. Boddens Hosang, *Establishing Boundaries: Christian Relations in Early Council Texts and the Writings of Church Fathers* (Leiden: Brill, 2010).

[45] See Becker and Yoshiko Reed, "Introduction: Traditional Models and New Directions," in *The Ways That Never Parted* (see endnote 41), p. 2;

see also the many contributions to the present volume.

[46] Ephraim Isaac, *The Ethiopian Orthodox Täwahïdo Church* (Trenton/London/Addis Ababa: Red Sea Press, 2012), p. xi.

[47] Ibid., p. xi. When I was in Addis Ababa for the celebration of the Ethiopian millennium in 2007, I was amazed how Professor Isaac was admired by "the athlete of the millennium" and the leading diplomats in the United Nations and in Ethiopia. Both men named "Isaac" are considered more than a brother by Christians. Moreover, the 14th-century *Kebra Nagast* claims that all world leaders are descendants of Israel (p. 245).

[48] Certainly, elephants could have come from Africa.

[49] This question has become an obsession of Johnson Thomaskutty; see, for example, his blogposts at http://ntscholarship.wordpress.com/

[50] Periplus maris Erythraei [a first-century merchant], *The Periplus of the Erythraean Sea: Travel and Trade in the Indian Ocean* (New York: Longmans, Green and Co., 1912). Most likely this is a first-century account of trade from Egyptian ports to Indian ports. The "Erythraean Sea" denotes the "Red Sea" but the Persian Gulf is included in the account of ancient navigation and commerce. From India, notably Barygaza and Muziris (near Cochin), centers of Roman trade, are exported many items, including fine linen, ivory, silk and precious stones (e.g., pearls and sapphires); *Periplus*, chapters 41–56.

[51] As A.F.J. Klijn stated: "[D]er Apostel Paulus nei in Edessa gewesen ist." See Klijn, *Edessa, Die Stadt des Apostels Thomas* (Neukirchen-Vluyn: Neukirchener Verlag, 1965), p. 29.

[52] See Hans-Joachim Klimkeit, *Gnosis on the Silk Road: Gnostic Texts from Central Asia* (New York: HarperCollins, 1993). In these ancient texts there are often striking parallels to the Odes of Solomon, 1 Enoch and the Qumran scrolls; for example, see *Hymn to the Living Soul* ("Sons of Truth," "Father of Light") on p. 51, *Hymn to the Third Messenger as Sun God* ("a Helper," "the Sons of Darkness" [see p. 164] versus "the Sons of the Day") on p. 58.

[53] In the early fourth century "the parting of the ways" was not Christians from Jews; it was east from west. At the funeral of Habbib, who was horrendously tortured but would not break God's first commandment, Jews joined with Christians to honor this brave martyr. See J.B. Segal, *Edessa: The Blessed City* (Oxford, Clarendon Press, 1970), pp. 85–86.

[54] See the scholarly discussions focused on Palmyra and Dura-Europos and the caravan routes. Adiabene is farther east even past Nisibis.

[55] See Josephus, *Antiquities* 20.2–4. The mother of King Monobazes II and Izates, Helena, and her family were buried in the "Tomb of the Kings" on Saladin Street near the American Colony hotel in Jerusalem. These easterners were beloved in Jerusalem; they supported the Jews against the Romans. The golden menorah given to the Temple by Helena was taken to Rome and is commemorated on Titus's arch (see p. 163). Jacob Neusner rightly sees that the Judaism known to Aphrahat derives from the Adiabenian converts to Judaism. Neusner, *Aphrahat and Judaism* (Leiden: Brill, 1971), pp. 144–149.

[56] Josephus, *Antiquities* 15; *Fathers According to Rabbi Nathan* 2.27; see also Joachim Jeremias, *Jerusalem in the Time of Jesus*, trans. F.H. and C.H. Cave (Philadelphia: Fortress Press, 1969), pp. 67–68; and the contributions in *Hillel and Jesus*, eds. James H. Charlesworth and Loren L. Johns (Minneapolis: Fortress Press, 1997).

[57] See Robert Murray, *Symbols of Church and Kingdom* (Cambridge: Cambridge University Press, 1975), pp. 7–12.

[58] Segal, *Edessa* (see endnote 53), p. 100.

[59] Almost all who wrote the preceding chapters miss this development.

[60] One of the advantages of the perspective brought by E. Mary Smallwood, and others, is to open our eyes to the Jews in all areas of the Roman world. See Smallwood, *The Jews Under Roman Rule*, Studies in Judaism in Late Antiquity 20 (Leiden: Brill, 1976).

[61] Gabriele Boccaccini, *Middle Judaism* (Minneapolis: Fortress Press, 1991), esp. 15.

[62] See, for example, Marius Heemstra, *The* Fiscus Judaicus *and the Parting of the Ways* (Tübingen: Mohr Siebeck, 2010).

[63] Political and economic concerns cannot be discussed in a brief chapter like this one, yet they help contextualize the issues. For example, when Hadrian built the elegant temple to Venus (Aphrodite) in the early second century, he did so to celebrate Venus, his own religion and Roman politics. In the process, he obliterated the site of Jesus' crucifixion and burial. To what extent was an anti-Jewish and anti-Christian position part of his building program?

[64] Paul seems to have persuaded James, who was head of "the circumcision party," that circumcision was not mandatory for gentile converts. See Jerome Murphy-O'Connor, "Why Did James Agree with Paul on Circumcision?" in *Paul: A Critical Life* (Oxford: Oxford University Press, 1997), pp. 138–141.

[65] Despite his perspicacity, E.P. Sanders errs when he includes the observance of Shabbat as one of the Jewish customs ridiculed by gentiles; see Sanders, *Paul, the Law, and the Jewish People* (London: SCM Press, 1983), p. 102. Some gentiles were drawn to Judaism because of the ability to have one day off from work each "week." Recall Philo (*Life of Moses* 2.21), Josephus (*Against Apion* 2.282), the *Corpus Papyrorum Judaicarum* 13, and Juvenal (*Satires* 14.96): "Some [gentiles] have had a father who reveres Shabbat (*sabbata*)." See the marvelous discussion by Menahem Stern in *GLAJJ*, vol. 2, pp. 102–107.

[66] Peter Schäfer also rightly points to the need for a better "more differentiated and sophisticated model" for exploring the parting of the ways; see his *The Jewish Jesus* (Princeton, NJ: Princeton University Press, 2012), p. 84.

[67] Contrast Seth Schwartz's claim that Jesus' group "was a movement, or rather a loose collection of related groups ... in which the Torah ... was definitely of secondary importance." Schwartz, *Imperialism and Jewish Society, 200 B.C.E. to 640 C.E.* (Princeton, NJ: Princeton University Press, 2001), p. 91.

[68] Jerome, *Epistles* 112.13 (*Patrologia Latina*, ed. J.P. Migne, 22.0924, pp. 746–747).

[69] The New Testament attests to riots against Paul by synagogue leaders (and other Jews) in Asia Minor and Macedonia, at precisely the same time, as Williams states (p. 155). She also clarifies that synagogal congregations included gentiles, Godfearers, proselytes, converts and conceivably also those non-Jews who believed Jesus was the Messiah. Gentiles attracted to Judaism may be represented by many terms: "Fearers of God," "Fearers of Heaven," *sebomenoi* and *phoboumenoi*.

[70] Pamela Watson wisely cautions that a putative parting, if the "Christians" fled to Pella, is not supported by any archaeological discovery in Pella (see Chapter IV). For decades, many of us have pointed out in numerous conferences that *realia* almost always cannot be linked to belief systems.

[71] John P. Meier, *A Marginal Jew* (New York: Doubleday, 1994), vol. 2, pp. 453–454. Indeed, Jesus, the master of parables, becomes the parable. See *Earthing Christologies: From Jesus' Parables to Jesus the Parable*, eds. James H. Charlesworth and W.P. Weaver, Faith and Scholarship Colloquies (Valley Forge, PA: Trinity Press International, 1995).

[72] See Segal, *Edessa* (see endnote 53), p. 69.

[73] Sometimes lost today is the recognition that "heresy" and "orthodoxy" are anachronistic terms, especially before the fourth century C.E., and that such terms represent an etic view. Walter Bauer proved that "heresy" often antedated "orthodoxy" in some regions (but those terms are misleading). See Bauer, with Georg Strecker, *Orthodoxy and Heresy in Earliest Christianity*, trans. and eds. Robert Kraft and Gerhard Krodel (Philadelphia: Fortress Press, 1971).

[74] What categories should be used for the Therapeutae and those who worshiped and studied in the so-called temple at Leontopolos (Heliopolis) that ceased in 73 C.E.?

Index

Note: Page numbers in *italics* refer to illustrations and captions.

Ishmael ben Phiabi (High Priest), 90
Ishmael, R., 226
Israel
  notions of, 318n13
  Paul's definition of, 35
Izates, 287–288, 366n55
Jackson-McCabe, Matt, 299
Jacob of Kfar Samah, 222, 224–226
Jacob of Kfar Sikhnin, 223, 224, 225–226
Jaffa, 245
Jairus, daughter of, 9
James
  on believers-in-Jesus, 308n82
  circumcision controversy, 116, 366n64
  Davidic genealogy, 63–64
  death, 363n16
  distinction between Jews and gentiles, 63–64
  execution, 31, 43
  guidelines for gentiles, 38, 61, 116, 117
  home of, 139
  leadership of Jerusalem church, 38
  letters attributed to, 45, 124
  martyrdom, 257, 287
  preaching about Jesus, 63–64
  requirements for followers of Jesus, 70
  respect for Jewish scruples, 257
Jamnia (Yavneh), 92, 103, 228, 257
Jechoniah, 346n61
Jerash (Gerasa) synagogue, 245
Jeremias, Joachim, 14
Jerome
  on Jews cursing Christians, 99, 231
  knowledge of Hebrew, 293
  on Nazoraeans, 198–200, 201, 202–203, 343n30
  on people wishing to be both Jews and Christians, 297
  references to Minaeans, 49
  Sun symbolism, 268
Jerusalem
  Byzantine cross reused in synagogue, 252, 253
  Christianity, 143
    70–132 C.E., 97
  complaints about Paul, 37
  gentiles, 98
  impact of fall of Jerusalem on, 42–43
  impact of Temple destruction on, 43
  leadership, 96
  migration to Pella, 74–75
  Roman period, 134
  fall of, 42–43, 160
Judaism
  burials (70 C.E.–135 C.E.), 91
  pilgrimages, 154
  post–70 C.E., 91
  prohibition against Jews, 98, plate 3
  rebuilt as Aelia Capitolina, 92, 93, 94
  reconquest (629 C.E.), 252
  Roman Legion X Fretensis, 90–91, 92
  Roman siege, 90
Jerusalem council, 257
Jerusalem Talmud, 361n8
Jerusalem Temple. see Temple
Jesus
  abolishing sacrifices, 305n36
  archaeological evidence, 5
  baptism by John the Baptist, 7, 197
  biblical dietary laws, 16–17
  building a church, 21–23
  in Capernaum, 139, 139
  as charismatic healer and exorcist, 8–10, 223–226
  charismatic Judaism, 15–20
  as charismatic prophet, 4–5
  as charismatic teacher, 10
  childhood, 5, 16
  childlike attitude toward God, 19–20
  contact with Temple of Jerusalem, 16
  crucifixion
    date, 329n3
    as Day of Atonement sacrifice, 50–51
    faltering of faith, 14
    Jewish attitudes toward, 30
    Jewish responsibility, 29
    reasons for, 23–25
    Roman responsibility, 29–30

Samaritans, 104, 282

Samuel the Small, 229–230, 308n90

Sanders, E.P., 284–285, 366n65

Sarah, 55

sarcophagus, 79–80

Sardis, 241, 243

Sassanid empire, 131–132, 252, 276, 277–278

Saul. *see* Paul

Schäfer, Peter, 350n4

Schmidtke, Alfred, 347n74

Schremer, Adiel, 148

Schumacher, Gottlieb

  anchorite cave, 79, 80–81, *81*, 86

  Briekah (site), 101

  Khan Bandak-Ghadiriyeh, 101

  Pella theory, 78–79, 80, 82, *82*

  theory disproved, 83

Schwartz, Seth, 148, 320n40, 328n21, 366n67

Scribes, 1, 202–204

Scythopolis (Beth Shean), 103, 109, 361n8

Sebaste, 104

sebomenoi (God-worshiping people), 62, 68–69

Second Jewish Revolt (132–135/6 C.E.)

  Bar-Kokhba's fame, 30

  causes, 92–94, plate 3

  coins, 92–93, *94*

  consequences, 87, 169

  as disastrous, 12

  Jewish-Christians, 97

  places of refuge, 93, *95*

  scale of, 334n99

Second Temple Judaism

  Christian Jews as unacceptable (*minim*), 49

  differing praxis, 27–28

  disappearance of, 42, 87, 363n1

  factionalism, 46–47, 282

  Jesus movement, 28

  red heifer sacrifice, 90

  relation to Rabbinic Judaism, 28–29

Segal, J.B., 295

Sejanus, Aelius, 153

Seleucid period, 76

Semeia (source of Jesus' sayings), 284n

Sepphoris

  Christianity, 134, 136, 145, 146

  dating of structures, 327n18

  Hellenization, plate 8

  Judaism, 91, *147*

  Mona Lisa of the Galilee (mosaic), plate 8

  Nile Festival Building mosaic, plate 9

  renamed Diocaesarea, 91

  theater, *135*

  zodiac mosaic, *147*

Septuagint, 57

Severus, Septimius, Emperor (Rome), 122

Severus, Sulpicius, 42

Shabbat. *see* Sabbath

Shadrach, plate 12

Shammai (rabbi), 202–203, 204, 283

Shanks, Hershel, 140, 296

Shechem (Neapolis Flavia), 104, 317n96

Shema' (God as one), 31, 49, 304n25

Shephelah, 93, *95*

Shmuel (*amora*), 278, 361n8

shofar (ram's horn), 175, *175*, 245, 247

Shu'fat (salvage site), 89

Sibyl (Greco-Roman prophetess), 57

Sibylline Oracles, 57, 59–60

Sicarii, 2

sickness, association with sinfulness, 8

Simon Magus, 130

Sirat, Colette, 338n3

Smith, Robert Houston, 79–80, 86, 312n14

social organization and parting in East and West, 269–279

  Christian position, 272–275

  geographic divide, 275–279

  Jewish position, 270–272

  relationship to government, 275–279

Socrates (Christian historian), 182, 339n18

Son of God

  angels as, 15

  Jesus as, 7, 15

  Jewish Jesus movement, 15

  as metaphor, 15

Sons of Darkness, 282

Temple
  administration, 92–93
  continuation of Temple concept after fall of Jerusalem, 90
  destruction by Titus (70 C.E.), 42–43, 159
  Hellenist dismissal of, 32
  as idolatrous, 32
  importance to Judaism, 34
  Jesus as replacement for, 47
  Jesus' disturbance, 23–24
  Qumran sect's questioning of, 33–34
  sacrificial cult, 32
  Second Jewish Revolt, 92–93
  tax, 330n20
  warning inscription, 22, 23, 303n46
Ten Commandments, 19, 124
Tenth Roman Legion. see Roman Legion X Fretensis
Tepper, Yotam, 317n95
Teppler, Yaakov, 99
Tertullian, 168, 190, 307n64, 343n27, 346n63
Testaments of the Twelve Patriarchs, 303n9
Testimonium Flavianum, 315n51
Theodotus, 33
Theophilus of Antioch, 120, 121, 122
theophoboumenoi. see Godfearers
Therapeutae, 180, 183
Thomas (apostle), 294
Thomas Aquinas, 360n55
Thomas, Infancy Gospel of, 290
Three Youths in the Fiery Furnace, 177, plate 12
Tiberias, 91, 100, 102, 134, 136
Tiberius, Emperor (Rome), 4, 153–154
Titus, Emperor (Rome), 42, 90–91, 108, 159, 161–162
Toldot Yeshu (The Life Story of Jesus), 248
Torah, 2, 120, 124
Tosefta
  applicability of laws concerning land of Israel in Syria, 109
  Birkat ha-Minim, 227–228, 230
  description of, 217
  halakhic status of Syria, 319n22
  minim, 216, 221–227, 230–231
  relationship to Mishnah, 217
  Yerushalmi as alternate version, 229
Trajan, Emperor (Rome), 91, 122, 167
Transjordan, 74
Tyre, 145
Upper Galilee, 143, 144
urban areas, 143, 146, 149
Valentinus, 168
Venus temple, 98
Vermes, Geza, 297, 299, 365n42
Verturia Paulla (convert to Judaism), 173–174
Vespasian, Emperor (Rome)
  anti-Jewish program, 159–161
  "Capture of Judea," 159–160, 160
  civic rights of Antiochene Jews, 108
  Colosseum construction, 332n59
  fiscus Judaicus, 44, 160–161, 211
Victor (Bishop of Rome), 261
Vigna Randanini catacomb, 170, 174, 175, 176, 335n117, plate 10
Villa Torlonia catacomb, 170, 176, plate 11
Vuong, Lily, 299
Wadi Hamam synagogue, 141
Wadi Jirm, 76, 77, 79, 82, 82–85
Watson, Pamela, 367n70
Weber, Max, 279
Werline, Rodney, 65
West Church, Pella, 78, 79–80
Williams, Margaret, 298
Wright, N.T., 291, 365n38
Yakir, Rabbeinu, 361n8
Yannai (synagogue poet), 247–248
Yavneh. see Jamnia
Yehoudieh, Tell el-. see Leontopolis
Yerushalmi, 228–229. see also Jerusalem Talmud
Yeshua ben Galgula, 89, 97
Yeshua ben Pantira, 223, 224, 226. see also Jesus
Yishmael, R., 221, 222–223, 224–225
Yohanan ben Zakkai, 92, 202
Yosi, R., 219, 221
Zadokite priesthood (Sadducees), 2, 96, 220
Zealots, 2
Zechariah (priest), 6
Zetterholm, Magnus, 118
Zion, Mount, 244